A PROFILE HISTORY OF THE UNITED STATES

GILMAN M. OSTRANDER

Associate Professor of History
Michigan State University

McGraw-Hill Book Company, New York • San Francisco • Toronto • London

PREFACE

A justly renowned historian of the old school faced a problem which is faced by historians of all but the most esoteric subjects, when he was obliged to include in his narrative much information which ought to have been common knowledge among his readers. His problem was that of presenting those twice-told tales without offensively implying ignorance on the part of the reader. To relieve himself of this embarrassment, he hit upon the not very subtle device of introducing these commonplaces with the phrase, "As every school boy knows. . . ."

"As every school boy knows" would do very well as the subtitle for this textbook. It has been written expressly for the student, who, by the time he has been graduated from high school, has gone back to 1492 and worked his way up to the present in one or two, if not even more, American history courses. Such a student, upon arriving in college, will despair to find himself back again on Watling's Island with Columbus, confronted with a bigger textbook than ever, through which he must march once more past the old, familiar milestones—1607, 1776, 1861, and so on—leading to the present time and to the end of the course.

Fortunately for that student, there is much in American history which is not comprehended in the philosophy of a course taught according to a single textbook, with its four causes for this and its three consequences of that. Often, major generalizations in a textbook conceal a vast amount of ignorance on the part of the textbook writer, except in those special areas where that writer has concentrated his attention during his career as an historian. In much of his writing, he must necessarily rely heavily upon the findings of specialists in those areas where he has no knowledge founded upon his own first-hand research. Even when dealing with a subject upon which he is the world's leading authority, he must painfully foreshorten the truth, as he has found it, in order to fit the material into its allotted space.

Consequently, the adept student of a textbook is in a position to bring many of the broad generalizations of that book into question through his reading of the relevant authorities in specific areas. And further, in any major library there will be materials by which the student can test conclusions of those very authorities who enabled him to refute the vulnerably "omniscent" text.

The present text is deliberately briefer than other college texts. It has been written as a concise, genral summation of what America's history has been, according to the most recent historical studies, and the purpose of its brevity is to detain the student as little as possible from embarking on his own investigations. This book is created in the spirit of Carl Becker's admonition that every man should be his own historian, examining main points of controversy and reaching his own informed conclusions.

As a means of furthering the aim of providing the student with the materials for enlarging the scope of his inquiry, suggestions for further reading in many specific areas have been placed at the end of each chapter. These bibliographical sections include most of the relevant paperback readings in many phases of American history. The sections comprise, among other things, impressive evidence of the much-talked-about paperback revolution in publishing. More importantly, the books which are listed have achieved their paperback distinction in one of two ways. Either they were among the most readable works in the field, or they were recent, brief, and authoritative. In both cases, they have been selected from a vast literature because it was supposed that they would attract the interest of people who are intellectually inquisitive. In addition, most of the recent general works among them contain comprehensive general bibliographical essays in the area of their subjects.

Where the accompanying comments are enclosed in quotation marks, these remarks have been drawn from reviews in one or another of the two main scholarly journals dealing with American history: the *American Historical Review* and the *Mississippi Valley Historical Review*. No one who is at all familiar with the differences of opinion among informed persons in many general areas of history will accept the comments as final judgments. They do, however, represent the opinions of the scholars who are best equipped to render them.

It may be objected—indeed, it often is objected—that an area of knowledge cannot be worth much if its authorities continue endlessly their researches without reaching final truths, except on small matters of fact. But, unless society becomes wholly reliant upon scientific authoritarianisms, its main alternative will be reliance upon the nonabsolute truths of history. Or—to descend from that more abstract dichotomy to the present concerns of everyday life—the American who is confronted throughout life with newspaper editorials and politicians' speeches will find his way among them much more satisfactorily, if he has his own informed opinion about what Washington, Jefferson, or Lincoln really meant or about what the First or Fifth or Fourteenth Amendment means.

American history will always have a special appeal for Americans; since Americans are the ones who live it. When Aeneas, in the court of Dido, observed works of art depicting events from the Trojan War, he was enlivened—despite the disastrous conclusion to those events—by the thought that he was a part of what he saw. History tends to appeal to people more strongly when they gain the sense of having, themselves, taken part in it. America is today playing a role of vastly greater importance in the world than it did in previous generations, and its history, as a whole, has become increasingly significant, and increasingly interesting, as a consequence.

If students use this text for its intended purpose, I hope they will criticize it as constructively and as charitably as some of my colleagues have. I wish especially to thank David Donald, William Harbaugh, Ari Hoogenboom, Madison Kuhn, Jean Withers Ostrander, Norman Rich, and Paul Varg for reading all or parts of the manuscript and putting me much straighter on many points than I had formerly been. I wish to thank also the University of Missouri Press for premitting me to draw on my book *The Rights of Man in America, 1606–1861* (1960) for this text.

Gilman M. Ostrander

CONTENTS

I

They steered a westerly course past the cape and found great
shallows at ebb tide, so that their ship was beached and lay some
distance from the sea. But they were so eager to go ashore that
they could not bear to wait till the tide rose under their ship. They
ran up on the shore to a place where a stream flowed out of a
lake. . . . When Spring came, they made the ship ready and sailed
away. Leif gave this country a name to suit its resources: he called
it Vinland.

The Vinland of this Norse saga was probably Nova Scotia,
and the year was probably 1002. When Leif Ericson returned
with tales of his discoveries, other Vikings sailed to America from
Greenland. They may have made the trip intermittently during the

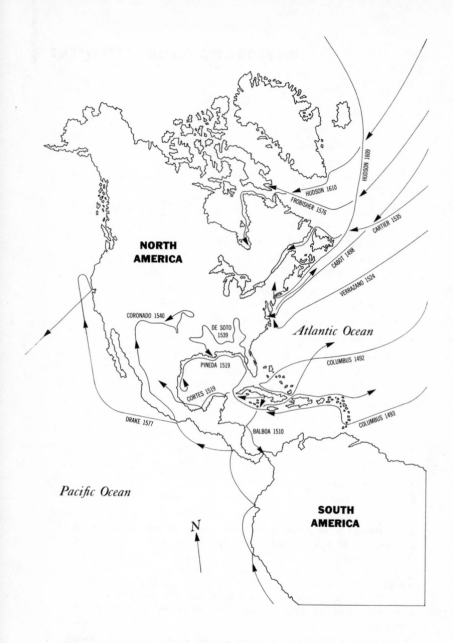

NORTH AMERICA

HUDSON 1609

HUDSON 1610
FROBISHER 1576

CARTIER 1535

CABOT 1498

VERRAZANO 1524

CORONADO 1540

DE SOTO 1539

Atlantic Ocean

PINEDA 1519

COLUMBUS 1492

CORTES 1519

DRAKE 1577

BALBOA 1510

COLUMBUS 1493

Pacific Ocean

N

SOUTH AMERICA

**Voyages of Exploration and Discovery
during the Fifteenth, Sixteenth, and Seventeenth Centuries.**

next three centuries, or perhaps none of them, including Leif, ever came at all; no conclusive evidence has been uncovered to confirm those fourteenth-century sagas. Claims made for early Irish and Portuguese landings in America have nearly nothing to go on but speculation. It was half a millennium after Leif's reputed discovery before Europe was made aware of the existence of two huge continents hidden beneath its western horizons.

European Society   Until the close of the fifteenth century awareness of the New World would have served a European little better than knowledge of Europe would have served an American Indian. For one thing, it was not until the fifteenth century that ships were evolved in Europe fit to make the voyage. The Vikings of Leif Ericson's day, Europe's foremost sailors, possessed single-masted open vessels capable of sailing into the wind, and other Europeans soon copied them. In the thirteenth century the modern rudder came into being, and in the fourteenth and fifteenth centuries the three-masted sailing ship was developed, which remained the basic type for the next five hundred years.

In any event, Europe until the fifteenth and sixteenth centuries was altogether too disorganized to engage in such large-scale undertakings as the establishment of permanent settlements in America. In theory and in spirit, fifteenth-century Europe was united in its allegiance to one God and in its obedience to one universal church. Europe was Christendom, shining forth in a pagan world, united against Mongol and Moslem and certain of its own final triumph.

But the Catholic Church was itself rent with discord, divided for a time between rival Popes and hopelessly incapable of maintaining peaceful order within its diocese. Underlying the jumble of empires, kingdoms, principalities, dukedoms, and knights' castles, the basic unit of organization remained the great estate, with its thousands of scattered acres, its hundreds of serfs and semi-serfs, and its primitive barter economy. The manorial system was a sprawling, sluggish resistance to political change and economic improvement.

It was in the coastal city-states, especially those in the Mediterranean, where men were moved by the enterprise and change of the commercial revolution. Efforts during the late Middle Ages to win the Holy Land from the Moslem had brought Europeans in closer contact with the commercial civilization of the Middle

East and with the spices, silks, porcelains, carpets, and metal work of the Orient. Europe was dependent for its luxuries upon this Eastern trade, and the city-states of Italy—Venice, Pisa, Florence, Genoa—were enriched and civilized by it.

The gold florin was first minted in Florence in 1252; Venice began coining ducats in 1280. Joint-stock companies operated in Italy in the fourteenth century, permitting risks to be shared and larger accumulations of capital to be amassed. Renaissance Italy in large measure evolved the methods necessary to the discovery and exploitation of the New World. The perpetually quarreling city-states themselves failed to provide the political basis for such colonial undertakings, but to a remarkable extent Italy provided the bankers, map makers, shipbuilders, mathematicians, captains, and sailors who opened the New World to those national states which emerged in Western Europe during the fifteenth and six-teenth centuries.

The new national monarchies owed much to the commercial revolution which tore at the web of feudal restrictions and which created middle class support for the kings in opposition to the feudal barons. Kings drew upon this revolutionary middle class for the lawyers and administrators and for the money to staff and finance their growing governments. Gunpowder was introduced from China, and new inventions made money more readily con-vertible into power, including firearms, blast furnaces to build heavy armaments, and artillery to break down the walls of castles. The Crusades had brought Western monarchs in contact with Ori-ental despotism and they applied this experience, notably in the areas of taxation and military arts, to the creation of absolute mon-archies in the West. The crusades at the same time appear to have aroused in Western soldiers a sense of national loyalty which strengthened the state and the crown against the Universal Church and against the provincial lords.

The European national state was a new development in human history, creating an order of power not shared by the world's dy-nasties and empires. Geographically Western Europe was but a peninsula on the great Eurasian continent, and one which con-tinued to be divided and distracted by incessant national wars, but now it went forth in confidence to dominate the world.

First of these new monarchies was Portugal. Securely bounded by mountains and ocean, Portugal achieved a sense of national unity in the victorious twelfth- and thirteenth-century struggles against the Moors, and it went on to strengthen its nationality under a long line of capable kings. Spain emerged in the fifteenth century victorious against the Moors, and it achieved political unity with the unification of Ferdinand's Aragon and Isabella's Castile. In France, meanwhile, Louis XI was moving energetically against the nobles, and in England Henry Tudor survived the Wars of the Roses to bring that nation under strong central government.

Spain, supreme among the nations for a century, entered upon a centuries-long decline late in the 1500s. The Spanish Armada met defeat in 1588, and the Netherlands rose in revolt to win independence from Spain a generation later. With the decline of Spain, a new era of colonization began. The Dutch, the French, and the English set forth almost simultaneously at the opening of the seventeenth century to compete in the exploitation of the New World. By then Spain and Portugal had enjoyed more than a century's start on them, and Spain was entrenched in an empire which extended from Santa Fe to Buenos Aires.

II

Exploration   In a prison in Genoa at the close of the thirteenth century Marco Polo, the traveler, dictated his *Book of Various Experiences* from which Europe learned for the first time of the vast Asian empire of Kublai Khan. Polo told of the power and wealth of the court at Peking and of such unknown lands as Tibet, Burma, Japan, Java, Madagascar, and Zanzibar. His work fired the imaginations of Europeans who in the course of the Crusades had acquired their first intimations of distant realms, rich and fine beyond their own understandings. Trade with Arab merchants of the Middle East sifted into Europe manufactured goods and spices which brought great wealth to the merchant princes of the Italian city-states. To find a direct route to the Spice Islands became the burning wish of European monarchs and merchants in the fifteenth, sixteenth, and seventeenth centuries. In the course of those three centuries European explorers ranged the globe seeking avenues to this wealth other than the one which Europe was unable to win eastward from Alexandria in its struggle with Islam.

Beginning early in the fifteenth century, Portugal, under the direction of Prince Henry the Navigator, sent out expeditions almost annually which explored the Azores and made their way down the coast of Africa. In 1488, Bartholomew Diaz emerged from a storm to find that he had rounded the Cape of Good Hope and was on the eastern coast of Africa. A decade later Vasco da Gama set forth beyond the Cape to win the Eastern trade for Portugal. On the Malabar Coast of India, amid bloody struggles with the established, marvelously polyglot Eastern traders, the Portuguese captured the colony of Goa, which they retained until 1961. From there they proceeded around the subcontinent of India to China and the East Indies winning the trade for Portugal.

The possibility of an alternative route to China, westward across the Atlantic, meanwhile, was one which suggested itself as theoretically possible on the basis of both the knowledge and the misinformation of late fifteenth-century Europe in world geography. That the world was round was widely known and taught in the European universities. As to its size there were differences of opinion, and errors in calculation, as in the case of Behaim's globe of 1492, sometimes reduced the world to a size which made a China trade appear practicable. Christopher Columbus of Genoa was apparently more optimistically misled than most investigators in his calculations. He estimated the distance from the Canary Islands to Cathay to be about 2,500 miles, and it was he who first seriously conceived the idea of the Western route.

Portugal was the logical nation to advance such a project, but the Portuguese knew too much to accept the global miscalculations of Columbus. Portugal therefore turned him down, but after eight years of campaigning, Columbus won the support of Queen Isabella of Spain, and, in 1492, on a smooth sea, under pleasant skies the *Nina*, the *Pinta*, and the *Santa Maria* sailed in the course of a month and three days from the Canary Islands to the Bahamas. Then, and on three subsequent trips to the Caribbean, as he himself boasted, he "placed under their Highnesses' sovereignty more land than there is in Africa and Europe." He furthermore established the colony of Hispaniola which became the starting point for the incredible conquests of the next two generations.

In 1513 Vasco Nuñez de Balboa moved in twenty-five days through 45 miles of jungle at Darien to discover the Pacific. In 1519 Ferdinand Magellan set forth from Seville on the greatest voyage of discovery in history to find the route to the Spice Islands.

Moving down the coast of South America, Magellan discovered the treacherous straits that bear his name, and the navigation of which alone took longer than had the entire first voyage of Columbus. Outriding storms and mutiny, he sailed his fleet off into the Pacific, where he was three months out of sight of land before his ships arrived at Guam. From there they sailed to the Philippine Islands, where Magellan was killed in the course of native warfare but not before he heard his Malayan servant converse with natives in the Malayan tongue and so knew he had achieved the exploring feat of the ages. Three years after setting sail, one of the five ships and 18 of the original 239 men rounded the world and returned to Spain.

In the twenties and thirties the Spanish conquistadores, soldiers of fortune directing their own private enterprises, swiftly subdued the great empires of Latin America with small companies of men. In America, as in India and the Orient, such incredible conquests were made possible in part by internal rivalries, which brought tribes to the side of the European conqueror. In part they were achieved by virtue of a spirit of absolute self-assurance in what surely must have appeared ludicrously impossible situations.

Hernando Cortés, invading Mexico in 1519 with a force of 550 men, seventeen horses, and ten cannons, marched to Mexico City and overthrew Montezuma II and his Aztec empire (aided by the Aztec conviction that he was Quetzalcoatl, the conquering king, so it was believed, of a former century who would one day return to reassert his authority). So it was also with Pizarro against the Incas in Peru, with Montejo in Yucatan, with Alvarado in Guatemala, and with Jimenez de Quesada in New Granada. Within two decades by these slender means the main conquest of Latin America was complete, and the Spanish Crown in company with the Catholic Church moved rapidly to assert centralized authority over the territory which private adventurers had brought within its power.

If Portugal lost the main opportunity by refusing the offers of Columbus and Magellan, it nevertheless gained from the Pope, following the first voyage of Columbus, sovereignty over all American lands within somewhat more than 1,000 miles of the Cape Verde Islands, a decision which gave Portugal her title to Brazil. Then in 1500, whether accidentally or by design, Pedralvarez Cabral landed on the coast of Brazil and claimed it for Portugal. As with the Spanish, private initiative conquered the territory before the Crown moved in to assert centralized authority. In 1580 Philip II united Spain and Portugal under one rule and so was the sovereign of America. Northern America, however, rejected by the Spanish because of its seeming lack of gold and silver mines and fountains of youth, lay open to the nations of Northern Europe.

Though Spanish explorers ranged through much of what became the United States, the uninviting nature of the plains regions as well as the lack of precious metals had discouraged their settlement north of Santa Fe. The first Europeans after the Norsemen to penetrate the North Atlantic seaboard apparently were nameless French, English, and Portuguese fishermen interested in cod rather than conquest. The great French explorer Jacques Cartier was apparently not surprised to come upon a group of Breton fishermen in the course of his discovery of the St. Lawrence River in the 1530s. These fishermen were among the many sailors who went among new lands and returned without leaving a mark on history. Ambitious kings were not moved to found empires by a desire for fish, even if perhaps they should have been. On the other hand, there were tall tales told by the Indians of gold and silver and also of a nearby western ocean which held out promise of a northwest passage to the Orient. In the course of this search Cartier discovered Quebec. He found no gold and silver, however, nor any northwest passage, and France left the region to the fishermen until the settlement of Quebec in 1608 by Samuel de Champlain.

England, with earlier claims in North America than France, was similarly slow to capitalize on them. In 1497, a year after the second American voyage of Columbus, another sailor from Genoa, Giovanni Caboto, was commissioned by Henry VII of England and sailed to Cape Breton, where he claimed the land for the English King. The delighted Tudor monarch presented a gift of £10 "to hym that founde the new Isle." During the following century, English fishermen came increasingly to dry their catch on the banks of Newfoundland, while English sea dogs familiarized themselves with the Americas in the course of wide-ranging raids upon Spanish and Portuguese colonial ports.

In the 1560s John Hawkins entered the slave trade between Africa and South America in the face of the Spanish monopoly of the trade. In 1577 his flag captain Francis Drake sailed on his three-year freebooting voyage around the world, while Martin Frobisher discovered Hudson's Strait. Sir Walter Raleigh and Sir

Humphrey Gilbert tried vainly to establish permanent American colonies by their own private efforts and fortunes, to find to their sorrow that "private purses are cold comforts to adventurers," and Spain remained a fearsome hazard to any English colonizing venture. Then the defeat of the Spanish Armada opened new possibilities, the accession to the English throne in 1603 of James I brought peace with Spain and with Scotland, the joint-stock company was being successfully applied to various areas of English trade, and England was at last in a position to profit from tight-fisted Henry VII's ten-pound investment.

III

Settlement of Virginia In 1606 James I issued two business charters: one to the Virginia Company of London, authorizing settlement of what later became southern Pennsylvania, North Carolina, Virginia, and Maryland; the other to the Virginia Company of Plymouth, covering what later became New England and the middle colonies. The patents overlapped each other, probably to provide altercations which would place the Crown in the role of mediator. Both were joint-stock companies, financed by private subscription, and both, hopeful of rich returns in gold and silver, immediately organized expeditions and sent out colonizing parties.

Inexperienced and ill-provided, the New England settlement of the Virginia Company of Plymouth foundered, and the survivors were returned to London. The Jamestown settlement of the London Company, as the Virginia Company of London was called, equally inexperienced and almost as poorly served, faced similarly grueling hardships. A motley band of gentlemen and prisoners, the first settlers were more interested in futile searchings for gold than in the homely task of grubbing a living from the new soil. English grains did not transplant well in American soil, and the settlers were reluctant to adjust to the native diet, mainly Indian corn. Disregarding the instructions of the company, the settlers founded the town on a swampy, malarial site along the James River. More than half the settlers died during the first year, and only the energetic leadership of Capt. John Smith saved the lives of the rest. Thereafter, for the next decade, the settlement survived under a regime of military discipline.

It had nevertheless been intended from the first that the English settlers in America, contrary to the practice of all the other colonizing nations of Europe, were, as the original London Company charter declared, to "enjoy all liberties, franchises, and immunities . . . to all intents and purposes, as if they had been abiding and born, within this our realm of England." Accordingly in 1619 the company sent a new governor to Virginia with instructions to call an assembly "freely to be elected by the inhabitants . . . to make and ordain whatsoever laws and orders should by them be thought good and profitable." Self-government was introduced to America that summer with the meeting of the first Virginia House of Burgesses.

The second meeting of the assembly in 1621 was assured by the company that orders would not bind the colony unless ratified by the assembly. The assembly in its turn asserted rights in matters of taxation and administration exceeding those claimed by Parliament. As a practical matter, however, effective authority continued to rest with the company officials. The time of trials appeared over when, in 1622, a surprise Indian raid wiped out virtually all the settlements outside Jamestown. The disaster played into the hands of the opposition to the company leadership. In 1624 the company's charter was revoked, and Virginia became a royal colony, the governor and council thereafter being appointed by the king.

Tobacco made the experiment pay. First raised successfully as a commercial product in 1613—it is said, by John Rolfe, the husband of Pocahontas—tobacco became an immediately successful money crop with a rapidly increasing market in England. The company officers were concerned lest this new development bring down upon the colony the wrath of King James I, who looked upon smoking as "lothesome to the eye, hatefull to the nose, harmefull to the brain, dangerous to the Lungs." They were concerned also that concentration on the tobacco crop would destroy the possibility of a self-sustaining economy, for it continued to be necessary to supply the colony with foodstuffs from England. Attempts to introduce manufacturing and varied farming largely failed, however, as the artisans and farmers sent over for the purpose deserted their former occupations to benefit from the one main source of profit.

Recruited mainly from the English yeomanry, the early settlers of Virginia arrived commonly as indentured servants, working for five years in the service of an employer to defray the cost of their passage. Thereafter they were freemen for whom land was easily obtainable. There were a few well-to-do Englishmen among the early settlers, who acquired large plantations along the James River. They were exceptional however. The more representative farm in the early years was one of three or four hundred acres, scattered along the navigable portions of the rivers. These farms were worked by individual families with the assistance of perhaps two or three indentured servants. African Negroes were first brought to Virginia in 1619, but for its first three generations the colony relied primarily on white labor.

Unlike most of the later English mainland colonies, Virginia was not intended as an asylum where refugees might conduct themselves in ways which were considered unacceptably un-English in the homeland. It was the wish of the Virginians to recreate the English countryside as nearly as possible in America, and they did so more nearly than any of the later colonies. The royally appointed governor and his council comprised almost a local nobility, reserving to themselves the right to wear gold braid and, more importantly, reserving to themselves most of the lucrative political positions.

The House of Burgesses was the Virginia House of Commons, elected initially by all adult males but later only by property holders. Justices of the peace, appointed also by the Crown, played much the same key role in local government in Virginia as in England. The Church of England was established in Virginia, and the vestrymen, soon a self-perpetuating group, responsible for the morals of the community and care of the poor as well as for the upkeep of the church, shared local responsibilities with the justices and like them were drawn from the "better sort" in the community.

In 1632 King Charles I granted a slice of northern Virginia to the court favorite George Calvert, Lord Baltimore, whose son, Cecilius, two years later succeeded in establishing on the basis of his own personal resources the colony of Maryland. Planned as a haven for Catholics from English persecution, Maryland for some reason recruited its population from the first largely from English Protestants. Consequently religious disputes broke out before the first ships, the *Ark* and the *Dove,* had landed, and the struggle continued between the Catholic leadership and the Protestant majority. A solution to the difficulty was found in 1649 in the Toleration Act, granting religious freedom to trinitarian Christians, but troubles continued and actual civil war broke out during the time of Cromwell and the Great Rebellion in England. The Toleration Act was repealed for a time, and even after it was passed again into law, various acts were passed limiting Catholic political participation.

It had been the intention of Baltimore to fashion a more thoroughly aristocratic government and society than had existed in England for centuries, and he, himself, devised his own charter for this purpose, choosing as his pattern the fourteenth-century charter of the bishop of the palatinate of Durham. As absolute lord and proprietor his ownership of the land was unrestricted, and he possessed the right to make any laws he wished, subject to the "advice, assent, and approbation of the freemen of the province." This arrangement, which gave the Calverts greater authority than kings enjoyed in England, was looked upon as a reasonable application to America of a feudal authority such as had been wielded in the medieval English marches, at the time when England had had its own frontier areas and had endowed lords with great powers in exchange for the performance of military duties.

In America the system faltered at once. Amid the religious struggle, isolated from the seat of royal power, faced with an abundance of land and a shortage of settlers and obliged to seek the approbation of the freemen, Cecilius Calvert soon made new terms with his colonists. The charter terms obliged him to put up with an elected assembly, and in 1639 he assented to the demand of the assembly that it share with him the right to initiate legislation. Within a dozen years the settled custom had developed of annual sessions, triennial elections, and a two-house legislature, the lower house being composed of freemen whose consent was required for all laws. Maryland and Virginia, created for different purposes under sharply contrasting charters, rapidly developed systems of society and government which were quite similar in major respects, the result of a common culture adjusting to a common geographical setting with the results that flowed from its tobacco economy.

IV

Settlement of New England

The addition of one hundred and one souls was lost to Virginia in 1620 when the *Mayflower* missed its course and landed to the north on Cape Cod. Moving across the bay this band of Pilgrims founded a colony which they called Plymouth, the name of the English city from which they had sailed. As Separatists, the majority of the Pilgrims represented the farthermost advance of the Protestant Reformation in early seventeenth-century England. Not content with the separation from Rome which the Church of England had accomplished in the 1530s, the Separatists removed themselves from the Church of England itself and covenanted together in completely autonomous religious bodies. From the point of view of the English Church and Crown, this was at least as lawless a course as the refusal to recognize the civil authority of the state. Consequently Separatist leaders were executed, while their followers were driven underground or out of the country.

Those who sailed on the *Mayflower* were enjoined by their pastor, Mr. Robinson, to remember that according to the true religion each man was a priest unto himself and should conduct himself in that spirit. Guided by this injunction, and by the determination to curb the non-Separatists among them, the Pilgrims, upon planting their colony, drew up the Mayflower Compact promising to abide in their civil affairs by the principle of direct democracy. The Mayflower Compact remains a wonderfully simple and clear-cut demonstration of the democratic tendencies which from the first were inherent in Protestant Christianity. Materially, Plymouth contributed little to the development of New England, and after several generations it merged with Massachusetts. Its important contribution was in its initiation of that tradition—symbolized in the *Mayflower*, the Mayflower Compact, Plymouth Rock, and Thanksgiving —by which later Americans came to interpret themselves.

Unlike the Pilgrims, the Puritans of the Massachusetts Bay Company, who commenced to arrive a few years later, considered themselves unseparated from the Church of England. They thought of themselves as loyal communicants, who wished to save the Church by purifying it of false Roman Catholic accretions. But, despite their professions of loyalty, this reforming zeal made them unwanted by the English hierarchy and by the Crown, and they therefore removed to New England, where they might create a New Zion, a recreation of Christianity as it was revealed in the Bible and as they supposed it to have been practiced in the days of the early church.

Much more powerfully placed in England than the Pilgrims, the Puritans succeeded in acquiring from the King a business charter similar to that of the Virginia Company, one which placed their company in complete charge of a large territorial concession. Fearing that the company might fall into the hands of unsympathetic stockholders, radical Puritans among the company shareholders themselves departed from England to Massachusetts, taking their charter with them in 1630 and so breaking all direct legal connection with the homeland. This questionably legal act placed them, in their own view, in virtual independence of the English Crown. The Great Migration of 20,000 came in the first generation, as compared to the 6,000 that had arrived in Virginia during its first generation of settlement. Then, with the outbreak of civil war in England in 1642, the migration largely ceased. Most New Englanders at the time of the American Revolution were descended from that first generation.

Salem was settled in 1628, and in 1630 one thousand additional settlers, including the company officers bringing with them their charter, settled Boston and other towns. John Winthrop, who dominated the company and the colony for a generation, favored a highly centralized government ruled by himself and his board of assistants or magistrates. A legislative body was created of the magistrates—company officials elected by the stockholders to the board of directors, called the General Court—and representatives elected by the freemen. The company admitted as freemen only a select group among the adult males who were members of one of the authorized Puritan churches, thereby probably eliminating a majority of the adult males as voters. The issue of whether the magistrates could set aside the votes of the elected deputies resulted in 1644 in the dividing of the General Court into two separate houses.

Local government meanwhile was permitted to develop of itself to an extent. The result was the town meeting form of government, where church members gathered in the meeting house, as the church was called, to decide upon local affairs and to rotate among themselves numerous civic duties. In 1647 the General Court admitted nonfreemen to active, although nonvoting, participation in local affairs. In 1648 nonfreemen were permitted to take part in any town meeting, council, or court proceeding in the colony. In the same year the Commonwealth of Massachusetts published its *General Laws and Liberties*, a conglomeration of General Court legislation, Mosaic law, and altered English common law. Within a generation the colony had altered itself from a company to a commonwealth, based on a working compromise between the authoritarian theocratic principles of the leaders and the demands of the majority.

New England Puritanism, although basically Calvinist, did not accept Calvin as the one indisputable authority, and, among other differences, placed much less emphasis on the doctrine of pre-destination. The Puritans believed that with Adam's fall, all mankind had sinned and deserved everlasting damnation. Christ's sacrifice, however, opened salvation to all who truly loved Christ and desired to seek Him. The desire came more readily to some than to others, but none could be certain that he was saved. However, those who had reason to believe that they were on the way to grace, if their evidence was acceptable to the congregation, would be admitted as one of the visible saints.

These saints would band together to worship autonomously under a pastor of their own choosing, as they believed had been the practice in the primitive Christian church. Election was achieved by faith alone and not by good works. Still, good behavior was evidence of sanctification; in practice the Puritans compromised in this matter. They compromised further in 1662 in the Halfway Covenant, which admitted the children of church members to a nonvoting membership in the congregation, while denying them communion. This covenant marks that decline in Puritan fervor which was a theme of sermons throughout the seventeenth century and into the worldly eighteenth.

The compromise did not extend to open deviation from religious orthodoxy. In 1635 Roger Williams was driven from Massachusetts for questioning the authority of the Church, and shortly thereafter Anne Hutchinson was driven after him into exile. Williams, a promising, apparently orthodox, minister caused trouble soon after his arrival when he questioned the authority by which the colony had preempted land from the Indians. If this were not subversive enough, he proceeded to question the authority of the ministry in matters of dogma.

It was the novel contention of Williams that religious truths were not certainly revealed to man in the Bible, and that therefore no priesthood was warranted forcing its dogma upon others. He further argued that men must be brought willingly to religion; that it could not be forced upon them. Anne Hutchinson, on the other hand, was an Antinomian, believing herself to be in direct mystical communication with God. Beyond freeing her from the necessity of submitting to church mediation, this placed her in a position to

judge on the eligibility of the Boston ministers, most of whom failed
to pass muster. Her following in the colony was so large that in
1636 it succeeded in electing its candidate, Henry Vane, as governor over Winthrop. The orthodox rallied their forces, however,
reelected Winthrop the next year and in 1638 banished Anne
Hutchinson forever from the colony.

Williams founded Providence, while Mrs. Hutchinson's party
founded Portsmouth. Friction in Portsmouth resulted in the founding of Newport, friction in Providence resulted in the founding of
Warwick, and a disharmonious union of the four towns was officially confirmed in 1663 by royal charter as the colony of Rhode
Island and Providence Plantations. Founded on the principle of
complete religious liberty and—incidentally—household democracy, the head of each home being a voting member of the community, Rhode Island was a precocious manifestation of the liber-
tarianism which, in the coming years, was to emerge from the
Protestant religious struggles in England.

Connecticut was founded mainly by orthodox Massachusetts
Puritans and separated peaceably from the mother colony. In 1639
four towns united themselves under the Fundamental Orders of
Connecticut, and in 1662 Connecticut received a royal charter,
which granted it a remarkably high degree of autonomy and which
annexed to it the more radically Puritan colony of New Haven. Attempts to colonize upper New England, meanwhile, had been
checked by troubles with the Indians and by legal disputes over
ownership. Massachusetts succeeded for a time in acquiring title to
New Hampshire, while remaining in control of Maine throughout
the colonial period.

The Puritanism of the first settlers, reviving itself in varying
sectarian forms during the centuries to come, was to remain a
fundamental aspect of the American character. Glorified by some
writers as the source of American self-reliance and moral strength,
it has been denounced by others as a narrowly repressive influence
upon the thought and conduct of the nation. Few would deny
the abiding strength of its influence, however. Its original character, therefore, has remained a matter of continuing significance
and controversy.

Since historical scholarship centered in New England down almost to the close of the nineteenth century, Puritanism tended
to receive highly sympathetic treatment, except for the occasional
Puritanical self-castigations of writers such as Charles Francis

Adams, Jr. Against this generally fixed assumption of superiority there was bound to be a reaction from what New England scholars had always treated as the provinces. Most eloquent and influential among the critics of New England Puritanism in the early twentieth century was Vernon L. Parrington, writing his *Main Currents in American Thought* (1930) from the distant University of Washington. To Parrington the history of New England was one of a swift decline from a bigoted but nevertheless heroic "Hebraized theocracy" to an arid, narrowly provincial society, reduced in its intellectual life to "unamiable bickerings."

Against the attacks of Parrington and others, notably James Truslow Adams and Thomas Jefferson Wertenbaker, a new generation of New England historians has kept up a continuous counteroffensive. Kenneth Murdock's *Increase Mather* (1926), although not widely influential at the time, initiated the new trend with a biography which revealed a remarkable breadth of learning in a leading New England minister whom Parrington dismissed as having "satisfied his intellectual curiosity by extolling the sufficiency of the creed of the fathers." Samuel Eliot Morison, in *Puritan Pronaos* (1936) and *Harvard College in the Seventeenth Century* (1936), found early New England to have been the colonial center of enlightened and comparatively tolerant inquiry, and this by virtue of the very intellectualism of Puritanism.

Perry Miller followed with a massive construct of *The New England Mind: Seventeenth Century* (1939), supported by a companion volume, *The New England Mind: From Colony to Province* (1953). The philosopher Ralph Barton Perry set forth, during World War II, to trace the nation's free institutions to Puritan roots in *Puritanism and Democracy* (1944). Writings in this vein continue, and, although they have no doubt failed to efface the popular image of the puritan as a witch-hunter and a blue-nosed dry, they currently hold the field in the area of scholarship.

V

Settlement under Charles II   In 1642 rebellion broke out in England against the King, and the English settlement of America was interrupted during the course of the struggle, which continued to the coming to the throne of Charles II in 1660. During

Charles's reign, which lasted to 1685, the second series of colony plantings took place, which resulted in the establishment of New York, Pennsylvania, New Jersey, and North and South Carolina. Interested in colonies mainly as a means of paying off obligations, Charles granted the Carolinas to eight aristocratic supporters in 1663, New York to his brother, the Duke of York, in 1664, and Pennsylvania to William Penn, son of a royal creditor, in 1681.

The intricately aristocratic intentions of the "true and absolute Lords Proprietors" of the Carolinas was indicated in their "Fundamental Constitutions," issued in 1669, by which the colony was divided into three counties and each county in turn subdivided into eight seignories, eight baronies, four precincts, and an indefinite number of large manorial estates. A fixed hierarchy was established of palatine, landgrave, cacique, and so on down to leet men, who, with their descendants, were to remain perpetually in a state of serfdom. At the bottom were the slaves, over whom the masters were given complete authority by law. The Fundamental Constitutions never received the "assent and approbation of the freeman" required by the charter and so never went entirely into effect. However, they remained a guide for the proprietors during the first generation of settlement and a disturbance to the settlers.

As it turned out, the aristocratic character of the southern portion of the grant, which became South Carolina, was dictated less by the intentions of the proprietors than it was by the geographical environment, which invited the introduction of slaves on a large scale and which brought great profits from the culture of rice. In 1719, after endless struggles with the proprietors, the South Carolinians performed a dignified revolution, which was accepted by the English Crown, and the province continued thereafter as a royal colony.

The northern part of the Carolinas, lacking the marketable cash crop of rice and, more important, lacking such port facilities as were provided South Carolina by the Ashley and the Cooper Rivers, followed from the first a separate history, after 1694 under separate governments. Beyond these difficulties the North Carolinians faced neglect from the proprietors and hostility from Virginia, with which North Carolina competed to some extent in the tobacco trade. Consequently the development of North Carolina was relatively slow among the colonies and its general economic condition relatively bad.

Originally founded by the Dutch as New Netherlands in the 1620s, New York was taken in war by the English in 1664. The Dutch at the opening of the seventeenth century were the most powerful maritime people in the world, and they might well have won North America for themselves had their interests not been concentrated elsewhere. The main concern of the Dutch East India Company, however, was wresting the spice trade from the Portuguese and establishing trading centers in the East Indies. The explorations of Henry Hudson on the Hudson River and in Hudson Bay were for the purpose of finding the northwest passage which would facilitate the trade with the Far East. Founded in 1621, the Dutch West India Company acquired various American possessions, including for a time Brazil, in addition to the settlement of New Netherlands. The company was much more concerned with raiding Spanish and Portuguese towns and treasure ships, however, than it was with establishing flourishing colonies.

The settlers of New Netherlands, possessing none of the rights of self-government which their English neighbors enjoyed, suffered under the tyranny or thievery of a succession of governors ending with Peter Stuyvesant, who lost the colony to the English. In a largely unsuccessful effort to attract settlers, the company offered vast tracts of land, great manorial authority over the tenants and the title of Patroon to any who would bring 500 families of tenants to New Netherlands. As a result of this system and of the more successful English adaptation of it, rural New York was divided into lordly estates where aristocrats ruled the countryside in a fashion not to be seen elsewhere in the northern mainland colonies.

In the course of war with the Dutch in 1664 the disgruntled colony fell into English hands without a struggle and was turned over to King Charles's younger brother, the Duke of York, under a charter which omitted the usual statement concerning the assent of freemen to the passage of laws. Of all the Thirteen Colonies, New York alone failed to summon a legislature during its first generation of existence. This was made possible in part by an exceptionally able governor, Richard Nicolls, who ruled the colony under "the Duke's laws," a combination of New England, English, and Dutch law. It was made possible in part also by the assent of the Dutch settlers, who had never enjoyed representative institutions in the colony, and who were better governed and securer in their rights under the conqueror than they had previously been.

The trouble came from English settlers who had moved to Long Island from New England and who complained of the "slavery" of being taxed by a nonrepresentative government. An assembly was finally summoned in 1683.

Meanwhile the Duke of York assigned a portion of his grant, New Jersey, to two friends. One of these sold his portion to two Quakers, and later on the widow of the other sold the rest to a group of proprietors. The subsequent colonial history of the Jerseys was confusing and litigious. The influence of the Quakers tended to predominate in West Jersey; the Puritan influence was marked in East Jersey, settled mainly from New England and Long Island.

In 1681, Charles II deeded a large grant of adjacent territory to the English courtier and convert to Quakerism, William Penn, in lieu of debts owed Penn's father. Penn, connected already with the West Jersey venture, set forth in Pennsylvania on a "Holy Experiment," the establishment of a community based upon the principles of political liberty and religious freedom. It was to be an asylum for Quakers, persecuted in England and in all American colonies except Rhode Island, but beyond that it was to be a refuge for those throughout Europe persecuted for their religious beliefs.

The Quakers, or Society of Friends, were a religious sect founded by George Fox amid the religious turmoil which accompanied and followed the English Civil Wars. The Quakers brought Protestantism to its logical conclusion with the announcement of the priesthood of all men and women. Quakerism placed reliance for religious authority not first of all upon Scripture, but upon the divine inner light of each individual conscience. While not original with the Quakers, the doctrine of the inner light was given a uniquely central position in their belief, dispensing with the need for priest, for formal church service, or for explicit dogma. In colonial America, Quakerism for a time became the dominant religion in Rhode Island, New Jersey, Delaware, Pennsylvania, and North Carolina, and it appeared that it might become the dominant American religion. It lacked organization and, subsequently, with the winning of prosperity and social status, it lost its proselytizing zeal. During the eighteenth century it was overtaken by the more evangelical sects.

Penn presented his design in 1682 in the "Frame of Government" based upon the belief, blasphemous from the Puritan point of view, that, though men might be evil, man was not innately so. "Governments," he declared, "like clocks, go from the motion men give them, so by them they are ruined too. . . . Let men be good, and the government cannot be bad. . . ." He thereupon provided a two-house legislature, both of them elective, which set about at once to give Penn troubles. Obliged to return to England, Penn for a time lost much of his control over the colony, and his charter was at one point revoked and later restored.

The Frame of Government was altered on several occasions and finally in 1701 Penn issued the "Charter of Privileges," establishing the only unicameral government among the Thirteen Colonies and reasserting the principle of religious freedom. He remained steadfast in his purpose to create the freest and most flourishing of the English mainland colonies. The Charter of Privileges remained the Pennsylvania constitution throughout the rest of the colonial period and provided the liberal pattern, with the coming of the Revolution, for the most democratic constitution of any of the new states. Delaware, meanwhile, had been leased to Penn by the Duke of York for ten thousand years and, early in the eighteenth century, was established as a separate colony.

The last of the Thirteen Colonies to be established, Georgia, was founded in 1733 by the philanthropist James Edward Oglethorpe, partly to provide a buffer colony against the Spanish in the Floridas and partly to provide an asylum for prisoners in England whose only crime had been that of indebtedness. This model colony prohibited slavery and rum, and it limited holdings to fifty acres—restrictive conditions which stunted its growth during the twenty years it remained a private colony. Thereafter, as provided by the original charter, it reverted to the Crown. The idealistic laws were repealed, and the first main development of the colony took place.

VI

The Imperial System

The little seventeenth-century English nation performed a seemingly impossible achievement in establishing itself on the long coastline from Maine to South Carolina when one considers that it took place during a century of furious political, social, economic, religious, and military strife at home. Actually it is within the context of this domestic disruption that the great English success on the American mainland is to be understood. Most importantly it provided the colonies with the abundant population which the Dutch were unable to entice to New Netherlands and which the much more populous France was unable to attract to Quebec. Religious discontent, and to a lesser degree economic discontent, populated New England during the absolutism of Charles I and the "Romish" regime of Archbishop Laud.

The Puritan ascendancy in England during the next generation ended the impulse to emigrate to New England, but, in turn, it served to double the population of Virginia from 15,000 to 30,000 in a new migration which included mainly yeomen and mechanics escaping disorganized conditions in England. This subsequent migration included also a sprinkling of aristocratic cavaliers. The aristocratic Randolphs established themselves in Virginia during this period, as did the Washingtons. Then, following the restoration of the Stuarts, Pennsylvania gained much of its population from religious refugees, not only from England but also from the Germanies, and so, to a greater or lesser extent, did all of the colonies south of New England.

England was not the only nation of Europe which had discontented subjects, but the English, unlike any other colonizing power, combined persecution at home with toleration abroad. Queen Elizabeth, at a time when Catholic subversives were being drawn, quartered, and disemboweled before shrieking mobs, contemplated a Roman Catholic colony in America, where English Catholics would be free from persecution and whereby the English Queen would be rid of potential enemies of the Crown. The French did not permit the potentially subversive Huguenots to emigrate to Quebec; nor did the Spanish permit their Jews and Protestants to escape to Spanish America. The English were alone in this tolerant policy, and the result was a thriving population of about 250,000 in the English-American colonies by the close of the seventeenth century.

The outbreak of the English Rebellion in 1642 came in the nick of time to preserve the Massachusetts Commonwealth in its independent position. In 1636 Charles I took legal steps to have the Massachusetts charter annulled. He won the court case, but the Massachusetts General Court refused to abide by the decision. The Crown replied by appointing Sir Ferdinando Gorges, a man with large experience in the colonizing of America, as Governor General of New England. Gorges had not yet reached New England, however, when the Rebellion broke out, and soon a Puritan leader, Oliver Cromwell, emerged who had much "pity" for New England and left it in possession of its autonomy.

A notable instance of New England independence was the founding of the New England Confederation in 1643, on the basis of no authority from England, among the colonies of Massachusetts Bay, Plymouth, Connecticut, and New Haven. Organized in defense against the French, the Dutch, and the Indians, the Confederation continued, theoretically at least, until 1691, defeating the Narragansett Indians, concluding a treaty with New Netherlands, and adjudicating various boundary disputes. It was weakened from the first by intercolonial jealousies, however, and with the revocation of the Massachusetts charter in 1684 it became substantially inoperative.

In Virginia the English Rebellion resulted in the temporary deposing of the Royalist Sir William Berkeley as governor, to be followed in office during the interregnum by three Puritans. But the Puritan government in England did not stir itself to get rid of Berkeley as a citizen of Virginia or to support the Puritans who followed him. The pro-Royalist assembly refused to be dissolved and instead increased its authority.

In Maryland the English Rebellion was the occasion for a rising of Protestants under William Claiborne against the Catholic leadership. In control of the colony for several years, the insurgents nevertheless failed to receive substantial English support, and Lord Baltimore soon regained authority. In 1654 revolt broke out again, the proprietary governor was deposed, and the Toleration Act was repealed. In 1657, however, a personal appeal to Cromwell by Lord Baltimore resulted in the return of his proprietary authority and reenactment of the Toleration Act. Cromwell did envision a "Western Design" to Protestantize America, especially in the West Indies. A result was the capture of Jamaica from the Spanish. Beyond that little was done, however, as events absorbed Cromwell's energies in Europe.

Pressure from Dutch competition in the carrying trade during the period of Cromwellian authority did result in the Navigation Act of 1651. The first general law controlling colonial commerce, the act excluded from trade within the empire the ships of foreign nations. No provision was made for enforcement, however, and the law was widely evaded. In 1660, following the Restoration, a further Navigation Act was passed confirming the prohibition of foreign ships, and restricting to trade within the empire certain "enumerated articles," including tobacco and indigo. In 1663 the Staple Act was passed requiring that all foreign commodities destined for the colonies be landed first in England. In 1668 a Council of Trade was created and in turn supplanted in 1675 by a further supervisory agency, the Lords of Trade. Overworked members of the Privy Council, these Lords of Trade were distracted from their responsibilities to the American colonies. Their one main achievement was the creation of the plan for the Dominion of New England.

English pressure against New England following the Restoration was resumed in 1676, when Edward Randolph was sent to Boston to investigate charges of violations of the Navigation Acts and to consider doing something about the government of Massachusetts before "all hopes of it may be hereafter lost." Following Randolph's hostile report, legal proceedings were brought against Massachusetts which resulted in the revocation of her charter in 1684. Henceforth it remained a royal colony.

Plans for consolidating New England under central royal authority were worked out, and in 1686 Sir Edmund Andros arrived as Governor General of the resulting Dominion of New England. A year later Connecticut, New York, and New Jersey were added to it. No provisions were made for elective assemblies, and Andros prohibited town meetings, except for one meeting annually to elect selectmen and assess property for tax purposes. His efforts to consolidate the region were not altogether effective, but the opposition was even less so, until the coming of the Glorious Revolution in England in 1688.

In 1688, the openly Catholic King, James II, in a bloodless revolution, was driven from the country and the Protestant leader of the Dutch Republic, William of Orange, with his English wife, Mary, were jointly declared King and Queen of England. The parliamentary appointment of the new monarchs was an assertion of parliamentary supremacy which was amplified by, among other things, the passage of the Bill of Rights, limiting the power of the King.

The result in America was a series of little glorious revolutions and the passage of a series of colonial bills of rights, all of which were set aside by the Privy Council. In Boston, Andros, Randolph, and other Dominion officials were jailed, and a government was created which restored the old charter and pledged allegiance to William and Mary. In New York the Andros administration, headed by Governor Francis Nicholson, was overthrown in a rebellion led by a German immigrant, Jacob Leisler, who was apparently motivated largely by anti-Catholic sentiment.

In Maryland the delay of Lord Baltimore in acknowledging William and Mary was met with the overthrow of his authority by a Protestant Association, which controlled the colony for two years. Disturbances occurred meanwhile in North and South Carolina which were, however, not directly connected with the Glorious Revolution. It appeared to many, especially in New England, that a new age was at hand, when "our glorious deliverer," William III, would usher in a new age of liberty.

A good many expectations were disappointed. Massachusetts was retained as a royal colony, although only the Governor was royally appointed and not the magistrates. In New York Leisler was executed and a royal governor appointed in his place. In the long run the most profound impact of the Glorious Revolution upon intercolonial relations probably was in its creation of an abiding imperial misunderstanding. The English at home saw the Revolution of 1688 as vindicating the principle of parliamentary supremacy, throughout the colonies as well as in England. The colonists in America, who had staged their own little revolutions, saw them as vindicating the principle of legislative supremacy, including the supremacy of their own provincial assemblies. This misunderstanding between the homeland and the colonies continued into the eighteenth century and into the American Revolution.

BIBLIOGRAPHY FOR CHAPTER ONE

For the purpose of following the exploits of sailors, conquistadores, voyageurs, and wilderness scouts, two excellent alternatives are available: J. B. Brebner, *The Explorers of North America, 1492–1806* (1933) and Bernard DeVoto, *Course of Empire* (1952), "the saga of the conquest of a continent . . . reported almost as though the author had been in the canoe or on the sailing vessel with each adventurer into the wilderness." Kenneth MacGowan, *Early Man in the New World* (1950) concerns itself with America's Indian civilization before the coming of the white man.

Wallace Notestein, *The English People on the Eve of Colonization, 1603–1630* (1954) "gives ample evidence that it has been written by an authority with great erudition. On every hand are signs of extensive knowledge of a wide range of sources. The supporting data are well chosen. The style is easy and the various chapters leave a very clear impression. The illustrations are extremely valuable and will be new to most readers." E. M. W. Tillyard, *The Elizabethan World Picture* (1943) is a brilliant, brief description of the cosmography of sixteenth-century England. For the religious background to the settlement of New England see Maurice Powicke, *The Reformation in England* (1941) and the classic by R. H. Tawney, *Religion and the Rise of Capitalism* (1926), an examination of the much mooted hypothesis that the Reformation was basically the spiritual rationale for the new economic order.

C. M. Andrews, *Our Earliest Colonial Settlements* (1959) is a short account by a great authority stressing institutional developments. Carl Becker, *Beginnings of the American People* (1915) is a summary of colonial history through the Revolution by one of the outstanding literary stylists among American historians.

The moving Bunyanesque *Of Plymouth Plantation* by Governor William Bradford remains the most appealing contemporary account of early New England. By contrast Governor Winthrop's history of the Massachusetts Bay Colony presents its author in a less sympathetic light. A recent effort to repair this picture is E. S. Morgan, *The Puritan Dilemma: The Story of John Winthrop* (1958), which one writer found to be, among other things, "the clearest, most easily digested, and painless presentation of Puritan dogma this reviewer has ever encountered. . . . Using the life of John Winthrop as a springboard, Morgan sketches the puritan beliefs, shows how they differed from other religious views of the time and how they influenced the economic, political, and intellectual lives of the faithful."

Alan Simpson, *Puritanism in New England and Old* (1955) is the best introduction to a formidably large, abstruse, and contentious literature on the subject. "In these brief essays Alan Simpson has given us one of the great books of our times. . . . He holds that the Puritans have shaped our society by their contributions to our systems of limited government, self-government, education, and morality. Their weakness was the egotism of their righteousness." Perry Miller, *The New England Mind: The Seventeenth Century* (1939) is a massively ambitious attempt to codify New England theology into a comprehensive, monolithic system. In common with Simpson and Morgan, Miller writes from a staunchly partisan point of view against the hostile writings of earlier historians. Most influential among these earlier critics was V. L. Parrington, *The Colonial Mind 1620–1800* (1927), the first volume of the earliest comprehensive study of American intellectual history. Witty and colorful and filled with vivid character sketches, Parrington's pioneer study is also the repository of much guesswork and misinformation. The generation of research which it stimulated has made possible a more sophisticated presentation of the hostile point of view by T. J. Wertenbaker in *The Puritan Oligarchy* (1947). "Writing avowedly as a Southerner disliking both the Puritans and the overemphasis which he feels historians have given them, he has still, within these intentional limits, tried to appraise them fairly. . . . His synthesis carries weight. It cannot be disregarded by any future student of our colonial beginnings." Perry Miller and T. H. Johnson, eds., *The Puritans: An Anthology of Their Writings*, 2 vols., is a very substantial sampling. P. L. Ford has edited *The New England Primer*.

The subject most felicitous for the purposes of the critics of Puritanism was, of course, the Salem witch trials. The champions of Puritanism, on their part, have, to an extent, disarmed this criticism by placing the phenomenon in the context of the times, when witchcraft was almost universally believed in and when, in Europe, persons were accused and executed for the crime by the hundreds. In Marion Starkey, *The Devil in Massachusetts* (1949), "The whole story is told with a restraint which never lapses into denunciation and with a sense of drama which never descends to melodrama . . . the most understanding account of the Salem witch trials that has been written." The critics have also dwelt long upon the persecution of the leading dissenter from Massachusetts orthodoxy, Roger Williams, whom they have presented as an early champion of democracy. Against this interpretation, Perry Miller in *Roger Williams* (1953) argues that the man was thoroughly theological in his orientation and all but oblivious to the political implications of his ideas.

The overemphasis upon New England, about which Wertenbaker complained and to which he contributed, is even more marked in the paperback field. No study is as yet available of the early history of the Chesapeake region or of the middle colonies. Verner Crane, *The Southern Frontier, 1670–1732* (1929) is the best general account of the early history of the Carolinas.

COLONIAL EXPANSION 2

I

England at the turn of the eighteenth century possessed about two dozen colonies in America, and of these the mainland colonies were by no means the most prized. Sugar had by then supplanted gold and silver as the world's most valuable commodity, more valuable than ever had been those spices of the East that had started the whole thing. The tremendous expansion of the production of sugar was continually outrun by the demand, and great fortunes were to be made on small lots of sugar cane, such profits to the English Crown, as well as to the planter, as to diminish other colonial wealth by comparison. St. Kitts was the first of these sugar islands; it was settled by the English in

CANADA
(French until 1763)

QUEBEC

FORT ONTARIO
FORT OSWEGO
FORT NIAGARA

FORT ALBANY

PORTSMOUTH
SALEM
BOSTON
PLYMOUTH

NEW YORK

FORT DUQUESNE
FORT PITT
FORT NECESSITY

PHILADELPHIA

L O U I S I A N A (French Possession)

W I L D E R N E S S

JAMESTOWN

Atlantic Ocean

CHARLESTON

SAVANNAH

F L O R I D A (Spanish Possession)

ST. AUGUSTINE

——— Boundries of present day States
••••• English Colonies
- - - - Spanish Possessions
——— French Possessions
••••• Proclamation line of 1763

Gulf of Mexico

Early American Colonies and the Proclamation Line of 1763.

1623. Settlement of Barbados followed several years later, and then additional small islands such as Nevis and Montserrat. Adm. William Penn, father of Pennsylvania's founder, captured Jamaica, largest of the English Caribbean possessions, in 1655.

The West Indian planters tended to think of themselves as Englishmen away from home, who, when they had made their fortunes, would return to the homeland, purchase land in the country, and take the seat in Parliament to which their new landed estate would virtually entitle them. Planters in Virginia and South Carolina tended to think likewise, perhaps, in the early stages of colonization, but they were clearly no longer of that mind by the middle of the eighteenth century. This contrast in outlook came from the Virginians and Carolinians being attached to a new continent as the West Indian planters were not.

The West Indian planters consolidated their holdings into fewer and larger plantations and soon came to the limit of their opportunities; the continental planters, constantly extending their holdings, did not begin to see the end of the opportunities lying westward. Early English West Indian history followed a course similar to that of the English mainland colonies, including defiant Puritanism in religion and defiant democracy in politics, but with the completion of settlement and the consolidations of plantations, all of this changed. The slave population increased, the white population decreased, and a good many of the most successful of the planters went home to England.

One result of this tendency was a rising West Indian political strength in England in the eighteenth century. By mid-century more than forty members of Parliament had a vested interest in West Indian sugar and therefore in any legislation which would be to its benefit. The tobacco planters of the Chesapeake and the rice planters of South Carolina had no such representation, not to speak of those farmers from the mainland areas which produced little that was thought to be of value by the English government. In the imperial scheme, therefore, the mainland colonies in the eighteenth century were almost bound to get the worst of it, however much the English government might want to be fair all around.

The most egregious example of this favoritism was the Molasses Act of 1733, which, among other things, placed a prohibitive tax on molasses imported to the mainland from the non-English West

Indies. The purpose of the tax was not to protect the molasses trade of the English West Indies, for they used up their own molasses production in their own rum industry. Its purpose was to deprive New England, and especially "mobbish Boston," of the molasses necessary to compete with the West Indian rum industry on the mainland rum market. This striking example of partiality in the imperial system was softened, characteristically, by the fact that little was done to enforce it.

England, in common with other colonizing nations, attempted to govern its colonies according to a set of notions which go by the name of mercantilism. During the three-quarters of a century before the Revolutionary War, England and France were at war with each other almost as often as not, and mercantilism was essentially economic warfare. The agricultural and industrial revolutions had not yet demonstrated their ways of increasing productivity, and it was therefore assumed that a nation could substantially increase its riches only at the expense of another nation or through colonial acquisitions.

Colonies should be so regulated as to prevent their most valuable products from escaping into foreign hands, and most particularly into enemy hands in time of war. Colonies should further serve to make the empire as a whole self-sufficient, for purposes of national security, by producing raw materials not available at home. On the other hand, colonies should not injure the economy of the homeland by duplication and competition.

So far as the mainland was concerned, South Carolina produced rice, which was not grown in England, and, on the basis of bounties paid by England, indigo for dyes. Virginia and Maryland produced tobacco, prized on the world market. Therefore the Chesapeake received special economic consideration, including a prohibition against tobacco-growing in England. Newfoundland served admirably in the fishing industry, which was also prized as the nursery of the British navy. For the rest there was not so much to be said from the English point of view.

North Carolina and New England produced naval stores—pitch, tar, and timber—which served to strengthen British sea power; while the middle colonies, New York, New Jersey, and Pennsylvania grew the food and raised the horses needed in those colonies to the south which were devoting their attention to cultivating the prized staple commodities. Each area had its part to play in the imperial economy, but from the English point of view the parts played by New England and the middle colonies were relatively humble ones. And increasingly in the eighteenth century, these areas came to engage in manufacturing pursuits which competed with English interests.

The effort to regulate all for the good of the whole which began with the Navigation Act of 1651 continued into the eighteenth century. The Navigation Act of 1660 originally prohibited the export from the empire of sugar, tobacco, cotton, and dyestuffs. Later rice, molasses, naval stores, beaver skins, furs, and copper were added. Then, as the colonies increased in population, a new kind of mercantilist legislation was enacted. Initially important as sources of raw materials, the colonies became increasingly important as markets for English manufacturers. When this came to be the case, laws were passed discouraging the colonists from making for themselves what they would otherwise buy from England.

In 1699 the Woolens Act was passed, prohibiting intercolonial commerce in woolen goods. In 1732 the Hat Act was passed prohibiting intercolonial commerce in hats. In 1750 the Iron Act was passed prohibiting the construction of new slitting and rolling mills, plating forges, and iron furnaces. These acts naturally annoyed the colonists, but it does not appear that they felt the need to obey them. Indeed, the assemblies of Massachusetts, New York, and Pennsylvania passed legislation encouraging the construction of new iron mills after the parliamentary prohibition had gone into effect.

In an effort to enforce its economic regulations, Parliament in 1696 passed a new navigation act giving greater power and responsibilities to customs officers and naval officers in America and imposing fines upon colonial governors who failed to enforce the laws. In the same year the Lords Commissioners of Trade and Plantations—known as the Board of Trade—was created as an advisory board of Privy Councilors and English merchants to oversee imperial trade. This agency gave comprehensive and detailed attention to colonial affairs, while the Treasury officials, Admiralty officers, the War Office, and the Secretary of State for the Southern Department, all concerned themselves with colonial matters in one connection or another.

Altogether, however, it amounted to something less than a comprehensive and effective system. During the first half of the

eighteenth century, the English government proceeded on the
assumption that its imperial laws were not really enforceable and
that, anyway, things were going along all right as they were. This
was the spirit behind the policy, associated with England's first
Prime Minister, Robert Walpole, known as salutary neglect. Under
this dispensation colonists obeyed or violated regulations pretty
much as it suited them.

II

The Colonial Economy The great majority of mainland colonists made
their livings by farming, and from frozen Maine
to sultry South Carolina, America offered a wider range of agricultural pursuits than Europe provided. Agriculturally the colonies were
divided into rather distinct regions: timbered and rocky New England, the fertile bread colonies of New York, Pennsylvania, New Jersey, and Delaware, where the main production was foodstuffs and
livestock, the Chesapeake region of Maryland and Virginia concentrating on tobacco, the South Carolina rice fields, and the backcountry which included most of North Carolina and the western areas
of the colonies generally, engaged mainly in subsistence farming.

Richest among all of these farming areas were the rice fields of
South Carolina. Slave labor was the indispensable basis there from
the first, since the wretched, lethal conditions in those malarial
swamps were not such as to invite any workers who had a choice
in the matter. Rice plantations were found to be most efficiently
operated on a relatively small scale, and the major planters owned
a number of these, each with its slave force under the direction
of an overseer.

To escape the fevers, those who could afford to withdrew for
six months of the year to the only city south of Philadelphia,
Charles Town, which became an extraordinarily exclusive and
prideful community. By contrast to the rich rice swamps, the
South Carolina backcountry, until the introduction of cotton, provided for little more than subsistence farming, and the colony was
sharply divided between "opulent and lordly planters, poor and
spiritless whites, and vile slaves." Charles Town supported also
a merchant aristocracy, while the planters themselves engaged in
commercial enterprises.

In good times tobacco might be profitably grown in the Chesapeake region both on small farms and on vast plantations, but as a hand crop it required much labor, and therefore only slave owners did really well with it. The amount of land was less important than the amount of labor, for the acreage devoted to its planting was small, even on large plantations. Its culture rapidly exhausted the soil, however, and the land-hungry Virginia planters acquired, in some cases, several hundred thousand acres of land.

Unlike the South Carolina planters, they lived on their land and generally superintended the operation of their own plantations. The plantations were directly connected with England by water transportation, and the planters dealt directly with English factors. The idea, later current in the South, that a gentleman did not engage in trade, was not one which was current among the colonial planter gentry. No need for a middleman existed in Colonial Virginia and Maryland, and therefore no towns of any size developed in the region.

New York and Pennsylvania were economically the most varied of the colonies. Albany, New York, remained the fur-trading center that it had been since the Dutch had enlisted the services of the Six Nations. Pennsylvania led in the iron industry, which existed to some extent in all colonies. The lumber industry was important throughout the area, and Philadelphia and New York City were engaged in a wide variety of manufacturers. Grain, horses, and cattle for the southern mainland colonies and the West Indies made up the greatest part of the export trade.

Throughout most of New England, except for limited areas such as the Connecticut Valley, the land was suitable only for subsistence farming, and those who were ambitious to rise above the level of plain if ample subsistence moved into areas of activity other than farming. Forests were among New England's most obvious assets, and shipbuilding early became a leading industry, and with it fishing and shipping. New England constructed ships for English purchasers suitable for transatlantic voyages, but New England merchants, for themselves, concentrated their energies in the coastal and West Indian trade, where geographically they held the advantage over their English competition.

The idea that there existed a triangular trade by which New England merchants traded rum for slaves in Africa, slaves for molasses in the West Indies, and molasses for rum in Boston is a

myth, based upon a single instance (and as it turned out an unprofitable one) of such a voyage. Rhode Island merchants did engage
in a fairly sizable slave trade, but on the whole New England
merchants, such as the Browns of Providence and the Hancocks
of Boston, preferred the substantial and safer returns to be found
closer to home.

Farming generally, and frontier farming especially, was conditioned by the abundance of land, the lack of profitable markets,
and the medieval farming methods which the American farmers
brought with them from England. Foreign observers were almost
uniformly severe in their criticism of colonial farming, reserving
their praise for non-English settlers such as the Swedes and the
Germans. From the Indian the Americans learned, most important
of all, to grow corn, which remained the staff of life throughout the
colonial and well into the national period. From the Indians they
learned also to avoid the necessity of clearing the land by simply
girdling the trees and allowing them to rot by themselves and
blow down.

Intertillage—the growing of a variety of crops in the same
fields—was also adopted from the Indians. But beyond what he
was taught by the Indians the frontier farmer did not go far.
Draft animals and farm implements were rare. Plows were of wood
and did no more than scratch the surface. Owing to the easy
availability of land the farmers stripped the soil with no concern
for the saving of its fertility, until soil exhaustion in the tobacco
region produced a notable crop of scientific farmers, including
George Washington and Thomas Jefferson, by the close of the
colonial period.

Foreign observers bestowed upon colonial cities some of the
praise they withheld from colonial farms. The spectacle of a developed metropolis in the American wilderness rarely failed to
evoke surprised admiration. Philadelphia by the middle of the
eighteenth century had supplanted Boston as the major colonial
city, and its broad and busy streets and handsome architecture
were matters for wonder. Founded in 1683, Philadelphia by the
eve of the Revolution, with a population of more than 30,000,
was about as large as any city in Great Britain except London.
In population New York followed Philadelphia at the close of the
colonial period with a population of about 22,000 and after it
Boston with 17,000. Although Boston had decisively lost its stand-

ing as the metropolis of the colonies, New England contained a much larger urban population than any other region, with a number of lesser cities and towns, of which Newport was the largest. These cities in the wilderness gave evidence of a complexity and maturity in American colonial society which the English government failed to take into account.

III

Immigration

The most important colonial developments during the first half of the eighteenth century went largely unnoticed in England, because they caused no imperial crises. The main change was the change in size. Between 1700 and 1775 the population of the colonies increased by roughly ten times, from about 250,000 to about 2,500,000. Meanwhile, the population of England increased by less than 30 per cent. By the eve of the Revolution, Englishmen at home still outnumbered those in the mainland colonies by three to one, but colonial leaders were aware that the day would come when America would outstrip England, and they were made the more confident and assertive by their awareness of America's growing importance within the empire.

In addition to the natural increase in population—in a farming age when large families were economic assets—America gained heavily from two waves of immigration; one from northern Ireland and one from Germany and Switzerland. During the seventeenth century, thousands of lowland Scots had been settled in northern Ireland for the purpose of bringing that country more firmly under Protestant English control. Nevertheless as Presbyterians these Scotch-Irish were made to suffer the same political and legal disabilities as did the native Celtic Catholics. Beyond that, again in common with the native Irish, the Scotch-Irish suffered from discriminatory economic legislation, especially the Woolens Act of 1699. Unlike Massachusetts or Pennsylvania, Ireland was close enough to England so that the navigation acts could be enforced, and with devastating effect. The consequence was mass starvation and an eighteenth-century migration to America of perhaps 300,000, beginning in the second decade of the century. The first main migration was to New England, but the stony

welcome received by the Irish Presbyterians persuaded later groups
to choose the middle and southern colonies. New York welcomed
them as New England did not, for the large landholders were
eager to attract tenant farmers, but New York soon gained a bad
reputation for victimizing the immigrants and for keeping them
from acquiring their own land.

The most hospitable port, and the one through which most
Scotch-Irish passed, was Philadelphia. From there many were
sent to the southern colonies, while others took advantage of the
favorable Pennsylvania land policy to take up farms to the west.
Their westward advance was halted by the Appalachian Mountains, which provided the Indians with an impenetrable line of
fortifications. Coming up against these mountains the settlers
turned southward and, beyond the reach of the seaboard government, took up land without much regard for the matter of legal
titles.

Migration from Germany began in the late seventeenth century
in response to the promotional work of William Penn, but the
large-scale migration from both Germany and Switzerland began
at the same time as that of the Scotch-Irish in the second decade
of the eighteenth century. Many of the Germans were refugees
from religious persecution, and these tended to arrive in groups of
religious congregations under the leadership of their pastor, as
had the New England Puritans originally. Like the Scotch-Irish
they settled in all of the colonies south of New England but concentrated in Pennsylvania where they were able to acquire land
on attractive terms. By the close of the colonial period, they made
up about one-third of the entire Pennsylvania population.

Held together by their distinctive language and religious beliefs,
they formed closed societies of their own within the dominant
Anglo-American society. The Scotch-Irish, lacking the barriers of
language and religion, were less exclusive. Nevertheless, they were
"clannish, contentious, and hard to get along with," in the view
of the older settlers and did not readily assimilate.

In addition to these main waves of migration, American society
was increased by a small but significant influx of Welsh Quakers,
French Huguenots, and Iberian Jews, the latter two groups exerting a considerable influence in the colonial cities where they were
concentrated.

By the eve of the Revolution, as a consequence of these population movements, there existed in all the colonies from New York to Georgia a separate western society, largely non-English, certainly nonsupporters of the established Church of England, and generally at odds with the seaboard community over matters of religion, taxation, representation, and Indian defense. Even before they won their independence from England, the English colonies themselves had acquired their own colonial areas, which, in a number of cases, were suffering many of those same abuses which the seaboard communities complained of in the hands of England.

IV

Great Awakening Perhaps the most striking impact of this non-English migration upon American culture was in the field of religion, for it was accompanied by a series of "great awakenings" which engulfed all the colonies and which laid the basis for the main evangelical sects of the nineteenth century. The religious activities encompassed in the term, great awakenings, varied widely from the revivalism of the English evangelist George Whitefield to the soberer Calvinism of the Dutch Reformed Church minister, Theodore Freylinghuysen.

Most of the German immigrants were Lutherans or Reformed Church members. Many were pietistic Protestants belonging to sects such as the Moravian, which had reacted against the cold formality of the Lutheran Church and which placed emphasis upon the need for spiritual rebirth accompanied by agonies of repentence in order to achieve salvation. They were characterized by this emotional approach and by their following of an extremely austere moral code. In America, keeping to themselves, they did not directly influence other American religious movements. They influenced the development of the Methodist Church, however, through its founder John Wesley, whose religious views were profoundly affected by his experience with Moravian Brethren in Georgia in the 1730s.

The earliest leader of this religious resurgence was Freylinghuysen, who arrived in New Jersey in 1719, organized private prayer meetings, recruited lay helpers, and captured the Dutch Reformed Church from an affluent leadership which had fallen away from a belief in the harsher doctrines of Calvinism. Freylinghuysen was influential also, through William Tennent, on the early history of the American Presbyterian Church, formed mainly of Scotch-Irish Pennsylvanians and New York Yankees.

Tennent ran a Log College in Pennsylvania where he trained an evangelical ministry which carried the Gospel throughout the colonies. The emotionalism of the Log College ministers and their emphasis upon predestination and the damnation of sinners affronted the genteel Presbyterian leadership and for a time split the Church, but by the eve of the Revolution the Church was reunited under the leadership of Tennent's followers.

Baptist revivalism, meanwhile, spread through Virginia under the leadership of former Congregational ministers who had been brought to the new calling by the persuasive English evangelist, George Whitefield. Persecuted in Virginia for not obeying the licensing laws, the Baptists rapidly gained adherents there and elsewhere. Virginia was the scene also of the beginnings of Methodism under the leadership of the Anglican minister Devereaux Jarrett.

In New England Jonathan Edwards aroused consternation among the Congregational ministers by conducting revivals and delivering such hellfire and damnation sermons as the famous "Sinners in the Hands of an Angry God." Edwards made his mark in the fields of philosophy and theology, however, rather than as a revivalist leader. His successes in the latter field were but temporary and were eclipsed even in New England by those of Whitefield and of William Tennent's son Gilbert.

The awakenings occurred during a time of relative religious complacency among the older denominations. This was especially true of the established churches, which was to say the Church of England in all of the colonies south of Pennsylvania and the Congregational Church throughout New England, except Rhode Island. Church establishment meant that the church was supported out of public taxes. Beyond that it meant that the church functioned, not only as a religious institution, but also as an arm of the government, which had been the case with the church in England from the reign of Elizabeth.

The New England Puritans, it is true, had from the first observed the principle of separation of church and state to the extent that the ministers did not hold public office. Still they had busied themselves with public affairs in an advisory capacity to an extent which might justify applying the term theocracy very loosely to New England. This ministerial influence remained after the initial religious fervor had somewhat declined.

Wherever the Church of England was established it acted from the outset as a vital agency of local government, recording births, marriages, and deaths, and caring for the poor. Virginia had been founded by Puritans, just as had New England, and the first two generations had been obliged to conduct themselves according to a moral and religious code almost as straitlaced as that of a New England colony. Long before Devereaux Jarrett started on his reforming mission, however, the Virginia churches had become social and political as well as religious agencies of the aristocracy which hardly attempted to carry religion to the people as a whole. And what was true in Virginia became true of the church as it was established in one after another of the southern colonies. This tendency toward religious complacency among the eighteenth-century gentry is apparent only in comparison with the seventeenth century, for by modern standards religion continued to play a vital role in their lives.

V

Enlightenment Upper-class America was little affected by the awakenings except in reaction against them. Among the men who emerged to lead the Revolution, orthodox believers such as Samuel Adams and Patrick Henry were exceptional, for the most basic development in eighteenth-century thought had been the acceptance of modern science and a corresponding decline in the authority of revealed religion.

The first generation of American settlers had lived intellectually in the universe of Aristotle and Ptolemy, as that universe had been Christianized by medieval scholar-priests, notably St. Thomas Aquinas. The earth had stood at the center of this universe, fixed and immovable, while around it had circled the celestial bodies, kept in motion by Christianized occult spirits and by God, the Unmoved Mover, who on occasion had hurled comets through the skies as portents to the humans on earth whom He had created in His own image and who were acting out the central purpose of His universe.

A century and a half later the generation of Americans who fought the Revolution lived in the entirely different universe of Newtonian science, a universe no longer guided by occult spirits, but one which operated according to mathematically comprehensible, physical laws of gravity and inertia. The earth in this universe had lost its central position, being but one of the planets in the solar system, moving according to the same physical laws which applied to all of the universe.

Astronomy was enthusiastically studied by American clergymen, among others, on the grounds that it would reveal the workings of God to man. The inevitable result was the reluctant relinquishment of old beliefs. The New England minister Increase Mather, for instance, found himself obliged to concede that comets followed scientifically predictable courses and were not those interruptions of natural law that he had originally believed them to be. Americans were in a position to make positive contributions to the science of astronomy because they viewed the heavens from an earthly location distant from that of European scientists and observatories, and they took enthusiastic advantage of this fact. A still more important American contribution to science was in the field of natural history, and Americans ranged the colonies collecting specimens of plant and animal life and contributing their findings to European scientists, notably to the great Swedish naturalist Carl Linnaeus. American enthusiasm for science was institutionalized in 1769 in the founding of the American Philosophical Society in Philadelphia.

To the enlightened men of the eighteenth century, the rational character of the universe demonstrated the rational nature of its author. He was no longer a mysterious God of Wrath, but rather a benevolent Creator who, having at a given moment in time devised the universe, had allowed it henceforth to move of itself without divine intervention. Everything in creation served its purpose in a great chain of being, descending from God to the lowest form of animal life on earth, and every living thing contained within itself a distinct principle of life necessary for its own perpetual survival.

It was an essentially static universe which had changed little since the beginning of time and would change little throughout eternity. To the rational man, the nature and purposes of God were to be understood best, not through the revealed word of the

Bible but rather through a study of the natural world that God had created. This altered religious attitude was variously and somewhat indiscriminately called natural religion, theism, unitarianism, and deism. It was in the spirit of this religious view that John Adams wrote Thomas Jefferson, "Had you and I been forty days with Moses on Mount Sinai, and admitted to behold the divine Shechinah, and there told that one was three and three one, we might not have had courage to deny it, but we could not have believed it."

From this view of the universe eighteenth-century Americans derived what they considered to be self-evident truths concerning the nature of man and of society. Man's rational faculties equipped him to govern his own affairs and rendered unsuitable for him a blind and unreasoning submission to authority. While man was not omniscient, he was endowed with capabilities sufficient for him to cope with his own human problems. A rational Creator would not conceivably have done less for him.

All men were born equal, not in the sense of sharing equal capabilities or of sharing the right to an equal station in society, but in the sense that all possessed equally certain natural rights, implicit in the very nature of man. The chief of these natural rights were the rights to life, to liberty, and to that property which represented the fruits of man's labor and therefore a part of him. The true purpose of all government was that of protecting men in these rights. This was the objective standard by which all governments could be judged as legitimate or illegitimate by their citizens.

Therefore, as the Declaration of Independence argued, "when a long train of abuses and usurpations, pursuing invariably the same object, evinces a design to reduce them under absolute Despotism, it is their right, it is their duty, to throw off such Government, and provide new Guards for their security." The legalistic, characteristically undoctrinaire colonists were drawn reluctantly to this line of argument, as the Declaration also points out, but once convinced of the need for revolution they were confident that the natural rights political theory which they shared with the enlightened thinkers of Europe would make self-evident the rightness of their cause. The American Revolution was in this respect a major event, from the point of view of Europeans as well as of Americans, in the history of the Age of Enlightenment.

In Benjamin Franklin, America produced the perfect embodiment of the Enlightenment and probably the most famous and honored philosopher which the Enlightenment produced either in Europe or America. Epitome of the universal genius, Franklin was the model businessman, civil leader, and philanthropic benefactor. He was the politician who, beyond manipulating Pennsylvania politics with great success, found it well within the scope of his abilities, while on his way to the Albany Congress in 1754, to draw up a Plan of Union by which a comprehensive reordering of the entire British imperial system would be arranged. He was among the most distinguished and effective diplomats America has produced. He was a man of letters who wrote a classic *Autobiography;* the universal authority who composed pamphlets on political theory, education, demography, economics, and religion; the musician who, beyond mastering four musical instruments, went on to invent one of his own, the armonica, for which Beethoven and Mozart composed special music. His inventions included the Franklin stove, smokeless street lamps, the lightning rod, and bifocal glasses. In science his contributions included original observations concerning heat conduction, winds, whirlwinds, lightning, and the origin of the Gulf Stream, and, as the crowning achievement of his career, his original researches in the field of electricity.

Numbers of other Americans were almost as remarkably many-sided as Franklin, among them Thomas Jefferson, the lawyer, political theorist, statesman, agricultural scientist, natural historian, inventor, musician, classical scholar, and man of letters. They reflected the faith of the age that the rationally ordered universe would reveal itself to the rational man who was willing, as Jefferson put it, to subject himself to the drudgery of a patient pursuit of facts and a cautious combination and comparison of them.

Impressive as were the contributions of individual Americans, however, colonial America made its main contribution to the history of ideas in the Age of Enlightenment by what it did rather than by what it thought. Pennsylvania was a demonstration of the perfect society, and the Revolution was a demonstration of right principles in action to European philosophes.

Colonial America produced its writers, composers, painters, and architects, but American conditions, generally speaking, did not favor the development of the arts. The best painters, Benjamin West and John Singleton Copley, were drawn irresistibly to England, where the rewards for their genius were so much richer than in America. The foremost colonial composer, William Billings, was unable to eke out a living for his numerous family through his prolific compositions of religious music; nor were there patrons at hand to help him out. In colonial society such men had to be jacks of several other trades as well in order to survive.

Colonial architecture, although mainly derivative of English architecture, almost immediately, and of necessity, developed its own distinctive regional characteristics. The greater extremes of heat and cold in America called for alterations as did the need and opportunity to make substitutions in building materials, chiefly wood. Professional architects did not develop until the mid-eighteenth century, but carpenters with their books of proportions met standards of simple attractiveness which were never again to be attained in America. With the accumulation of wealth in the eighteenth century, elegant houses made their appearance. Brick and stone replaced wood in houses which emulated the contemporary Georgian style of England. William Byrd II's Westover remains as the most beautiful example of this American Georgian style. Imposing public buildings made their appearance also, without the grunting effort to achieve grandeur which was to characterize public structures in the national period. Graceful and useful, colonial public buildings such as the Old Colony House in Newport and Independence Hall in Philadelphia tended to resemble large private homes.

In the field of literature, little effort was made in the colonies to rival the rich creativity of seventeenth- and eighteenth-century England. The writing of poetry was a common practice among educated Americans, but the colonial period produced only one poet, the Congregational minister, Edward Taylor, who is regarded very seriously by critics. At the time of the development of the novel in England, Americans were content to accept what England offered without adding contributions of their own.

Colonial American writing was concentrated in the fields of religion and history, where the Americans felt they had a unique contribution to make. Among religious works perhaps the most ambitious was that by the Boston minister, Cotton Mather. His *Magnalia Christi Americana* is an account of New England Puritanism describing "in heroic mood the principles and personal characteristics of the fathers." Mather, however, with his ornate style and ostentatious display of erudition, is unpalatable to the taste of a modern reader in this, as in most of the 400 books and pamphlets to come from his pen.

The field of history provided the most rewarding opportunities for colonial writers, as they themselves were obviously aware. Writing of a new world and the founding of new societies, these men possessed subject matter of interest to European readers, and, beginning with John Smith's account of the founding of Virginia, a sizable literature of American history was created. William Bradford's *Of Plymouth Plantation* is in marked contrast to Mather's *Magnalia* in the affecting simplicity of style, and its appealing quality helped to establish the Pilgrims as an important part of the American tradition.

Virginia produced valuable historians in Robert Beverly and in Thomas Jefferson, whose *Notes on Virginia* displayed an incredible fund of information on the subject, presented in the felicitous Jeffersonian style. Probably the most distinguished historian colonial America produced was Thomas Hutchinson, the last royal governor of Massachusetts and author of the extensive *History of the Province of Massachusetts Bay*. Letter writing was a developed art in America as in England and in this area the colonists offered such graceful correspondents as Thomas Jefferson and Benjamin Franklin.

Education in colonial America was fostered largely for religious purposes and thrived best where religious zeal was strongest. New England therefore led in its educational facilities on both the grammar school and college level. After the establishment of church and government in New England, wrote Edward Johnson in his *New England's First Fruits,* "One of the next things we longed for, and looked after was to advance *Learning* and perpetuate it to Posterity; dreading to leave an illiterate Ministry in the Churches, when our present ministers shall lie in the Dust."

Accordingly a system of public education was developed in Massachusetts which was formalized in 1647 in a law providing for a free grammar school system and compulsory attendance in order that the "ould deluder Satan" should be prevented from keeping "men from the knowledge of the scriptures." Harvard College was founded in 1636 for the purpose both of training ministers and of educating the upper classes generally. Latin grammar schools were provided for those who intended to go on to college. Although the religious motive was dominant, the schools were publicly supported and the teachers were recruited from outside the ministry. Yale was founded to supplement Harvard in 1701.

Elsewhere education was somewhat more haphazard. In New York the Dutch had instituted a public school system which was gradually replaced by private schools sponsored by various religious sects. Quaker schools predominated in Pennsylvania, amid a number of other sectarian schools. In the southern colonies there were both private and publicly supported schools, but the rural character of those colonies and the relative lack of religious zeal worked against the development of effective systems.

William and Mary was founded in 1693 in Virginia under the auspices of the Anglican Church, which also founded King's College, changed to Columbia College with the Revolution, in 1754. The mid-eighteenth century saw the founding by various sects of Princeton, Brown, Queen's College, later changed to Rutgers, and Dartmouth. The University of Pennsylvania, in part one of Benjamin Franklin's many civic enterprises, was founded as a nonsectarian institution.

The educational standards of these institutions, generally speaking, were those of the English grammar schools and colleges. Nevertheless the wilderness environment was obviously not conducive to education and culture. John Adams no doubt was indulging in one of his characteristic overstatements when he declared that a native inhabitant who could read was "as rare as a comet or an earthquake," but certainly many Americans did without the luxury of literacy.

VI

Colonial Society   Eighteenth-century colonial society looked to England for its patterns of behavior, including New England, which by then had lost much of the impulse to maintain a New Zion. English society was aristocratic, and accordingly American society was also aristocratic to the extent that conditions permitted. Americans thought naturally in terms of ranks and stations, and since most of America was rural, it was the rural English class system which was emulated. To begin with, however, class lines were less rigid in England than on the European Continent and in America they were much harder to maintain than in England.

The attempt to create a formal aristocracy if not a nobility was repeatedly tried in upper New England, New York, Maryland, Virginia, and in the Carolinas, but never with any great success. The nearest approach to success was in New York, with its great landed estates, and in South Carolina with its rich rice lands. When Lord Say and Sele and other Puritan aristocrats offered to emigrate to New England if the government could be reformed to provide for a hereditary house of lords, John Cotton was delegated the task of explaining to them that there was only an upper class of gentlemen in Massachusetts, of which he and the other leaders were members, and it was not intended that another class should be raised above them.

On the other hand, in Massachusetts as elsewhere, the attempt was made to observe fine class distinctions. The Massachusetts General Court in 1651 prohibited "excess in Apparel . . . especially amongst people of mean condition," going on to express its "utter detestation and dislike that men or women of mean condition should take upon them the garb of Gentlemen." The difficulty remained of deciding who fit where. In every settled community there existed the "better sort" consisting of planters and merchants and, in New England, of the ministry; beneath these "gentle folk" were the "middling sort" of yeomen, small merchants and successful craftsmen; beneath them the "plain people," the subsistence farmers and artisans; beneath them the "meaner sort," indentured servants, tenant farmers, drifters, and finally, at the bottom of the scale, the Negroes, virtually all of whom were enslaved in the northern as well as the southern colonies.

Titles were of importance to people in fixing these distinctions, but they could not be exactly applied. "Esquire" was a title reserved for councilors and magistrates, and "squire" generally referred to a broader group including justices of the peace. "Gent." followed the name of a larger classification of members of the well-born ruling social group, often including ministers. "Goodman" or "Goodwife" was the customary form of address for the substantial yeoman or artisan. "Mr." was a decided cut above Goodman as a mode of address, and in at least one case a Bostonian was officially deprived of the right to be addressed as "Mr." in punishment for a criminal offense. The established churches were among the strongest supports to class distinctions, often ranking the community precisely by the order of seating arrangement.

Politically most of the colonies were relatively democratic by English standards, although this varied widely in the colonies as indeed it also did in England. The vote was limited to free white male property holders, the assumption being universally held that only those persons had a right to take part in the political life of the community who had a "stake in society." The property qualification ranged from twenty-five to one hundred acres in most colonies, although in South Carolina it was three hundred. Personal property met the requirement in some colonies. There were further restrictions based on religion, especially against Catholics and Jews, and there were other antidemocratic circumstances such as the distance to the polling places, which were as much as a day's journey from the voter's residence, plural voting, and the practice of voting by voice.

Apparently, however, it was less the election laws that were undemocratic than it was the spirit of the people. Indeed the voting restrictions do not seem to have been seriously regarded in many areas. Governor Hutchinson of Massachusetts complained that "there is scarce ever any inquiry" into the qualifications of the voters. The fact was, however, that the overwhelming majority of the people did not vote, whether or not they were qualified to do so. Consistently in Massachusetts and Connecticut before and during the Revolution, the major issues were decided by about 2 per cent of the population or about one out of eight legal voters. Men in colonial America, unlike their descendants in the nineteenth century, were willing to leave political matters to their betters.

Colonial political history in the eighteenth century was a continuous struggle between the assemblies and the governors, with the advantage generally going to the assemblies. Despite the authority and social prestige of the governors and the power they received from patronage and from the support of the councils, their fiats were often nullified in practice. The distance from England was a source of weakness, and the viceroys were subjected to strong pressures not to violate the feelings of the best people of the community. In most of the royal colonies the governors were subjected to economic pressures as well. Except in Georgia and Virginia the governor was, practically speaking, dependent for his salary upon grants of money by the assembly, and the assemblies followed the practice of paying the governor in annual grants in order to limit his independence.

Within the assemblies no clear permanent party lines developed during the colonial period. In New England the assemblies tended to divide on the issue of paper money, between the merchant interests on the one hand and the farmers and lesser merchants on the other. In New York politics remained chiefly a struggle for power among the leading families, with New York City providing a disturbingly democratic element. In Pennsylvania the Quakers with German support controlled the assembly until the middle of the century against the proprietors, who by then had joined the Anglican Church. By contrast to New York, Pennsylvania was democratic in the countryside and oligarchic in Philadelphia. In the tobacco colonies the division was chiefly between the large and small planters, and in South Carolina the chief contests were between the merchants and the major planters, the plain people being largely unrepresented.

Most of the colonial assemblies, in their turn, experienced growing western opposition to seaboard control in the decades before the Revolution. In three colonies, Pennsylvania, New York, and North Carolina, the opposition broke into active, if ineffective, insurrection, while the latent western opposition in Massachusetts later erupted into Shays' Rebellion during the period of the Articles of Confederation. Western resentment fed on complaints of overtaxation, support of an established church which most westerners did not attend, underrepresentation, unreasonable legal expenses, graft, government influence in land speculation, and inadequate Indian defense.

In New York the tenant farmers rose in arms against their landlords to be suppressed swiftly by British redcoats. In Pennsylvania the unwillingness of the assembly to defend the frontiers inspired the abortive march of Paxton's Boys on Philadelphia. In North Carolina the western Regulators were aroused by a variety of grievances: chiefly maladministration of western counties and wholesale government corruption. The Regulators were defeated at the Battle of Alamance, but they were not without their effect on North Carolina politics. One result was the manifestation of strong loyalist sentiment in western North Carolina during the Revolution. Another was the development of militant democratic sentiment among

the westerners, a sentiment which the eastern Whigs felt obliged
to appease in drawing up the first state constitution.

Western South Carolina enjoyed no regular government at all to
the very eve of the Revolution. Only in 1769, in response to desperate western appeals, did the South Carolina assembly finally
create four grossly underrepresented western counties. The aristocratic patriots of South Carolina, while fighting England in defense
of their liberties, refused to make any substantial concessions to
western demands. Elsewhere, with the coming of the Revolution,
however, eastern patriots seeking unity against England were willing to satisfy some of those grievances of westerners which were so
embarrassingly similar to their own.

VII

Colonial Wars — French Canada, originating with the founding of Quebec in 1608, had extended its claims southward by
the close of the seventeenth century to include the whole of
the Ohio Valley. Comparatively unsuccessful in attracting settlers, New France became outnumbered fifteen to one by the English colonists. Its population was a centrally directed military force,
however, as compared with the undisciplined, incorrigibly civilian,
and—from the English point of view—generally ungovernable society to the south. The French settlements in the Ohio Valley were
communities of farmer-soldiers, who farmed chiefly as a means of
supporting semimilitary establishments. Concerned with fur trading
rather than farming, the French colonists were in a better position
than the English to win support from the Indians, and they
strengthened this attachment by intermarriages. The Algonquin
Indians were a great source of strength to the French. The Iroquois, by contrast, supported the English mainly because their
Algonquin enemies were on the other side, and the Iroquois therefore proved much less dedicated allies.

The English colonists, for their part, during time of war became
reluctant militiamen, who would serve only for short terms and who
were untrained as soldiers. They proved themselves to be first-rate
fighters on many occasions, but they often refused to fight beyond
the boundaries of their own colony or during the seasons when they
were needed on the farm. While French Canada remained in con-

stant danger of conquest from the time of settlement to final defeat
in 1763, the English could count on safety in numbers, and they
acted accordingly.

The hopelessly unsoldierly conduct of many American militiamen during these wars was one of the reasons why the English
government set forth with such confidence in 1775 to suppress the
rebels. Military men who had fought in America were able to ad-
vise the government that the colonials could always be counted on
not to fight. Four wars with New France appeared to them to put
this fact beyond question.

The first of these, King William's War, began in 1689, when
William of Orange, leader of the coalition against Louis XIV of
France, was crowned King of England. Fitfully waged in America,
this world conflict was temporarily concluded in 1697. War was
resumed in 1702, and the American phase, Queen Anne's War, was
small-scale and sporadic on both sides. Aside from the border colonies of New England and the Carolinas, the colonials may hardly
be said to have involved themselves.

Thirty years of peace followed the conclusion in 1713 of that
war. The next one, King George's War, 1740 to 1748, also was, in
America, small-scale and inconclusive, except for one successful
major campaign, the conquest of Louisbourg by a large New England force. The return of Louisbourg to France at the conclusion
of hostilities served to dampen enthusiasm among the colonists for
further such heroic exertions in the decisive war that was soon to
come.

The French and Indian Wars—the American phase of Europe's
Seven Years War, 1756 to 1763—unlike its predecessors, had its
origins, not in a European declaration of war, but in the conflict
which developed between contending French and English colonials
in the disputed Ohio Valley in 1754. From the beginning the scale
of fighting in America was much greater than in any of the previous wars, and for the first three years the major victories were all
on the side of the French.

Then the masterful William Pitt as Prime Minister of England
took command of a conflict which had spread to the continent of
Europe and to the subcontinent of India. European allies financed
by England drew off French troops. The colonial and the English
armies were both greatly augmented, and England moved on the
offensive. On September 13, 1759, Quebec fell in the decisive

battle of the war in America. Although the general war continued for four more years, the great battle between the forces of Wolfe and those of Montcalm, as it proved, settled the issue on the North American mainland.

At the close of the French and Indian Wars, for the first time in English colonial history, no major power arrayed itself along the English frontier. Until then the presence of the French enemy had created to some extent a colonial reliance upon English redcoats. With the defeat of New France the colonists freed themselves of this need for military support, and Britain removed the one force which had made the British connection essential to the colonials. "With the fall of Quebec," wrote the historian Francis Parkman, "began the history of the United States."

BIBLIOGRAPHY FOR CHAPTER TWO

Until a generation or so ago historians tended to look upon the first half of the eighteenth century as a rather uneventful interruption between the ages of settlement and of revolution. More recently the growing interest in economic, social, and intellectual history has given rise to a growing literature concerning significant developments of this period which the institutional historians had tended to disregard. The most recent survey of these developments is L. B. Wright, *Cultural Life of the American Colonies, 1607–1763* (1957), which includes detailed discussions of the literature on the subject. It is especially good on the middle and southern colonies. V. L. Parington, *Colonial Mind* examines changes in political, social, and religious thought, as does T. J. Wertenbaker, *The Golden Age of American Culture* (1942).

S. E. Morison, *The Intellectual Life of Colonial New England* is a reprint of his *The Puritan Pronaos* (1935), a brief and immensely knowledgeable survey, covering mainly the last quarter of the seventeenth and the first quarter of the eighteenth centuries. Morison argues that the Puritans, above all other English colonists, were responsible for preserving humanistic culture and initiating scientific inquiry in America. Covering the same ground in greater detail, Perry Miller, *The New England Mind: From Colony to Province* (1953) "treats the intellectual and literary history of New England, with attention focused almost steadily upon the Massachusetts Bay Colony, from about 1600 until 1730. . . . Many readers will find much new material in this book, some of which may provoke vigorous dissent. Mr. Miller is penetrating; he is sometimes pungent; he is firm—and occasionally free—in his opinions." The life of New England's leading intellectual is best approached through Ola Winslow, *Jonathan Edwards* (1940); his thought is best analyzed in Perry Miller, *Jonathan Edwards* (1949). A good anthology of his writings is C. H. Faust and T. H. Johnson, eds., *Jonathan Edwards*. For an authoritative and readable general discussion read K. B. Murdock, *Literature and Theology in Colonial New England* (1949).

The great classic of the American enlightenment, Benjamin Franklin's *Autobiography* is available in various paperback editions; and Verner Crane, *Benjamin Franklin and a Rising People* (1954) "presents a reliable, informative, well-balanced, and interesting portrait. . . ." Carl and Jessica Bridenbaugh, *Rebels and Gentlemen: Philadelphia in the Age of Franklin* (1942) is a colorful account of life and thought in the colonial metropolis. D. J. Boorstin, *The Lost World of Thomas Jefferson* (1948) is concerned with the ideas of leading members of Philadelphia's American Philosophical Society, including Jefferson. "The book's aim is to discover the dominant spirit of the Jeffersonian view of the world—not . . . the ideas of Jefferson alone, but the atmosphere of Jeffersonian ideas . . . a valuable study of eighteenth century thought in most of its contexts. [The] method of approach is fresh and original. . . ." Carl Bridenbaugh, *Myths and Realities: Societies of the Colonial South* (1952) is an absorbing pioneer study.

The outstanding account of immigration in the early period is M. L. Hansen, *The Atlantic Migration, 1607–1860* (1940). "No one will question its significance in interpreting the American heritage. Although the many economic and social forces which determined the migration of Western Europeans are explained and integrated more satisfactorily . . . than in any preceding work, it is the individual that stands out. . . . In style and accuracy the author's . . . achievement is outstanding. . . . erudite and human explanation of America's origins." An excellent brief beginning to a relatively little explored subject is Bernard Bailyn, *Education in the Forming of American Society: Needs and Opportunities for Study* (1960), "a trenchant revisionist interpretation of colonial educational history . . . [and] a lengthy critical commentary on sources. Both essays are urbane, stimulating, and beautifully written, and promise to exert a profound influence on future work in the field." Among anthologies of colonial literature is R. H. Pearce, *Colonial American Writings*. M. C. Tyler, *A History of American Literature, 1607–1765* (1878) is an American history classic.

REVOLUTION AND CONSTITUTION 3

I

"The having all North America to ourselves by acquiring Canada
dazzles the eyes," wrote a "Gentleman from Guadaloupe" in 1761,
"and blinds the understandings of the giddy and unthinking
people . . . yet it is easy to discover that such a peace might
ruin Britain. . . ." At issue was the question of whether to retain
French Canada or the French sugar island of Guadaloupe at war's
end, it being understood that one or the other would have to be
returned to France. To the gentleman from Guadaloupe the folly
of creating a united North America was clear as day, for "such a
country at such a distance could never remain long subject to Britain . . . they are always grumbling and complaining against Britain,
even while they have the French to dread, what may they not be
supposed to do if the French is no longer a check on them. . . . "

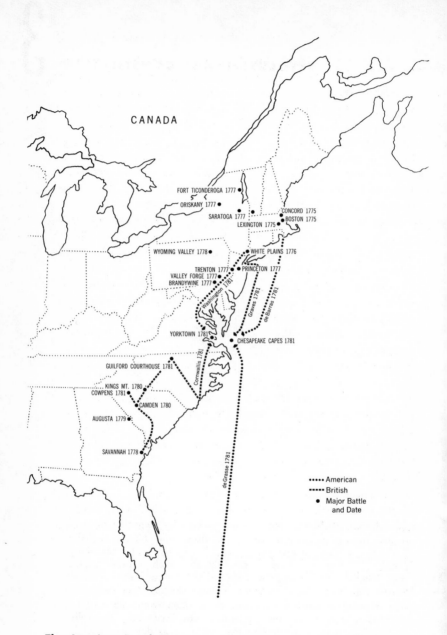

CANADA

FORT TICONDEROGA 1777 ●
ORISKANY 1777 ●
SARATOGA 1777 ●
● CONCORD 1775
● BOSTON 1775
LEXINGTON 1775 ●
WYOMING VALLEY 1778 ●
● WHITE PLAINS 1776
TRENTON 1777 ●
VALLEY FORGE 1777 ●
BRANDYWINE 1777 ●
● PRINCETON 1777
Washington 1781
Graves 1781
de Barras 1781
YORKTOWN 1781 ●
● CHESAPEAKE CAPES 1781
GUILFORD COURTHOUSE 1781 ●
Cornwallis 1781
KINGS MT. 1780 ●
COWPENS 1781 ●
● CAMDEN 1780
AUGUSTA 1779 ●
SAVANNAH 1778 ●
de Grasse 1781

····· American
---- British
● Major Battle
  and Date

**The American Revolution:
Major Lines of Advance and Chief Battle Sites.**

Colonial Reorganization Against this argument, the affable American colonial agent in Britain, Benjamin Franklin, felt
obliged to take exception. Such fears of American independence
were groundless, he argued. On the contrary the acquisition of
Canada would serve to remove imperial stresses which already
were beginning to appear. The opening of Canadian farmland,
Franklin explained, would serve to consume colonial energies and
so delay the day when declining agricultural opportunities might
force Americans into lines of economic activity which would compete with English manufacturing and commercial interests.

After an extended debate, and pressured by the West India
sugar interests which were opposed to bringing the rich French
sugar island into the empire, Parliament returned Guadaloupe and
retained Quebec. Thirteen years later, as the gentleman from
Guadaloupe had predicted, the American colonists declared their
independence from England. By that time some Englishmen were
calling on their government to return Canada to France and "turn
the French Indians loose" on the colonists again, but these men
had become wise too long after the fact.

Guadaloupe would have brought immediate revenue to Britain.
Canada brought heavy expenditures and these, moreover, to a
government which already had gone deeply in debt to finance the
most expensive war of its history. Nor did the removal of French
power permit military economies to the extent anticipated, for the
former Indian allies of France remained on the rampage, and
England faced the expensive prospect of subduing the conquered
regions.

The prospect was the more dolorous to members of Parliament
for the fact that the main source of revenue for the government remained the land tax, which bore with disproportionate weight
upon members themselves. Naturally they were concerned to find
some means of distributing the burden more equitably and so they
were led to consider taxing those American colonists who, as it
turned out, had been the chief beneficiaries of the war. It had
never been a part of the British mercantilist practice to supplement the national revenue through taxation of the colonists, and
the Grenville administration, which assumed power in England in
1763, did not altogether admit to such a motive. It argued, rather,
that the military helplessness of the colonies required Britain to
retain troops in America, and that, such being the case, it was en-

tirely reasonable to tax the colonists in order to support a part of the burden of the colonists' own defense.

The time seemed propitious, in fact, for a general overhauling of the imperial system. In their contribution to the war effort the colonies had done much less than might reasonably have been expected of them. Worse than that, colonial merchants had extended the length of the war by trading briskly with the enemy throughout the conflict. On the other hand, the efforts of the British government under Pitt to exert greater control over the colonies and to suppress smuggling had provided valuable experience which could be made use of in time of peace.

Previously the navigation laws had been but indifferently enforced, partly because effective enforcement seemed to involve insuperable difficulties and prohibitive expenses. The fact that successful smugglers late in the war were making up to 4,000 per cent profits, however, indicated the surprising extent to which this trade had been suppressed. Thus faced with serious postwar problems and at the same time armed with valuable wartime experience in ways of meeting these problems, the British government set forth to put the whole empire in good operating order.

George III came to the throne in 1760, and it was he more than anyone else who was responsible for the new imperial policies which led to the Revolution. And until the Boston Tea Party offended him, George was not altogether unsympathetic to the colonial point of view. Until then he certainly did not associate himself with any aggressively coercive colonial policy. The trouble with George III was that he was much more concerned with small matters of domestic politics than he was with the great imperial problems, and that he therefore neither informed himself thoroughly on imperial matters nor appointed able and well-informed men to carry out the new programs. It was his main purpose to recover the royal authority which his two predecessors had permitted to pass into the hands of Parliament. Conceding the sovereignty of Parliament, he set forth to do this by building a King's party in the House of Commons through which he could rule the nation.

Opposition to these royal pretensions came from various discordant factions led by ambitious and powerful lords and known as the Whigs. There was a certain Tory element in Parliament which always automatically voted on the side of the King, on the grounds that it was disloyal and blasphemous to do otherwise. To this group George III added enough followers to gain control of the House of Commons by use of the royal patronage, by the conferring of numerous titles, and by influencing elections, especially in the rotten boroughs where members were elected by a handful of votes. British politics under these circumstances was intensely personal, picayune, and not characteristically divided by great issues. Who got a local franchise was apt to seem more important at the moment than how to handle the Indian problem in America.

Upon coming to the throne in the midst of the war, George III dismissed the brilliant and experienced William Pitt as Prime Minister and shuffled his cabinets busily during the next few years. There was the Newcastle ministry until 1762, the Bute ministry until 1763, the Grenville ministry until 1765, the Rockingham ministry until 1766, and the Pitt-Grafton ministry until 1770. By that time George III, firmly in control, was able to place the pliant Lord North in office and keep him there until he was forced out by the disastrous conclusion to the American Revolution.

Of these men Pitt was much the best equipped to deal with the problems of empire. Unfortunately he was taken by insanity several months after assuming office and thereafter took no part in the conduct of the government. George III, himself, was suffering the early stages of those recurring fits of madness, which later on incapacitated him altogether, and a number of the Friends of America, since they got drunk nightly on port wine, must have suffered terrible hangovers during parliamentary debates. Because of these circumstances the American colonies did not receive the consideration which their importance to England warranted.

II

Grenville Acts   The most immediately pressing American concern at the close of the French and Indian War was the Indian problem. There were three main Indian language groups along the Anglo-American frontiers. The Muskhogean Indians occupied the southern frontier, and of the tribes in this group the Creek Nation was the most formidable, occupying the territory from Georgia to the Mississippi. Too loosely organized for any effective counterthrust against the white colonists, the Creeks occasionally united even less effectively with the neighboring nations such as the Seminole, Catawba, Chickasaw, and Choctaw.

Later, however, during the Revolutionary era, the Creeks gained a remarkable leader in Alexander McGillivray, the son of a Scotch-Indian trader who, through the matrilineal system, could claim status as a full-blooded Creek. Accepting pay simultaneously from the English, the Spanish and the Americans, McGillivray played one off against the other so effectively as to secure the sovereignty of the Creeks for a generation after the northern tribes had been settled on reservations.

To the north the Algonquin Indians occupied most of Canada and the Ohio Valley and all of New England. Their firm alliance with the French had been secured early by the French interest in fur trading and by the relative lack of French interest in farming. The traditional enemies of the Algonquin were the Five Nations or Iroquois confederacy of Cayuga, Mohawk, Oneida, Onondaga, and Seneca tribes in Upper New York, the third major Indian group. The English inherited the alliance which the Dutch fur traders had earlier made with the Iroquois, but they never succeeded in controlling their Indian allies as effectively as the French did theirs.

In 1763 the Algonquins found a leader in Pontiac, a chief of the Ottawas, aided by the mystical Delaware Prophet, who envisioned a vast Indian confederacy extending across the language groupings. The alliance with the southern Indians failed to be achieved, and the barbaric intricacies of tribal custom prevented Pontiac from holding his local alliance together for long. Northern Indians rose up in the Conspiracy of Pontiac, however, and in 1763 his warriors succeeded in capturing every English fort west of Fort Niagara but the one at Detroit.

The uprising was not put down until 1765. In the meantime a hastily prepared proclamation of 1763 was issued by George III dealing with the Indian problem as well as all of the territory acquired from France. Civil governments were established in Quebec, East and West Florida, and the Island of Grenada, and the proclamation line was drawn down through the Appalachian Mountains beyond which land was not to be granted and settlers were not to go.

The proclamation was protested by Americans on various grounds but most seriously on the grounds that it deprived colonies of their rights to territories which were assigned them in their charters. Most directly affected were Virginians and Pennsylvanians, including Franklin and Washington, who had invested in land companies in the Ohio Valley, These objections were tempered, however, by the belief, which Washington shared with others, that the proclamation was no more than an emergency measure which would be rescinded when the crisis was past. It was only later that the proclamation came to be looked upon as a part of a comprehensive plan to coerce the colonies.

Even before the Pontiac rising the English government had decided to maintain 10,000 troops in America for purposes both of Indian defense and of maintaining order among the newly acquired Spanish and French populations, and it was considered by them to be reasonable to expect the American colonies to assume from a third to a half of the expenses involved. One means by which this could be achieved was through the added revenue which would derive from strict enforcement of the trade laws. The navy was given greater authority than previously to inspect trading vessels, and crews were given half the prize money for the capture of smugglers.

The greatest source of revenue lost to the Treasury through smuggling was in the rarely collected tax on non-English molasses, and in 1764 the Sugar Act was passed to remedy this. The Sugar Act, which taxed a variety of commodities brought into the colonies from foreign areas, lowered the duty on molasses from 6d. per gallon to 3d., in order to permit the trade to continue, and then Parliament passed a series of enactments increasing rewards, facilitating searches and seizures, and providing legal immunities for enforcement officers.

The news of this act, according to Governor Bernard of Massachusetts, "caused a greater alarm in this country than the taking of Fort William Henry did in 1757." Merchants were convinced that the act would destroy their vital trade with the non-English West Indies, and they argued this point convincingly and at length in memorials to Parliament, amid deepening depression conditions. Similar memorials were sent by merchants from the middle colonies and from Charleston. The Massachusetts Assembly passed a resolution declaring the act to be a violation of the principle of no taxation without representation and calling for united colonial opposition to the act.

The Massachusetts resolution was not effective in achieving its purpose, because, in the first place, the act injured few economic interests in the colonies south of Pennsylvania, and, in the second place, the merchants who were most directly concerned did not want to argue their case in the inflammatory terms of their rights as Englishmen. They were much happier appealing to the business sense of Parliament by demonstrating that large business losses would be suffered by England from the resulting decline in purchasing power in the American market for British goods. But while the merchants were waiting for their bread-and-butter arguments to sink home, the Sugar Act, according to James Otis of Massachusetts, "set people to thinking, in six months, more than they had done in their whole lives before."

Following the Sugar Act, Parliament passed the Colonial Currency Act, prohibiting the use of bills of credit as legal tender and so threatening to deprive the colonies of their main form of currency. Then in 1765 Parliament managed to alienate the colonies completely, as it had failed to do with the Sugar Act, by passing the Stamp Act. Passed after a dull and perfunctory discussion, this enactment provided that colonial expenses would be defrayed in part by taxes in the form of stamps or stamped paper to be paid for in specie and to be used for numerous items, including newspapers, business documents, and legal papers.

Unlike the Sugar Act, the Stamp Act was a direct tax for the exclusive purpose of revenue, and, again unlike the Sugar Act, it struck at practically everybody of consequence in all the colonies and struck with especial force at the most influential members of society: the merchants, the planters, the lawyers, and the newspaper editors. The colonists were virtually unanimous in their conviction that such taxation, by a parliament in which they were not represented, was unconstitutional, and they rose angrily to prevent its operation. Parliament had considerately provided a period of grace before the law would go into effect. It never did go into effect.

In the Virginia House of Burgesses Patrick Henry was successful, after a close fight, in passing a series of resolutions denouncing the practice of taxation without representation and recalling to the English government the "liberties, franchises and immunities" which Americans possessed by virtue of being Englishmen and also by their charter rights. The resolution, in company with a number which failed to pass the House, was at once circulated through the colonies. Then in "mobbish Boston" radicals staged violent anti-Stamp Tax demonstrations which the authorities were powerless to restrain. Rhode Island followed with a mob which drove the King's officers from their houses.

Riots spread through the colonies. Stamp officials were tarred and feathered, and a new political force, the lower-middle-class Sons of Liberty, made its appearance. The Sons appeared in all thirteen colonies, and everywhere they received strong aristocratic support. In New York, De Lanceys and Livingstons sponsored them, and in South Carolina Henry Laurens, mobbed by rioters in the middle of the night, identified nine aristocratic acquaintances of his beneath the "soot, sailors habits, slouch hats &c." Meanwhile colonial leaders assembled in New York in the Stamp Act Congress to resolve that the act had "a manifest Tendency to subvert the Rights and Liberties of the Colonists."

Amazed and shocked by the violent American reaction, Parliament, which had passed the act with no expectation that it would arouse great commotion, now repealed it by a vote of more than two to one, four months after it was supposed to have gone into effect. Beyond that, Parliament repealed the Sugar Act and reduced the molasses duty to one penny. A Declaratory Act accompanied the Stamp Act repeal, asserting Parliament's right to tax the colonists, but this point was disregarded amid the rejoicing over the repeal. The Quartering Act, passed at the time of the Stamp Act, provided under certain circumstances for the quartering of troops in privately owned barns, taverns, inns, and unoccupied houses. Its continued operation caused trouble in Massachusetts and New York, but the colonists generally took the view that they had won their point and all was well.

Nevertheless, the Stamp Act crisis left lasting changes in American society which bode ill for the well-being of Britain's American empire. In the course of the crisis radicals gained control of the Massachusetts Assembly under the leadership of James Otis and of the Virginia House of Burgesses under the leadership of Patrick Henry. The Sons of Liberty, called into existence by the crisis, continued on afterwards alienating many of their original aristocratic sponsors by their violence and by the radicalism of their demands, which included broadening of the suffrage and other political and social reforms. They continued on under more plebeian and more radical leadership in the urban centers of the the Northern colonies, corresponding with each other and looking for ways to cause further trouble.

Originally the colonists had been virtually united in their opposition to the Stamp Act, but they were never united again. The issue was drawn by the lawless and violent manner in which the act had been opposed. Sides were taken on this issue, and they remained roughly the same sides which later divided into the Revolutionary patriots and the Tory loyalists.

The Stamp Act crisis brought the American newspaper into existence for the first time as an independent political force. Previously the colonial newspapers, beginning with the *Boston News Letter* in 1704, had been published "by authority" and had served as the official organ of the government. Their editors, if they wished to stay out of jail, had done nothing to bring themselves unfavorably to official notice. In 1733 the cause of freedom of the press had won a victory when John Peter Zenger, editor of the New York *Weekly Journal,* was acquitted of the charge of libeling the governor of the state. Acquittal was on the grounds—not acceptable at that time in English common law as a defense against libel charges—that the statements had been true.

The Zenger case had had no direct effect upon the law of the land, but subsequently all colonies passed laws giving juries, not judges, the right to determine libel. Until 1765, however, newspapers had ventured little into political controversy. Then, injured more by the Stamp Act than perhaps any other element in the colonies, they struck out with political cartoons and ringing editorials which were widely circulated and widely popular. Following this first taste of power, the newspapers remained in the forefront of controversy. The large majority of them continued to take the radical side and later to support the Revolution.

It was during this period that the American lawyer rose suddenly to achieve a political power probably uniquely great among the nations of the world. Until the middle of the eighteenth century the role of lawyers was a minor one and their position in society was quite low. Yet twenty-five of the fifty-six signers of the Declaration of Independence were lawyers and so were thirty-one of the fifty-five men who attended the Constitutional Convention. Life in seventeenth-century America had been too simple for the complexities of the common law, but during the eighteenth century the westward expansion, with its endless opportunities for litigation in land law, provided incentives for the legal profession as did the growth of commerce.

Most illustrious among the common people who chose the law as an avenue of advancement was John Adams, who made the decision after some hesitation. "The study of law," he wrote a friend, "is indeed an avenue to the more important offices of State and the happiness of human society is an object worth the pursuit of any man. But the acquisition of these important offices depends upon many circumstances of birth and of fortune, not to mention capacity, which I have not and I can have no hopes of being useful in that way." The event which did much to prove John Adams wrong was the American Revolution, freeing America from aristocratic English control and placing American lawyers firmly in the seats of power. Ambitious American lawyers brought the law to the side of liberty and the American Revolution. Once in power, these lawyers took the side of property and position just as effectively against the threatening advance of democracy. The history of the American bar helps to explain why the Revolution came in the first place and why it then took the moderate course that it did.

III

Townshend and Coercive Acts — There remained for Parliament that same English debt and those continuing expenses of maintaining soldiers in America. With Pitt's withdrawal from the Pitt-Grafton Cabinet which succeeeded that of Grenville, the real leader became Charles Townshend, serving as Chancellor of the Exchequer, and therefore responsible for preparing the 1767 budget. "Champagne Charlie," as he was known to the bon ton, had a great reputation as a wit. He took an unusually supercilious view of the American colonists and their little problems and funny arguments. He playfully mocked castles down by taking advantage of a distinction which he mistakenly thought they made between internal and external taxes: internal taxes being those placed on goods within the colonies and external taxes being those placed on goods as they were being imported. In 1767, therefore, against the advice of other members of the Cabinet, he introduced the Townshend Acts, placing import duties on English painters' colors, lead, paper, glass, and tea in order to raise a rather paltry £40,-000 in annual revenue. In addition a board of customs commissioners was created which proved far more effective than had the older Naval Office, and the New York Assembly was suspended until it complied with the Quartering Act.

For a time Townshend's laugh appeared to be the last laugh.

The New York Assembly knuckled under with an appropriation for quartering the soldiers; colonial leaders, who had been shocked by the Stamp Act riots, held back for a time, and merchants, deciding that they would not be materially injured by the duties, showed no disposition to stand irresponsibly on principle. For six months after passage of the duties calm prevailed before the storm. The storm broke with the publication by the wealthy and rather conservative Quaker lawyer, John Dickinson, of *Letters from a Farmer in Pennsylvania,* the most influential of all pre-Revolutionary tracts before the writings of Thomas Paine. Concerned to resolve the conflict rather than inflame it, Dickinson attempted to prove that the taxes were constitutionally incompatible with the British imperial system. Edmund Burke had spoken admiringly of the Americans as "smatterers" in law, and the legalism of Dickinson's argument was typical of the American approach to the problem. The essays were immediately acclaimed on both sides of the Atlantic, and a whole literature of writings began to be added in their support.

Two months after the appearance of Dickinson's *Letters* the Massachusetts Assembly, under the direction of Samuel Adams, drafted a circular letter and sent it to the other colonial legislatures protesting the new duties. The assembly was ordered to rescind the circular letter, and, when it refused by an overwhelming vote to do so, it was dissolved. A law was passed which provided for the sending to England for trial persons suspected of treason, and two additional regiments were sent to Boston. The Boston town meeting remained in operation, however, and the Boston merchants were finally moved to accept a Non-Importation Agreement boycotting the goods covered by the Townshend duties. They were reluctantly followed by the merchants of New York and Philadelphia. The Virginia House of Burgesses passed the Virginia Resolves against the duties and against the law providing for the trying of Americans in England. It then adopted nonimportation and was accordingly dissolved.

The colonists never regained the first fine careless rapture of their opposition to the Stamp Act. The merchants moved reluctantly and were sometimes caught at violations by the Sons of Liberty, who made themselves the chief enforcers of nonimportation. In Boston in 1770, excitement momentarily reached a new pitch when redcoats fired on a mob killing five, but outside Massachusetts this "massacre" caused little commotion. Meanwhile Lord North had taken office as Prime Minister, and, deciding that a tax on English goods was prejudicial to English interests, pushed a measure through Parliament repealing all the duties except that on tea, which was retained, George III wrote, "to keep the right" in the matter of parliamentary authority.

In the colonies cannons exploded in celebration, as had happened following repeal of the Stamp Act, and to most people all seemed well. Nonimportation was broken first by New York, which had suffered most from it, a defection which, according to the New York Sons, would be "a stench in the nostrils of every true-born American, till time is no more." Amid a half-hearted boycott on tea and the shrill frustration of radicals such as Samuel Adams, three years of relative quiet descended upon the empire. Imperial affairs were not critically disrupted either by the burning of the British revenue boat *Gaspee* in Rhode Island or by the British assumption of the responsibility for paying the salaries of the governors and judges in Massachusetts. Radicals, meanwhile, organized committees of correspondence to achieve intercolonial unity while they waited their opportunity for new assaults against the home government.

Their opportunity came in 1773 in the form of the Tea Act, bestowed by the British government upon the East India Company, with its needy stockholding following in Parliament. Under the terms of the act, the East India Company was permitted to ship tea directly to the American colonies and so avoid the English duties. This piece of favoritism enabled that company to undersell even native American smugglers on the American market. Sharp protests were heard from Charleston, Philadelphia, and New York, and then from Boston came the splash heard round the world. Radicals, disguised as Indians, boarded East India Company ships in Boston harbor. They dumped a fortune in tea into the bay, and revolution was in sight. This violation of the natural right of private property, which shocked many colonists, roused Parliament to a righteous fury and resulted in the Coercive, or as the Americans called them, Intolerable Acts. These in turn roused the colonists to call the First Continental Congress for the purpose of organizing against England.

The Coercive Acts consisted of the Boston Port Bill, closing the port to trade until *somebody* paid for the tea; the Massachusetts

Government Act, arbitrarily altering the provincial government in violation of charter rights; the Administration of Justice Act, permitting the trial in England of persons accused of a crime in a colony; and a new Quartering Act, making local authorities responsible for the quartering of troops in areas to which they were sent, if barracks were not available. Additional troops were sent to New England, and General Gage was made governor of Massachusetts "to put the rebels in their places."

At the same time, although independently of the Coercive Acts, the Quebec Act was passed, incorporating the Ohio Valley into the province of Quebec in violation of colonial charters and extending wide religious and political liberties to the Catholic French Canadians. The Quebec Act, except perhaps for the extension of the province to include the Ohio Valley, was an honest implementation of promises made the French in the Treaty of Paris of 1763. The colonists, however, had good reason to suspect it as an attempt to destroy colonial independence by building up Canada as an opposing force, and the act was lumped together with the rest of the acts in their minds as part of a comprehensive program of coercion.

The Quebec Act may have been motivated by the intention to divide and thereby conquer; the Coercive Acts certainly were. Under them Massachusetts was singled out for discipline, and it was apparently supposed that other colonies, since they were not affected, would keep fairly quiet while Massachusetts was being made an example of. Events quickly pointed up the error in this reasoning. Pamphlets appeared such as Jefferson's *A Summary View of the Rights of British America*. Resolutions of sympathy were passed in various cities, and the Sons of Liberty, with their committees of correspondence, went into action. The New York Sons called for a renewal of nonimportation, and the Virginia House of Burgesses, meeting in a tavern after being dissolved for approving something Thomas Jefferson said, did likewise.

Faced with this new radical challenge, the conservative New York oligarchy bypassed the New York Committee of Correspondence and organized its own group, the Committee of Fifty-one. The Committee defeated the radicals partly by holding meetings in the early afternoon when workingmen found it hard to attend. It moved to circumvent the committees of correspondence by calling for the meeting of a continental congress. Such a congress, according to conservative calculations, would be controlled by prudent men who could act in unison to curb radical elements in individual colonies. These calculations left out of account the incendiary radicalism of the Southern aristocrats, especially the new order in Virginia. They left out of account also the increasingly bellicose program of the British government, which was rapidly driving moderates into the radical camp.

The colonists responded with the First Continental Congress which met in Philadelphia in September, 1774, representing all the Thirteen Colonies except Georgia. The first victory went speedily to the radicals with the endorsement of the Suffolk Resolves, drawn up by the people of Suffolk County, Massachusetts, including Boston, calling for a preservation of the people's liberties. The conservatives, hurrying to stave off disaster, joined in support of a plan proposed by Joseph Galloway, of Pennsylvania, providing for an American parliament, inferior to the British Parliament but in charge generally of intercolonial matters. Any legislation affecting America would require concurrence of both parliaments. It was similar to the Albany Plan proposed by Franklin in 1754 to unify the colonies in the face of the French threat. It was similar also to plans subsequently suggested by a number of other men including Jefferson and John Adams. One objection to it when Franklin had proposed it had been that Parliament would not accept it, and there was still no assurance, and probably no likelihood, that Parliament would accept the Galloway Plan. In any event it was rejected by a vote of six colonies to five, and from that point on the radicals had it their own way.

A Declaration of Rights and Grievances was passed criticizing Parliament for a whole catalog of errors, and an Association was created to enforce the cessation of all trade with England and the British West Indies, the voters in all communities being charged with electing committees to enforce the boycott and, after September, 1775, nonexportation as well. A job lot of petitions and memorials was then composed, and the congress adjourned, voting to meet again the following May if grievances had not been redressed by that time.

Conservatives still hoped for a middle road out of the crisis, but the radical Patrick Henry departed from Philadelphia happily convinced that a situation had been created from which war would certainly result, and the Battle of Lexington and Concord occurred three weeks before the meeting of the Second Continental Congress to prove him right. The Second Continental Congress when it met in May, 1775, was faced with the fact of war, and it continued on as the wartime government of the Thirteen Colonies until replaced in 1781 by the government of the Articles of Confederation.

For more than a century after the American Revolution, American historians were in cordial agreement as to its causes and character. It had been a righteous struggle for freedom against English tyranny. The classic, scholarly account of colonial and Revolutionary history in this tradition was George Bancroft's multivolume *History of the United States*.

It might be supposed that English historians writing on the Revolution would have arrived at different conclusions, but they did not. Lord Acton spoke the opinion of liberal English historians in the nineteenth century when, comparing it with the English Revolution, he found it a "more glorious Revolution, infinitely more definite and clear-cut, with a stronger grasp of principle, and depending less on conciliation and compromise. . . ." Beyond that, a school of English historians has emerged in the twentieth century, led by Lewis Namier, which places blame squarely upon George III and the British Parliament for the narrow provinciality and piggish self-interestedness which underlay their management of the empire.

It was among historians in America at the close of the nineteenth century that a new school of thought arose which was more sympathetic to the British side in the struggle. These revisionists, most notably Charles M. Andrews, found the British imperial system to have been one which, on the whole, was advantageous to the American colonial interests. They looked upon the Revolution, rather regretfully, as rising, not out of English tyranny, but rather out of the world-wide struggle with France and the consequent maladjustments in the imperial system. This is the main thesis underlying the vast study by Lawrence H. Gipson, still in process of completion.

Hard on the heels of the imperial school came the economic determinists, asserting that the Revolution was the attempt of "the American merchant and planter-capitalism" to free itself from the restraints of imperial economic control. Fashionable especially in the Depression period of the thirties, this school has failed to win influential adherents during the past generation. However, a somewhat similar, but less starkly economic, view has gained support among urban-oriented historians beginning with Arthur Mier Schlesinger, Sr., in his *Colonial Merchants and the American Revolution* (1918). These historians tend to see the colonies as having outgrown, socially as well as economically, the role demanded of them by the British government. Most recently the leading advocate of this thesis has been Carl Bridenbaugh in various writings including *Cities in the Wilderness* (1938) and *Cities in Revolt* (1955).

It is as a mainly political controversy, however, that the Revolution continues to be chiefly viewed. That is not to say that the historians, viewing it in this light, have patched up their differences. At issue, for one thing, is the question of who was oppressing whom. In 1909 Carl Becker, in a study of New York politics during the pre-Revolutionary era, reached the conclusion that the struggle was not one for home rule so much as it was a contest to see who should rule at home. Basic to the crisis, he and others after him argued, were the class and sectional struggles within the colonies which deranged the imperial system. The leading current spokesman for this interpretation is Merrill Jensen, as against a new group of writers who see the Revolution as a defense of thoroughly democratic institutions already successfully established in colonial America. Most influential among this latter group has been Robert E. Brown in his *Middle Class Democracy in Massachusetts and the Revolution* (1955).

Daniel J. Boorstin, meanwhile, has returned to the original view that the Revolution was most basically a constitutional controversy over the principle of "No Taxation without Representation." Far from seeing this as the stirring issue which it had seemed to earlier historians, however, he looks upon it as having been "a pretty technical legal problem," and he looks upon the Revolution as having been, "In the modern European sense of the word, . . . hardly a revolution at all."

IV

Independence   In April, 1775, General Gage sent troops to Concord to confiscate rebel military stores. The mission was accomplished at the cost of 273 dead and wounded, as the redcoats ran the gauntlet of minutemen from Concord back to Boston. On May

10, the day the Second Continental Congress convened, Ethan Allen captured Fort Ticonderoga, and two days later Benedict Arnold captured Crown Point. In June the capture of Breed's and Bunker's Hills in Boston cost the British more than a thousand casualties. British reinforcements had arrived, increasing British troops in America to about 10,000. In June the Congress named George Washington commander in chief of the Continental forces. Subordinate generals were later named and provision was made for the creation of a navy and for the issuance of letters of marque and reprisal for privateers. Congress then drew up the Olive Branch Petition expressing its loyalty to the King.

More than a year passed before the revolutionists were driven to abandon their hopes for reconciliation and to declare their independence of England; yet at no point during that period did the British government give them any basis for hoping that their main demands would be met. In England their cause was supported by William Pitt, now Lord Chatham, James Fox, and Edmund Burke. But Pitt, though he praised the Continental Congress as a valuable addition to the imperial system, insisted that the colonies recognize the theoretical right of Parliament to tax them, which the revolutionists were bound not to do. Under any circumstances Chatham, Fox, and Burke were powerless amid outraged public opinion and in a Parliament by now securely controlled by George III and Lord North.

Several months before Lexington and Concord Lord North presented the government's offer: the colonies would not be taxed if they would raise the funds themselves for the administration of the colonies and for their share in the common defense. His offer conceded nothing concerning the English right to tax its colonies, nor did it propose withdrawing troops from the colonies. It served only to convince the rebels of the hopelessness of negotiation. The Continental Congress made no further formal attempt at reconciliation. Held together by no traditional loyalties except English loyalties, the revolutionists continued to toast the King and argue for their English liberties as they armed for independence.

It was Thomas Paine, recently over from England, who broke the cake of custom early in 1776 with his *Common Sense*, presenting the natural rights argument for revolution and attacking monarchy in general and the "royal brute" George III in particular. This first published argument for independence was read every-

where in the colonies within a month and exerted an immense influence. In June, Richard Henry Lee presented before Congress a
Virginia resolution calling for outright independence. After a sharp
debate the resolution was approved by a vote of seven colonies to
five, and a committee was appointed to draw up a declaration of
the fact. On July 2, the Congress announced to the world that
"these United Colonies are, and of right ought to be FREE AND
INDEPENDENT STATES," and two days later the prepared Declaration
of Independence was formally signed.

Jefferson, as author of the Declaration, presented the natural
rights argument for revolution which, in the view of the signers,
was a self-evident one. All men, they believed, were created equal,
not in native ability nor in their equal share of the world's goods
nor in their right to participate in government, but in their equal
possession of that God-given right to life, liberty, and property.
Governments were formed for the purpose of securing these rights
for them. Therefore that government which failed of its purpose
lost its reason for being. This social compact theory of government
was derived from English and European writers such as John Locke
and Samuel Pufendorf, but it was strengthened in America as nowhere else by actual experience. From the Mayflower Compact to
the establishment of the latest frontier community, men had joined
together in a state of nature to form governments, on the basis of
written social compacts. What was theory to European philosophers
was common practice to American settlers.

Although undeniably a revolutionary document, the Declaration
presented a more conservative argument, in the minds of its signers,
than would appear from a modern reading of it. By "consent of the
governed" the signers meant consent of the property-holding taxpayers. By "pursuit of Happiness" the signers meant the right to do
with their property as they liked, subject to such necessary limitations as they placed upon themselves through their governments.

That the signers viewed the words of the Declaration in this
rather conservative light is demonstrated by the conservative state
constitutions which they proceeded to draw up. The phrase "pursuit of Happiness" was a Jeffersonian touch which gave warmth to
the document while in no way binding the signers or the new nation
(although the phrase afterwards crept into various state constitutions, where it remained as a perplexing problem for the state
courts). But the Declaration, whatever the sober intentions of its

signers, was inescapably a revolutionary document, and although it bound no one to anything but independence, it remained as a consecrated statement of revolutionary purpose to which American radicalism thereafter could always appeal.

Ten of the states completed their republican constitutions within the year. New York and Georgia followed in 1777 and Massachusetts, the only state to submit its constitution to the people for ratification, in 1780. In most cases they were basically republican translations of the colonial charters, with bills of rights added. Where they departed from precedent it was generally to weaken the executive and strengthen the assembly, liberty being associated in the patriots' minds with assemblies; tyranny, with kings and governors.

The most radical of the constitutions, that of Pennsylvania, created a one-house legislature, annually elected and sharing administrative authority with a plural executive. Without having to depart far from the Charter of Privileges of 1701, the Pennsylvania constitution expressed the radical Whig belief that government ought to represent the unobstructed will of the people. The most influential of the conservative constitutions, that drawn up for Massachusetts mainly by John Adams, demonstrated the conservatives' fear of faction, whether of the popular majority or of the privileged minority. It provided for an independent judiciary, a strong, indirectly elected executive, an upper house designed to represent property interests, and a lower house representing the people and holding power to levy taxes. The judiciary, the executive, and each legislative house held separately the right to veto, to check and balance the conflicting factions in society.

Perhaps the most significant innovation in most state constitutions was the addition of those bills of rights which the Privy Council had denied the colonies. The first of these, and the model for the first nine amendments to the Federal Constitution, was the Virginia Bill of Rights, chiefly written by the libertarian aristocrat George Mason. Proceeding from the Lockian compact theory of government, the Virginia Bill of Rights listed the liberties necessary to a free people: prohibition of hereditary offices, an independent judiciary, no taxation without representation, trial by jury, the right of the accused to confront opposing witnesses, the right of the accused to refuse to testify against himself, prohibition of general warrants for searches and seizures, prohibition of excessive bail, freedom of the press, the right to bear arms, subordination of military to civil power, and the free exercise of religion according to the dictates of conscience. Mason's eloquent list influenced French revolutionary thought more than perhaps any other document of the American Revolution. It demonstrated a concern for individual liberty among slaveholding aristocrats in the eighteenth century such as was rarely matched by equalitarian democrats in the nineteenth.

One general trend which exerted a democratizing influence on state governments was the removal of state capitals westward. It had been Jefferson's opinion that in theory the western counties had their fair share of representation, but that in practice the distance to Williamsburg meant that they were consistently underrepresented. In 1776 Jefferson proposed the transfer of the capital from Williamsburg to Richmond, and the move was approved three years later. North Carolina and Georgia, with no regular permanent capitals before the war, established them inland at Raleigh and Augusta. The capital of South Carolina was moved from Charleston to Columbia in 1789. The trend was slower in the northern states, New York and Pennsylvania each delaying for two decades.

Each state was an independent nation over which the Continental Congress had no legal authority. Congress decided on the number of troops which each state was supposed to contribute to the war, but the state was under no legal obligation to comply. Similarly Congress requisitioned the states for money and then took what it was given, which was never nearly enough. With victory in sight the war was nearly lost in 1781 for lack of money, until Congress was rescued by the newly appointed superintendent of finance, Robert Morris. Congress assumed command of the Continental Army and the direction of foreign affairs, but in domestic political matters it could do no more than recommend and hope.

V

War for Independence From first to last, the War for Independence was a remarkably chancy fight, not only as to the probable outcome—which was always in doubt until after Yorktown in 1781—nor merely because it was a struggle which was marked over and over again by very close shaves, but also in that, in the context of eighteenth-century warfare, it was full of imponderables. In the age of enlightened despotism nobody had been expected to fight for love of country. The people had had nothing to do with the many wars of the age, which had been fought by highly disciplined professional soldiers maneuvering in set formations under the suspicious scrutiny of their officers.

Had the Americans played by these rules, England would have made short work of Washington's amateurs with her professional army and her overwhelming naval superiority. With this disproportionate power the British were able to take major northern cities with relative ease, and had they been content with this they might, just by holding on, have in time stopped the rebels short of complete independence. They had orders to put down the rebellion, however, and when they moved into the country to accomplish this they were subjected to guerrilla tactics of farmer-soldiers which they were not trained to cope with.

Conflicting loyalties confused the struggle throughout. The Americans were bitterly divided between patriot and loyalist, at least 80,000 loyalists and perhaps more fleeing the country in the course of the Revolution. The southern planters were largely united on the patriot side, but in the northern states, except among the merchant gentry, the aristocratic leadership was predominantly loyalist, while many frontier regions were overwhelmingly anti-patriot. But the loyalists were unable to unite and organize upon a clearly understood program behind forceful leaders as were the patriots. England also was divided on the issue of the Revolution. There were Friends of America not only in Parliament but also in the British army, many officers being unwilling to fight against their countrymen in America. Doubts concerning the reliability of British soldiers was a major British motive for relying heavily upon Hessian mercenaries.

To the British went the advantage of the centrally organized government pitting itself against a league of independent states, but this advantage was offset by the corruption and incompetence which characterized the government of Lord North. The venality and incompetence of the Admiralty under the loathsome Lord Sandwich is generally regarded as unique in the annals of the British navy, while the War Department was mismanaged by Lord George Germain, who, among his many disqualifications for the position, could count the fact that he had himself been cashiered from the army for cowardice. The Americans had their share of incompetents and cowards also, but in George Washington they possessed the incomparable leader of the age. Washington's greatness as a national leader and the resulting confidence which even the Continental Congress came to place in him did much to offset the lack of a true central government and a national tradition and so made victory possible.

Driven from New York in the summer of 1776, Washington raised the perilously low morale of the army that winter with brilliant sallies at Trenton and Princeton. The initiative nevertheless remained with the British on the basis of their great naval and military superiority, and in the spring of 1777 Lord George Germain approved a campaign to end the war by dividing the colonies at the line of the Hudson River. General "Gentleman Johnny" Burgoyne was to move south from Canada by way of Lake Champlain, Col. Barry St. Leger was to move east from Lake Ontario, Gen. William Howe was to send a detachment north along the Hudson, and the three forces were to converge on the American Northern Army and destroy it. Several things went wrong. St. Leger met the Mohawk Valley militia and retreated into Canada, Howe was unable to act until it was too late, and the sizable force sent by Burgoyne to collect needed military supplies was beaten by the Green Mountain Boys at the Battle of Bennington.

Burgoyne's delayed advance permitted the strengthening of the Northern Army, and at the Battle of Saratoga Burgoyne surrendered his entire army of 5,000. This proved to be the decisive battle of the war, for it did much to convince the French to come into the war on the American side. Howe, meanwhile, had captured Philadelphia, and Washington retreated to spend that famous bitter winter in Valley Forge, the summer soldiers and sunshine patriots having by then deserted in large numbers. A year of indecisive fencing followed, and the British, having failed in their main northern attempt, shifted their attention to the South.

The revolutionists from the first had looked upon French military assistance as a likely possibility, and four months before their declaration of independence they sent Silas Deane to Paris to see what could be arranged. The French responded with generous supplies of cannon, guns, gunpowder, and clothing. In September, Deane, with Benjamin Franklin and Arthur Lee, was appointed to negotiate a commercial treaty with France, while a half dozen other European states were similarly sounded out. Nothing was achieved until news arrived of the Battle of Saratoga and of new favorable terms of settlement being considered by the British government. In February, 1778, a treaty of alliance was concluded providing that if France were drawn into the war, France would make American independence the essential object of the war and that neither nation would make peace with England before consulting the other. A commercial treaty was additionally concluded. France entered the war in June and was followed by Spain in 1779 and Holland in 1780.

The French were to play the major part in the eventual American victory, but they were woefully slow in arriving, as the British directed their attention to the southern states. The British captured Savannah in September, 1778, and royal government was returned to Georgia. In 1780 they launched the main southern campaign with the capture of Charleston by Sir Henry Clinton and the devastating defeat of the American army at Camden under Horatio Gates by General Cornwallis. Then, with everything apparently going their way, British cavalry forces with Tory supporters moved overboldly into the backcountry and were annihilated at Kings Mountain, ruining Southern Tory morale and raising up bands of farmer-fighters under Andrew Pickens, Thomas Sumter, and Francis Marion. Gates was replaced by the able General Nathanael Greene, and the British, defeated at Cowpens and weakened by a costly victory at Guilford Courthouse, were driven back to the coast. At this encouraging point the French joined with the needed military and naval support to bring the American war to its conclusion.

General Rochambeau arrived in Newport with 6,000 men in the summer of 1780 where he waited for a year until the arrival, essential to his usefulness, of the French fleet under the command of the Comte de Grasse. In August, 1781, Grasse sailed for the Chesapeake, a Franco-American army moved southward from New York, and by the end of September Cornwallis was penned up at Yorktown by the French fleet and combined French and American forces of 16,000. On October 19, 1781, he surrendered his entire force. The war in America was over, except for frontier fighting in the Northwest and a general mopping up of American merchantmen by the British navy.

Defeat in America discredited the personal rule of George III, toppled his minister, Lord North, and brought the Friends of America to power in time for them to conclude the hostilities with a treaty which gave the United States terms much more generous than they had any good reason to expect. The treaty negotiations were complicated, to say the least of it, by the French alliance and the further alliance between Spain and France. Congress appointed a commission to negotiate the peace by consultation with the French.

Suspicious, with good reason, that the French intended to appease Spain at American expense, the commission violated its instructions in entering into negotiations directly with England. The resulting agreement signed in November, 1782, went into effect September 3, 1783, when the Peace of Paris was concluded, bringing the general war to a conclusion. By the terms of the treaty Britain acknowledged American independence and conceded to the United States the territory extending north to the Great Lakes, west to the Mississippi, and south to the Floridas, which England returned to Spain. The treaty was based on extremely sketchy geographical knowledge, however, and in important matters it was ambiguously worded. It took sixty years of diplomatic negotiation to decide what it meant.

VI

The Critical Period   Once independence had been decided upon, nobody supposed that the Second Continental Congress, summoned for quite a different purpose, was a suitable government for the new nation. The Virginia resolution of June, 1776, while calling for independence, called also for a plan of confederation to be prepared and transmitted to the colonies, and Congress appointed John Dickinson to prepare the plan. The committee returned a month later with a report which for more than a year was not acted upon because of the military situation and also because of disagreements among the states. They mainly disagreed over whether western lands belonged to the states with charter rights to them or whether they belonged to the nation as a whole. In November, 1777, however, thirteen Articles of Confederation and Perpetual Union were submitted to the states for ratification.

The Articles provided for a unicameral Congress, in which each state would count for one vote. The Congress possessed the power to declare war, make peace, control foreign policy, appoint military officers, regulate Indian affairs, fix standards of weights and measures, determine the value of coins issued by the state as well as by the national governments, and decide on interstate disputes. On all decisions of importance a majority vote of nine states was needed, and on all amendments to the Articles unanimous agreement of the states was required. No executive branch was created except for a Committee of the States, each being represented by one delegate. Drawn up chiefly by the conservative Dickinson (who had refused to sign the Declaration of Independence on the grounds that there still remained lines of legal argument to be explored), the Articles put into writing the authority which the Second Continental Congress had already assumed. It was therefore not in itself any matter for controversy, except among those nationalists who clamored for a stronger central government.

It was the disposition of the western land which remained at issue, the argument of the states without western claims being that these belonged to all who were fighting the common fight. If the charter claims had been honored, Virginia would have had the right to rule a territory, extending to the Great Lakes, greater than that of all the other states combined. The Articles were speedily approved by most of the states, but Virginia's Chesapeake neighbor, Maryland, held out on the western lands issue until her point was won. New York, with the weakest claims to western land, conceded first, Virginia capitulated in January, 1781, Maryland signed a month later, and the Articles went into effect.

At the outset the period of the Confederation appeared to be opening upon an age of triumph. It began brilliantly with the decisive victory at Yorktown, lifting the American states from a long, doubtful contest into a world of astonishing promise. With the generous treaty of peace two years later the world was to be edified by a new nation of noble Romans, guiding their own self-reliant republican destinies by the pure light of Scripture and by the self-evident truths of the Declaration of Independence. Freed from the restrictions of the British imperial system, American enterprise saw boundless possibilities for profit in commercial agriculture, commerce, manufacturing, banking, road and canal building, and land speculation. Before the Revolution the royal governments had been the selfish guardians of British interests. The governments were now in the hands of the people and so could be trusted to help the people to enrich themselves.

Such buoyant hopes were bound to be deflated in the course of everyday events. Not everybody shared the widespread enthusiasm for the new republican ways or for independence, and even at the moment of victory many of those who had worked hardest for the cause had good reason to suspect the new system of inconsistency. The army at the close of the war, unrewarded and ill-cared for, was ominously restless. The older aristocracy, momentarily discredited, still held great power in most of the states, and after the war it was daily strengthened by returning loyalists.

Peace had hardly been declared when republicanism was threatened by the army. The main force of the army was wintering at Newburgh on the Hudson at war's end, idle and exasperated by the lack of supplies and by the failure of Congress to fulfill pledges. The officers had been promised half-pay for life, after the European custom, but Congress delayed taking official action. As the army grew increasingly restless, right-wing politicians like Alexander Hamilton came to view it as a potentially useful political instrument. The narrowly aristocratic Gouverneur Morris was enthusiastic about such a prospect. He wrote John Jay that he was "glad to see things in their present train. Depend on it, good will arise from the situation to which we are hastening . . . although I think it probable that much of convulsion will ensue, yet it must terminate in giving government that power, without which government is but a name."

The crisis reached its climax in March with the circulation of the anonymous Newburgh Address. Were the men in the army to be the only sufferers in the Revolution? It would not be so "if you have sense enough to discover, and spirit enough to oppose tyranny under whatever garb it may assume; whether it be the plain coat of republicanism, or the splendid robe of royalty. . . ." If there was any real danger of a *coup d'état* in an antimilitaristic nation of armed men, it was ended by Washington's admonitory address to his officers, who thereafter disbanded peaceably without waiting for their demands to be met. Widespread fear of the military was aroused all over again when the Order of the Cincinnati was organized as a hereditary secret order of the officers of the Revolution. Sam Adams was convinced that it was an attempt to establish, in as short a time as had ever been known, a military aristocracy, and radical enlisted men hurried to organize their own Sons of St. Tammand, or Tammany Societies, in opposition. One of these latter

Tammany organizations did develop into a permanent political power, but the Cincinnati proved to be no more than another bogeyman for Sam Adams and others.

There remained the problem of the common soldiers. In Pennsylvania about eighty soldiers, ill-treated and unpaid, marched to Philadelphia, got drunk, and surrounded the building where Congress was convened. Congress suffered fear and embarrassment and fled to Princeton, finally taking up quarters in New York. It made known its attitude toward the military by defeating a bill to create a permanent standing army of 896 men. It authorized instead a permanent force of eighty men: twenty-five at Fort Pitt and fifty-five at West Point. Whereas the officers were finally voted five years' pay, nothing of a like nature was done by Congress for the enlisted men, although individual states responded to their demands.

While the end of the war brought vast new economic opportunities for American businessmen, it also ushered in a commercial depression of continental proportions, compounded by the merchants, who continued to import large amounts of goods at continually falling prices. In 1785 there was a sharp decline in prices for American agricultural produce. Then depression passed over into recovery. By the eve of the Constitutional Convention the nation had entered upon good times and was launched upon the world-wide commercial enterprise which independence had promised. The period of the Confederation was the occasion for the depression which created sentiment in favor of a strong central government; it was also the time of return to prosperity which helped to launch the constitutional venture so auspiciously.

Although businessmen roundly denounced the thirteen democratical states and the weak Confederation for practices inimical to a sound economy, the politics of the time was generally favorable to business except in the realm of financial legislation. In the area of interstate trade the state governments showed an impressive spirit of restraint, the main tendency of the duties being to protect against foreign rather than interstate trade. There were acrimonious disputes over the location of state borders, but these were peacefully settled. Most impressively the problem of western lands was settled with the acquisition of the national domain from the states and with the creation by Congress of an orderly system for land sales, for settlement, for territorial government, and for eventual statehood.

By the Ordinance of 1785, government lands were divided into townships six miles square, which in turn were subdivided into thirty-six sections of 640 acres. They were to be sold alternately by townships and by sections at one dollar per acre. By the Ordinance of 1787, government for the territories was established and the method of achieving statehood created. The initial government, appointed by the Congress, consisted of a governor, a secretary, and three judges. When the territory supported 5,000 adult males these would be permitted to elect a legislature, which would in turn nominate a legislative council, while administration of the territory remained in the hands of the appointed governor. At that stage the territory would be entitled to a nonvoting delegate to the Congress. When the total population reached 60,000, the territory might call a convention, draw up a constitution and submit it to Congress, which then had the authority to admit the territory as a state on an equal political basis with the original states.

With this Northwest Ordinance, it has been said, the American government fundamentally solved the problem upon which the British empire had broken. Early settlement of the Northwest Territory, meanwhile, was expedited little by the Ordinance of 1785 and much by grandiose schemes of land speculators. The Ohio Company was chief among the companies and individuals which acquired vast tracts of land, often on the claim of their being just rewards for Revolutionary War services. As it turned out, few made substantial profits on these schemes, but the activities of the companies resulted in the rapid settlement of what became the state of Ohio.

The yeoman farmers had been the main force of the armies during the Revolution, and they were the chief basis of society in the Confederation period. They were the most numerous voters, and they demanded that their grievances be met. Their economic demands were simple. They lived as they had always lived, in a subsistence and barter economy. They had debts and taxes, and they lacked the money to pay them. They were forced to bear a disproportionately heavy share of the tax burden through the payment of poll taxes, and foreclosure, perhaps debtors' prison, awaited those who could not meet their obligations.

Their remedy was cheap money, as it had always been. In colonial times the Privy Council had consistently fought the issuance of paper money. The Revolution, however, had been financed in large part by state and continental paper currency, which quickly became worthless and was no longer in use by the close of the war. Upon the ruins of paper money system the creditor group established a hard money policy which enhanced the value of the debts owed them by the people, the states, and the Confederation government. In all states the growing opposition of the small farmer-debtor classes was inflamed by the sharp price decline in agricultural goods in the mid-eighties.

Demands for issuances of paper money became the center of controversy in all states, and seven states responded with paper money bills. In New York, New Jersey, South Carolina, Rhode Island, and Pennsylvania the money was based on land and served a need which was not met again until the establishment of Federal farm loan banks in the twentieth century. In some states the paper currency system was used to fund state and national debts. In those states where the merchants complied with the law willingly the measures worked well enough. Debtors found the opportunity to pay their creditors, and the paper money held its value. In states where the measures were fought by the merchants, notably in Rhode Island, the consequences were disastrous to creditors and debtors alike.

The central and western farmers of Massachusetts, struggling to hold their farms and to stay out of debtors' prison, received no satisfaction from their legislature. In some western districts there remained no single citizen who could meet the property qualification for representatives, and those districts were obliged to go unrepresented. Slow to revolt in the period before the Revolution, these western farmers had been trained by Boston and Sam Adams to organize and fight. In 1786 they rose again. They took possession of the courthouse at Northampton and at Worcester. They drilled and marched, and at Springfield, under the command of Daniel Shays, they clashed with the state militia and retreated in disorder. Through a dismal winter, bands of insurgents wandered about the countryside. By spring the remnants returned to their homes, and Shays' Rebellion was at an end. Congress in the meantime cautiously began to raise troops, asserting the need for frontier protection against Indians. It moved too slowly and timidly, however, to be of any assistance to the state of Massachusetts, whose militia proved amply sufficient for the purpose.

Shays' Rebellion, ineffectual as it proved to be, was a straight-out example of violent class struggle. It struck fear into the hearts of the old Whig revolutionists. The rights of property were threatened, and everywhere the call went out for a sober counterrevolution. Until the eruption of Shays' Rebellion the aristocratic Rufus King had been an enthusiastic and powerful leader of the opposition to all attempts to give greater authority to Congress. But in 1787 King wrote, "Events are hurrying us to a crisis; prudent and sagacious men should be ready to seize the most favorable circumstances to establish a more perfect and vigorous Government." From the time of the rising of the western farmers of Massachusetts, King was a staunch Federalist. The nation had triumphed over England, and it had triumphed over its own army. The moment was at hand when it must stir itself to triumph over the masses of its people.

VII

Constitutional Convention   The men of the Constitutional Convention, the historian John Bach McMaster long ago wrote, "were brought together in response to the demands of the businessmen of the country, not to form an ideal plan of government but such a practical plan as would meet the business needs of the people." The founding fathers were predominantly the substantial men of the merchant-planter community, the economic beneficiaries of independence and of the Revolutionary War. They saw their interests threatened by the disunity of the states and by the leveling spirit of the times. Therefore they met in Philadelphia to halt the revolution and create a stable, orderly system of government. The new Federal union soon found these men struggling among themselves for control, but at Philadephia they were united by a common objective. What was wanted was, in Alexander Hamilton's phrase, "a solid coercive union," one which could levy taxes, control interstate commerce, maintain a uniform monetary system, protect private property, and secure the nation against a leveling revolution.

Even while the Articles were under consideration there were those who were dedicating their efforts to the cause of a more centralized government. None were in such a good position to appreciate the need for one than the army officers who had to deal with the Second Continental Congress. Among these, whose profession naturally imbued them with respect for authority, Washington and his aide Hamilton were early converted to a belief in a strong central government. In 1785 a dispute between Maryland and Virginia over water rights on the Chesapeake, which had vexed relations between them for 150 years, was conferred upon at Washington's home, Mount Vernon. The conference reached no agreement, but it was decided at the meeting that the time had arrived for a general conference of the Thirteen Colonies to discuss interstate problems, especially those in the commercial field.

The result was the Annapolis Convention in 1786, which was attended by representatives of only five states: Delaware, New Jersey, New York, Pennsylvania, and Virginia, although four other states appointed delegates which, for one reason or another, failed to show up. The Annapolis Convention discussions broadened into a consideration of the weakness of the Articles generally, and out of them, at the suggestion of Hamilton, came the call for an intercolonial meeting to be held the next year at Philadelphia to think over the whole question of the nature of the national government and to propose reforms for the consideration of the Congress and, after its approval, the state legislatures.

The delegates to this Philadelphia meeting were selected by the state legislatures at a time when Shays' Rebellion caused men of substance everywhere to fear for their safety. The legislatures, following the example of Virginia, rose to the occasion by appointing the most prominent and respected citizens of their states. Substitutions had to be found for some who refused the offer, but the substitutions, though men of smaller reputation, proved to be safe appointments. The few radicals among the delegates were right-wing radicals like Alexander Hamilton, holding monarchist or ultra-aristocratic views. The majority were in close agreement concerning the nature of the problem, and, except where the question of representation of the states entered in, the delegates did not disagree widely concerning the nature of the solution.

Except for the surprisingly large number of men who were still in their twenties, the delegates were the same patriots who had fought for American independence. A number of them were the same men who had signed the Declaration of Independence, and it is not to be supposed that they had repudiated their earlier views concerning the natural rights of man. But now they faced a new problem, during new times, of making rather than breaking. After all, the revolutionary state governments of 1776 had not relied on self-evident truths in constructing workable instruments of government, and the founding fathers had even less reason to do so. "Experience must be our only guide," the delegates were warned by the conservative John Dickinson, who at a similar stage in the French Revolution would have long since lost his ninth life. "Reason may mislead us," he further warned.

The delegates wanted a system of government strong enough to protect property interests, yet not so strong as to deprive the states of authority or the citizens of liberty. It was essential that such a government be kept from the control of "faction," whether popular or aristocratic. The aristocratic delegates had seen and read enough to know that unlimited power in the hands of an aristocratic faction would lead to corruption just as surely as if it were in the hands of the people. The delegates wanted a government which could withstand their own overweening passions as well as those of the people, but the popular threat was uppermost in their minds.

In meeting the problem the delegates used the Articles of Confederation as their chief working model, adopting much of it bodily. They had at their disposal thirteen working models of republican government, and the experiences of the state governments were frequently drawn upon. The key to the resulting document was its mechanism for avoiding, as James Madison, the Convention's most influential member, said, "The accumulation of all powers, legislative, executive, and judiciary, in the same hands, whether of one, a few, or many, and whether hereditary, self-appointed, or elective."

The Senate and the House of Representatives were designed to balance wealth against popularity as well as to balance the large states against the small states. The President could veto legislation, and the legislature by a two-thirds vote could still pass the bills into law. An independent judiciary was established, headed by a supreme court which at least some delegates assumed would have the right, contrary to practice elsewhere in the world, of declaring congressional laws unconstitutional. A separate principle of selection was devised for each branch of the government. The House was to be elected by the people as the states directed. The Senate was to be appointed by the state legislatures. The President was to be chosen by special electors, which the states might designate as they saw fit. All branches of the government would be bound by the Constitution, which imposed specific limitations upon the powers of each of them and declared itself to be the supreme law of the land.

The one main disagreement in the Convention, and one which threatened for a time to disrupt it altogether, was that one concerning the basis of representation in the proposed government, the less populous states desiring representation by states, as was the case with the Congress of the Confederation, and the more populous states demanding the apportionment of representation by population. Virginia, having led in the calling of the Convention, presented a plan of government which remained substantially the basis for discussion in the Convention. The Virginia Plan, largely the work of James Madison, called for a two-house legislature, both houses to be apportioned according to population, an executive, to be elected by Congress, and a Federal judiciary headed by a supreme court.

Against this proposal William Paterson of New Jersey presented a plan for a unicameral legislature, in which each state would have one vote, and a plural executive, to be elected by Congress. Where this New Jersey Plan departed from the existing system was in giving its Congress increased authority over finance and commerce and in creating a national judiciary. The solution of electing the upper house by states and the lower house by population ended the one conflict which might have broken up the Convention.

During the fight for ratification additional restrictions were demanded, and these were incorporated into the Constitution during the first Federal administration in ten amendments. The first nine of these comprised a bill of rights, limiting the power of government over the private citizen. The tenth specifically reserved to the states all powers not delegated to the Federal government. The Convention had rejected such a bill of rights when George Mason proposed one during the final sessions. The delegates apparently voted the proposition down because they felt that such an addition would merely duplicate existing state bills of rights and because it was late and they wanted to go home, not because they opposed a bill of rights on its own merits.

At each step of the way the Constitution was altered to meet specific, practical objections. In the course of meeting these practical objections, as Madison said, it was "forced into some deviations from that artificial structure and regular symmetry which an abstract view of the subject might lead an ingenious theorist to bestow on a Constitution planned in his closet or in his imagination." Nevertheless the deviations were not permitted to do violence to the basic political principles of the eighteenth century, republican, libertarian, antidemocratic, American whiggery.

The final draft might well have been more aristocratic than it was, except for purely accidental reasons. There were a number of delegates who wanted the president to be elected to serve during his lifetime. At one time four states voted for such a provision, and alternative terms of twelve and fifteen years received serious consideration. Property qualifications for legislators were abandoned only because the problem appeared too difficult to arrange nationally. The majority of delegates favored apportionment of representation in the House according to wealth as well as population. This arrangement was discarded largely because of the difficulties involved in measuring wealth. It was generally agreed that new states should be admitted to the Union, but it was by no means agreed that they should be admitted on a basis of equality with the older ones. The Constitution remained ambiguous on this point, and some delegates hoped that it would be interpreted in such a way as to leave political control permanently with the Atlantic states.

In drawing up an entirely new constitution, the Convention had exceeded the authority given it by the Confederation Congress, and it faced the difficult task of persuading the nation to accept what it had done. Realizing that a major source of opposition would probably be the state governments, which the proposed constitution deprived of sovereign powers, the Convention decided to bypass the state legislatures in seeking national approval by calling for special nominating conventions in the states. It further provided that when nine states had so ratified, the Constitution would become the law of the land.

The delegates who had remained throughout the Convention and signed the document—about one-third had abandoned the project or had remained to oppose it—hurried home to lead the fight for ratification. Most of the smaller states ratified with little opposition. The doubtful contests were fought in the large states, especially New York and Virginia. New York ratified by a narrow margin after a bitter struggle, which produced the classic *Federalist Papers* by Alexander Hamilton, James Madison, and John Jay. News of this victory was rushed to Virginia in time to influence the decision of that state in favor of ratification. North Carolina and Rhode Island delayed ratification until after the first Federal government had taken office in 1789, and Rhode Island, the one state which had not participated in the Convention, joined only under the coercion of the neighboring states. It remained to be seen what form of government would result from the implementation of this unique, concise, and in many respects ambiguous document.

The reputation of the Constitution naturally rose in the ensuing age of national self-confidence, and a patriotic account of its history was developed, which survived in the public mind without influential criticism for more than a century. The American states in 1787 were desperately caught in what John Fiske established to have been "the critical period" of the nation's history. Lack of a competent central government and weakness and irresponsibility in the state governments threatened the dissolution of the new nation. At that moment an assemblage of demigods gathered in Philadelphia and drew up the greatest document ever struck off by the hand of man, and the nation was placed at once upon the course of stability and progress.

In the years of the Progressive movement early in the twentieth century, some historians came to observe that the government under the Constitution was not as responsive to the will of the people as they thought suitable to a democracy. Several critical studies of the Constitution were written during the first decade of the century, and in 1913 there appeared *An Economic Interpretation of the Constitution* by Charles Beard. Taking each of the fifty-five members of the Convention, one by one, Beard listed property holdings, paying especial attention to the holdings in government securities. To some extent Beard allowed the weight of the evidence to speak for itself, refraining from bringing wholesale charges against the founding fathers. The implication was nevertheless clear that in the Constitutional Convention the rich men of the community had reordered the national system in such a manner as to secure and enhance their own economic interests. Attacked at the time it appeared on the grounds of faulty use of the historical evidence, the *Economic Interpretation* nevertheless quickly established itself as one of the most influential of all writings in the field of American history. It was followed in 1915 by Beard's *Economic Origins of Jeffersonian Democracy*, which employed the same techniques to argue that an economic class struggle existed from the time of the Convention between the rich planters and the rich capitalists, which later became the essential basis of the Jeffersonian and the Federalist parties. This thesis has received extensive support more recently from Merrill Jensen in *The Articles of Confederation* (1948) and *The New Nation* (1950).

At the same time, however, Beard's thesis has recently come under sweeping attacks. Robert E. Brown in *Charles Beard and the Constitution* (1956) subjected the *Economic Interpretation* to a devastating chapter-by-chapter criticism. Forest McDonald in *We the People* (1958) returned to the sources that Beard had used, and, on the basis of much more thorough research, flatly repudiated the Beardian thesis. The founding fathers did not, on the whole, represent the wealth of the nation, and where their personal economic interests were concerned, they voted, as often as not, against their own interests. Further study of those involved in the state ratifying conventions similarly failed to support Beard, in McDonald's view.

Certainly Beard's thesis has been severely shaken, in the minds of most historians, but it is not to be supposed that the last word has been—or perhaps ever will be—said in the controversy. In the meantime, rather remarkably, the *Economic Origins of Jeffersonian Democracy*, equally unflattering to the founders and open to the same criticisms, has been generally ignored by the controversialists.

VIII

Social Change   In the view of the Revolutionary leaders the Revolution was conservative and rather narrowly political in its purpose. They saw it as a defense against attempted alterations by England of the imperial system which they had inherited from their fathers. Revolutions take on lives of their own, however, and the Revolutionary era in America experienced profound social changes. To begin with, the West was reopened, and the crown lands were placed at the disposal of the state legislatures, which distributed them as popular demand dictated. Royal and proprietary quit rents were no longer collected, and feudal requirements were abolished, such as the right of the royal surveyor to reserve selected white pine trees on private land for the King's use.

All of these rules formerly had been violated, but now they no longer existed.

Many of the great loyalist estates were confiscated by the state legislatures and redistributed at public sales for very low prices. The largest of these holdings were the proprietary estates of the Penn family, but other enormous holdings were seized, such as the De Lancey estate and the three hundred square mile Phillips estate in New York and the Fairfax estate in Virginia. New York passed a law discouraging the sale of these estates in lots of more than five hundred acres, and the De Lancey estate was sold to 275 persons. Patriots of wealth and influence naturally gained most from the redistribution of land. Nevertheless, except perhaps for South Carolina, the tendency was at least modestly a leveling one. After the war land was given to soldiers in payment for services, and the Confederation period witnessed unprecedented land speculation and land settlement.

Furthermore, during the ten years after independence, all but two states had abolished laws entailing land to a single heir upon the death of the previous owner, and within fifteen years all states had abolished primogeniture, which declared the exclusive right of the inheritance of land to belong to the firstborn son. These laws formerly had often been ignored, but after the Revolutionary era they no longer existed.

Religious toleration had long been an accepted principle of life in most of the colonies, but the main beginning of religious liberty, with the separation of church and state, was a product of the Revolution. The Church of England was disestablished in all the Southern states, although the Congregational Church, which unlike the Anglican had represented the American cause, remained established in New England well into the nineteenth century.

The Revolution ushered in the first age of humanitarianism in American history. The first antislavery society, probably in the history of the world, was organized in Philadelphia five days before the Battle of Lexington and Concord, "at a time," the society noted, "when justice, liberty, and the laws of the land are general topics among most ranks and stations of men." During the 1780s slavery was abolished in one after another of the states north of Maryland, freeing about fifty thousand. In the meantime twice as many slaves were freed in Virginia through manumission as were freed in Massachusetts through abolition.

The age saw a proliferation of humanitarian reform societies, library societies, humane societies, charitable societies, temperance societies, societies for distressed prisoners, debtors, and mariners. Reform of prison conditions and of the penal codes was carried out, especially in Pennsylvania and in New York, which reduced the crimes for which death was inflicted from sixteen to two, murder and treason. Not much, perhaps, was accomplished by Revolutionary reforms, but the main reforms which occupied humanitarians in the nineteenth century all had their origins in the Revolutionary era.

BIBLIOGRAPHY FOR CHAPTER THREE

E. S. Morgan, *The Birth of the Republic, 1763–1789* (1956) "concisely and clearly covers the major topics and . . . offers a well-organized and attractively written survey . . . particularly to be praised because of the sensible and judicious views offered by Morgan. . . . It will also be stimulating and useful to older scholars." The book concludes with an equally stimulating essay on the historiography of the subject. L. H. Gipson, *The Coming of the Revolution, 1763–1775* (1954) is an interpretive study of the subject by the author of by far the most extensive colonial history ever written. "Professor Gipson is the leading spokesman of the "imperial" school of historians in America [and] he now gives us a brief account of the events leading to American independence as they appear to him after a lifetime devoted to study of the empire . . . emphasis on the imperial perspective eclipses another set of facts that would make colonial resistance appear less reprehensible . . . done with grace and style. . . ."

A. M. Schlesinger, *Prelude to Independence: The Newspaper War on Britain* (1958) is a detailed account of the remarkable, sudden rise of the newspapers in political influence with the passage of the Stamp Act. It is perhaps damning an absorbing book with hackneyed praise to declare it "an important contribution both to the history of the Revolution and the history of American journalism." E. S. and H. M. Morgan, *The Stamp Act Crisis: Prologue to Revolution* (1953) is a fast-paced account of a critical event. It is supported by E. S. Morgan, ed., *Prologue to Revolution: Sources and Documents on the Stamp Act Crisis* (1959).

R. G. Adams, *Political Ideas of the American Revolution* (1922) is the standard study of the subject. Carl Becker,

The History of Political Parties in the Province of New York, 1760–1776 (1909) proposed the influential thesis, now under attack from various quarters, that the central dispute leading to the Revolution was not so much over home rule as over who should rule at home. Becker's *The Declaration of Independence* (1922) is a brilliant exegesis of that document.

J. R. Alden, *The American Revolution, 1775–1783* (1954) is a conventional study, with a heavy emphasis on military campaigns. "He describes actions, analyzes strategy and tactics, assesses results, in such a way that a nonmilitary minded reader can follow them with understanding and interest." Howard Peckham, *The War for Independence* (1958) is a more thoroughly military history. The "judgments are generally conventional. Peckham's narrative is interestingly and often colorfully written . . . especially good on the British side of the Struggle. . . ." G. F. Scheer and H. F. Rankin, *Rebels and Redcoats* (1957) is made up of contemporary accounts of participants in the Revolution. S. F. Bemis, *Diplomacy of the American Revolution* (1935) is the standard text.

J. F. Jameson, *The American Revolution as a Social Movement* (1926) is a short (100 pp.) series of four lectures by one of the greatest, and at the same time one of the most literate, of all American historians. The thesis, which is explicit in the title, has been generally accepted on the basis of this little presentation. Two generations of ambitious monographers have hacked away at it to remarkably little effect. This great little book should be missed by no student of American history.

Merrill Jensen, *The Articles of Confederation* (1940) supports the Articles as democratic and more effective than most have conceded, an argument that Jensen amplifies in a later study. The successful creation of a national government is simply and briefly told by the outstanding authority on the subject, Max Farrand, in *The Framing of the Constitution of the United States* (1913), published in the same year as Charles Beard's devastatingly monotonous *An Economic Interpretation of the Constitution. The Federalist Papers* are available in several paperback editions, as are selected writings of Jefferson, Adams, and Hamilton. E. H. Cady, ed., *Literature of the Early Republic* (1950) is a good collection of writings from the age of Revolution and Constitution as well as from the early national period.

FOUNDING OF THE REPUBLIC 4

I

Among the makers of the modern world, two political leaders, Washington and Lenin, remain unrivaled by any third in their vast and enduring influence. Each brought an improbable revolution to triumph in a nation which in time would dominate half the globe. It is said that forces and not men make history; yet without the leadership of these two men the revolutions would not have succeeded which created American democracy on the one hand and Russian communism on the other. Beyond winning the Revolution and establishing the Republic, Washington, by his mere presence as presiding officer of the Constitutional Convention, influenced the shaping of the new government; for the men of the Convention acted upon the assumption that he would be the nation's first Chief

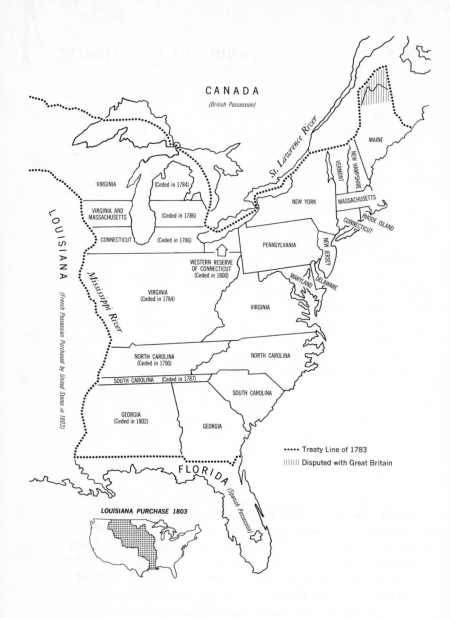

CANADA
(British Possession)

VIRGINIA

(Ceded in 1784)

VIRGINIA AND MASSACHUSETTS

(Ceded in 1786)

CONNECTICUT

(Ceded in 1786)

WESTERN RESERVE OF CONNECTICUT
(Ceded in 1800)

VIRGINIA
(Ceded in 1784)

NORTH CAROLINA
(Ceded in 1790)

SOUTH CAROLINA (Ceded in 1787)

GEORGIA
(Ceded in 1802)

LOUISIANA

(French Possession Purchased by United States in 1803)

Mississippi River

St. Lawrence River

MAINE

NEW HAMPSHIRE

VERMONT

NEW YORK

MASSACHUSETTS

RHODE ISLAND

CONNECTICUT

PENNSYLVANIA

NEW JERSEY

DELAWARE

MARYLAND

VIRGINIA

NORTH CAROLINA

SOUTH CAROLINA

GEORGIA

FLORIDA

(Spanish Possession)

····· Treaty Line of 1783
||||||| Disputed with Great Britain

LOUISIANA PURCHASE 1803

**Founding of the American Republic:
America at the Time of the Louisiana Purchase.**

Executive, and that as President he would invest the government with an immense prestige which would greatly facilitate its general acceptance.

It is difficult to keep in mind the fact that in the task of founding the Federal government Washington was the one indispensable man. He seems strangely missing in the struggles which marked his two administrations, returning only at the close of his Presidency to present his Farewell Address, prepared for him by his former Secretary of the Treasury Hamilton. Political activity appears to have been directed almost entirely by his subordinates, chiefly Hamilton and Jefferson. The all important fact about Washington, however, was that these other men were able to act out their parts as they did because Washington gave the government the strength to withstand the desperate factionalism of the opening years.

Already canonized for his equally indispensable role in the Revolutionary War, Washington was a unique political force by the time he served as President of the Constitutional Convention. As President of the United States he was the one man who could command a loyal opposition. Jefferson became the leader of the party which sought to defeat the program of the Washington administration; yet of the leader whose program he opposed Jefferson later wrote, "On the whole, his character was, in its mass, perfect, in nothing bad, in few points indifferent; and it may truly be said, that never did nature and fortune combine more perfectly to make a man great, and to place him in the same constellation with whatever worthies have merited from man an everlasting remembrance."

It was Washington's intention to select his advisers from the wisest and best part of the nation and to rule on his own responsibility by the light of their wisdom. For Secretary of the Treasury, he selected his trusted former military aide, Alexander Hamilton of New York; for Secretary of State, the minister to France, Thomas Jefferson. His other appointments were of comparatively little consequence, and, as it turned out, Jefferson's greater influence came to be felt as leader of the opposition after he had resigned from the Cabinet. It was Hamilton's program that Washington accepted as the basis for his administration.

The Hamiltonian System   It was Hamilton's opinion that the British royal government more nearly approached perfection than any other that history recorded. By comparison the American Federal Republic, to his way of thinking, was ramshackle and feckless. It rested upon the will of the people, which was to say upon the will of a great beast, senseless, self-seeking, and always dangerous to the stability of society and to the security of property. The salvation of the Republic lay in the creation of a responsible aristocracy, whose interests would be inextricably associated with the maintenance of a strong central government. These aristocrats would be every bit as venal and self-seeking as the common people beneath them, but theirs would be a socially useful avarice, serving to strengthen the government and maintain order.

Hamilton's measures, economic in character but also political in intent, were passed during the first two years of Washington's administration. Hamilton called for the assumption by the Federal government of the debts incurred by the states during the Revolution. These were to be funded together with the debts incurred by the Continental Congress and the government of the Articles of Confederation, and the consolidated debt was to be made redeemable in new government bonds at par value, even though at that time the state and national bonds sold on the market for but a fraction of their par value.

Opponents of the scheme argued the injustice of allowing speculators thus to make huge profits at the expense of the original patriotic holders of the bonds, at the expense of the nation as a whole and at the expense of those states which had already paid off their wartime indebtedness. Hamilton argued in reply that the measure was necessary to secure the credit of the nation. It was his further view that the system would make good citizens of the economically powerful speculators who held the new government bonds and that when their holdings of state bonds had been nationalized, their loyalties would be nationalized correspondingly. Hamilton had declared that it was "a fundamental maxim, in the system of public credit of the United States, that the creation of debt should always be accompanied with the means of extinguishment." In his funding measures, however, he provided only for payment of interest and not of the debt itself, perpetuation of the debt being essential to his system.

Successful in his funding program, Hamilton was also successful in creating the Bank of the United States, which would handle government money, would exert a controlling influence upon state banks and, again, would attach to the national government the interests of the mercantile community, which provided the main stockholders for the bank. The bank bill called for a subscription of 10 million dollars, one-fifth to be held by the government, with one-fifth representation, therefore, on the board of direction, and the rest to be subscribed privately. Finally, Hamilton instituted a series of excise taxes for the financial purpose of supporting the government and for the political purpose of impressing the power of the government upon the tax-paying population.

Hamilton also proposed, in his Report on Manufactures, a tariff high enough, not only to raise revenue, but also to protect American industry. This, he argued, would make the nation self-sufficient in time of war, provide markets for domestic farm produce, and provide employment for women and children of "tender years." In this he was frustrated, although a moderate tariff measure was passed in 1792. He faced the difficulty that his staunchest supporters, the commercial interests, opposed a tariff which would interfere with trade.

Amid the political storms it aroused, the Hamiltonian program succeeded brilliantly in its economic purpose of restoring the public credit. The new government bonds were soon selling at above their par value, commerce expanded rapidly, and the nation entered a period of heady prosperity. In his political views Hamilton was a reactionary, quite out of tune with the times. In his economic views he was a creative statesman, fashioning the practical program for a developing nation against which the economically reactionary Jeffersonians and Jacksonians were to struggle fruitlessly during the following generations.

Among the unlooked-for developments under the new Constitution, perhaps the most unwelcome was the appearance of the two-party system, which Hamilton's controversial program brought into being. "There is nothing I dread so much," John Adams wrote during the Federalist period, "as the division of the Republic into two great parties, each under its leader. . . . This, in my humble opinion, is to be feared as the greatest political evil under our Constitution." Adams had more reason than most to dislike political parties, but his sentiments toward them were shared by all the leading political figures of the time, including those masters of party organization, Hamilton and Jefferson.

Each of these two men thought of himself not as a party leader, but as a champion of rightly constituted government. Each thought of the other as the chieftain of a dangerous faction, subversive of good public order, a threat to the state. That was Jefferson's point of view when in his first inaugural address he said, "We are all Republicans; we are all Federalists." He meant that "faction" had been defeated and that the country henceforth would be in the hands of a truly national government rather than a party one. The bitterness of politics in the 1790s fed on this assumption that the fight was to the finish for permanent control of the nation. The assumption proved correct, for the Federalists never recovered from their defeat in 1800, partly because of the desperate spirit engendered by the assumption in the first place. Two generations passed before Americans came to accept organized political parties as a regular part of constitutional government.

In retrospect the division between Federalists and Republicans can be detected in the *Federalist Papers,* chiefly written by Madison and Hamilton during the New York fight for ratification. Although the co-authors worked effectively together, they actually produced two separate attitudes toward the Constitution. Madison's argument revealed the document as creating a balanced, limited government drawing its authority from the people. Hamilton defended it as the plan for an effective administrative organization, which would further the national interest and protect property against the injudicious political acts on the part of the states. These divergent points of view created no issues in the Convention, because Hamilton was in such a feeble minority position that he contented himself with announcing his position and standing aside while the Convention as a whole worked out a plan alien to his views and in harmony with those of Madison.

While conflict between the mercantile and agrarian interests was inevitable, it was Hamilton's militant partisanship which split the two interests into irreconcilable factions. He gathered in the support of the speculators by granting them opportunities such as they had never anticipated. Within twenty-four hours of Hamilton's first financial report the value of government securities had risen by 50 per cent, speculators were running to the woods to buy securities from the common people before the news spread, and congressmen, about half of whom were probably holders of public securities, began to speak of assumption at par as the minimum requirement of honesty.

Hamilton's program drove into the opposition agrarian leaders who had been nationalistic supporters of the Constitution and the Judiciary Act. Neither Madison nor Jefferson had opposed Federal assumption of the states' debts on some basis. Neither, for that matter, had given systematic attention to financial questions. Some of their planter-colleagues had, however, and the naked ruthlessness of Hamilton's program caused the landed interest to side at once with the political economy of such agrarian writers as John Taylor of Caroline.

The agrarians argued the injustice of enriching speculators at the expense of the nation, and beyond that they argued the evil of maintaining the debt for what amounted to purposes of political bribery. It should be paid off. They objected to the bank as a government-authorized monopoly which similarly would lend itself to political corruption. The government, they argued, should conduct itself like an honest business house and economize for the purpose of paying its debts. It should do so also as a useful exercise in self-limitation of powers. It should be beholden to no particular group in the nation and should benefit no particular group, least of all the small speculating interest as compared with the great farming majority.

When Hamilton's program divided the commercial North from the agrarian South, it also crystalized a long standing contrast in political outlook between New England and the Southern states. New Englanders were proud of their township, county, and state government regulations, which the people themselves maintained for the good of the whole. They spoke glowingly of the "steady habits of New England, which habits were formed by a singular machinery in the body politic." But to the Southern agrarian aristocrats, living as they did in comparative isolation upon splendid, self-sufficient estates, such complicated machinery of government seemed like the wheels and cogs of tyranny. The planters believed in centralized government for their own plantations; otherwise the best government was the one which governed least.

The first political parties were divided more clearly by divergent political theories than was perhaps ever again to be the case in the nation's history. It was therefore appropriate that the opposing leaders were each personally in such dramatic contrast to the other. Hamilton, a short, dapper, handsome, and vigorously forceful man, born under disadvantageous circumstances—the bastard son of a Scottish peddler, as the hostile John Adams had put it— leapt to prominence by virtue of his energy and brilliance, becoming General Washington's aide during the Revolution at the age of twenty, becoming the leading figure behind the calling of the

Constitutional Convention, and by his thirty-fifth year, almost single-handedly establishing the economic basis upon which the new government would rest. An almost arrogantly honest man, Hamilton created a system founded upon a firm faith in the fundamental dishonesty of man.

Against him, the descendant of the aristocratic Randolph family, Jefferson, became the chief philosopher and spokesman for government based upon the faith in the ability of men to govern themselves. A tall, homely, shambling figure of a man, Jefferson was probably not Hamilton's match in logical argument, and certainly not in his grasp of economic realities. The range of Jefferson's inquiring genius, however, was such as to make Hamilton's thinking appear narrowly provincial by comparison. A brilliant product of the Age of Enlightenment, Jefferson was a lawyer, statesman, political theorist, agricultural scientist, natural scientist, inventor, architect, classical scholar, educator, musician, and man of letters. Awkward in public speech, he was a master literary stylist, whose writings remain among the most eloquent expressions of continuing American ideals. Both Jefferson and Hamilton in different ways rather despised the arts of politics, and both were masters of political manipulation. Jefferson's politics were on the side of popular rule, however, and they were destined to triumph.

Hamilton began to initiate his program while Jefferson was still abroad, and it was Madison in Congress who rose first in opposition. Under Madison's leadership the anti-Federalists opposed Hamilton's assumption program and put forward an alternate proposal which would reward the original holders rather than the later speculators. Hamilton's assumption measure was defeated in the House, and its eventual passage was made possible only by a bargain with Jefferson. Jefferson, just returned from France, exchanged his influence in favor of Hamilton's measure for Hamilton's influence in favor of locating the national capital permanently in the South. After making this bad bargain, Jefferson and Madison were in a weak position to fight the excise taxes, which they disapproved of, because they were necessary to the financing of the funding program.

It was the creation of a national bank which they made the chief issue, arguing not only that it was dangerous and unjust, but also that it was unconstitutional, no specific provision having been made in the Constitution for a federally chartered bank. In reply

Hamilton argued that Congress had the "implied power" to establish such a bank, since the bank was necessary to the performance of functions which were specifically authorized by the Constitution.

II

The extraconstitutionality and novelty of the two-party system was sufficiently shocking in itself to eighteenth-century statesmen, but the evil was compounded by the violent revolutionary influences imported from France. On May 5, 1789, a month after the first Congress of the new Federal government took up its duties, the Estates-General met in France for the first time in 175 years. Revolution swiftly followed, and Americans gave it an enthusiastic welcome, in fact took positive pride in it. They congratulated themselves that the more enlightened part of the Old World was taking a lesson from the New. But as the Revolution grew increasingly violent, American conservatives became increasingly critical. They read Edmund Burke's *Reflections on the Revolution in France,* and they became convinced that the old champion of the American cause was right again. Americans began to take sides and argue heatedly about France. The argument remained largely academic until war broke out between France and England in 1793.

The French government, already at war with Austria and Russia, opened the year with the execution of the King, followed by a declaration of war against Great Britain, Holland, and Spain and an invitation to the peoples of Europe to rise up against their rulers. In November it announced the abolition of the worship of God and the organization of the Cult of Reason.

Within a few months of the French King's execution Citizen Genêt arrived in the United States as the new French minister to America. His orders were to make what capital he could of the fund of republican enthusiasm in America and of the military alliance of 1778, which still bound the United States to support France in war. Genêt was greeted with enthusiastic mass demonstrations wherever he went, to the point where he became convinced apparently that he, rather than Washington, represented the will of the American people. He busied himself with projects to make American men and resources felt on the French side. His irresponsible conduct was acutely embarrassing to Jefferson, who finally requested the French government to relieve Genêt of his duties.

Fast on the heels of the French declaration of war, there appeared in Philadelphia the first of those Democratic Societies which spread rapidly throughout the Union. Although less violent and more law-abiding than the old Sons of Liberty, these societies were disturbingly democratic in their behavior, and some of them functioned without the restraining influence of upper-class leadership. They were patterned upon the revolutionary Jacobin clubs in France, and they made Citizen Genêt's travels through America one long triumphal march.

In 1794 the Reign of Terror was at flood tide in France, and in that year farmers in western Pennsylvania demonstrated against the newly imposed excise tax on whiskey. They raised liberty poles, held mass meetings, and rioted. The violence lacked direction, however, and it failed to win support from the law-abiding and essentially middle-class Democratic Societies outside the immediate region.

Washington nevertheless was convinced that the Democratic Societies were behind it, and although he himself was a member of the Society of the Cincinnati, he did not suppose that anything could be "more absurd, more arrogant, or more pernicious to the peace of society, than . . . self created bodies . . . endeavoring . . . to form themselves into permanent censors . . . endeavoring to form their *will* into laws for the government of the whole. . . ." He sent Colonel Hamilton after the whiskey rebels at the head of an absurdly large militia. By the time Hamilton had reached the scene the local authorities had stepped in, and there was no organized opposition to attack. Cheated of his glory, Hamilton nevertheless charged ahead, making arrest and calling for "rigor everywhere." Under the impact of Washington's opposition and of the absurdities of Genêt, the rather flimsy Democratic Societies disintegrated, but the harsh suppression of the very little rebellion damaged the reputation of the administration and played into the hands of the opposition.

The French Revolutionary wars were full of both opportunities and dangers to the new Federal Republic. They distracted Europe from America while the United States was establishing itself, and at the same time they opened up great commercial opportunities to a neutral nation. Under the terms of the Franco-American treaty of 1778 France might have asked America to enter the war, but the United States was more valuable to France as a neutral supplier of the French West Indies.

The difficulty here for the United States was the difference of opinion between France and England as to the trading rights of neutrals, the French and the Franco-American treaty permitting the trade of neutrals with belligerents except in contraband, which did not include food and naval stores. The British, who had not previously accepted this dictum, issued orders-in-council in 1793 to bring in all ships carrying goods to French ports. Early the next year three hundred American vessels were captured in the Caribbean under these orders. News of the captures further aroused Americans, who already were convinced that the British were inciting the Indians against America in the Northwest, and the ensuing war crisis persuaded Washington to send John Jay to England to secure the peace with England which was so necessary to the new republic.

By the terms of the resulting Jay Treaty of 1794, Great Britain agreed to evacuate forts on American soil in the Northwest and to pay compensation at some future time for the capture of American vessels. Trade with the British West Indies was permitted, but on conditions which were unacceptable to the United States Senate. On the other hand Britain retained fur-trading rights with the Indians on American soil, and the British conceded nothing to the American claims concerning trading rights of neutrals. Washington, after some hesitation, submitted the treaty to the Senate, fearing that war with England would result from refusal to sign it, and the Senate, amid the angry outcries of indignant public opinion, approved the treaty by barely more than the necessary two-thirds majority. The Jay Treaty was followed in 1795 by a highly popular treaty with Spain, arranged by Thomas Pinckney, settling the northern boundary of Spanish Florida at 31° and opening the Mississippi, including the port of New Orleans, to American trade.

Declining to serve for a third term, Washington opened the way in 1796 for the party contests which had been checked to some extent by the great regard in which he was still held. Jefferson, as the acknowledged leader of the anti-Federalists, or Republicans as they came to be called, was their obvious candidate. Among the Federalists a split had developed between Hamilton of New York, who had already resigned as Secretary of the Treasury, and Vice President John Adams of New England. Adams won the candidacy against the opposition of Hamilton and by a margin of 71 electoral votes to 68, he won the Presidency. In this as in other early elections, the presidential electors were chosen by the state legislatures, and no election campaign was waged in the modern sense. The opposition candidate, Jefferson, since he received the second largest vote, won the vice presidency in place of the Federalist candidate, Thomas Pinckney of South Carolina, a peculiar situation which was prevented from repeating itself by the Twelfth Amendment to the Constitution passed in 1804.

The crotchety Adams, within the limitations of his own view of his office, was fairly effective as President. In foreign affairs he took a realistic and independent view of America's interests, successfully withstanding the pro-British influences within his party as well as the pro-French efforts of the opposition. In domestic politics he successfully resisted the intrigues of the politically astute Hamilton, to remain as the head of his party in 1800 and in a good position to win reelection. His distaste for politics and his distrust of popular rule, however, limited his effectiveness in a time of bitter party strife. He did little to organize a party behind him or to rid his administration of the Hamiltonian faction which opposed him, and, unlike Washington, he often absented himself from the capital for months at a time, remaining almost completely out of touch with his subordinates.

The most trying problems of Adams's administration, as in Washington's second term, were those in the area of foreign affairs. Angered by the Jay Treaty the French had stepped up their attacks on American commerce, and they refused to accept the minister appointed to the French court by Adams. To avoid a war with France, which would have been highly popular with the Hamiltonian faction, Adams sent a diplomatic mission to the French government. The members of the mission were told that they could not begin diplomatic discussions until they paid bribes to French officials, as was the fairly common European practice. The Americans indignantly refused and returned a report to President Adams, who submitted the report to Congress, except for the names of the French agents involved, whom he listed as Messrs. X, Y, and Z. The report of the "XYZ Affair," when published, set off a national salvo of martial indignation. It precipitated an undeclared naval war with France and roused Congress to pass the Alien and Sedition Acts.

The acts, unsponsored by the administration, were passed partly out of fury and partly for Federalist party advantage. Their purpose was to curb the political power of the new immigrants, who, it was noted, tended overwhelmingly to vote Republican, and to curb criticism of the government by the opposing press as well as by private citizens. The three Alien Acts extended the residence requirement for citizenship from five to fourteen years and empowered the President to jail or deport undesirable aliens. The Sedition Act provided fines and jail sentences for anybody who wrote or said something "with intent to defame . . . or bring into contempt or disrepute" any members of the government. No aliens were prosecuted under the Alien Acts, but more than two dozen men, most of them newspaper editors, were jailed under the Sedition Act.

The Jeffersonians, in their turn, attempted to combat this repressive legislation with the Virginia and Kentucky Resolutions, written by Madison and Jefferson, arguing the unconstitutionality of these laws and suggesting that the states had the constitutional authority to nullify them. They were disappoined in the hope that other state legislatures besides those of Virginia and Kentucky would pass similar resolutions, and their resolutions probably had little political effect on the presidential election that followed. They were to have a much greater political impact more than a generation later, when John C. Calhoun resurrected them in defense of the Southern states-rights argument.

Amid this atmosphere of mutual suspicion, John Adams in 1800 ran for reelection against Jefferson. As it turned out, the bitter issues of the time had no perceptible influence on the outcome of the election. Outside the state of New York, Adams was given a few votes more than he had received in 1796. He nevertheless lost the election because New York, which until then had voted solidly Federalist, was captured by the opposition under the direction of Tammany Hall and the brilliant political leader, Aaron Burr. As a consequence of this political coup, New York voted for Jefferson, with Burr as his running mate, and by that margin the Presidency changed from Federalist to Republican hands. Since each received the same number of electoral votes, the House of Representatives had the constitutional right to choose either man as President, and for a time it appeared that the anti-Jeffersonians might deprive the intended candidate of the office. This situation also was made impossible in the future by the Twelfth Amendment to the Constitution.

Thus narrowly slipped into office, Jefferson launched quietly upon what he afterwards liked to speak of as a "revolution." Adams, meanwhile, as his last act in office, launched a counterrevolution of his own with the appointment of stout Federalists to newly authorized judicial posts and most importantly the appointment of John Marshall as Chief Justice of the Supreme Court. Marshall was to outlast four Presidents in that position and to entrench federalism in the courts for a generation after it had been driven from the political arena.

III

The Administrations of Jefferson

Jefferson's first inaugural address is the classic document of eighteenth-century republicanism, with its faith in a libertarian society founded upon a self-reliant yeomanry and maintaining itself in perfect equipoise within the balanced government of the Constitution. Jefferson took the occasion to present "the essential principles of this government, and consequently those which ought to shape its administration." Jefferson's republicanism breathed the old-fashioned Whig spirit of John Locke. It comfortably retained from Locke the mutually contradictory tenets of majority rule and inalienable personal rights. Like Locke, Jefferson was able to incorporate this inconsistency in his beliefs, because although his conception of individual rights was vivid and specific, his conception of majority rule was hazy and general and not altogether distinguishable from the idea of the "common good."

Jefferson was far from being a democrat in the sense that the word came to be used in the nineteenth century. The first requirement of government in his view was not that it be completely representative but that it be limited. Although Jefferson was more optimistic in his view of human nature than were most of his colleagues, he believed with them that power inevitably corrupted, and that liberty was secure only where power was limited. To the extent that government was necessary, it should, so far as possible, be controlled by the people immediately affected. State governments should not assume the responsibilities which could be discharged by the counties, and the national government should accept as a self-limiting duty "the support of the State governments in all their rights, as the most competent administrations for our domestic concerns and the surest bulwarks against antirepublican tendencies." Although later interpreted by Southerners simply as a states-rights advocate, Jefferson was more truly an advocate of localized authority generally than he was a champion of state sovereignty.

It was the agrarian basis of American society, in Jefferson's view, that made the continuance of republican institutions possible. The yeoman farmer was the key to a free society. On the one hand, owning his own land and supplying for himself most of his own wants, he represented the freest class of men on earth. On the other hand his position in society did not give him the power to tyrannize others. And beyond this, Jefferson, despite his distaste for Rousseau's romanticism, had a mystical faith that "Those who labor in the earth are the chosen people of God, if ever he had a chosen people," and that "Corruption of morals in the mass of cultivators is a phenomenon of which no age nor nation has furnished an example."

The yeomanry ought to be charged with controlling their own local affairs and choosing the representatives who would speak for them in the larger areas of activity with which they were unfamiliar. Those who guided the national destinies, in Jefferson's view, should be drawn from the natural aristocracy, chosen not on the basis of having been born to high station, but on the basis of a natural superiority in virtues and talents, whatever their original station in life. Jefferson proposed a system of education which would bring forth this natural aristocracy by giving all boys a grammar school training and then, through successive weedings-out, bringing to college training at state expense the select group which had demonstrated its ability to assume the main national responsibilities. Jefferson's efforts to create such an educational system in Virginia failed, and the equalitarian educational system which later developed in democratic America, in the contrast it presents to the Jeffersonian system, is one good measure of the contrast between democracy as Jefferson understood it and democracy as it turned out to be.

As President, Jefferson set out at once to quiet the sectional conflict which had dominated the campaign with his conciliatory inaugural address and by his appointment of New Englanders as Attorney General, Secretary of War, and Postmaster General. For the two most important posts he chose two of his most brilliant Republican colleagues. James Madison, the architect of the Constitution, became Secretary of State, and Albert Gallatin of Switzerland and Pennsylvania became Secretary of the Treasury.

In replacing Federalist appointments Jefferson moved slowly out of regard for Federalist sensibilities and out of a distaste for the job, noting that "whenever a man has cast a longing eye on offices, a rottenness begins in his conduct." He did not extend his forbearance, however, to the "midnight judges" whom Adams had crowded onto the bench during his last hours and minutes in office. Jefferson's own brief and highly successful experience as a lawyer had left him distrustful of the law as a guardian of liberty, and the judicial tyranny which the Sedition Act had unleashed was fresh in his memory. He set forth at once, therefore, to replace Adams's appointments with his own and then to repeal the Judiciary Act of 1801 which had created these new positions.

Jefferson's anger at the midnight appointments was heightened by the appointment of his hated cousin, John Marshall, as Chief Justice, and Cousin John lost no time in getting in his own hard licks. At the first session of the Supreme Court, Marshall handed down the decision in the case of Marbury v. Madison, dealing with a "midnight appointment," Marbury, from whom Secretary of State Madison had withheld the position. The case appears to have been contrived in order to allow Marshall to lecture Jefferson through the medium of a judicial opinion and, more importantly, to enable Marshall to assert the authority of the Supreme Court to declare Federal laws unconstitutional.

After finding Madison's actions to have been legally indefensible, Marshall went on to declare that Marbury nevertheless could not gain his just deserts by applying to the Supreme Court for them. The authority by which Marbury had attempted to do so had been the Judiciary Act of 1789, which, Marshall ruled, was constitutionally faulty in this regard. It was "emphatically the province and duty of the judicial department to say what the law is," and "a law repugnant to the Constitution is void." The relevant clause of the Judiciary Act was therefore declared unconstitutional, and Marbury could not receive satisfaction.

This was the first case in which the Supreme Court asserted the right to declare a Federal law unconstitutional, and it was cleverly contrived to give no one a practical interest in challenging the decision. Having made his point, Marshall never again attempted to assert this authority. The next occasion upon which the Supreme Court made this claim was the Dred Scott decision of 1857, which was followed by an enormous uproar and after that by civil war.

Jefferson, no doubt with Marshall in mind as an eventual victim, acted through his congressional leaders to impeach Federalist judges, beginning first with an obvious incompetent by reason of insanity. Successful in this, House Republicans impeached a Supreme Court justice, Samuel Chase, who had conducted sedition trials in a most violently injudicious manner. Tried by the Senate, Chase was found innocent of crimes and misdemeanors. With this defeat, the Jeffersonians gave up the fight, and federalism continued its guardianship of the nation from the Federal judiciary.

Jefferson had much better fortune elsewhere during his first administration. He freed those imprisoned under the sedition law and returned them their fines. So far as the United States Bank was concerned, he was content to tolerate it until its charter expired in 1811. He applied himself, however, to ridding the nation of its debt, reducing the personnel of the government, cutting the army, stopping naval construction, and at the same time removing excise, stamp, and land taxes. He eliminated most of the ceremonies of his office to conform to his views on proper republican simplicity, aided by the removal of the national capital in 1800 from urbane, aristocratic New York to the Washington, D.C., mud flats.

His pure theory was subject to the corruptions of power, however, as he himself predicted it would be. In 1802 he wrote Secretary of the Treasury Gallatin that, since all banks were evil, whether chartered by the nation or the states, "Between such parties the less we meddle the better." But the next year he wrote Gallatin, "I am decidedly in favor of making all the banks republican by sharing deposits with them in proportion to the dispositions they show." Nevertheless he was probably as successful during his first administration in putting his ideas into action as any President has ever been. To a friend he wrote, "The path we have to pursue is so quiet that we have nothing scarcely to propose to our Legislature. A noiseless course, not meddling with the affairs of others, unattractive of notice, is a mark that society is going on in happiness." Of all Federal administrations in the nation's history, the first Jefferson administration governed least, a circumstance made possible by Jefferson's own great political skill as well as by his political convictions, and with notable exceptions such as his fury against the midnight judges, his imperturbable tolerance and forbearance.

During his first term Jefferson sinned seriously but once against his eighteenth-century republican decalogue. The opportunity presented itself to him to buy the province of Louisiana from France, and despite the absence of explicit constitutional authority, he hurried to accomplish it. Until 1800 Louisiana had been in Spanish hands, and Jefferson had thought that, from the American point of view, there could be no better custodian for it "Till our population can be sufficiently advanced to gain it from them piece by piece." In 1800, however, Spain returned it to the France of Napoleon Bonaparte, and when this dangerous development occurred, Jefferson moved to acquire for the United States at least the port of New Orleans which was vital to the Mississippi trade of the Northwest. In 1802 Spain, still in occupation, suspended the American right of deposit at New Orleans, and amid demands for war, Jefferson sent James Monroe to Paris to assist the American minister, Robert Livingston, in persuading Napoleon to sell New Orleans.

The French armies, having been demolished in Santo Domingo and resumption of hostilities impending in Europe, Napoleon decided to cut his American losses and sell all of Louisiana to the United States for 15 million dollars. The surprised American negotiators accepted, and the United States almost doubled its territory. Jefferson, the strict constructionist, with no specific authorization in the Constitution for such an act, rushed the measure through Congress before Napoleon could change his mind, later justifying the purchase as a response to a "higher obligation" than that of written laws.

For Jefferson the acquisition of Louisiana meant room for indefinite expansion of that farming population which in his view was the one firm foundation for republican institutions. To embittered New England Federalists, with visions of numbers of new states rising up in the West to overwhelm New England's already waning power in the Union, it was a ruthless violation of the Constitution and one which presaged the end of the Republic. As the election of 1804 was to show, however, Jefferson's program of sweet reasonableness was beginning to subvert even that stronghold of federalism. In 1804, against the Federalist candidate, C. C. Pinckney of South Carolina, he won the electoral votes of every state in the Union but those of Connecticut and Delaware.

IV

Westward Expansion While many New Englanders would have been happy to see the West depart from the Union to form some kind of savage nation of its own, many Westerners were for their part willing to end their unfriendly and seemingly unrewarding connection with the Eastern states. The transappalachian settlements, which in the year of Jefferson's election numbered 386,000 souls, had had their first beginnings on the eve of the Revolution, following the suppression of Pontiac's Conspiracy. In the early seventies two Virginia land speculators, James Robertson and John Sevier, led separate parties of settlers into what was then western North Carolina and later eastern Tennessee, creating the Watauga Association under which they governed themselves. In 1775 Richard Henderson of North Carolina organized the Transylvania Company which made settlement in what later became part of Kentucky. The history of these early settlements was marked by bickering among the settlers, very highhanded and legally questionable tactics on the part of their leaders, and constant jurisdictional disputes with the mother states and later with the government of the Confederation.

Ohio Territory in the Northwest, by contrast, was settled in a relatively orderly manner under the terms of the Ordinances of 1785 and 1787 and, in different areas, under the direction of various state governments and various authorized land companies. Connecticut retained a portion of northern Ohio, the Western Reserve, where New England society was transplanted under the auspices of the Connecticut Land Company and Moses Cleaveland, and Virginia retained a military district in southern Ohio, chiefly for the purpose of rewarding Revolutionary War veterans. Southeastern

Ohio went at bargain rates to the Ohio Company on the basis of a complicated piece of chicane which involved the creation of a second company, the Scioto Company, in which congressmen held stock. The Scioto Company earned nothing but scandal, while the backers of the Ohio Company failed to make the anticipated huge profits. The settlement of Ohio meanwhile proceeded briskly.

The early history of the New West was marked by struggles with the states and the United States which repeatedly threatened the dismemberment of the new nation. The key to Western settlement was the port of New Orleans, which controlled the whole Western system of water transportation. In 1785 the New Yorker, John Jay, was authorized by the Confederation Congress to arrange a treaty with Spain. The resulting Jay-Gardoqui Treaty exchanged commercial concessions in Spanish ports, which would aid principally New England and the middle states, for an American agreement to surrender its claims to the use of the Mississippi for twenty-five years. Although the treaty failed of ratification, seven states voted in its favor, and Westerners began seriously to consider the Spanish offer to admit them to the Spanish empire.

Amid these circumstances, Tennessee ruled itself as the independent nation of Franklin for five years, before it settled upon a working arrangement with the Union, and then it accepted as its chief leader the one man, John Sevier, upon whom the Federal government had not yet bestowed an official pardon. Tennessee in 1796 elected as its first Senator William Blount, who proceeded to conspire to capture Louisiana Territory and the Floridas for Great Britain. Expelled from the Senate for having been guilty of a high misdemeanor, Blount was enthusiastically received in Tennessee and elected presiding officer of the state senate. James Wilkinson was almost constantly involved in a bewildering variety of conspiracies from the time of his early career under Horatio Gates and Benedict Arnold until his death from opium in 1825 while representing the American Bible Society in Mexico; yet his justly deserved reputation as a traitor did not prevent him from receiving a Jeffersonian appointment as governor of Louisiana Territory, at a time when he was in the pay of the Spanish government.

Wilkinson was also involved in the most famous of the western intrigues, the schemes of Aaron Burr, apparently to form some sort of independent Western nation. Burr, politically discredited by the Hamilton duel and out of favor with Jefferson, had apparently already involved himself in a scheme to separate New York and New England from the Union. Failing in this, he moved west to investigate the possibilities of establishing a Western empire either under British or Spanish patronage.

Wilkinson, with whom he plotted, betrayed him to Jefferson, and in 1807 Burr was tried for treason by John Marshall. Jefferson's vindictive prosecution of Burr was one of the least creditable episodes in his political life. Marshall, for his part, turned the trial into a judicial attack on Jefferson and, incidentally to this, secured Burr's acquittal. The precedent established by Marshall in the process made future conviction for the crime of treason a near impossibility, and the courts thereafter were obliged to try traitors for the crime of espionage instead. With Louisiana and New Orleans in American hands and with Tennessee, Kentucky, and Ohio admitted to statehood, meanwhile, the Burr trial brought a close to the era of Western conspiracies.

The first of the Western states, Kentucky, drew up its constitution and entered the Union in 1792, after a sharp struggle in which representatives of the major property-holding interests substantially defeated the radical democrats. Drawing their program from the Pennsylvania constitution of 1776, the radicals fought for manhood suffrage, for abolition of slavery, for a one-house legislature, for the popular election of all local officials, and for the omission of a bill of rights. Opposition to the bill of rights was based partly on the protection such a bill would give to slavery as a form of private property. Partly, however, the radicals rejected it as an undemocratic restriction upon the will of the people.

For democrats in Kentucky as elsewhere in the West, democracy meant the full implementation of the will of the majority, unobstructed even by those guards to individual liberty which served the first purpose of government in the Jeffersonian view. This was to prove the fundamental difference which divided libertarian Jeffersonian republicanism from majoritarian Jacksonian democracy. In 1792, however, the Kentucky conservatives carried the day. While conceding the radicals unrestricted white manhood suffrage and a lower house elected directly and annually by the people, the conservatives suceeded in having the upper house and the governor chosen by an electoral college. The governor was given a wide power of appointment, the judges were elected for life terms, a bill of rights was included, and slavery was protected.

The Tennessee constitution of 1796 advanced beyond Kentucky in providing for the direct election of the governor and in providing that justices of the peace be chosen by the assembly. The least democratic feature of the Tennessee constitution, and the target of the radicals thereafter, was the life tenure of justices of the peace and the power invested in the justices to appoint most local officers. Slavery was protected, and a system of taxation was instituted which bore disproportionately upon the small landowners.

Ohio in 1803, on the other hand, where slavery had been prohibited by congressional law, drew up a thoroughly democratic constitution. The ballot was extended to all white male taxpayers resident in the state for a year. Both governor and legislature were popularly elected, and all town and township officers were chosen annually by the people. Judges were chosen by the legislature rather than by the governor. The model for the Ohio constitution was that of Tennessee; the removal of undemocratic restrictions of the Tennessee constitution was clearly facilitated by the absence of a slaveholding interest.

Viewing the nation's history from the prospect of the ivy-covered Eastern universities, American historians of the nineteenth century tended to view the Western development of the nation as a colonial development, peripheral to the main course of the nation's history. Then in 1893 young Frederick Jackson Turner, an instructor at the University of Wisconsin, came out of the West and changed that whole way of thinking, when he delivered before the American Historical Association the most influential paper in the whole history of American historiography: "The Significance of the Frontier in American History." For two generations thereafter Turner continued to write and speak on that theme, but all of his main points were contained in that original paper.

America was unique among the nations of the world, he argued, and it was the West that made it so. "The peculiarity of American institutions is the fact that they have been compelled to adapt themselves to the changes of an expanding people—to the changes involved in crossing a continent, in winning a wilderness, and in developing at each area of this progress out of the primitive economic and political conditions of the frontier into the complexity of city life." America became a new and democratic nation because, "In the crucible of the frontier the immigrants were Americanized, liberated, and fused into a mixed race, English in neither nationality nor characteristics," and "frontier individualism has from the beginning promoted democracy." He found that "The growth of nationalism and the evolution of American political institutions were dependent on the advance of the frontier"; that the main political issues of land, tariff, and internal improvements were created by the moving West.

Flattering to the American ego and congenial to the thought of that age of Darwinian evolution and environmentalism, the Turner thesis took hold and dominated American historiography for the next two generations. The reaction came in the 1930s in numbers of learned articles, critical of Turner's sweeping generalizations. Under the conditions of the Depression the need was felt to deny the doctrine that the promise of America had passed with the passing of the frontier. American civilization, Dixon Ryan Fox argued, was not the unique product of the frontier; it was the creation of Western civilization, which had succeeded in imposing itself upon the frontier environment. Nor was the nation beholden to the frontier for the formation of its democratic institutions. Thomas P. Abernethy found that the new Western societies, as compared with those older Eastern seaboard societies, were characterized by a majoritarian suppression of the liberties of the individual. Historians and economists joined in the attack upon Turner's assertion that the West had served as a safety valve for Eastern social discontent, pointing out that Western lands were not available to downtrodden Eastern workers and farmers.

During and after World War II the Turner thesis, with its strongly isolationist implications, further lost in attractiveness to American historians. It is also true that American historians in the mid-twentieth century tend to come from the cities, although two generations ago they tended to come from the farms. The city boys do not as readily make the association between free farming land and democracy as did the farmers' sons, and the thesis has suffered accordingly.

Recently one citified historian, Daniel J. Boorstin, has reconstituted the Turner thesis in a nonagrarian form in his *Genius of American Politics* (1953) and *The Americans; The Colonial Experience* (1958). While largely avoiding notice of the frontiersman and the farmer, Boorstin concludes, with Turner, that "The genius of American democracy comes not from any special virtue of the American people but from the unprecedented opportunities of this continent and from a peculiar and unrepeatable combination of historical circumstances." David M. Potter in *People of Plenty* (1954) sees "abundance" as the basic influence. Turner, despite the host of criticism which was raised against him, has permanently altered the course of American historical writing. This is evident in these generalizations of Boorstin and Potter.

V

War of 1812   Absolutely essential to the Jeffersonian system was an immaculate isolation from Europe in the areas of politics and war. The system did not admit of the maintenance of a large army and navy, because these would threaten the liberties of the people and impose burdensome taxes upon them. Jefferson demonstrated that he was no pacifist during his first administration by refusing to pay tribute to the pirate rulers of North Africa, as other European nations did, and as the United States had formerly done. He ordered the bombardment of Tripoli which—with the even more effective, privately initiated overland attack of the American consul in Tunis, William Eaton—led to a treaty with Tripoli meeting American conditions.

At the same time Jefferson held to the idealistic view that wars were unreasonable and, where the United States was concerned, unnecessary. The United States could remain neutral so far as Europe's wars were concerned, and it could force Europe to respect its neutrality by the peaceful and reasonable method of imposing sanctions on the violator. The famous Jeffersonian rule was friendship with all nations and entangling alliances with none. It was true that the birth of the Republic had been achieved through the original sin of a permanent entangling military alliance with France. Nevertheless, once independence had been achieved, Jeffersonians as well as Federalists wished so far as possible to conduct themselves as if no such alliance existed.

This had proved difficult for Washington and Adams, but Jefferson inherited from Adams the final settlement with France as well as a period of diplomatic calm in which to create his "quiet" system of government. Following his triumphant reelection, Jefferson embarked with understandable confidence upon a second administration during which his quiet system was to be wrecked beyond recovery by the international storms which he mistakenly supposed he could control.

In 1805 Lord Nelson broke French naval power at Trafalgar, and two months later Napoleon defeated the combined Austrian and Russian armies at Austerlitz. In the stalemated war of attrition which followed, between the mistress of the seas and the master of the continent, neutral trade was harried and destroyed by authority of British orders-in-council and Napoleonic decrees, inflicting terrible depredations upon American commerce. Since Britain controlled the seas, that nation was the more effective in carrying out confiscations, and to this violation of American neutrality Britain added the kidnapping of American sailors into the British navy. Impressment, as the practice was called, was vital to the manning of the British navy, given the uninviting conditions of navy life, and since there often was no good way of distinguishing American from British sailors, the English government refused to guarantee the security of Americans from being accidentally impressed.

In 1807 the British warship *Leopard,* in search of deserters, intercepted the American frigate *Chesapeake.* When the commander of the *Chesapeake* refused to permit a search party on board, the *Leopard* opened fire, boarded the ship and removed the alleged deserters. That the United States would declare war immediately seemed to many to be a foregone conclusion, but Jefferson had other plans. He was ambitious in wanting to give an enlightened demonstration of the superior effectiveness of peaceful coercion over war. He therefore replied to the *Leopard-Chesapeake* affair with the Embargo Act, closing all American ports to foreign trade, in the confidence that this would starve England into submission before it had destroyed the American economy.

When, after fourteen months of desperate depression, Jefferson's expectations were still disappointed, he consented to replacing the Embargo Act with the Non-Intercourse Act. This act opened trade with all countries but England and France, although promising to open trade with either of those countries when it would cease its attack on American shipping. Then Jefferson, "panting for retirement," departed for his plantation at Monticello, turning the problem over to his Virginia neighbor, close friend, and chosen successor, President Madison, who defeated C. C. Pinckney by 122 electoral votes to 47.

Under Madison, failure of the Non-Intercourse Act was followed by passage of Macon's Bill No. 2, ending nonintercourse but promising to revive it against France, if Britain rescinded her orders-in-council or against Britain, if Napoleon rescinded his decrees. The wily Napoleon persuaded Madison to restore nonintercourse with England by announcing the revocation of the disputed decrees without, apparently, the least intention of ceasing their enforcement. At that point an unlikely turn in the weather suddenly created for the first time the conditions under which the Jeffersonian policy of peaceful coercion might have proved an effective one. The British winter of 1811–1812 was the worst in a century and a half, and during that winter Napoleon extended his Continental system against England with increasing effect. The American market was vital to England as never before, and in June, 1812, the British suspended the orders-in-council. Two days later, and weeks before word could be received of the British capitulation, Congress declared war on England.

From the time of the Embargo in 1807 until that bad British winter of 1811, the Jefferson-Madison programs of economic coercion had consistently damaged the American economy much more seriously than those of either Britain or France. Until the embargo bill, American shippers, despite both British and French harassment, had been making unprecedented profits from neutral trade. With England's increased control of the seas after Trafalgar, neutral trade became much safer for neutrals who would submit to British inspection and regulation as American shippers were glad to do, considering the profits involved. Then that Virginian in the White House put an end to this traffic, plunging New England and New York in depression and permanently ruining many of the smaller shippers.

Depression struck also in the South and the West, but the brunt of the Embargo was sustained by the Northeast where federalism had lately been dying out, and, amid a now resurgent federalism, state legislatures hurled defiance against the Federal government in terms reminiscent of those Virginia and Kentucky Resolutions of Madison and Jefferson a decade earlier. The rapid spread of secessionist sentiment from New York north did not go unnoticed in England, where many lived who had never accepted American independence as the final solution. The possibility that Jefferson and Madison might drive New York and New England back into the British Empire made at least some English governmental officials wholly enthusiastic supporters of the Jeffersonian policy.

So far as most of the Northeast was concerned, nothing had happened by 1812 to reconcile that section either to a continuance of the program of economic coercion or, even less, to waging war with England in support of it, and that section of the country voted heavily against the declaration of war (the maritime areas of the Northeast, however, voting in its favor). The measure passed by a large margin on the strength of its popularity in the South and the West. The division of sentiment was reflected also in the election of 1812, when the mild leader of the "war party" Madison won reelection on the basis of Southern and Western votes against DeWitt Clinton of New York, who for his part carried every state in the Northeast but Pennsylvania and Vermont. Though ostensibly a war for "Free Trade and Sailors' Rights," the War of 1812 was most popular in those areas least affected by British regulation and impressment.

In the South and West the war was popular on patriotic grounds, for American sovereignty obviously was being violated, but there were also more tangible reasons for its popularity. In the Northwest the Indians had been removed from more than one hundred million acres of land by treaties which they did not entirely understand. They were spoiling for a fight, and in 1811 the Shawnee Chief Tecumseh announced the beginning of a general organization of northern and southern tribes against further white penetration. The Governor of Indiana Territory, William Henry Harrison, answered the challenge by moving against the Shawnees during the temporary absence of Tecumseh, only to be surprised in his turn by the forewarned Indians. In the resulting Battle of Tippecanoe, Harrison drove them back and burned their Prophetstown, but at the cost of heavy casualties and without breaking Tecumseh's power.

The frontiersmen, meanwhile, were absolutely convinced that the English in Canada guided by their fur-trading interest and their hatred of the United States were supplying the Indians with arms and sending them against the Americans. The Battle at Tippecanoe therefore inflamed anti-British feeling on the frontier and aroused frontiersmen to demand a war with Britain, a war which not only would end the Anglo-Indian menace but would also result in the American conquest of Canada. And while anti-British feeling was combining with land hunger to make this war popular in the Northwest, anti-Spanish feeling combined with land hunger to make war popular on the southern frontier where, under the weak Spanish administration, the Floridas had become nests of pirates, international adventurers, raiding Indians, and runaway slaves. In the elections of 1810 this Western war sentiment sent to Congress from the Western regions the "war hawks," who elected their leader Henry Clay as Speaker of the House and launched the campaign which ended with the declaration of war.

The unhappy experience of the United States with its state militia during the Revolutionary War had done nothing to diminish confidence in the system. With an ill-trained standing army of less than seven thousand men, the militia remained the main line of defense, and one which unhappily sorted well with the leadership it was given. Theoretically there were 694,000 of these "swords of the Republic," but despite repeated appeals, there were never more than 35,000 men in the war. This was hardly sufficient even against the motley opposition which England could spare from the Napoleonic conflict, but in addition to this, the campaigns were hopelessly bungled by the superannuated commanders.

With no chance of matching the British navy in sea battles, the attack on Canada was obviously dictated, and a three-pronged attack was planned at Detroit, Niagara, and Lake Champlain. General William Hull at the outset surrendered Detroit to a force half the size of his own, losing his personal belongings in the process, along with the Army war plans. At Niagara, the New York militia quit the fight when it crossed the state lines. At Plattsburg on Lake Champlain the militia made a twenty-mile hike, decided that was enough and went home. These were lessons which taught the Americans enough to make possible the winning of some of their subsequent battles under new commanders, notably the stirring American triumph at Niagara in the Battle of Lundy's Lane.

The real saving of the American cause, however, was due paradoxically, not to military victories, but to naval exploits. At the outset the American Navy gained some spectacular victories at sea in one encounter after another, based on the heavier broadsides of the American ships and the better spirit of the volunteer American crews. Soon, however, the British bottled up the American Navy in American harbors, where it remained for the rest of the war. Of much greater strategic importance was the tour de force of Oliver Hazard Perry in building a fleet on Lake Erie which gained control of the lake for the United States, and the naval victory of Thomas MacDonough on Lake Champlain, which gave the United States an almost invulnerable position of strength along the eastern

Canadian border. It was the strong position of the nation's fresh water navy which mainly decided the British government in favor of moderate peace terms.

Checked in Canada, the British, in the final stages of the war, used their naval superiority to invade the Chesapeake and burn Washington, D.C., while a further expeditionary force landed at New Orleans. At New Orleans, it met a large collection of militia under the direction of Andrew Jackson, fresh from victory at the Battle of Horseshoe Bend, where the power of the Creek Nation had been decisively broken. The British frontal attack against Jackson's fortified position resulted in more than two thousand British casualties to seventy-one for the Americans. As it turned out, the Battle of New Orleans occurred after the peace treaty had been signed at Ghent and so had no military value. It served, however, to wipe out memories of the many past defeats and usher in a period of perfervid patriotism.

The home front had proved every bit as incompetent in the struggle as had the front lines. The Bank of the United States had been allowed to die upon the expiration of its charter in 1811, and the war had resulted in inflation and in a public debt of 127,000,000 dollars. The Jeffersonian opposition to an extensive Federal road- and canal-building program without specific constitutional authorization had contributed to the breakdown of wartime transportation. The Jeffersonian military policy had disastrously weakened the nation at a time when the national security was in peril. And the Jeffersonians, who preached that those governments were best which governed least, had proceeded to govern New England commerce into extinction.

In 1814 the experimental American Federal Republic seemed to many to be about to fall apart, and Massachusetts sent out a call for a convention of New England representatives to discuss how that maligned and injured section should conduct itself in the course of this dissolution and possible conquest. Meeting at Hartford, Connecticut, the convention, under the circumstances, proceeded with moderation, proposing, not secession, but simply a number of constitutional reforms. Its emissaries had no sooner been dispatched to Washington, however, when the incredible news came of an overwhelming American victory under Andrew Jackson at New Orleans and of the Treaty of Ghent with England, signed two weeks before the Battle of New Orleans, restoring to the United States all that it had lost in the war and bringing the conflict to a close. Under the circumstances those emissaries had the discretion not to present their proposals, but in the ensuing rush of nationalism they and their confederates in New England were given ample reason to regret their most ill-timed action.

As for the Jeffersonians, the war obliged them to repudiate their main political tenets one after another. Wartime financial chaos resulted in the passage of a bill chartering a second United States Bank and signed reluctantly by President Madison, "Public Judgement necessarily superceding individual opinion." The nation emerged, saddled with a debt and therefore with monocratic bond-holders, to an extent hardly anticipated in the days of Hamilton.

The Jefferson policy of commercial warfare had resulted in the rapid development of American industry, especially the textile industry, made possible by the temporary absence of British competition. At war's end the British attempted to destroy those infant industries by dumping their own goods on the American market at reduced prices. The United States retaliated with the passage of a protective tariff such as Hamilton had earlier fought in vain to push through Congress. The Jeffersonians themselves, who had once urged America to leave its shops and mills in Europe, were brought to the support of at least moderate protection of American industry to give the nation a degree of economic independence from Europe which it had formerly lacked. The war had dramatized America's bad roads, and the Jeffersonians were now in favor of federally sponsored internal improvements, providing only that they be authorized by a constitutional amendment. This demand for constitutional authorization, wrote Jefferson himself, provided by 1816 "almost the only landmark which now divides the Federalists from the Republicans."

In this Jefferson was generous to a slain opponent. The Federalist party had in truth become a narrowly sectional party: cranky, obstructionist, and somewhat theocratic. From the time of its secessionist grumblings at the Louisiana Purchase, its leadership had become more and more narrowly provincial. During "Mr. Madison's War," not only had the Federalist party resisted all efforts to bring New England into the struggle, but Federalists had traded openly and briskly with the enemy. The Federalists climaxed their recalcitrance with the Hartford Convention. They continued their struggles into the twenties, winning victories locally and harrassing the Republicans nationally, but as an effective national political party they had destroyed themselves.

The triumphant conclusion of the war, meanwhile, was almost as disastrous to the spirit of Jeffersonian republicanism as it was to the old Jeffersonian program, for the boastful nationalism of the time affected even the Virginia dynasty. In 1816 the third successive Virginian, James Monroe, was elected President almost by acclaim, and four years later he swept the nation with but one dissenting electoral vote. A comparison of Monroe's first inaugural address with those of Jefferson and Madison is instructive. Theirs had both been chiefly concerned with the problem of defending individual liberty in a national state. Both Jefferson and Madison had been concerned also to conciliate sections of the country which evinced the disposition to fly off into independent nations of their own if things did not go according to their liking. Not so Monroe:

> To whatever object we turn our attention, whether it relates to our foreign or domestic concerns, we find abundant cause to felicitate ourselves on the excellence of our institutions. . . .
>
> Such then is the happy Government under which we live—a Government adequate to every purpose for which the social compact is formed. . . .
>
> Never did a government commence under auspices so favorable, nor ever was success so complete. If we look to the history of other nations, ancient or modern, we find no example of a growth so rapid, so gigantic, of a people so prosperous and happy . . . If we persevere in the career in which we have advanced so far and in the path already traced, we can not fail, under the favor of a gracious Providence, to attain the high destiny which seems to await us.

BIBLIOGRAPHY FOR CHAPTER FOUR

An excellent recent survey is available in J. C. Miller, *The Federalist Era, 1789–1801* (1960), containing a full discussion of the literature of the period, "a clear, readable combination of synthesis and original scholarship . . . perhaps the best short history of the Federalist period." More thoroughly Hamiltonian in its point of view than the rather Hamiltonian *Federalist Era* is Nathan Schachner's, *The Founding Fathers* (1954), "essentially a political narrative focused on individuals, bare of fresh interpretation, and with an undue stress on the dramatic. It is withal a lively and readable book, one that will attract the general reader and provide the undergraduate with an up-to-date text on the critical years of the American Republic."

Inclined to Jeffersonianism, on the other hand, is Adrienne Koch, *Power, Morals and the Founding Fathers* (1961), a series of essays on the leading figures; and Joseph C. Charles, *The Origins of the American Party System* (1956) is a "provocative, if at times intemperate, antifederalist interpretation of the administrations of Washington and John Adams." Marcus Cunliffe, *George Washington, Man and Monument* (1958) is a brief biography by a leading English scholar of American history. Nathan Schachner, *Alexander Hamilton* (1946) is a scholarly study and "an incisive and graphic narrative of Hamilton's career . . . a highly personal biography, its emphasis falling upon the individual to the neglect of the times." S. G. Kurtz, *The Presidency of John Adams: The Collapse of Federalism, 1795–1800* (1958) is, in common with several other recent studies, a strong defense of Adams as, in Kurtz's words, "a fitting successor to George Washington."

No survey of the Jeffersonian era is as yet available in paperback, but two excellent brief biographies are. Gilbert Chinard, *Thomas Jefferson, The Apostle of Americanism* (1939) is generally rated the best one-volume biography, while A. J. Nock, *Thomas Jefferson* (1926) is a fascinating tour de force, a biographical study of Jefferson's thought. C. M. Wiltse, *The Jeffersonian Tradition in American Democracy* (1935) is a study by the author of a multi-volume biography of Calhoun, and it places a correspondingly heavy emphasis upon the southern states'-rights aspect of Jeffersonianism. Merrill Peterson, *The Jeffersonian Image in the American Mind* (1960), ranging more widely, contains much interesting information which will be new to scholars as well as to students of American history.

Richard Hofstadter, *The American Political Tradition and the Men Who Made It* (1948) contains a chapter on Jefferson which is in substantial accord with the Nock interpretation. It contains also a chapter on the founding fathers, emphasizing their application of Calvinistic psychology to human affairs. Among the most influential historical writings of the past generation, *The American Political Tradition* is "primarily a series of reevaluations of American political leaders from the Founding Fathers to Franklin D. Roosevelt. Mr. Hofstadter brings to this task . . . a deft literary style. His estimates are fresh and original, shaped by requirements neither of myth nor of debunking." The essays are rather uneven in merit. These first two are among the best of them.

Henry Adams, *United States in 1800* is a reprinting of the famous introductory chapters to Adams's lengthy history of the United States during the administrations of Jefferson and Madison. A discussion of American society and thought, and its sectional variations, they reveal the science-minded historian Adams at his brilliant and egregiously unscientific best. Russell Nye, *Cultural Life of the New Nation, 1776–1830* (1960) is a pioneer work of synthesis, "a solid study where the problems are often new and sometimes great . . . a long step in the right direction." Since the publication of Nye's study, the history of the American intellect can no longer be suspended—as has tended to be the case—during the period between Jefferson's first inaugural address and Emerson's American Scholar address.

The inevitable and inviting point of departure for any study of the American West is the essays of Turner, beginning with the first and most influential of them, "The Significance of the Frontier in American History." Two volumes edited by Ray Billington are available in paperback: *Frontier in American History* and *Frontier and Section: Selected Essays by Frederick Jackson Turner*. A good sampling of the controversy which has ranged over the Turner thesis is given in the Amherst pamphlet, *The Turner Thesis*, edited by G. R. Taylor. The journals of Lewis and Clark are available in several editions. H. N. Smith, *Virgin Land: The American West as Symbol and Myth* (1950) is a novel and interesting undertaking which examines the West in terms of its impact upon America's creative imagination and its national aspirations. Francis Parkman, *The Oregon Trail* (1849) is a classic account of a trip westward by a young man who later became one of the greatest of American historians. A similar personal account of the Santa Fe trail is to be found in Josiah Gregg, *Commerce of the Prairies*, 2 vols. (1844).

Marquis James, *Andrew Jackson: The Border Captain* (1933) is a vivid account of Jackson's role in the War of 1812. No history of the war itself is available in paperback, but a good coverage of the interesting historical controversies surrounding the war—notably who in America wanted it and why—is given in Bradford Perkins, ed., *Causes of the War of 1812: National Honor or National Interest?*

RISE OF DEMOCRACY 5

I

Era of Good Feelings It is customary to speak of Monroe's two administrations, 1817–1825, as the Era of Good Feelings, a laughably inappropriate phrase to describe an age of confused politics and desperate politicians. During Monroe's tenure the nation suffered the worst depression it had ever experienced. Then, in the midst of that depression, it was frightened by sudden intimations of a coming civil war, during the congressional debates on slavery, inspired by the proposed admission of Missouri to the Union as a slave state.

The age was a dangerous one for individual politicians also. Among these, Thomas Hart Benton and his brother successfully

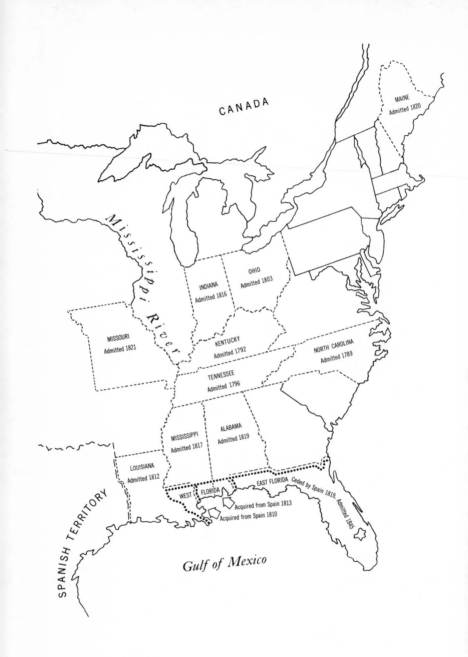

American Acquisition of the Floridas and the Admission of Missouri, Indiana, Mississippi, Illinois, Alabama, and Maine to the Union.

shot Andrew Jackson, who in turn killed another political opponent in another duel, as did Senator Benton, himself, on a different occasion. (Jackson had fought a bloodless duel with Governor John Sevier of Tennessee.) William H. Crawford, the Jeffersonian candidate for President in 1824, managed to kill the first member of the opposition to challenge him. He went on to survive, at the cost of a shattered wrist, a duel with an Indian fighter, employed by the opposition. A return match was demanded, which he refused, and shortly thereafter he was mercifully elevated and removed to the United States Senate. Nobody was hurt in the duel between Senator John Randolph of Roanoke and Secretary of State Henry Clay, although Randolph's cloak was ruined.

The period was an Era of Good Feelings in the superficial sense that organized opposition to the Jeffersonian Republicans collapsed after the suicidal Federalist Hartford Convention, and Monroe, as a consequence, won by a landslide in 1816 and won again without any opposition whatever in 1820. Era of Good Feelings refers also to the heady spirit of nationalism which filled the country following the surprising American victory at New Orleans and favorable peace terms at Ghent. The period of trial was over. The Republic was established, and Monroe, dressed in the high top boots and white periwig of Revolutionary times, presided above the fight as a symbol of the Republic itself, a nation certain of itself at last. It was a nation, however, which was caught in the throes of turbulent economic and geographical change and in the clutches of politicians who, released from the restraints of party discipline, were clawing their way savagely toward the Presidency in 1825.

So swiftly was the nation changing, that politicians found it impossible to measure the true interests of the sections they represented. In 1816 John C. Calhoun of South Carolina was an outstanding champion of the nation's first protective tariff, while Daniel Webster of Massachusetts was its staunch opponent. Twelve years later Webster was the leading spokesman in the Senate for the high protective tariff, and Calhoun was the author of the South Carolina Exposition, threatening to nullify within the state of South Carolina the tariff which had been passed that year.

Webster had originally opposed the tariff as a spokesman for the dominant commercial classes in New England, since the merchants, who had earlier been instrumental in defeating the Hamilton tariff proposals, naturally were opposed to a tax on trade. Even while Webster was fighting the tariff, however, New England's industry was beginning to rival its commerce in importance. At the same time that the War of 1812 had ruined New England shipping, it had created a protected market for American manufactures. Prominent Boston merchants had thereupon entered the textile industry on a large scale and with such success that they continued to make large profits in the postwar period, even under the pressure of British competition. By 1828 the transition had largely taken place. New England was by then the most industrialized area of the nation, and Webster, always the fiery champion of the upper dog, made himself industry's most eloquent spokesman.

Calhoun's early support of the tariff had been based upon nationalist sentiment and also upon the expectation that South Carolina would soon develop an important cotton textile industry which would benefit from protection. Even at the time the dominant opinion in South Carolina probably was against the tariff, but Calhoun was a logical man, and logic was on his side. In 1816 South Carolina was a leading producer of cotton, and it also possessed everything else necessary to make it a leading textile center: cheap slave labor, sources for skilled labor among the German and Scotch-Irish settlers in the piedmont, plentiful water power, and a commercial metropolis.

In 1828 it still had all of these things, but no textile industry was resulting from them. South Carolina was therefore dependent for its livelihood on cotton exports to England and France, and tariff protection meant only rising costs of manufactured goods imported from the North. By that time, although the nation's first railroad line was yet to be completed, the main national pattern of economic development had established itself, and politicians in all sections could speak on economic matters with assurance. The relationships between the sections themselves, meanwhile, were altering unpredictably as the West emerged suddenly to rival the Northeast and Southeast in political importance.

To the Hamiltonian nationalism of the postwar tariff and banking legislation was added the Hamiltonian nationalism of the Supreme Court under Chief Justice John Marshall. The Marshall

Court decisions tended consistently to strengthen the power of the Federal government over the states and at the same time to secure the protection of property rights against government regulation and to secure vested interests against free competition. Although Marshall never again attempted to set aside a Federal law after Marbury *v.* Madison, his Court declared state laws to be unconstitutional in thirteen cases from Wilson *v.* Mason in 1801 to Worcester *v.* Georgia in 1832. In this he was clearly following the intention of the founders, as was by no means so clearly the case when he invalidated part of a Federal law in Marbury *v.* Madison.

Unleashing judicial decisions like thunderbolts throughout his long tenure as Chief Justice, the gentle and kindly John Marshall was a veritable Wizard of Oz in the contrast between his public personality and his private one. Unaffectedly democratic in his tastes and habits, he was committed intellectually to the view that society could remain in good order only so long as it remained in the capable hands of "the wise, the rich, and the good." During most of his career on the Court, the majority of his fellow members were appointees of Republican Presidents, placed on the Court to fight Marshallian federalism. And Marshall took one after another of these capable men in hand and brought them up to become his dedicated followers, aided by the fact that the Supreme Court, as a centrally national institution, would tend to form the thinking of its members along centrally national lines.

The most famous and controversial of his rulings against the states was McCulloch *v.* Maryland in 1819 prohibiting the state of Maryland from taxing the Maryland branch of the United States Bank. The Constitution has nothing to say about banks or about the Federal power to charter any corporations, and it might therefore be concluded that by the terms of the tenth amendment these powers are reserved to the states. The Constitution does, however, empower Congress "to make all laws which shall be necessary and proper for carrying into execution the foregoing powers." To Marshall, in the decision of McCulloch *v.* Maryland, this meant: "Let the end be legitimate, let it be within the scope of the constitution, and all means which are appropriate, which are plainly adapted to that end, which are not prohibited, but consist with the letter and spirit of the constitution, are constitutional."

Having thus sweepingly established the authority of the Federal government to charter the bank, Marshall went on to declare invalid the Maryland tax. The states were not empowered to destroy a Federal instrumentality, and the power to tax was the power to destroy. Marshall made no distinction between a tax, such as the Maryland one, which was destructive in intent, and other state taxes which were neither destructive nor discriminatory. The result of this sweeping decision was that the doctrine of immunity from taxation of government instrumentalities, so fruitful of administrative difficulties, became firmly imbedded in constitutional law.

Business was afforded a constitutional protection against state interference in 1810 to an extent never contemplated by the founding fathers when, in the Constitution, they prohibited the states from passing laws "impairing the obligation of contracts." The original intent appears to have been to prevent impairment by the states of contracts between private persons. In Fletcher *v.* Peck, however, Marshall cited the contract clause as his authority to prohibit the state of Georgia from repealing a state enactment involving the corrupt Yazoo land sales.

Then, in 1819 in Dartmouth College *v.* Woodward, the state of New Hampshire was prevented from altering the charter which the college had received in 1769 from George III. Thus the Court decided that states cannot alter contracts made with private persons and, further, that a corporate charter is a contract. Business corporations by this decision came under the broadened protection of the contract clause. The importance to free enterprise of these decisions has probably been overemphasized however. At the time few business corporations existed. It was only later in the century that the importance of the Dartmouth College decision as a protection to vested interests came to manifest itself, and by that time corporation lawyers had found an even better legal protection in the "due process" clause of the Fourteenth Amendment.

The Marshall Court decided on only three cases involving the constitutional authority of the Federal government to regulate interstate commerce, the most famous of which was Gibbons *v.* Ogden in 1824. Marshall's decision in this case was a popular one, because it invalidated a state-authorized shipping monopoly, on the grounds that it came in conflict with a Federal coasting license law. In his decision Marshall was firm in his assertion of the sovereign power of the Federal government to regulate interstate commerce.

He further defined the control over commerce to comprehend government supervision over the product from point of origin to point of destination. By noticing the fact of an applicable Federal licensing law, however, he spared himself the necessity of asserting the exclusive authority of the Federal government in the area of interstate commerce. As in other of his decisions, his assertions of wide Federal authority escaped serious challenge, because, upon asserting them, he based his decision on a different and narrowly technical ground. Marshall was by all odds the nation's most powerful advocate of nationalism in the postwar period, which was not to say that his deviously forthright decisions always contributed to the good feelings of the era.

Postwar nationalism achieved its happiest expression in the field of foreign affairs under the direction of Monroe's fretfully undiplomatic Secretary of State John Quincy Adams. Chief among the nation's diplomatic triumphs were the Spanish-American Transcontinental Treaty of 1819 and the Monroe Doctrine of 1823, each of them related to the fact of rapidly failing Spanish power in America. The first quarter of the nineteenth century saw the disintegration of the Spanish empire in America, as Spain became distracted by internal revolution and by Napoleonic and British invasions. Forced to cede Louisiana to France in 1800, Spain lost all of mainland Latin America within the next generation to patriotic revolutionary forces, except for the Floridas which were wrested from her by the United States.

Stretched across the river systems which gave Alabama and much of Georgia access to the ocean, the Floridas had early been, with New Orleans, objects of American desire. An ingenious interpretation of the terms of the purchase of Louisiana permitted the Americans to persuade themselves that they had purchased West Florida with it, but the always land-hungry Jefferson was unable to persuade the Spanish. Madison was in a better position to do something about the Floridas as the revolution in Spain came to be accompanied by near anarchy in Spanish America. Part of West Florida was occupied in 1810 and at Madison's direction Congress followed this occupation with the declaration, directed chiefly against Britain, that the United States "cannot, without serious inquietude, see any part of the said territory [of the Floridas] pass into the hands of any foreign power." The United States occupied the rest of West Florida in 1813.

In 1817 the Spanish minister Luis de Onis sat down with Secre-

tary of State Adams to a series of discussions which Onis protracted for more than a year with the aid of successive new documents from the bottomless Spanish archives and in the vain hope
of receiving assistance from the European powers. In 1818, however, Andrew Jackson hurried the Spanish to a decision by invading East Florida in pursuit of marauding Seminole Indians. In
1819 the Spanish agreed to the Transcontinental Treaty, ceding
to the United States all of the Floridas, finally acknowledging
American possession of Louisiana Territory and in addition throwing in the weighty Spanish claims to the territory of the Pacific
Northwest. Adams would have insisted on Texas as well had he
been able to gain support from Monroe and from other Cabinet
members.

In the meantime formal recognition of the new Latin-American
republics presented a problem which Monroe attempted to solve
by joining England in a simultaneous statement of recognition. In
1822, four years after his proposal was made, having failed to receive British support, the United States extended this recognition
of Latin America on its own. A year later France invaded Spain,
and the faint possibility arose of a Franco-Spanish invasion of
Latin America. Faced with this threat to the new British markets
in Latin America the British Foreign Minister, George Canning,
proposed to the United States government a joint protest against
European intervention. Monroe and most of his Cabinet and advisors, flattered by the prospective partnership, were inclined to
accept.

Not so Secretary of State Adams. Wishing to avoid becoming
"a cock boat in the wake of the British man of war," Adams prevailed upon Monroe to decline the British proposal and instead
to make his own declaration unilaterally in a Presidential message.
It was Adams's correct assumption that Britain with its navy would
be obliged to support the doctrine out of self-interest, regardless of
whether or how the declaration was made. The result was the
Monroe Doctrine, declaring on the one hand that the United
States could not concern itself with intra-European politics or
wars, and on the other that the United States considered the
Americas to be no longer subject to further colonization by European powers.

The Monroe Doctrine was a statement of a policy which the
United States had been formulating from the first days of the

Federal government: in Washington's Farewell Address, in John Adams's termination of the French military alliance, in Jefferson's first inaugural address, and in the statement of Congress at the time of the American occupation of West Florida, opposing foreign occupation of the Floridas. Universally popular in the United States, the Monroe Doctrine remained the basis of American foreign policy throughout the nineteenth century, despite the entire lack, except during the Civil War, of any American military and naval force capable of enforcing it. No European nation recognized its validity, and one or another of them on occasion violated it with impunity. Nevertheless, while Britain wished to maintain open markets in Latin America and while she remained queen of the seas in an age of sailing vessels, it was almost all the long-range foreign policy the United States needed to have.

II

Advance of Democracy   The Monroe Doctrine was the diplomacy of a nation which had turned its back on Europe and was busily moving westward. From the War of 1812 to the Civil War, westward expansion and western state-making provided, among other things, an endlessly unsettling factor in the national political life. During the postwar period this proved most shockingly so in the case of Missouri. In the course of the congressional debates over admission of Missouri as a state, Representative James Tallmadge of New York proposed an amendment to the enabling act prohibiting the introduction of any more slaves into the new state. The Tallmadge amendment brought the slavery issue to the floor of Congress as a critical issue for the first time in the nation's history, and the fury that it aroused on both sides came, as Jefferson said, like a fire bell in the night, rousing both Northerners and Southerners to their first realization of the danger to the nation inherent in the slavery issue.

With the House of Representatives containing a decisive majority of free state representatives, the South came now to regard the Senate, divided in 1820 equally between free and slave states, as the special guardian of their peculiar institution. In a compromise handled by Henry Clay their anxieties were somewhat allayed by the admission of Missouri as a slave state, while northern feelings were quieted by the simultaneous admission of Maine as a free state and by the prohibition of slavery thereafter in all the rest of Louisiana Territory lying north of 36° 30″. That settled the issue in Congress for a generation, but the slavery question remained in men's minds on both sides of the Mason and Dixon line and lurked behind all of the other sectional controversies which divided the nation.

Westward expansion and western state making in the postwar period had ceased to inspire the awful forebodings among conservative Easterners which had followed the purchase of Louisiana. By 1824 even that most perfectly correct Bostonian Edward Everett had arrived at the conclusion that "by the wise and happy partition of powers between the national and state governments . . . all bounds seem removed from the possible extension of our country, but the geographical limits of the continent." Still, Everett and his friends were less than happy with the perceptible democratization of the nation which accompanied the westward movement. The six new states were Indiana, Mississippi, Illinois, Alabama, Maine, and Missouri, while Louisiana had entered the Union as a state in 1812, and of these all provided for adult white manhood suffrage except Louisiana and Mississippi.

In addition, by the eve of the War of 1812 universal white manhood or taxpayer's suffrage was the rule in New Hampshire, Pennsylvania, New Jersey, Maryland, North Carolina, and Georgia. It existed in South Carolina also, but under conditions which rendered it innocuous to the ruling group. Thus the adding of the new states would alone have created a preponderance of democratic governments among the states of the Union, but in addition, during this period, radicals called conventions in three of the populous older states, Connecticut, New York, and Massachusetts, and won them to the side of popular rule. After 1821, therefore, the few states which retained property qualifications remained anachronistic deviations from the accepted rule.

Connecticut conservatism was the victim of the unhappily timed Hartford Convention, which undermined the authority of established church and state. Deserted thus unkindly by their own special providence, the Connecticut Federalists bowed to the inevitable. They did not seriously resist the call for a state constitutional convention in 1818, and, rather than fight democracy to the death, they cooperated, hoping only to exert a moderating in-

fluence. They were not altogether unsuccessful in this. The reformed franchise stopped just short of manhood suffrage, being
extended to men who served in the militia or paid a state tax or
held a freehold estate valued at $7. The Congregational Church
was disestablished, and religious tests for officeholding were abolished. Separation of the branches of government were effected,
and the judicial and tax systems were reformed. When the deed
had been accomplished, the Federalist party of Connecticut condemned the new constitution officially and, attempting to make a
political issue of the matter, fell from power.

Nor were the Federalists in Connecticut's neighboring states
spared in the hour of triumph. If the ruling groups in those states
could have withstood the force of triumphant nationalism, they
were unable to withstand the outraged popular sentiment aroused
by the panic of 1819. Unexampled wretchedness swept the nation
and nowhere more fiercely than in New York City. Bank failures
and business foreclosures discredited the whole crew of speculators who, it was charged, operated the state governments in their
own interest. Pools of unemployment widened in the cities in a
way that had never before been seen. Something had to be done.
Where the people controlled the state governments they demanded
popular aid; where the state governments were in the hands of
oligarchies, the people demanded control.

In New York a long standing opposition to the Council of Appointment sparked the movement for constitutional revision. Set
up by the state constitution of 1777 to limit the power of the
governor, the five-man council controlled appointments to fifteen
thousand public offices. Under DeWitt Clinton this council had
become the basis for the most effective spoils system in the nation,
and in 1818 the anti-Clinton Tammany Society called for a convention to eliminate the council which their opponents controlled. By
delaying for a year Clinton brought upon himself the added discontents of the panic, and the resulting convention was composed
overwhelmingly of anti-Clinton Democrats.

The Council of Appointment was abolished along with a Council of Revision and then, against the wishes of the Tammany men
who had called the convention, property qualifications for the
vote were removed. While straight-out adult white manhood suffrage was not achieved, as the radicals wished, the new constitution extended the vote to all adult white male residents of the

state who had lived in the state one year and who had paid taxes or served in the militia or worked on the highways.

On one point it was the conservatives who fought successfully for a broadening of the suffrage against the opposition of the radicals. They secured the vote for all adult male Negroes who owned a freehold worth $250 and paid a tax upon it. The conservatives and the radicals both reasoned that the wealthy men of the community were in a position to gain these votes. Democratic reforms continued inexorably in New York during the next generation. In 1826 unrestricted white manhood suffrage was achieved and the office of justice of the peace was made elective, and within the next decade the office of mayor became elective in all New York cities.

Massachusetts in the meantime had subjected John Adams's constitution of 1780 to the same criticism and had altered it along similar lines, extending the vote to all adult, white, male taxpayers, amid the somber warnings of John Adams himself as well as those of Joseph Story and Daniel Webster. In both Massachusetts and New York the defenders of property qualifications consistently had had the best of the debate. The democratic reformers could not meet the argument that voting was a privilege and not a right. If voting were a right, they were asked, then why deny it to women, Negroes, and Indians? Since the reformers were almost universally opposed to extending the vote to these elements of the population, they were obliged to make their defense, not on generous grounds of democratic theory, but on such narrow grounds as taxpayers', militiamen's, and road workers' rights. Nevertheless they were sustained by the democratic spirit of the times, and although they may have lost the arguments, they won the decisions.

So far as the western farmers were concerned, the panic of 1819 may well have been the severest depression ever to be experienced before or since. Later depressions found most farmers in possession of the title to their own lands. In 1819 most western farmers were still in the process of making payments on their land, and the panic faced them with the prospect of mass eviction and the likelihood of debtors prison. In Tennessee they found their spokesman in Felix Grundy, who pushed through the legislature various relief measures, including a bill establishing a state loan office to tide the debtors through the depression. In state after state the debtors grasped control of the government as they had not done since the depression days of the Confederation. When the Bank of Kentucky suspended payments, the legislature passed a stay law and established a new bank, authorized to issue bank notes to the amount of 3 million dollars. At the same time the legislature voted a mere 7 thousand dollars toward establishing a bank, a sum sufficient to pay for the printing of the notes.

Most of the state legislation proved ineffectual, and the only significant legislation produced nationally by the panic was the Land Act of 1820. Earlier a series of enactments in 1796, 1800, and 1804 had reduced the minimum size of the purchase from 640 to 160 acres and had reduced the minimum price per acre from $2 to $1.64. The minimum down payment had been lowered from 50 per cent to 25 per cent, and the time for further payments had been extended from one to four years. The Land Act of 1820 made possible the purchase of 80 acres of government land for $100. A relief act also was passed assisting those who had been unable to meet the earlier requirements.

III

Triumph of Jackson

The panic had no effect whatever on the unopposed reelection of President Monroe, and Monroe, for his part, all but ignored the panic in his second inaugural address. In the course of his second administration prosperous times returned to the nation, and the panic was not an issue in the election of 1824. It was in this apparently placid atmosphere that a few gentlemen from Virginia and a few machine politicians from New York got together, as they had regularly done since 1800, to select the next President and Vice President. Beginning with the Jefferson-Burr collaboration, this tight little Virginia-New York alliance had controlled every election. The Virginia group was made up of a small knot of newspapermen, bankers, judges, and planters, organized during Jefferson's first administration into the secret Richmond Junto. In New York, where politics was bitterly factional, control had changed hands over the period from Burr to DeWitt Clinton to Senator Martin Van Buren, who in 1824 controlled New York politics through an exclusive political combination known as the Albany Regency. The South and West had consistently followed where New York and Virginia led, and so had Pennsylvania, the most democratic state in the Union, which had consistently been too riven by political battles to produce a favorite son of its own.

With the extraconstitutional development of the party system, the practice had been followed of delegating the formal task of nominating presidential candidates to a caucus of the congressmen of each party. Since the Republican party was unopposed in 1824, it seemed evident that the caucus candidiate would be the next President. And so he might have been, had not the chosen candidate, Secretary of the Treasury William H. Crawford, been stricken by paralysis a year before the election. In the event, Crawford's apparently hopeless condition created a vacuum which sucked in favorite sons from around the nation including Henry Clay, John C. Calhoun, DeWitt Clinton, and John Quincy Adams. With no clear political differences to divide them, and with no hope of receiving the caucus nomination, they all campaigned against the caucus as a usurpation of the rights of the people. So hot did the issue become that when Congress met to nominate Crawford only 66 members attended out of a total of 261 congressmen, and the system was never again used. It was replaced by the nominating convention, originated in 1824.

It was the first Pennsylvania nominating convention which brought Andrew Jackson abruptly to political prominence, but it was the supporters of Clay and Calhoun, not those of Jackson, who called for the convention in the first place. Indeed until the convention Jackson was not taken seriously as a candidate by experienced politicians, and not a single one of them in Pennsylvania supported his candidacy. He was looked upon as a backwoods figure who did not fit the aristocratic Washingtonian mold of the Presidency. It was true that he stirred the common people, but as one leading Pennsylvania politician put it, this was but "an effervescence that can accomplish nothing," for the common people did not have a hand in the selection. This line of reasoning changed overnight when the convention met and nominated Jackson by a vote of 124 to 1.

In 1824 the presidential electors, who originally had been appointed by the state legislatures, were chosen by popular vote in all but six of the twenty-four states. In the election of 1824 Jackson won a plurality, but he fell short of a clear majority, and in the electoral college he received only 99 of the 261 votes. As the Constitution directed, therefore, the names of the first three candidates, Jackson, Adams, and Crawford, were presented to the House of

Representatives for a vote, Calhoun having bowed out of the contest to win the vice presidency and Clay having finished fourth. Adams received the support of Clay in Congress and won on the first ballot. Then Adams appointed Clay Secretary of State, and Adams was hardly in office before the next presidential campaign was under way, waged chiefly on the issue of an alleged "corrupt bargain" between Adams and Clay by which the people had been robbed of their first choice for President.

John Quincy Adams's main historical function as President was to facilitate the transition to democracy by a stern abstention from the vulgar mechanics of politics. The author, shortly before his election as President, of a brief history of political parties in America, Adams was quite unaware of the nature of party politics as it was developing during his time in office. As had Washington and John Adams before him, he saw himself as a patriot President, above party, ruling with the advice and assistance of the best and wisest in the nation. His chief political advisors Clay and Webster urged him to use the patronage to strengthen the National Republican party which had supported his candidacy, but Adams refused to cooperate. He even permitted his political enemy John McLean to remain in charge of the richest source of patronage as Postmaster General on the grounds that McLean was a competent administrator. "Mr. Adams," the political boss Thurlow Weed later wrote, "during his administration, failed to cherish, strengthen, or even recognize the party to which he owed his election; nor as far as I am informed, with the great power he possessed did he make a single influential friend."

The opposition, meanwhile, moved aggressively to organize for victory behind the new leader, Andrew Jackson. Among the "eleventh hour men" who had leapt aboard the Jackson bandwagon following the Pennsylvania nominating convention, the leading figure, and the chief organizer of the Democratic party, was Senator Van Buren of New York. Van Buren toured the South to bring Southern gentlemen rather reluctantly to the side of the upstart aristocrat Jackson. He faced the equally difficult task of uniting the Clinton and Tammany factions in New York, assisted by the timely death of DeWitt Clinton, who had nursed trouble-making vice-presidential ambitions. And finally Van Buren devoted his energies as United States Senator to the task of creating an effective anti-Adams alliance.

Adams brought to the Presidency a vision, which was shared by no other prominent figure in public life, of a strong national government providing for the general welfare through a coordinated program of national development. He favored a moderate protective tariff and extensive internal improvements financed out of Federal funds. The government would promote the improvement of agriculture, commerce, and manufactures. Beyond that it would establish a national university, would finance scientific expeditions, and would patronize "the elegant arts, the advancement of literature, and the progress of the sciences, ornamental and profound." It was a program which held attractive features for some groups in the country, such as manufacturers who would receive tariff protection, but it was presented in such an elevated and disinterested manner as to appeal to almost nobody. No other President in American history was ever so out of tune with his times as Adams, with the possible exception of Hoover during the Depression years. For the "Little Magician" Van Buren he was an easy mark.

The Senate, which would have almost nothing to do with Adams's program, made history during his administration chiefly by its acrimonious and largely meaningless debate on whether to send representatives to a Pan-American congress in 1826. The heat of the arguments appeared in retrospect to have been quite artificially created. The debate ranged to such subjects as the institution of slavery and the frightful character of slave insurrections. It produced sharp exchanges between senators and the President, and it confirmed the Calhoun faction in its opposition to the administration and joined it to the Van Buren group in support of Jackson, who under any circumstances was plainly going to win the coming election.

As the election approached, the Jackson men helped to create for campaign purposes a "tariff of abominations" which would win support of farmers in the Northwest with duties on wool and flax and support from the middle states with a tax on iron, with the acquiescence of the antitariff South, which had no other party to turn to. The "tariff of abominations" was one of the trickiest maneuvers of the wily Van Buren, but it was altogether unnecessary for the triumph of Old Hickory, who captured every state outside the Northeast and won by the most overwhelming popular mandate of any President in the nineteenth century.

With his defeat Adams was dropped by the National Republicans and so was his ambitious program. "My own system of administration," he confided to his diary, ". . . had been undisguisedly abandoned by H. Clay, ingloriously deserted by J. C. Calhoun, and silently given up by D. Webster." Thus defeated by enemies and disowned by friends, the indomitable Adams entered alone upon the most remarkable period of his career. He entered Congress as the representative of Quincy, Massachusetts, against the wishes of his family who thought it a demeaning office for a former President to hold. And there, until struck down on the floor of the House by an apoplectic stroke in 1848, he fought a single-handed battle for civil rights and against the extension of slavery. Refusing to join the abolitionists and with no political organization behind him, he forced his will upon the government, to become by all odds the most powerful opponent of slavery in the political world of his time.

IV

Jacksonian Democracy   Jackson in office was the visible sign of the people's triumph. His inauguration is remembered, not for what he said, which was very little and to no clear point, but for the motley crowd of farmers and mechanics who obtruded themselves upon a ceremony which formerly had been reserved for gentlefolk. Traveling by horse and by foot over roads made all but impassable by the spring rains, these common people converged on Washington by the thousands, some of them coming as far as 500 miles for the occasion. Muddy and unmannerly, they crowded their way, uninvited, into the postinauguration reception, threatening to reduce the White House to shambles, until they were diverted by tubs of punch hastily carried to the White House lawn. They announced their sovereignty to the world.

There were hostile observers who found this inauguration of democracy disgraceful and fittingly so. As the French observer Alexis de Tocqueville noted, many Americans of wealth, position, and education privately despised democracy. Publicly, however, they were compelled to accept the prevailing democratic shibboleths. Privately they might be guided by sensible and decorous religious conventions; publicly they were obliged to conduct themselves in such a way as to give no offense to the prevailing mores of the evangelical religions. They might profess to despise a society which made money the naked measure of social position, but new rich were coming constantly on the scene, and there seemed to be no way to keep them out. And however much certain rich men might despise the democratic process, the age of Jackson taught them the hard lesson that if they desired the political power to which they felt their position entitled them, they would have to go to the people to get it. As a class the aristocracy had become separated from the national character, which was democratic.

What followed Jackson's White House reception was anticlimax. It turned out that Thomas Jefferson had disturbed himself unnecessarily over the possibility of a Jacksonian *coup d'état* against the Republic. The new President and his chief lieutenants thought of themselves, not as political innovators, but as good, safe Jeffersonians whose duty it was to safeguard the people against dangerous centralizing tendencies in the national government. Where Jackson departed from the Jeffersonian tradition, the difference was often largely a matter of style. Where Jefferson believed that a good government was one which operated so quietly as to go almost unnoticed, Jackson acted on the principle that a good democratic government ought to trumpet forth in the name of the people now and then.

Where Jefferson, fearing the city mobs, placed his reliance upon those "who labor in the earth," Jackson presented himself as the champion of the workingman as well as the farmer. In practice, however, the two men followed very similar policies toward those who labored in the shops and mills. The Jeffersonians had eagerly made common cause, both with the urban radicalism of the Democratic Societies and with the urban political machinery of the Tammany Society. Jackson, on the other hand, while drawing political strength from these same elements, showed no marked interest in the problems which were peculiarly those of the city worker. Most Americans were still farmers in Jackson's day, and most of the laborers in whose name Jackson spoke were those who labored in the earth.

The most startling novelty to occur during Jackson's first year in office was his defense of the spoils system, when he argued that rotation in office freed the nation from the threat of an entrenched bureaucracy and that "The duties of all public offices are, or at least admit of being made, so plain and simple that men of intelligence may readily qualify themselves for their performance." Certainly

this conception was a world apart from Jefferson's natural aristocracy, but it was also true that Jackson proved reluctant to follow
his own advice, and that the turnover in personnel under him was
roughly comparable to that which had taken place under Jefferson.
It was not until the 1840s that the spoils system came into its own.

There remained more basic differences between Jeffersonian republicanism and Jacksonian democracy. Jackson rejected the Jeffersonian idea that government was a necessary evil and by its very
nature an abridgment of liberty. "There are no necessary evils in
government," he declared. "Its evils exist only in its abuses. If it
would confine itself to equal protection, and, as Heaven does its
rains, shower its favors alike on the high and the low, the rich and
the poor, it would be an unqualified blessing." Jefferson, with his
generation, feared the tyranny of the majority. Jackson supposed
that the nation was secure against tyranny so long as it was under
majority rule. As the first President literally to represent the popular will, Jackson conceived of himself as the embodiment of the
majority and in its name the special guardian of the Constitution.
It was in this emphasis upon the sovereign will of the majority that
the Jacksonians departed farthest from the Jeffersonians.

Jackson led a party without a political program of its own, and
it was no doubt the deep desire of his political lieutenants that he
avoid ever arriving at a program. He had been elected by high-
tariff and low-tariff men, by broad nationalists and states' rights
men, by inflationists and hard-money men, and by friends and foes
of extensive Federal internal improvements. Under such circumstances the interests of the party seemed best served by doing as
little as possible about anything. Jackson himself seemed to think
that he possessed a political program and, furthermore, that he had
presented it to the public in his first annual message to Congress.
The message contained no specific recommendations for domestic
legislation, however, and it led to the passage of no bill.

The Peggy Eaton episode may well have been the most important event, so far as the Presidency was concerned, of Jackson's
first three years in office, when the chivalrous President used the full
weight of his office to defend the wife of his friend the Secretary
of War John Eaton against the snobbery and aspersions of Washington society. The event was important, because it contributed to the
political break between Jackson and Vice President Calhoun, the
husband of Washington's leading socialite. Until the Eaton affair

Calhoun had reason to suppose himself the heir apparent to Jackson; afterwards the widower, Van Buren, partly by the kindly attentions he paid Mrs. Eaton, won the gratitude of Jackson which later helped him to the Presidency. As the most important event to follow the democratic revolution of 1828, however, the Eaton episode was significantly lacking in ideological import.

Jackson's most vigorous executive action in those first years was the Maysville Road bill veto, which placed Jackson in opposition to federally financed intrastate internal improvements, on grounds of both economy and constitutionality. Jackson broke no new ground with the veto; he merely reaffirmed a principle established by several of his predecessors. Nor did the veto commit him to any very clear policy in the field of internal improvements, for subsequently he signed other similar measures on the grounds that they were national rather than local in scope, and the Federal internal improvements program did not diminish during his administration. Jackson's treatment of the tariff question was similarly vague, cautious, and middle-of-the-road. He signed both the tariff of 1832 and the compromise tariff of 1833, but neither of them was passed as an administration measure. They were associated rather with his presidential rival Clay and so hardly could serve to separate the Jacksonians from their political opponents.

Until the last months of Jackson's first administration the initiative in political affairs continued to be assumed, not by the President, but by the Congress, as had been the case since 1809 when Jefferson went home to Monticello. The Senate remained the main center of activity as it had been during the Adams administration, and here, during the winter of '29 to '30, from a somewhat peevish discussion of how to sell Federal land the debates rose in an awesome crescendo of magniloquence to the grand debate between Webster and Senator Robert Y. Hayne of South Carolina on the fundamental nature of the Union.

Hayne, in the course of a two-and-one-half hour oration, discussed New England's treason during the War of 1812 and other controversial subjects. He made his main impact, however, by a defense of the nullification doctrine that sovereignty rested with the states, not with the Federal Union, and that therefore the states possessed the authority to nullify within their boundaries unconstitutional Federal laws, such as the tariff of abominations. Webster of Massachusetts, declaring that "I will grind him fine as a pinch of snuff," held the floor for four hours, several days later, to deliver what came to be one of the most admired of American orations, on the loyalty of New England, the treasonableness of the nullification doctrine, the horrors of civil feuds, the glory of the flag, and "Liberty *and* Union, now and for ever, one and inseparable!"

The possibility that South Carolina might act at any moment to nullify the tariff of 1828 gave urgency to the debate. That state suffered an economic depression which was due mainly to soil depletion and to the ruinous new competition from the richer new cotton lands of the lower Mississippi Valley. About this nothing could be done, but the Charleston gentry came to believe it could do something to free itself from the added burden of the protective tariff. Taking its text from the Virginia and Kentucky Resolutions, it threatened to call a state convention which would pass an ordinance declaring the tariff to be of no effect within the state. Among these angry men, Calhoun had developed the nullification argument most fully in his *South Carolina Exposition,* anonymously written and officially approved by the state legislature in 1828. Calhoun went beyond the contention that the Union was a compact of independent states to describe the machinery by which states could nullify laws.

Jackson, from whom the nullificationists hoped to receive support, made known his disapproval in a famous Jefferson Day dinner toast: "Our Union, it must be preserved," to which Calhoun made the equally famous reply, "The Union—next to our liberty, the most dear." The break between Calhoun and Jackson on the personal level, meanwhile, was precipitated by the Peggy Eaton episode and then made irrevocable by the revelation that in 1818 Calhoun as Secretary of War had recommended Jackson's punishment for his invasion of Spanish Florida. With these developments Van Buren replaced Calhoun as the man Jackson would name his successor, and Calhoun, with nothing now to lose by it, came forth as the main leader of nullification. Congress responded in 1832 to the general dislike of the tariff of abominations with a tariff reform which, while adjusting rates downward, did so less in response to Southern complaints than to such objections of Northern industry as the inclusion of duties on imported raw materials.

South Carolina moved at once. A newly elected legislature ordered the calling of a special convention which in turn voted overwhelmingly to nullify the tariff and secede from the Union if the Federal government attempted enforcement. Jackson, returned to office by another landslide vote, issued a Nullification Proclamation promising to meet treason with force, and the Senate passed a Force Bill empowering Jackson to use the armed forces for the purpose. Henry Clay at the same time introduced a compromise tariff calling for major reductions in duties over a nine-year period. Jackson signed the new tariff bill simultaneously with the Force Bill. South Carolina thereupon withdrew its nullification ordinances, and passed a further one against the Force Act and victory was claimed by all sides.

In truth, however, the Charleston fire-eaters had suffered a humiliating defeat from which some of them did not recover. The anticipated support from other Southern states had not been forthcoming; while strong Unionist sentiment in western South Carolina would probably have ignited civil war in the state, had the nullification ordinances been carried out. From that time until the Civil War a group of men in Charleston remained, as the state's leading historian has said, like a foetus in a bottle, unchanged by passing events, waiting for the opportunity which finally came to them to lead the South out of the Union.

V

The Bank War   Had Jackson not been presented by Congress with a bill rechartering the United States Bank in 1832 he would have entered the campaign for reelection as little involved in any real political issues as he had been four years earlier; for the leaders of the opposition, Clay and Webster, had supported, and even led, the fight against nullification. As it happened, Nicholas Biddle, director of the bank, upon the advice of Webster and others, called for a new charter four years before the expiration of the existing one. Biddle and Congressional leaders, knowing Jackson's hostility to the bank, reasoned that political considerations would force Jackson to sign the bill, if it were presented to him before the election. Jackson instead returned the bill to Congress with what has remained the most famous veto in American history, and he launched an attack upon the bank which continued throughout his second term, serving, more than any other circumstance, to crystalize the national political forces at last into two separate organized political parties of Whig and Democrat.

The early history of the second United States Bank had been in sorry contrast to the brilliant beginnings of the first. Greedy for high profits, its directors had extended credit incautiously and then on second thought had called in bank notes so suddenly as to help precipitate the panic of 1819. This sudden contraction of credit had been followed by a run of failures among flimsy state banks, and then, amid farm foreclosures and business failures, the branches of the United States Bank gathered in large amounts of property from the bankruptcies it had helped to create. In Cincinnati, for instance, the bank actually acquired a large part of the city in house lots, hotels, business firms, warehouses, and iron foundries.

For the time being the bank survived the depression-born hostility and reformed its ways under more responsible management, but the sentiment had been created which supported Jackson a decade later in his fight against the bank. In 1823 Nicholas Biddle of Philadelphia, a Jeffersonian Republican who voted for Jackson in 1828, became president of the bank and administered it in a manner which has since won him high praise from financial historians. He continued, however, to incur the wrath and suspicion of many in the country, both among those who wanted credit on easier terms than the bank permitted and those who accused it of dishonest profits through the manipulation of credit. On the one hand there remained the state banking interests whose lending activities were curbed and on the other there were the hard-money men of the Old Republican school who would have liked to have abolished all banks and restricted financial transactions to payments in gold and silver.

Jackson, it turned out, was of the old school, distrustful of all banks and in favor, not of a nationally chartered bank, but simply of a bank of deposit attached to the treasury and deprived of the lending function. Upon taking office he let Biddle know that, while he appreciated the services the bank had performed for the government, he distrusted all banks and beyond that was convinced, despite McCulloch v. Maryland, that a federally chartered bank was unconstitutional outside the confines of the District of Columbia. His vaguely threatening remarks concerning the bank in his first message to Congress inspired congressional investigations, which, however, came to nothing. Supporters of the bank were therefore given good warning and so were led to the tactical error of demanding the rechartering of the bank four years early.

Jackson's veto was vigorously forthright in style and electric with ideology.

It is to be regretted that the rich and powerful too often bend the acts of government to their selfish purposes. Distinctions in society will always exist under every just government. Equality of talents, of education, or of wealth can not be produced by human institutions . . . but when the laws undertake to add to these natural and just advantages artificial distinctions, to grant titles, gratuities, and exclusive privileges, to make the rich richer and the potent more powerful, the humble members of society—the farmers, mechanics and laborers—who have neither the time or the means of securing like favors to themselves, have a right to complain of the injustice of their government.

This line of argument, although it represented the dominant economic radicalism of democratic America, was by no means new, nor was it peculiar to American democratic thought, except in its aversion to titles and in its pointed concern for the farmers, mechanics and laborers. With those exceptions this statement might well have been presented more than two centuries earlier amid loud cheers to that Elizabethan House of Commons which in 1601 successfully forced the Queen to rescind certain chartered monopolies. The Bible of economic liberalism, Adam Smith's *The Wealth of Nations,* was published in the same year that Jefferson wrote the Declaration of Independence. *The Wealth of Nations* was the economic declaration of independence for the British businessman, who went on to win England to free trade over the opposition of the landed interests during the second quarter of the nineteenth century. Jacksonian America, meanwhile, experienced a somewhat similar struggle with the sides roughly reversed. The landed interests of the Cotton Kingdom won a partial victory for free trade over the opposition of the tariff-minded business community. Economic liberalism was not accepted by the American businessman, and if it was accepted privately by Jackson he did not advocate it as President.

Jackson did place himself at the forefront of the antimonopoly fight with his bank bill veto, but he did so in a highly qualified manner. The veto lashed out at the principle of monopoly itself, but specifically it was an attack upon a national, as opposed to a state, monopoly. Indeed one of Jackson's arguments against the bank was that it infringed upon the rights of the less powerful banks which had been chartered by the states. The monopolistic state banking interests fully appreciated this argument, as their strong support of Jackson indicated in 1832. On the other hand his veto message brought him also the strong support of the radical hard-money antimonopoly Democrats—the Locofocos as they were called—who until then had been indifferently enthusiastic about the old hero of New Orleans. This Locofoco movement, while attacking monopolies in general and the United States Bank in particular, was not proposing *laissez faire*. The Locofocos accepted government control, and they did not oppose government support for private enterprise. They simply wished, as Jackson said, to live under a government which would "shower its favors alike on the high and the low, the rich and the poor."

Against this collection of mutually antagonistic but uniformly enthusiastic Jackson supporters, the National Republicans held a national convention, nominated Henry Clay, denounced Jackson for his bank bill veto and went down to resounding defeat. Meanwhile, several of the most promising younger politicians in the anti-Jackson camp, notably Thurlow Weed and William H. Seward of New York and Thaddeus Stevens of Pennsylvania, disgusted with the National Republican party under Adams, had broken away to join an odd little party which apparently seemed promising at the moment.

The Anti-Masonic party had its origins in 1826 in the disappearance and suspected murder of a Mason named William Morgan who was planning an exposé of the Masonic order. Suspicion that he had been murdered by fellow Masons aroused the old American hostility to secret societies, and on this issue alone a new party was created which placed its candidate, William Wirt, in the election of 1832. Wirt won a few thousand votes and the party disintegrated. Its historical importance is in the training in grass roots politics it gave to the future leaders of the Whig party, who were determined to out-Jackson Jackson in popular election techniques and who finally succeeded in doing so in the election of 1840.

The bank bill veto could not deprive the bank of its four more years of life, and Jackson's second administration was dominated by the continuing fight and by administration efforts to find some practical alternative to the institution. Jackson removed government funds from the bank and distributed them in "pet" state banks, although he had to replace his Secretary of the Treasury to do it. The withdrawals were necessarily gradual for they would in turn require the bank to call in those loans to private banks which had been made on the basis of the government deposits.

Biddle, for his part, called in loans more rapidly than was necessary in order to create an economic crisis for which the administration would be blamed. Pressure from the business community forced him to stop the practice, and the nation moved swiftly from depression to an inflationary boom encouraged by the added capital provided by government deposits in state banks and by release of state banks from the restraint of the United States Bank.

The government further encouraged the boom by permitting public land to be purchased with paper money issued by the state banks and then permitting the land to be used as collateral for the purchase of further land. In response to the appeals of hard-money men within his party, notably Senator Benton, Jackson in 1836 issued the Specie Circular, requiring gold and silver for the purchase of public land. Then he retired and left the ensuing depression in the hands of his successor.

VI

Rise of the Whigs   Times had never been better, though, than they were during the Presidential campaign of 1836, and the anti-Jackson forces, in the opinion of their younger leaders, were doing nothing constructive to meet the problem of Jackson's popularity. "Our party as at present organized," wrote Thurlow Weed in 1834, "is doomed to fight merely to be beaten. . . . The longer we fight Jacksonianism with our present weapons, *the more it won't die!*. . . . With Clay, Webster, or Calhoun, or indeed any man identified with the war against Jackson and in favor of the Bank, or the Bank's shadow, the game is up." The new Whig party of which he spoke, created out of the bank war and the nullification crisis, was essentially a coalition of the National Republicans who had gone down to defeat with Clay and the broadcloth party of Southern gentlemen.

From the point of view of economic self-interest, the Southern cotton planters probably had less reason to oppose Jackson than they had to oppose the Northern and dominant wing of the new Whig party. They were offended, however, by the vulgar equalitarianism of Jacksonian democracy and by the spirit of assertiveness it engendered in the leathershirt class in the South. And, however much Southern planters outside South Carolina might disapprove of the attempted unilateral nullification of the tariff, they were nevertheless sensitive to any attack upon the principle of state sovereignty, and ever more so as the slave states assumed a smaller and smaller minority position in the nation. Taking the name Whig as the opponents of "King Andrew I," this coalition of Northern high-tariff nationalists and Southern free-trade states righters did what it could to combat the party of popularity.

Clearly the unpopular party and unable to agree on a campaign platform, the Whigs in 1836 attempted to win the Presidency by conducting the election in the manner originally intended by the founding fathers, who, never anticipating the rise of political parties, had supposed that the presidential electors would split their votes among favorite sons, and that the House of Representatives would choose among these. The Whigs ran Webster in New England, William Henry Harrison in the middle states and in the West, Hugh L. White in Tennessee, and Willie P. Mangum in South Carolina (where electors were still chosen by the legislature).

The stratagem failed, for Van Buren received a clear majority of the electoral votes, but it did produce one hopeful omen for the Whigs. Wherever Harrison had run, he had stirred excitement among the people. Long out of the political limelight, Harrison was best remembered for his part in the Battle of Tippecanoe twenty-five years before, where he had managed to avoid defeat at the hands of the wily Indian warriors. With no more than this to recommend him, he had won more than a half million votes. Harrison and some of the younger Whig politicians kept this in mind as the panic of 1837 broke upon the nation. Hopefully, at a time of rising unemployment and business failures, the younger Whigs gathered their strength behind Harrison in the 1840 convention. Amid extravagant praises of the unhappy presidential aspirant Clay, the nomination went to Harrison, while the vice-presidential nomination went to the Virginia aristocrat John Tyler as a sop to the Southern wing of the party.

In the campaign that followed Thurlow Weed was the leading figure. Under him the Whigs developed grass roots organizations and centralized direction. They levied campaign contributions so vigorously as to arouse in Horace Greeley the fear that they would "drive our rich men out of politics." All that was needed was a campaign issue, and this was provided by a campaign slur against

Harrison in a letter to a Baltimore newspaper: "Give him a barrel of Hard Cider, and settle a pension of $2,000 a year on him, and my word for it, he will set the remainder of his days in his Log Cabin, by the side of a 'sea coal' fire and study moral philosophy."

Omitting the damaging charge that their candidate was a student of moral philosophy, the Whig politicians grasped the rest of the statement as an issue entirely sufficient to their purposes. They launched a nationwide circus performance working endless variations on the theme that their candidate was a man of the people, born and living in a log cabin and content to drink hard cider. As for Harrison himself, that dignified country gentleman whom the professionals would have preferred to see stay home moved about the country giving long, meaningless speeches in which he referred from time to time to his log cabin background. In vain did the Democrats protest that Harrison had been to the manner born, while Van Buren was a poor boy who had made good. The Whigs got their point across, and they got out the vote in unprecedented volume. On the basis of a vote more than half again as large as in 1836, the Whigs won handily, even though Van Buren received 400,000 more votes than he had won in his victorious 1836 campaign.

Following his election, Harrison was brought forward by the Whig politicians to deliver an inaugural address which he had written by himself despite Daniel Webster's protests. Harrison, it appeared from his inaugural, wished, as John Adams and John Quincy Adams had before him, to become a patriot President after the model of George Washington. He would select his aides from among the most capable members of society regardless of party, and he hoped that his administrations would be such as to bring an end to party conflict. A month later, exhausted by the furious onslaught of office seekers, President Harrison died of pneumonia, and his place was taken by Vice President Tyler, states'-rights advocate, opponent of the tariff, and enemy to any Whig scheme for the reconstitution of a national bank. After a fruitless struggle to force the Northern Whig program through Congress over Tyler's vetoes, the Whigs in Congress caucussed and wrote their President out of the party. The Northern Whigs had been poorly rewarded for their exertions, but they had learned at last how to make Presidents in democratic America.

Jacksonian democracy began at least as early as the Kentucky

constitution of 1792 and completed itself with the triumph of the
Whigs, by Jacksonian means, in 1840. That this had come to pass
was agreed upon by contemporaries, and upon this point historians
have subsequently remained in agreement. Upon the question of
the meaning of Jackson and Jacksonian democracy, however, the
historians have disagreed almost to the point of chaos.

James Parton, the first scholarly student of the subject, stated
the problem, so far as it concerned Jackson himself, when he
noted that Jackson could be called both

> a patriot and a traitor. He was one of the greatest of generals,
> and wholly ignorant of the art of war. A writer brilliant, elegant,
> eloquent, without being able to compose a correct sentence, or spell
> words of four syllables. The first of statesmen, he never devised,
> he never framed a measure. He was the most candid of men, and
> was capable of the profoundest dissimulation. A most law-defying,
> law-obeying citizen. A stickler for discipline, he never hesitated to
> disobey his superior. A democratic autocrat. An urbane savage.
> An atrocious saint. [Parton plainly meant this as a judgment on
> most Americans as well.]

The democracy that Jackson fronted was at least as unsuscepti-
ble of analysis as was Jackson himself. To the French observer
Alexis de Tocqueville it meant an equalitarian society, stifling to
individual liberty and to individual creative achievement but full
of brute creativeness and energy. Tocqueville, an aristocratic
Frenchman, was so deftly polite about it as to be accepted by the
Americans he criticized, but he was not altogether sympathetic. He
flattered Americans by depicting them as breaking the ground for
the burial place of old, aristocratic, refined civilization. The leading
American historians throughout the nineteenth century came, generally with less *savoir-faire,* to pretty much the same conclusion.
More concerned with the domestic political issues than Tocqueville, they grudgingly conceded to Jackson credit for defending the
integrity of the nation and for standing in favor of free enterprise.
And then they damned him for all else.

It was during the Progressive era, while Beard was unfrocking
the founding fathers, that Jackson was ordained by historians
as a high priest of American democracy. Frederick Jackson Turner
presented him as the epitome of the West, which was to say the
expression of American democracy. Casting aside the questions
which Tocqueville had raised, other historians, notably Vernon

L. Parrington and Claude Bowers, further bolstered Jackson's reputation as a champion of the people against privilege.

The Jackson of the Progressive era entered the New Deal and emerged gloriously once again, but in new raiment. Arthur Mier Schlesinger, Jr., in *The Age of Jackson* (1945) presented the man and the movement as the triumph of the nation's working classes, prefiguring the ideological struggles of the 1930s. In Schlesinger's work the basic struggle between the man and the dollar remained, but the hero in the struggle became the Eastern workingman rather than the frontier farmer.

Schlesinger's book stirred up a hornet's nest, which, as yet, is far from settling itself. Articles have been written to demonstrate that Eastern workingmen—for whatever they were worth politically at the time—were mainly against Jackson. Statewide studies have demonstrated that the Jacksonian Democrats were composed of a conglomeration of disparate and often contradictory elements like any other successful American national party. Bray Hammond has exposed Jackson as the tool of the state banking interests against the United States Bank. Other historians have entered this active arena. John Ward in *Andrew Jackson, Symbol for an Age* (1955), deals with Jackson, as the title indicates, as a catalytic agent in a democratizing America. Marvin Meyers, in *The Jacksonian Persuasion* (1957), sees Jackson as the embodiment of the ancient republican virtues in an America caught in the disturbing throes of the industrial revolution. These writers disagree on much, but there is little disagreement upon the fact that something happened in America at this time which heralded a new order, not only in America, but in the whole world.

BIBLIOGRAPHY FOR CHAPTER FIVE

F. J. Turner's survey, *The Rise of the New West, 1819–1829* (1906), is organized around the author's frontier thesis and remains good and rewarding reading. A more recent general account for the period following is provided by the biographer of various Whig statesmen from New York, G. G. Van Deusen, in *The Jacksonian Era, 1828–1848* (1959), "a clear sound survey of American politics from the first election of Jackson through the election of Zachary Taylor. . . . The reader expecting a [Whiggish and New York] bias will not be altogether disappointed, although it is a bias of emphasis rather than interpretation." Under the circumstances, this is the mildest of criticisms; for, to avoid the charge in this contentious area of American history, it would be necessary to confine one's work to the bare chronology of events. A clear birds-eye view of this long-standing and ever shifting controversy is offered in an excellent anthology edited by James Bugg, *Jacksonian Democracy, Myth or Reality.*

During the past generation the focal point of the controversy has been A. M. Schlesinger, Jr., *The Age of Jackson* (1946). Interesting for its striking thesis concerning the central role of the eastern workingmen in the Jacksonian movement, it is "lively and pungent, written with an attention to epigrammatic conciseness that lends itself to readability, though it is occasionally overstretched in the creation of a flashing phrase."

Marvin Meyers, *The Jacksonian Persuasion* (1957), analyzing the movement through the writings of leading spokesmen, sees as the main theme a desire to return to the golden past of Jeffersonian America. Gilman Ostrander, *The Rights of Man in America, 1606–1861* (1960) sees the movement in its broadest outlines as a majoritarian and equalitarian departure from the relatively more libertarian and aristocratic philosophy of Jeffersonian democracy. A good sampling of what various of the Jacksonians themselves thought they were about is to be found in J. L. Blau, ed., *Social Theories of Jacksonian Democracy* (1947). Lee Benson, *Concept of Jacksonian Democracy: New York as a Test Case* (1961) is an examination of the subject which attacks all the simple generalizations to the point of rendering the term almost meaningless.

Adopting the approach of H. N. Smith's *Virgin Land,* John Ward, *Andrew Jackson, Symbol for an Age* (1955), "has employed the insight provided by the political and intellectual historian, the literary critic, and the political philosopher as effective aids in the examination and evaluation of Andrew Jackson and the society in which he lived . . . a fresh, stimulating and provocative essay in a field that had come to seem barren and worthless from too much cultivation."

Marquis James's biography, *Andrew Jackson: Portrait of a President* (1937), is a vivid, uncritical, and indifferently accurate account with colorful details. M. L. Coit, *John C. Calhoun* (1950) is "Well-written, the product of much research in manuscript collections, newspapers, and contemporary travellers' accounts . . . an excellent synthesis of the life and times of John C. Calhoun . . . a warm, sympathetic account."

An insight into the overshadowed Jacksonian opposition is to be had in Clement Eaton, *Henry Clay and the Art of American Politics* (1957). Its "great virtue is not the presentation of new viewpoints or new materials . . . but rather the skill displayed in selecting pertinent matter from a huge mass . . . and presenting the story in a form and style to please the general reader."

Tocqueville's *Democracy in America* is available, abridged and otherwise, in various paperback editions, the best of which is the two-volume Vintage edition by Phillips Bradley. Tocqueville has overshadowed other contemporary foreign observers whose observations were often equally cogent and usually more amusing. A number of the best of these are in paperback: Michael Chavalier, *Society, Manners and Politics in the United States* (1839), Francis J. Grund, *Aristocracy in America* (1839), Harriet Martineau, *Society in America* (1837), Frances Trollope, *Domestic Manners of the Americans* (1832), and Charles Dickens, *American Notes* (1842).

SOCIETY AND THOUGHT
IN DEMOCRATIC AMERICA

6

I

Social and Economic Change   The United States, still overwhelmingly agricultural when Jackson entered the White
House, was industrializing during the pre-Civil War decades at a
velocity which outdistanced the understandings of contemporaries.
Agrarian America at the opening of the nineteenth century made
its livelihood by methods which did not differ radically from those
employed by its ancient Saxon forebears. Nor had industry per-
ceptibly altered society, outside areas in New England, at the time
Jackson took office. Indeed the decade between 1810 and 1820 experienced a relative decline in the nation's urban population. Society as Thomas Jefferson and John Adams had experienced it had

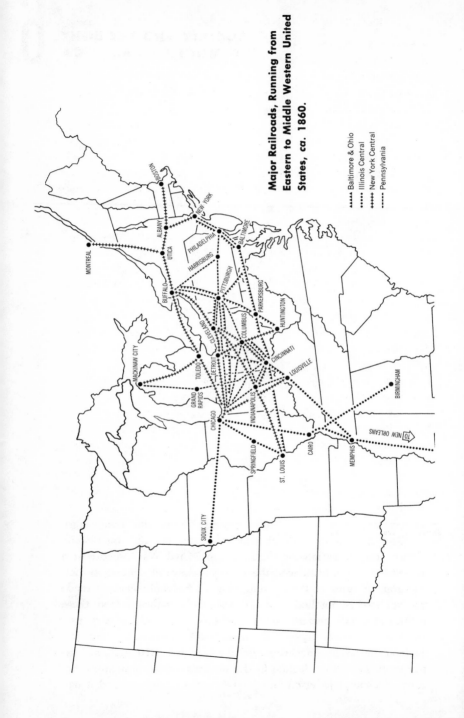

Major Railroads, Running from Eastern to Middle Western United States, ca. 1860.

▲▲▲▲ Baltimore & Ohio
•••• Illinois Central
+++++ New York Central
---- Pennsylvania

BOSTON
NEW YORK
ALBANY
UTICA
MONTREAL
PHILADELPHIA
BALTIMORE
HARRISBURG
BUFFALO
PITTSBURGH
PARKERSBURG
CLEVELAND
COLUMBUS
HUNTINGTON
MACKINAW CITY
DETROIT
TOLEDO
CINCINNATI
LOUISVILLE
GRAND RAPIDS
CHICAGO
INDIANAPOLIS
BIRMINGHAM
SPRINGFIELD
ST. LOUIS
CAIRO
MEMPHIS
TO NEW ORLEANS
SIOUX CITY

remained essentially changeless with respect to the daily rounds necessary to subsistence, and therefore they were bound to suppose that it would continue to be so. Progress for Jefferson meant improvement of conditions as they existed, not the radical alteration of the physical conditions under which men lived.

In the year of Jackson's election as President the last surviving signer of the Declaration of Independence, Charles Carroll of Carrollton, formally declared the coming of the industrial revolution by turning the first spadeful of dirt to begin construction on America's first railroad, the Baltimore & Ohio. From that time to the end of the century, railroad construction continued in America at a pace unheard of elsewhere in the world, providing the main stimulus for the rise of heavy industry in America as elsewhere, but, more than that, in common with canals and improved waterways, opening up nationwide markets to mass purchasers, mass producers, and mass distributors. When it did that, it struck down the ancient, rural economy upon which American society and government had been founded. Commercial farming replaced subsistence farming over large areas, household manufactures were abandoned, local craftsmen were ruined by the country store, and modern America came into being.

Mount Pleasant, Ohio, in 1815 may be taken as typical of American society before the coming of the railroad. A town of five hundred persons, excluding journeymen, laborers, and transients, Mount Pleasant supported three saddlers, three hatters, four blacksmiths, four weavers, six shoemakers, eight carpenters, three tailors, three cabinetmakers, one baker, one apothecary, two wagon makers, two tanners, one manufacturer of wool-carding machines, one operator of a machine for spinning wool, a manufactory for spinning thread from flax, a nail manufacturer, and the operator of two wool-carding machines. Within a six-mile radius there were nine merchant mills, two gristmills, twelve sawmills, one paper mill, and a woolen factory. All of this was in addition to the household manufacturers, where most of these processes were duplicated and where many additional ones were performed. This was the typical homespun economy which the railroad was rapidly obliterating in the 1840s and 1850s.

For farmers who acquired new commercial markets, the development brought a higher standard of living but also diminished independence. Commercial farming brought rich returns during good times and severe hardships during the depression of 1857. But even in good times it brought unwonted reliance upon world market prices and upon other uncontrollable outside economic factors. Naturally unwilling to return to the old simplicities of subsistence agriculture, farmers were outraged to find that they had been robbed of their birthright of independence. In 1858 farmers attended meetings to demand state and federal regulation of railroads, of grain elevators, and of financial institutions. They called for the organization of cooperatives to drive out the thieving middleman and restore to those who labored in the earth the just fruits of their toil. This incipient farmers' revolt was nipped in the bud by war, bumper crops, and soaring farm prices, but the farm protests which made up so much of late nineteenth-century history were clearly foreshadowed in this early reaction.

The craftsman, like the commercial farmer, tended on the one hand, to benefit economically from the industrial revolution in most cases, and, on the other, to feel the loss of the independence he formerly had enjoyed. Earlier in the century it had been customary for the journeyman mechanic, whether a cobbler or a tailor or a saddlemaker, to be paid, not for his hourly labor, but for his "price," that is to say, for the commodity he produced. Typically he had worked on equal terms with a small group which included the proprietor of the shop.

During the forties and fifties a change was taking place which saw the proprietor replaced by a hired manager, the work force increased, the production broken down into specialized operations, and the mechanic paid an hourly wage. When that began to happen, bitter complaints were everywhere raised against "wage slavery." The National Typographical Society declared in 1850, "It is useless for us to disguise from ourselves the fact that, under the present arrangement of things, there exists a perpetual antagonism between Labor and Capital . . . one striving to sell their labor for as much, and the other to buy it for as little as they can."

Craftsmen had organized into local unions as early as the Confederation period. In the nineteenth century they continued to organize locally and on occasion to strike, although strikes and union organizations were considered illegal under common law and subject to criminal action. This legal interpretation began to soften, a landmark in the trend toward union recognition being a prounion decision of the Massachusetts Supreme Court in 1842, Commonwealth *v.* Hunt. The first major interunion activity had taken place in the late twenties when unions in the major cities of the Northeast united and formed Workingmen's parties, influenced by radical intellectuals and supporting broad programs of general reform. These Workingmen's parties existed for but a few years, however, and few of the unions themselves survived the depression of 1837.

Then during the fifties craft unions were organizing once more, this time not to advocate general reform but for the purpose of strengthening the mechanics' bargaining position against the employer. These unions in turn were overwhelmed by the depression of 1857, and labor entered the Civil War in a disorganized and demoralized condition. Unskilled workers, in the meantime, were unable to make the first beginnings at organizations, and they made their grievances known in fruitless, bloody riots. The standard of living of skilled as well as unskilled labor, submarginal by modern standards, was distinctly higher than in England and Western Europe and it tended to rise as the worker moved west from New York to Pittsburgh to Chicago.

At the other end of the economic scale the industrial revolution was providing capitalists with the means to acquire unprecedented riches. Until the coming of the railroad, millionaires had been extreme rarities. At the close of the War of 1812 there were two distinctly rich men, Stephen Girard and John Jacob Astor, and a small handful of others who had stretched their fortunes into seven figures. Millionaires were not at that time numerous enough, however, to form a society of their own. Their numbers, of course, had considerably increased by the eve of the Civil War, but the plutocratic industrialist was still in the future, and commerce remained, as it had always been, the main source of wealth, its possibilities vastly increased by the transportation revolution. Two of the nation's richest men on the eve of the Civil War were H. B. Claflin, the drygoods merchant, and A. T. Stewart, the department store owner.

But while the railroad tycoons had yet to emerge out of the violent process of railroad consolidation, the way was rapidly being prepared for them. During the fifties the Pennsylvania Railroad bought out the competing Pennsylvania canal system, New York Central was formed of seven independent lines, and Baltimore & Ohio extended its system to Wheeling, West Virginia. By 1861

Congress had granted 18,000,000 acres of land to the states for railroad construction, and the Illinois Central had become the chief landowner in Illinois, with the practical prospect of realizing from land speculation those fortunes which during the period of the Articles of Confederation, the operators of the Ohio and Scioto companies had awaited in vain. The first commercial oil well was drilled in the fifties, and the iron ore of the Lake Superior region was mined then for the first time. In 1860, for the first time in the nation's history, the value of mining and industrial production exceeded that of agriculture, although this did not occur again for a number of years.

The most dramatic manifestation of the accelerating change was the rising city. New York doubled its population during the fifties to become a city of more than one million people, and prodigious increases were sustained by the other eastern cities. During the same ten years, Chicago quadrupled, while the port cities of the Great Lakes generally experienced unmanageably swift growths, accompanied inevitably by blatant lawlessness, violence, epidemics, and poverty. Political machines battened on corruption, while desperate problems such as sanitation, slum conditions, and police protection received half-hearted, ill-considered attention. Many who had become otherwise reconciled to democracy were convinced that safeguards against universal manhood suffrage were needed in the cities. Doubts about the possibility of urban democracy were heightened by the fact that the greater part of this new population was acquired from abroad, mainly from Ireland.

Immigration to America, a constant factor during the colonial period, had virtually ceased during the first two generations after the Revolution. Then, with the close of the Napoleonic Wars in 1815, there had been a steady upswing of immigration during the twenties and thirties. The forties saw an abrupt increase, most of it from Ireland and Germany. The German immigration was made up largely of substantial farmers who were able to purchase lands in the Upper Mississippi Valley, transport themselves and their equipment there by way of the Erie Canal, and form themselves into transplanted German communities. This immigration included also a significant number of professional people, many of them refugees from the failure of the German revolutions in 1848. These people were in a position to establish themselves in the newly emerging western cities such as Cincinnati and Milwaukee. The Irish, on the other hand, were helpless victims of the potato famine, the wholesale destruction by disease of their basic source of subsistence. Penniless and starving, the majority of the Irish-American population during the next generation placed itself at the mercy of the steamship company agents, escaped to America and took the first employment offered. The Irish built the canals and railroads, performed sweated labor in the cities, and served as menials in the households of older Americans, who, for these reasons, and on grounds of anti-Catholic sentiment, looked down upon them as inferior beings.

Until the German-Irish immigration, Catholics had made up no more than an insignificant fraction of American society. Even so, anti-Catholic riots had occurred earlier, and anti-Catholic literature had been circulated, warning of concerted "Romish" plans to overthrow Protestant Christian American democracy. Americans were convinced that Protestantism and democracy were two parts of the same thing, while Catholicism and authoritarianism were inseparable. The massive Catholic immigration, therefore, aroused hatreds and fears among native Americans. Nativism bellied forth in 1854 in political victories for the new Know-Nothing party, a party based upon no clearly understood principle except anti-foreign and anti-Catholic sentiment. It immediately gained a national following, winning its main victories in Massachusetts against the Irish and in California against the Chinese. For a time this new party was taken up by many seasoned politicians as the party of the future, but it lacked any positive program or strong organization, and it passed from the scene.

Mid-century American society, while it was celebrating the triumph of its democratic institutions, was undergoing antidemocratic transformations to which its politicians, writers and thinkers remained largely oblivious, with a few diverse exceptions such as John C. Calhoun, Herman Melville, and Horace Mann. The rich were getting richer and the poor, poorer, while those in the middle, the craftsman and the landowning farmer, were bettering themselves economically at the expense of their independence. The immigrants of the new age were providing the original immigrants with a servile class to look down upon, and for the well-to-do among the older Americans they were providing a new index to social status, position in society coming increasingly to be judged by the number of servants in the household.

An observer of American society earlier in the nineteenth century had supposed that "No country of the same wealth, intelligence, and civilization has so few menial servants (strictly speaking) in families of persons of the greatest property," as the United States; and, of the servants that were available, another wrote, "Europeans, especially Englishmen, settling in the United States, who lived decently at home, have a universal complaint to make about the 'impertinence of servants,' meaning chiefly *women* and girls hired to do house work. . . ."

> These girls will not call the lady of the house *mistress* or drop a *curtesy* when honored with a command; and, if they do not like the usage they receive, will be off in an instant, and leave you to manage as well as you can. . . . These girls who behave as they ought, soon get married and raise up families for themselves. This is what they *calculate* upon, and it is this calculation that makes them "saucy."

This kind of independent spirit, which had refused to live below-stairs in the aristocratic Federalist era, was being pushed into the scullery in the age of democracy.

II

Cultural Nationalism — Patriotic American intellectuals shared hopes, far too extravagant for fulfillment, that under free republican institutions the arts and sciences would flourish more richly than under the benighted monarchies of Europe, and in this optimistic mood a crusade for cultural independence followed fast upon the struggle for political independence. "America," declared Noah Webster, "must be as independent in *literature* as she is in *politics*, as famous for *arts* as for *arms*," and the poet Francis Hopkinson was of the opinion that "The world looks toward us as a country that may become a great nursery of arts and sciences." More than that, it was the view of Samuel Cooper that only in America, where liberty "unfetters and expands the human mind," could the sciences really flourish. As the transition took place from an aristocratic to a democratic society, however, these expectations were increasingly disappointed. The democratic temper, in fact, proved vaguely hostile to the arts and sciences; while from the moralistic, evangelical point of view, which was characteristic of democratic America, the pursuit of truth or of beauty simply for its own sake was downright immoral.

Science, however, began to receive a larger place in the college curriculum. In 1802 Benjamin Silliman was appointed professor of chemistry and natural history at Yale and remained for fifty years as the most influential of academic scientists, founding the *American Journal of Science and Art* in 1818. The importance of science continued to increase slowly in the colleges, especially Harvard and Yale; while the Federal government, as well as the state governments, came gradually to provide opportunities for scientific research. The United States Coast Survey, organized in 1832, engaged in important work in geography, geology, biology, and ethnology, while the director of the Naval Observatory and Hydrographic Office, Matthew Maury, gained a distinguished reputation internationally for his work in oceanography. In 1846 Congress used the bequest of an Englishman to found the Smithsonian Institution for the encouragement of research and the maintenance of museums of art and science, appointing the greatest American scientist of the age, Joseph Henry, as its first director.

While democratic America distrusted science for its purity, it distrusted the arts for the opposite reason. The old Puritan hostility to the theater on moral grounds was very much present in the evangelical America of the mid-nineteenth century and naturally inhibited the development of the theater. A number of American playwrights emerged, notably William Dunlap, and more than seven hundred American plays were produced before the Civil War; yet English plays and English actors tended to dominate the American theater. The narrow morality of evangelical America, which was more grimly good in its behavior than the colonial Puritanism ever had been, severely limited subject matter and treatment. A certain amount of low life was permissible on the stage, however, if its purpose was to depict the drunkard's doom, just as novels like *Charlotte Temple,* which went through more than 150 editions, might linger long on the subject of seduction, if the novel served the edifying purpose of demonstrating that the wages of sin were death.

America had little in the way of a classical musical heritage, and in this respect it was almost entirely dependent upon Europe. The one American concert artist who received high recognition in his own country, Louis Moreau Gottschalk, gained it by first making a reputation for himself in Europe, traveling the path which still often remains the shortest one to success in the American musical world. The one American composer to achieve a lasting reputation, Stephen Foster, wrote melodies which were immediately popular, but it was not supposed that he was making a permanent contribution to American music. In architecture the patriotic need was felt for public buildings which would reflect the republican spirit, and a pretentious classicism developed which architects in recent generations have been trying to do something about. America borrowed ideas also from Gothic castles, Norman keeps, Chinese temples, and Swiss chalets without successfully achieving the American forms some of them sought.

In the field of painting, America during the Revolutionary era produced a number of distinguished portraitists, including Benjamin West, John Singleton Copley, and Charles Willson Peale, whose sons, Titian, Raphaelle, Rembrant, and Rubens Peale, themselves became talented artists. Depending for their livings on fairly wealthy sitters, however, these artists did not work in an atmosphere which reflected the republican spirit, and the cause of cultural nationalism was better served in Jacksonian America by a school of *genre* painters, notably William Sidney Mount of Long Island and George Caleb Bingham of Missouri. Taking American scenes as their subject, these artists won wide popularity. Similarly the lithographers Currier and Ives enjoyed enormous popular and financial success by appealing to the American interest in and affection for the scenes of the American nation.

It was in the field of literature that Americans were best equipped by their English background to distinguish themselves, and it was there that they were most ambitious to make their mark. The call for literary independence from England went up with the Revolution and remained a dominant theme of American literary history down to the Civil War. The Jeffersonian newspaper editor, Philip Freneau, in addition to writing reams of political doggerel, composed lyric verse which established him as the leading poet of the early period. Less successful but highly regarded at the time in England as well as America were the more pompous "Hartford Wits," led by Timothy Dwight, president of Yale, celebrating America in elephantine epic poems. America's first professional novelist, Charles Brockden Brown, was conspicuous for his patriotic determination to make his living entirely by writing at the turn of the century, but after a half dozen failures he gave up the attempt.

Probably the most successful effort of this early period to contribute to a distinctly American literature was *Modern Chivalry,* by Judge Hugh Henry Brackenridge of Pennsylvania. A lengthy picaresque novel modeled from *Don Quixote,* it was a delightful lampooning of American democratic society. From the point of view of literary craftsmanship the leading American writer of the day was Washington Irving, whose *Knickerbocker History of New York* appeared in 1809. Irving, in common with a number of his contemporaries, received a warm and ready reception abroad. It was also true of these writers, as of later ones, that critical acclaim from abroad was a prerequisite for acceptance at home. "We do not praise a thing," the poet and newspaper editor William Cullen Bryant, later complained, "until we see the seal of transatlantic approbation upon it."

The War of 1812, accompanied as it was by a warlike attack in the British literary quarterlies on American cultural pretenses, redoubled the desire for literary independence. As the call continued to go forth during the next two generations, two distinct literary capitals emerged in America, which took two fairly distinct attitudes toward the matter. New York produced a distinguished number of writers who were consciously patriotic in their sense of literary mission. Boston produced a perhaps equally distinguished number, who tended to view the bumptious crusade for an American literature with genteel indifference. Boston displayed virtually its entire claim to distinction in the membership of the Saturday Club, organized in the 1850s, which included the poets Henry Wadsworth Longfellow, Oliver Wendell Holmes, Ralph Waldo Emerson, John Greenleaf Whittier, and James Russell Lowell, as well as the novelist, Nathaniel Hawthorne, the historians, John Lothrop Motley and William H. Prescott, and the orator Edward Everett. These members tended to be politically conservative except for Hawthorne, who, as a Jacksonian Democrat, was "on the side of barbarism & vandalism" according to Everett. Two literary figures of the Boston area conspicuous by their absence were the nonconformist poet and essayist Henry David Thoreau and the historian and Jacksonian Democrat George Bancroft.

New York produced a more diverse array of talent over a longer period of time beginning with Freneau, Bryant, Brown, and Irving and continuing with the poet and essayist James Kirk Paulding, the novelists James Fenimore Cooper and Herman Melville, and the poets Walt Whitman and Edgar Allen Poe. Poe, though a Virginian, was chiefly associated with New York in his literary ac-

tivities. These writers were all of them without exception Democratic in politics, and, in various degrees, committed to the fight
for literary emancipation. New York supported its own cliques of
genteel, literary Anglophiles, but these enlisted none of its major
writers.

Cooper, who achieved immediate acclaim with his early novel,
The Spy, remained as popular as he was productive until, disillusioned with American society, he began to write savage criticisms
of American democracy, notably in *The American Democrat.* He
ended his life reviled but still widely read. Melville, similarly,
turned from democratic partisanship to gloomy criticism, notably
in *Mardi* and the later poem, *Clarel.* Popular overnight as a writer
of stories of the South Sea islands, *Typee* and *Omoo,* he lost his
reading public as his writings became increasingly allegorical. His
masterpiece, the Faustian *Moby Dick,* remained virtually unread
for three quarters of a century.

Poe was most influential in his own day as a literary critic. His
reputation as a poet and short story writer was always qualified
because he was thought to be an immoral man and his works were
thought to be unwholesome. He became thereafter important to
French literature, which was influenced by poems such as *The
Raven* and grotesque stories such as *The Fall of the House of
Usher.* Whitman, the writer most robustly dedicated to an indig-
enous American literature, was given the poorest American reception of them all. He was hailed as a great poet by Thoreau
and Emerson, but most of the literary world either ignored him or
denounced him as a writer of dirty and disorganized verse. His
Leaves of Grass, a gargantuan paean concerning all aspects of
American society, appeared in print in 1855, but only because
Whitman was a printer by trade and could put up the type himself. A strong influence on twentieth century poetry, *Leaves of
Grass* alienated Whitman's generation by its unacceptable treatment of sex and by its free verse form.

The Boston group, by contrast, comparatively unoriginal and
always observing the proprieties, enjoyed, on the whole, an early
and continuing success. Oliver Wendell Holmes won popularity
through such easily memorable verses as *Old Ironsides* and *The
Chambered Nautilus.* Longfellow, technically, perhaps, the most
proficient poet of his generation, appealed to the sentimental
America's interest in her own past, in *Paul Revere's Ride* and ap-

pealed to her moralistic nature in verses which affirmed the belief that, "Life is real! Life is earnest! And the grave is not its
goal. . . . " Lowell gained a high reputation both as a critic and
as the writer of a great deal of poetry. His greatest popular success was in the field of plain doggerel: *The Biglow Papers* and *A
Fable for Critics*. The Quaker Whittier, who amply demonstrated
his real genius with his quiet character study in verse, *Snowbound,*
dissipated his talents in polemical writings against slavery, a contentious form of writing for which his gentle style was not well
suited.

Emerson, who probably was at his best as a poet, gained his
greatest popularity as a public lecturer. His lectures were culled
from his daily journals and then refined once more into his essays,
which for the most part were little more than a series of discon-
nected, but often brilliant, aphorisms. The essays gained their artistic unity from their concentration on the one simple theme of
Emersonian transcendentalism: that God exists in all nature, and
that man, in his conduct, is ultimately responsible to his conscience,
or soul, which is an aspect of the omnipresent Divinity. Sometimes spoken of as the philosopher of democracy, Emerson
preached a pantheism and a doctrine of conscientious individualism which was quite unacceptable to the majority of Americans.
He himself was an eloquent speaker and also an obviously devout
and good man, and his respectability was never questioned. His
friend Thoreau, whose life represented transcendentalism in action,
however, was considered a disagreeable character by Emerson's
Boston colleagues. Thoreau's nature essays, especially his *Walden,*
gained steadily in popularity after his death, but during his lifetime his books went largely unread.

Hawthorne had the satisfaction during his lifetime of being
generally acknowledged as America's greatest writer and of hearing his novel, *The Scarlet Letter,* hailed as the greatest work in all
of American literature. It is true that he fell short of being a great
popular success in his own country. Most of his writings were
too dark and allegorical and followed too sternly the theme of
man's duty to society. Hawthorne remained a Puritan in his writings, accepting the Puritan psychology of original sin and moral
determinism while rejecting the theology. His reputation among
such diverse literary figures as Poe and Melville was uniquely
high, each of these men concluding that with Hawthorne Ameri-

can literature had finally achieved an undoubted measure of greatness. It is probably true to say that in the twentieth century Melville's reputation has risen above that of all his contemporaries
including Hawthorne, but in the nineteenth century Hawthorne
was the pride of the literary patriots.

The struggle for cultural independence had been waged with
but indifferent success in the sciences and the fine arts, but in
the field of literature it was brought to a brilliant climax of creativity by the eve of the Civil War. The first five years of the 1850s
saw the appearance of Emerson's *Representative Men,* Hawthorne's
The Scarlet Letter and *The House of Seven Gables,* Melville's
Moby Dick and *Pierre,* Thoreau's *Walden* and Whitman's *Leaves
of Grass.* With the exception of the 1920s no other period in
American literary history rivals this one for creative productivity.

If American writers had won their independence from England,
however, the American reading public had not yet done so. For
its choice in tasteful reading it continued to take its cues from
English criticism, whether of English or American writers. When
it read for pleasure it turned to the "women's books," sentimental
novels by such now forgotten writers as Elizabeth Oakes Smith,
Mary Jane Holmes, Caroline Lee Hentz, and Sarah Josepha Hale.
Hawthorne, who was apparently content on the whole with his
American reception, was moved during one moment of exaspera-
tion to complain that "America is now wholly given over to a
d--d mob of scribbing women, and I should have no chance of
success while the public taste is occupied with their trash. . . ."
It was not until the 1920s that the American reading public freed
itself entirely from dependence upon English literary arbiters and
enthusiastically embraced the writings of the so-called lost generation, with their many-sided literary onslaughts upon American culture.

III

Evangelical Religion   "Religion in America," wrote French observer Alexis
de Toqueville of the Jacksonian period, "takes
no direct part in the government of society, but it must be regarded as the first of their political institutions; for it does not
impart a taste for freedom, it facilitates the use of it. . . ." In common with other foreign observers he was struck by the paradox

that churches in America, receiving no support from the state, nevertheless exerted a much greater influence upon society than did state churches in Europe. They had succeeded in enforcing upon society an outward conformity to the popular religious tenets, whether sincere or hypocritical, which deterred people from doing things which their free institutions permitted them to do. It was this achievement, in Tocqueville's opinion, that made the continuance of the free institutions possible. The Americans about whom he wrote might have rejected so utilitarian a defense of their religious beliefs, but they would certainly agree on the main point. Evangelical Protestantism and democracy had emerged together in the nineteenth century, and in the American view they were two inseparable parts of the same thing.

Organized Christianity had probably exerted less influence upon American society during the first generation of independence than at any other time in American history. It was during this reign of "infidelity"—the spread of religious liberalism among the upper classes and of "nothingism" among the common people—that America established its independent political institutions and organized its Federal government, and it was during this period that the principle of the separation of church and state was won, by men who opposed the pretensions of organized religion as the exclusive custodians of divine authority. Consequently when, in the early nineteenth century, American society was converted to the religions of the Great Revival, the spirit of American society assumed in religion just as it did in politics a character never intended by the founding fathers. Democratic America pledged its allegiance to a different God than the God of the Enlightenment. It worshipped the God of Wrath, accepting the literal word of the Bible and the total depravity of man and viewing human progress single-mindedly in terms of the mysterious process of personal salvation.

Amid this emotional and anti-intellectual torrent, upperclass, literate America retained the religious tradition it had inherited from the Enlightenment. Though in some quarters, especially among the transcendentalists, its religious outlook took on the emotional and irrational coloring of the romantic movement, it nevertheless remained closely akin to the moderate deism of the founding fathers. The religious spirit of American democracy was compounded of these antagonistic liberal and evangelical religious currents. Together they preached the good moral life. Each believed in the perfectibility of man. Each was convinced that America had been especially chosen by divine providence for a special world mission. Each worked in its own way for an American millennium. America belonged to both, and neither was entirely easy with the other.

It was the French Revolution with its cult of reason which had initially inspired the counterattack against religious infidelity. Deism, which formerly had been the religious persuasion of gentlemen, became during the French Revolutionary era, the dogmatic belief of the sort of lower middle class radicals who were associated with the Democratic Societies. Thomas Paine, who had lost some of his American friends by his defense of the French Revolution in his *Rights of Man,* lost more of them with his defense of dogmatic Deism, in his *Age of Reason,* written in France while Paine was himself as thoroughly involved in the French Revolution as he had formerly been in the American one. The association of radicalism in religion with radicalism in politics caused such formerly indifferently dedicated Christians as Hamilton to gain an appreciation of orthodox religion which until then they had lacked. Hamilton even toyed with the idea of a Christian party to combat Jeffersonian tendencies.

In both New York and Massachusetts the Federalist leadership was liberal in religion, and therefore no such conservative alliance as Hamilton envisioned between religion and politics was possible in those states. The Connecticut leadership, however, was orthodox in both spheres, and there at the close of the century Timothy Dwight, president of Yale College, led the crusade for revived religion. Encouraging the revivalism which had been sanctioned by his grandfather Jonathan Edwards, Dwight nevertheless guarded against individualistic tendencies, stressing the duty of obedience to civil and religious authority. Within Connecticut Dwight and his colleagues were wholly successful. In 1816, the year before Dwight's death, the Fairfield County Bible Society could declare that "The present has been emphatically called the age of Bibles and Missionaries. The atheism of Voltaire and his associates, is gone down, almost with their dust to the grave. The blasphemies of Paine are remembered only to be abhorred."

In 1798 the Connecticut Home Missionary Society was formed to carry Calvinism and federalism to the savage West, and, even earlier, Presbyterian missionaries from Hampden-Sydney and

Washington Colleges in Virginia were active in the new Southwest. In 1801 a Plan of Union was drawn up uniting the Congregationalists and Presbyterians for missionary purposes. The advantage, as it turned out, was with the Presbyterians, with their greater organizational strength on the one hand and their lack of reliance upon state support on the other. Congregationalism remained primarily a New England religion which did not transplant well outside its protected area. But even while the arrangement worked to the advantage of the Presbyterians, the resulting "Presbygationalism" resulted in doctrinal and organizational difficulties which left the Presbyterian Church more rent by factionalism, perhaps, than any other frontier religion.

In any case neither sect was a match for the Baptists and the Methodists in the West. Both the Congregationalists and the Presbyterians were too closely associated with the aristocratic doctrine of predestination, and the insistence of both upon formally trained ministers limited them, especially the Congregationalists, to a distinctly eastern and elite ministry, ill at ease and distrusted in western society. On the other hand the Baptists were democratic in both organization and in the belief shared by many, although not by all of them, in the equal opportunity of all to achieve salvation. They chose their preachers from their own members, argued out their own doctrine, and cared for their own souls, as well as for those of their neighbors, in a manner which won the ready approbation of moral Westerners. At monthly meetings attended by all members, the individual churches meted out discipline to erring members. Religious disputes resulted in the splintering into quarreling sects, but, in the case of American religions, in division there was strength.

The Methodist church, similarly preaching the doctrine of salvation open to all, was highly centralized in its organization but generally democratic in local church matters, while the Methodist ministry itself was recruited from among the people it served, without requiring an esoteric training in theology. The anti-intellectual bias was never as pronounced in the Methodist Church as it was in the Baptist one however, and its ministers were obliged to follow a minimum course of study upon which they were examined before they could be ordained.

The camp meeting was the great agency of the evangelical churches, especially the Methodist, for saving souls and winning church members. Thousands of people gathered together for days at a time to sing hymns, drink in the exhortations of the preachers, and work themselves up to the experience of salvation. To the Westerners living among the lonely terrors of frontier life the horrid descriptions of hellfire and damnation touched a responsive chord. The frenzies of revivalistic emotion produced peculiar re-actions—talking in tongues, barking, jerks, running, jumping, and passing out. Such excesses were generally discouraged by church leaders, and yet it was impossible to draw the line between the true experience of salvation and the fraudulent one marked by emotional excesses. The test of salvation came later, after the heated confession of sins, in the orderly life of moral earnestness which characterized the soul truly saved from the burning pit. Re-vivalism at the same time swept the Eastern cities as well. It was in the Broadway Tabernacle in New York that Charles Grandison Finney's preaching exerted the widest influence. By mid-century the Baptists and Methodists made up somewhat more than half of the total membership of the Protestant churches in America.

The impact of the forest environment of upstate New York upon the westward moving heirs to New England Puritanism pro-duced such an intensity of religious enthusiasm that it earned for the area the name of the "burnt-over district." The Anti-Masonic party which came out of this area was almost as much a religious crusade as it was a political organization, and upstate New York sent forth a remarkably large number of the evangelical leaders who led religious revivalism nationally, including the most influential of them all, Charles Finney. Spiritualism came out of this area, convincing many well educated and prominent Americans of the possibility of communicating with the dead through auto-matic writing, seances, and the like. Of more enduring importance were two religious developments in this region which resulted in the permanent formation of the Seventh Day Adventist Church and the Church of Jesus Christ of the Latter Day Saints, or Mor-mon Church.

The founder of Mormonism, Joseph Smith, according to his own account, was told in a vision of the coming of a new dispensation of the Gospel such as had previously occurred following fallings away from true religion. In a subsequent vision the Angel Moroni appeared, revealing gold plates hidden not far from the Smith home, containing the Gospel as it had been given to the ancient Americans. These, Smith said, were later delivered to him and translated into the Book of Mormon in 1830. Founded on the faith that the Book of Mormon was equal in authority to the Jewish Scriptures, the church sent out missionaries through New England and into the West.

Opposition to the church in New York drove the Mormons to Missouri, where bloody warfare with the older settlers brought out the state militia against them. Escaping to Illinois in the winter of 1838 to 1839, the Mormons founded the town of Nauvoo. The church at this time had attracted many more women than men, and in 1843 the practice of polygamy was initiated by Smith, although not officially proclaimed by the church for another decade. Polygamy split the church, aroused the surrounding countryside, and resulted in the murder of Smith, precipitating a struggle over the leadership of the church. Brigham Young won the support of the majority, which shortly thereafter made that remarkable hegira across the plains to the prophesied "Land of Zion" on the shores of the Great Salt Lake. In the 1850s Brigham Young was appointed governor of the Territory of Utah by President Fillmore, and for two generations thereafter the theocracy of Deseret remained a defiant enclave within the United States until the practice of polygamy was discontinued in 1890 and Utah was admitted to the Union as a state six years thereafter.

The Seventh Day Adventist Church developed from the activities of the Millerites, whose leader, William Miller, became convinced from his reading of the Bible that the day of judgment was at hand and that it would occur in 1843 or 1844, when, amid destruction, Christ would descend to earth and separate the saved from the damned. Millennialism, belief in the imminent Second Coming, has had a history almost as old as Christianity. It had been important to orthodox religious thought in New England at the turn of the nineteenth century, the question as to the exact time of the Second Coming being a subject of lively debate between theological and intellectual leaders such as Timothy Dwight. Thereafter it gradually ceased to command the attention of the scholarly world. Nevertheless Miller's views were far from being novel, except perhaps in the nearness of the predicted date. Miller attracted a large following, much of which remained after the failure of the predicted Second Coming to take place. Eventually the Millerites formed themselves in a number of different sects of which Seventh Day Adventism became the most numerous.

IV

Humanitarian Reform The millennialist spirit, of which Millerism was the most direct and dramatic manifestation, in one form or another permeated American social thought in the mid-nineteenth century. For some, like Miller and Joseph Smith and like Alexander Campbell, the founder of the Christian Church, it was a literal belief. For others it was a metaphorical truth, translated by them into a faith in the perfectibility of society, or at least of American society, through application of the true principles of Christianity and of democracy.

The belief that Americans were the new chosen people and that America was destined to become a heaven on earth inspired a bewildering variety of reforms and panaceas. "We are all a little wild here with numberless projects of social reform," Emerson wrote Carlyle in 1840. "Not a reading man but has a draft of a new Community in his waistcoat pocket." At a convention in Boston of the Friends of Universal Reform, Emerson found "Madmen, madwomen, men with beards, Dunkers, Muggletonians, Come-outers, Groaners, Agrarians, Seventh Day Baptists, Quakers, Abolitionists, Calvinists, Unitarians, and Philosophers. . . ." There were phrenological enthusiasts who would achieve the social millennium by molding children's heads in such a way as to eliminate mental evils and foster socially benign thought processes. There were others who would harness mesmerism or animal magnetism or phrenomagnetic manipulation or the principle of amativeness to the perfection of society.

It was the confident view of these reformers that the application of the one principle they advocated was sufficient to make over the world. Sylvester Graham, the dietary reformer, for instance, did not see the goal of his crusade as limited to the mere improvement of the health of the nation. Dietary reform, Graham asserted, "lies at the foundation of all others" as the basis for the perfect society. Nor were these hopeful faddists generally to be found on the lunatic fringe of society. More often it was among the better educated American idealists that they won their earliest and warmest supporters.

The most extreme manifestations of this millennial hopefulness were the utopian communities which sprang up throughout the nation in the 1840s as pilot experiments which would lead the way to a general utopian reform of society. In 1825 Robert Owen, the English industrialist, at New Harmony, Indiana, founded such a community, which was swiftly disrupted, partly through internal dissension but more through popular reaction to Owen's criticism of those two most basic American institutions, private property and marriage. It is indicative of the boundless optimism which characterized the utopians that Owen should have supposed this sober-sided American society to "have been prepared in the most remarkable manner for the New System" which by popular American standards was one of licentious, atheistic communism.

A generation later the most numerous among the socialist experiments were those forty or more which were based upon a mathematically exact plan of society drawn up by the French utopian socialist Charles Fourier upon the fundamental assumption of the social benevolence of unrestrained human passions. Among the utopian communities, Brook Farm gained lasting fame from its association with leading literary figures in New England, but almost all of them passed rapidly from the scene. In practice they had been nowhere nearly as wild as they were in theory. Their utopian socialism was a world apart from the scientific socialism of class warfare which Karl Marx was formulating in Europe, and their freedom from restraint in most cases was based upon the confident assumption that, if a person were properly brought up, he would naturally behave himself without being told to.

There were also more hardheaded reformers who doubted that dietary reform would end war and crime and who saw that the tasks confronting American idealists were daily becoming more difficult as the nation underwent increasingly rapid industrialization and urbanization. On the whole, however, idealistic Americans concerned themselves remarkably little with the sweeping changes through which they were living. Massachusetts, the most highly industrialized of the states, was also a main center for humanitarian reform; yet, exceptional were the reformers like Horace Mann who saw the need for radical measures to cope with the problems of the industrial revolution. To many idealistic Americans the Catholic immigrant was a dark threat to the vision of a pure Protestant Christian democracy; while the festering sores of the multiplying city slums were the consequence, not of social and economic factors, but of sin and sloth, to be cured only through the moral improvement of the slum dwellers.

Charity was a Christian duty, and aid to the starving was therefore extended. Robert M. Hartley, secretary of the New York Association for Improving the Condition of the Poor, probably was the most effective administrator of philanthropy of his day; yet he was moved to dedicate his life to the cause by a sense of Christian duty unsupported by any real sympathy for what he called the "debased poor." These, he said, "love to clan together in some out-of-the-way place, where they are content to live in filth and disorder with a bare subsistence, provided they can drink, and smoke, and gossip, and enjoy their balls, and wakes, and frolics, without molestation." Some others, such as the Unitarian minister Theodore Parker, took a much more sympathetic attitude, but even Parker was at a loss to suggest any solution except more charity and understanding. Poverty was an affront to the American faith in the efficacy of self-help. America ideally was the land of opportunity for all who would live according to the Gospel and who were willing to put an honest hand to the plow. Mid-century American humanitarianism was nourished by America's rural past, and it was handicapped by this orientation in its efforts to attack the evils of industrial society.

Revived by the advance of democracy and lashed by the panic of '37, the humanitarian reform movements which had been initiated during the Revolutionary era reached a climax of activity in the forties and fifties. During this period the elimination of the prison penalty for indebtedness was completed along with numerous additional reforms in the state penal codes. In most states the death penalty was eliminated for dozens of crimes, while punishments such as branding, cutting out the tongue and cropping the ears were widely abolished. Widespread prison reform resulted in better living conditions for prisoners, although treatment remained harsh. Special and more humane treatment of the insane was achieved in Massachusetts under the instigation of the Unitarian reformer Dorothea Dix, and it was emulated in other states. More impressive than these were the reforms achieved in the field of education, reforms which were especially congenial to the American ideal of self-help.

Early nineteenth-century public education differed widely from state to state. New England had originally established a strong public school system, but its motivation had been strongly theological, and it had declined with the declining authority of religion, private schools emerging in its place for those who could afford them. South of New England there existed mixed systems of public, parochial, and charity schools. Generally speaking, a boy in the middle states stood a better chance of gaining a basic education than one from the Southern and Western states and stood a poorer chance than a boy from New England. In the Northwest Territory the Confederation government, in the Ordinance of 1875, had provided a method whereby the settlers would support their own educational system, but the law rarely had been acted on in good faith. Education was least well provided for in the Deep South and remained so down to the Civil War.

Revitalizing of public education occurred in New England under the leadership of Horace Mann of Massachusetts and Henry Barnard of Connecticut and Rhode Island. Mann argued that, education being necessary for the maintenance of a Christian republic, it must follow that "the property of this commonwealth is pledged for the education of all its youth, up to such a point as will save them from poverty and vice, and prepare them for the adequate performance of their social and civil duties." Amid bitter clerical quarrels over the question of religious instruction, Mann won his point in Massachusetts against businessmen who did not want to be taxed and farmers who did not want to lose temporarily the labor of their sons. New England by the eve of the Civil War provided the pattern for public education which was being emulated in varying degrees elsewhere in the nation. Girls shared to some extent in the programs of elementary education, but they were initially barred from the colleges. Troy Female Seminary was opened in 1821, and a number of additional women's colleges were established prior to the Civil War. Oberlin College became coeducational in 1833, and other institutions, especially state colleges, followed suit.

The temperance crusade was among the most popular reforms of the day, drawing its strength mainly from the evangelical churches and preaching of the coming millennium when drunkenness, the one main source of society's ills, had been washed from the land. Beginning early in the century as a true temperance movement to convert society to sobriety through voluntary moderation or personal abstinence, it turned from voluntarism to the objective of legal prohibition in the 1840s, after a long discouraging struggle with stubborn drinkers and weak backsliders. The first legislative success was the Maine prohibitory liquor law in 1846. Encouraged by this, the prohibitionists passed "Maine laws" during the next decade throughout New England, in Delaware, Indiana, and in the territories of Minnesota and Nebraska. To the corresponding secretary of the American Temperance Union it seemed that total victory was in sight. "The North will not give up," he declared, "and the South keep not back; and men in other countries are already hailing and welcoming this as one of those moral revolutions which occur, under God, in the course of ages, to root out sin and sorrow, and usher in millennial glories."

That year of 1855 proved to be the high point of success, however. With the slavery controversy, the Civil War, and the postwar Gilded Age, prohibition lost the ground it had gained and did not recover its initiative for another generation. Most of its leading advocates were also abolitionists. Indeed the antiliquor and antislavery crusades were united in the minds of many evangelical reformers as the "twin evils" of the age, the two main impediments to salvation; for the drunkard, like the slave, was deprived of the freedom necessary for the regeneration of his soul. When the slavery controversy came to dominate American politics and abolition came to be seen as the most important of all national reforms, the temperance movement lost the urgency it had formerly had among many of its own chief spokesmen.

V

Abolitionist Movement The abolitionist movement developed in the 1830's, but the conservative antislavery movement had begun during the Revolution and had been nationwide in scope. Southern gentlemen during the Age of Enlightenment had shared a vision of humane and happy society, which entailed abolition of the barbarous, inhumane, degrading institution of slavery. Slaveholders such as Washington, Jefferson, Madison, and George Mason had addressed themselves earnestly to correcting this evil, but they were never able to advance beyond the hopelessly impractical and equally inhumane solution of wholesale expulsion to Africa. The American Colonization Society, organized to send freed Negroes to Liberia, absorbed the devoted attention of Southern humanitarians, while at the same time demonstrating completely the futility of this most advanced Southern solution to the problem.

Southern disapproval of slavery in the late eighteenth century was fortified by unfavorable economic conditions. In the worn-out tobacco lands of the Chesapeake region, the institution had become unprofitable—in fact a terrible burden—to slaveholders, who were obliged to maintain their slaves, even when profitable employment for them could not be found. In the nineteenth century, however, this economic problem vanished in the face of the expanding cotton economy and, to a lesser extent, the acquisition of sugar plantations with the Louisiana Purchase. The invention of the cotton gin and the introduction of a new strain of cotton at the close of the eighteenth century opened up a cotton bonanza which increased prodigiously in the forty years preceding the Civil War. The cotton plantation, extending itself rapidly through the Southern wilderness, once again provided profitable employment for the multiplying slave force, which reached 3,500,000 by the Civil War period, out of a total Confederate population of nine million. In the fifties the price of slaves was on the rise, and demands were being made for a reopening of the African slave trade, legally closed in 1808 in accordance with the ruling originally written into the Constitution.

In 1832 the Virginia House of Burgesses conducted one final discussion concerning the possibility of abolishing slavery. Frightened by the bloody Nat Turner slave insurrection in Southhampton County, Virginia, the legislature sought for a solution, and then gave it up altogether as, indeed, the Deep South had done from the first. In an influential report on the question, Thomas R. Dew, a professor at William and Mary College, examined slavery from the point of view of history, of the nature of civilization, and of religion. He found the institution to be essential to civilization, in complete accord with international law, and enjoying the support of Biblical authority. During the next generation Southern scholars and ministers devoted their energies to documenting and amplifying Dew's argument. The most important of these later writers, George Fitzhugh, advanced beyond Dew to assert the racial inferiority of the Negro, as Dew had not done, and to derive a further main argument from this.

The South self-consciously reoriented its political and legal institutions accordingly. Southern constitutions no longer declared their governments to be founded on the self-evident truth that all men were created equal and endowed with inalienable rights. The new Southern constitutions followed the new form of declaring that all freemen, when they form a social compact, are equal in rights. Those outside the compact had the right to life and to virtually nothing else. The states proceeded to legislate new systems of laws rigidly defining the place of the slave in society and narrowing the degree of freedom he might be allowed by his master. The "peculiar institution" of slavery varied greatly according to region and according to master on the eve of the Civil War, but the tendency was toward an even stricter control.

On January 1, 1831, William Lloyd Garrison in Boston printed the first issue of *The Liberator*, declaring, "I shall strenuously contend for the immediate enfranchisement of our slave population. . . . I am in earnest—I will not equivocate—I will not excuse—I will not retreat an inch—AND I WILL BE HEARD." Garrison was an agitator, out to stir up hatred of slavery in the complaisant North. With no practical program and for a long time no organization of his own, he demanded immediate and unconditional emancipation. He was heard, and more widely in the South than in the North. His writings, reprinted in Southern newspapers, did much to convince the South of what it was ready to believe, that all Northerners were abolitionists and that all abolitionists were violent fanatics. In New England Garrison won the support of a rather small but highly valuable following, including literary figures such as Emerson who, refusing to join abolitionist organizations, nevertheless lent their talents to the cause.

A second equally dedicated but more moderate abolitionist movement began in the early thirties under the leadership of a follower of Charles G. Finney, Theodore Weld, who with two wealthy New York philanthropists, the Tappan brothers, founded the American Anti-Slavery Society in 1833. Moving West, Weld for a time attended Lane Seminary in Cincinnati and then was expelled for his abolitionist leanings. Removing to Oberlin with likeminded students, Weld transformed that college, soon to receive Finney as president, into the most important ministerial training ground in the nation for abolitionist leaders. Closely associated with the Quakers, Weld and his followers advocated a program of gradual, compensated emancipation, which would achieve abolition without singling out the slaveholders to make the sacrifice for a cause which was the responsibility of the whole nation. Southerners, however, refused to make distinctions among varieties of abolitionists.

The abolitionists recruited some of their most effective supporters from the South, notably the Quaker Grimké sisters from South Carolina and James G. Birney from Kentucky and Alabama. These left the South, necessarily, for by the thirties the slightest hint of antislavery sentiment had ceased to be tolerated there. This was true of the upper South also. There were few Southern abolitionists —if indeed there was any other—like big Cassius Marcellus Clay of Kentucky, who fortified his newspaper office with cannon, kept his bowie knife handy and occasionally in use, and stayed put. Even in the North, to be an avowed abolitionist was to be in constant danger of mob violence. Down to the outbreak of the Civil War Northern opinion was violently against the abolitionists and expressed itself repeatedly in mob actions against antislavery meetings and known abolitionists.

Until the Kansas-Nebraska Bill of 1854, when the issue of slavery once again became one of its extension into the free West, the most widespread opposition to the system in the North was based, not upon the institution itself, but upon limitations on Northern rights demanded by Southerners for the purpose of defending their institution. When Southern congressmen passed a "gag rule" in the House prohibiting the presentation of antislavery petitions, Representative John Quincy Adams fought it year in and year out until he aroused Northern sentiment to enforce its repeal in 1844.

And when Southern slave-catchers pursuing runaway slaves used the broad terms of the Federal law of 1793 to return South with Northern free Negroes instead, the Northern states, some of which had passed laws prohibiting the immigration of free Negroes in the first place, passed "personal liberty" laws which made the identity of a runaway slave virtually impossible to establish legally. The invalidation of such laws by the Southern-dominated Supreme Court aroused the indignation of Northerners who were little concerned about the plight of the distant and racially unacceptable slaves. The abolitionists appealed to the rights of Northern whites in the case of the gag rule and the personal liberty laws, and they did so again in the cases of the new fugitive slave law of 1850 and the Kansas-Nebraska act of 1854. By these tactics they were successful at last in broadening one important aspect of the antislavery cause into a popular movement.

BIBLIOGRAPHY FOR CHAPTER SIX

T. C. Cochran and William Miller, *The Age of Enterprise: A Social History of Industrial America,* revised edition (1961) is an interesting account of the impact of the developments in business and industry upon society and thought. Roger

Burlingame, *The March of the Iron Men* (1938) covers somewhat the same subject in a more popular vein.

V. W. Brooks has written a chatty series of books on the whole course of American literature, of which one, *The Flowering of New England* (1936) is in paperback. Here the Concord transcendentalists and the Boston Brahmins are seen intimately in their natural habitats. Edmund Wilson, ed., *The Shock of Recognition: The Development of Literature in the United States Recorded by the Men Who Made It* (1943) vol. I, is a collection of essays about writers by other writers, which provides insights into the literary aspirations of the period. O. B. Frothingham, *Transcendentalism in New England* (1896) has been reprinted, as the most complete study of the transcendentalists. Perry Miller, ed., *The Transcendentalists* is an anthology. V. L. Parrington, *The Romantic Revolution in America, 1800–1860* (1927) is the second volume of the trilogy, which places the literature of the period in the social context.

A. F. Tyler, *Freedom's Ferment: Phases of American Social History to 1860* (1944) is a straightforward, comprehensive account of the main humanitarian and utopian movements. H. S. Commanger, ed., *The Era of Reform, 1830–1860* (1960) is an equally comprehensive, although snippety, documentation of these movements.

E. B. Greene, *Religion and the State: The Making and Testing of an American Tradition* (1941) is a brief historical account of a currently contentious subject about which remarkably little is known. The literature concerning the enormously important developments in evangelical religion has not been accorded paperback honors except for the *Autobiography* of Peter Cartwright, the salty narrative of a hardhitting frontier Methodist preacher.

I

Westward Expansion
Considering the overriding influence of the westward movement in the nation's history, the Federal government concerned itself little with its Western possessions during the early years of the nineteenth century. President Jefferson, it is true, an enthusiastic westward expansionist, planned a scientific expedition overland to the Pacific in 1803, remarkably enough while Louisiana Territory was still a French possession. Under direction of two army officers, Meriwether Lewis, and William Clark, the expedition set forth from St. Louis in May, 1804, ascending the Missouri River during the next six months into North Dakota. After a winter among the Mandan Indians the party con-

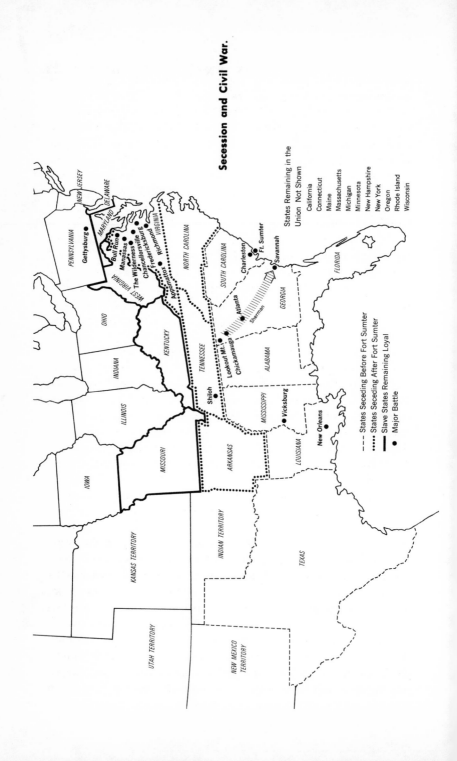

Secession and Civil War.

PENNSYLVANIA
Gettysburg

NEW JERSEY

MARYLAND
DELAWARE

OHIO

WEST VIRGINIA

VIRGINIA
Bull Run
Manassas
The Wilderness
Chancellorsville
Fredericksburg
Richmond
Appomattox

NORTH CAROLINA

SOUTH CAROLINA
Charleston
Ft. Sumter

INDIANA

ILLINOIS

KENTUCKY

TENNESSEE
Lookout Mt.
Chickamauga
Shiloh

Atlanta
Sherman
Savannah

GEORGIA

ALABAMA

IOWA

MISSOURI

ARKANSAS

MISSISSIPPI
Vicksburg

LOUISIANA
New Orleans

FLORIDA

KANSAS TERRITORY

INDIAN TERRITORY

TEXAS

UTAH TERRITORY

NEW MEXICO TERRITORY

States Remaining in the
Union Not Shown
California
Connecticut
Maine
Massachusetts
Michigan
Minnesota
New Hampshire
New York
Oregon
Rhode Island
Wisconsin

- - - States Seceding Before Fort Sumter
· · · States Seceding After Fort Sumter
――― Slave States Remaining Loyal
● Major Battle

tinued on during the next year to the mouth of the Columbia. The return trip to St. Louis was made by September, 1806. Hugely successful, returning with rich geographical and scientific information, the expedition was followed by others during Jefferson's second administration, but nothing approaching systematic and comprehensive exploration was undertaken. Then in 1819, the year of the Transcontinental Treaty, an expedition was sent out which reported the Great Plains to be a great American desert, unfit for habitation. Thereafter for another generation the government mainly left western settlement to the free enterprise of trappers, farmers, and missionaries.

The idea of the gradual expansion of the nation to transcontinental proportions was one which, in the opening years of the century, seemed almost too fantastic for consideration. There were many who had had doubts about the feasibility of maintaining a republic on the scale of the original thirteen states, not to speak of extending it to the Pacific. Even Jefferson, while envisioning the gradual movement of farmers into the vast West, did not see this in terms of an eventual transcontinental nation, but rather as "free and independent Americans, unconnected with us but by the ties of blood and interest, and employing like us the rights of self-government." The governing on representative principles, of a nation which took months to traverse, presented unimaginable obstacles. Even so ardent an expansionist as Senator Thomas Hart Benton of Missouri looked upon the Rockies as marking inevitably the Western limits of the nation, until the coming of the railroad changed his ideas.

The Mexican government, completing its long struggle for independence from Spain, had incomparably less reason than the United States for supposing that it could assert its authority effectively over an even more extensive territory extending from Upper California to Central America. The Spanish missions in much of this area were secularized following Mexican independence and the garrisons withdrawn and, lacking an expansive population of its own, the Mexican government granted concessions to foreigners who would nominally pledge their allegiance to the new nation. To Moses Austin of Connecticut, Pennsylvania, Virginia, and Missouri, it bestowed a large territorial concession in Texas, confirmed by the Mexican Congress in 1823 and settled in that year by Moses' son Stephen. Within a decade the American colony, under the strict proprietary rule of Stephen Austin, had increased to 20,000. Austin appears to have taken his Mexican citizenship seriously, but in the thirties the American settlement swelled beyond his ability to control it, and the antislavery policy of the Mexican government threatened the slave property of the many immigrants.

In 1835 President Santa Anna of Mexico abolished the federal form of government, prohibited further American immigration, and made large grants in Texas to Mexican supporters. The Americans thereupon formed a provisional government of their own against which Santa Anna promptly rode at the head of the Mexican army. At the Alamo in 1836 he wiped out the entire garrison of 200 men and moved on to complete the destruction of the new Lone Star Republic. A Texan army under Sam Houston was waiting for him at the San Jacinto River, however, and the resulting American victory brought the war to a conclusion. Santa Anna himself was captured, and he never again attempted to regain the Texan province. Houston was elected president of the republic, which requested admission to the United States.

During the negotiation of the Transcontinental Treaty John Quincy Adams had been the nation's most forceful advocate of the acquisition of Texas from Spain. In 1836, however, Adams, now in the House of Representatives, was a leading opponent of the extension of slavery. By that time the new Northern sentiment to which Adams appealed naturally opposed the acquisition of new slave territory. Under the circumstances, President Jackson remained cautiously correct in his dealings with Texas, extending it American recognition following congressional approval on his last day in office. President Van Buren opposed annexation out of deference to antislavery sensibilities, and the Texan government thereupon began to approach France and England for the political support which they had been denied by the United States. Under these new circumstances, and with Tyler of Virginia as President and Calhoun of South Carolina as Secretary of State, Congress was persuaded to annex Texas in 1845 by a joint resolution.

The nation, which in the election of 1844 confronted the issue of Texan annexation, faced also the much longer-standing issue of whether to annex Oregon country and, if so, how much of it to annex. During more than two generations of Canadian border controversies with England, the American governments had taken an attitude almost of indifference toward the question of the Pacific

Northwest. Despite the good American claims to it, it had seemed so far away as to appear impossible of absorption into the American republic. Little was known about it, but on the basis of the scanty available reports it was not thought to be an especially inviting country. More serious, meanwhile, were the eastern border disputes, marked by violence and threats of war along the northern frontiers of New York, Vermont, and Maine.

From 1798 to 1842 British and American commissions worked to reach agreements on boundary lines which had been so ambiguously worded in the treaty of 1783 and which at the same time had been based upon much inexact geographical knowledge. The close of the War of 1812 found little accomplished, and newly appointed commissions continued discussions leading to an arbitration by the King of the Netherlands which the United States refused to accept. Border relations continued uneasily, threatening to disrupt into war in 1837. In that year Canadian troops sank the American steamship *Caroline* on the American side of the Niagara River, and the state of New York tried, but acquitted, one Alexander McLeod, over British protests. This was followed in 1839 by the informal Aroostook War between American and Canadian lumberjacks, and again rising war sentiment. Both the British and the American governments were peaceably disposed, however, and Lord Ashburton arrived from England determined to arrive at a final settlement.

The resulting Webster-Ashburton Treaty of 1842 split the difference between the British and American claims concerning the Maine boundary, despite better evidence for the American contention, and then accepted the American position concerning the northern boundary of Vermont and New York, despite the fact that this position was based upon an inaccurate survey. The solution was facilitated by the fact that each side held secret possession of a map which favored the claims of the opposing nation. In 1933 a further map was discovered, indicating that the American claims regarding the Maine boundary had, in fact, been correct.

Settlement of the Oregon question, meanwhile, hinged from the English point of view largely upon the business policy of the Hudson's Bay Company, which, in 1821, had received a monopoly of trading rights in the Northwest. Interested primarily in the fur trade, the Hudson's Bay Company was anxious to discourage the settlement of farm communities, whether British or American, in the fur bearing regions of the Northwest. Although the English were in the area earlier than the Americans, the Americans had the better claim to the territory south of the Columbia River, on the basis of Captain Gray's discovery of the Columbia in 1792 (weakened by the lack of evidence that he claimed it officially in the name of the United States) and the Lewis and Clark expedition, which had explored the area in the next decade. These good American claims were strengthened in 1819 by acquisition of the Spanish claims, extending back to the Papal bull of 1493 and buttressed by subsequent Spanish explorations.

The main early American effort to occupy the region was the establishment by John Jacob Astor of the trading post of Astoria. With the outbreak of the War of 1812, however, Astor was obliged to sell out to the more powerful British interests in the area. Several unsuccessful American attempts at settlement in the 1830s served to publicize the area as potentially rich in agriculture, abounding in fish and game, and providing the forest environment to which American settlers had been accustomed during two centuries of farming. Of special influence was the missionary Jason Lee who settled in the Willamette Valley in 1834.

Government in Oregon until 1843 was provided by the Hudson's Bay Company under the direction of Dr. John McLoughlin at Fort Vancouver. McLoughlin followed a friendly policy toward American settlers, while at the same time using his influence to direct them to areas south of the Columbia River, the vague British-American agreement concerning the territory being at that time the temporary one of "joint occupation." In 1842 the first extensive American migration took place along the Oregon Trail through Laramie and South Pass in Wyoming. In 1843 these settlers in the Willamette Valley established their own provisional government, and in 1844 their numbers had increased to about 2,500. With the area ruined for the fur trade by farmers, the Hudson's Bay Company withdrew its headquarters to Vancouver Island, and the main British motive for delaying final settlement was removed. Until this point the American government, its attention focused on Texas, had largely ignored the fact of American settlement of Oregon, although Webster and Ashburton had discussed the question informally in 1842. Then the rising volume of migration along the Oregon Trail thrust the question abruptly into politics and joined it to the controversy concerning admission of Texas in the election campaign of 1844.

II

War with Mexico   In the election of 1844 the seasoned politicians Henry Clay and Martin Van Buren, still fighting the old bank war, were caught unaware by the enthusiasm for expansion. Consequently they were done out of the Presidency by a comparatively little known congressman from Tennessee, James K. Polk, running on the program of extending the national borders north, south, and west. As former governor of Tennessee and then Speaker of the House, Polk was far from being entirely a political unknown, it is true. Nevertheless he was the first dark horse in American election history, winning the nomination with the support of Jackson after the failure of Van Buren to receive the required two-thirds vote of the convention. Polk won the election in a close contest which would have gone the other way had not Clay lost sufficient votes in New York to an abolitionist candidate, James G. Birney of the Liberty party, to throw that state, and with it the nation, to Polk.

Although Polk was a Southern slaveholder, he was, like the slaveholder Jackson, a thoroughgoing nationalist who refused to be influenced by the slavery controversy in his expansionist aims. During the campaign the annexation of the free territory of Oregon had been rather secondary to admission of slaveholding Texas as a political issue. Robbed of the credit for acquiring Texas, Polk moved single-mindedly and with complete effect toward his other expansionist objectives, in areas where slavery was highly unlikely to penetrate. His first act was to reach agreement with England concerning the Oregon question, in order to free himself for his more grandiose designs against Mexico.

Despite extravagant claims made on both sides during the half century that the Pacific Northwest was under discussion, the area really at issue had been the area from the Columbia River north to the 49th parallel including the southern tip of Vancouver Island. The Americans had at one point agreed to the 49th parallel, and when the British Foreign Minister suggested this line except for the British retention of all of Vancouver Island, Polk was happy to accept. Amid a certain amount of aggressive talk about "54°40' or fight," which didn't mean much of anything, the treaty was ratified by Congress in 1846, in the same year that the Mormons set forth from Nauvoo for the promised land of the Great Salt Lake.

Although little had been said about it during the campaign, it was the rich and mysterious land of California more than anything else that fired Polk's ambitions for America's larger future. Of California little was definitely known at the time Polk became President. In 1840 Richard Henry Dana, Jr.'s *Two Years before the Mast* had appeared giving a detailed account of southern California life and glimpses of the San Francisco Bay region. In 1844 John C. Fremont gained a reputation as a modern Marco Polo by his account of his California travels, and the American consul in Monterrey, California, Thomas O. Larkin, was doing his best to acquaint the government with its Far Western opportunities. To the vision of the apparent richness and variety of California was joined the old dream of the Western route to Cathay. That the San Francisco Bay provided excellent harbor facilities was universally attested to; while by 1846 the practicality of a transcontinental railroad was past doubt. With the acquisition of California, and whatever intervening territory existed, the quest of Columbus would be brought to a most successful conclusion by President James K. Polk.

Attempts had already been made during the administrations of Jackson and Tyler to purchase California from Mexico, but what was now known was that Mexico was hardly even in possession of the land. The Catholic missions, through which the Spanish had extended their control, had lost their authority, and power was exerted locally by individual land barons such as the Swiss-American, John A. Sutter, in the Sacramento Valley. That France or England was prepared to capture California was a fear, fully justified in the case of England, which gave urgency to Polk's aims. In 1845 he sent John Slidell to Mexico with the authority to buy Upper California and points east. When the Mexican government would not receive Slidell, a California revolution was arranged at the suggestion of the Polk administration by American and pro-American settlers under the leadership of Larkin, only to be spoiled by the intervention of the exuberantly incompetent Fremont. Fremont later joined in a second effort which established the Bear Flag Republic, but by that time Mexico and the United States were already at war.

Following the Mexican rejection of Slidell, Polk ordered General Zachary Taylor into territory disputed with Mexico between the Nueces River and the Rio Grande. In April, Mexican troops attacked some of Taylor's men. In May, Polk sent a war message to

Congress declaring that the Mexicans had shed American blood on American soil. Congress responded overwhelmingly with a declaration that war existed between the two countries. So little was known about the vast territory of Utah, New Mexico, and California which Polk proposed to acquire, that his strongest support came from the slave states and strongest opposition from Northern antislavery opinion, although as it turned out the whole region was geographically destined to be free territory.

California was quickly placed under American control through the naval action of Commodore Sloat at Monterrey and the taking of San Diego and Los Angeles by Colonel Kearny, marching overland from Independence, Missouri. The main line of attack against Mexico under the command of General Zachary Taylor, meanwhile, was south from the Rio Grande to Mexico City. A brilliant victory by Taylor at Monterrey made him a possible Whig presidential candidate, and Polk altered the main strategy to an attack on Mexico City west from Vera Cruz under the direction of General Winfield Scott. While Taylor was beating Santa Anna in the north at Buena Vista, Scott captured Vera Cruz in March 1847, won a major victory in the battle of Churubusco in front of Mexico City in August and a month later stormed the hill of Chapultepec and occupied the Mexican capital.

Following the victories at Buena Vista and Vera Cruz, Polk sent the chief clerk of the State Department, Nicholas Trist, with Scott's army to negotiate the peace. Polk's terms were the Rio Grande boundary, cession of New Mexico and California, and right of transit across the Isthmus of Tehuantepec. Scott arranged an armistice for negotiations, invading Mexico City afterwards when Santa Anna decided, on the basis of the terms, to return to the fight. Trist, recalled by Polk following the breaking of the armistice, remained against instructions to negotiate the treaty of Guadalupe Hidalgo in February 1848, by which the Mexicans capitulated to Polk's terms. Polk, in turn, against a rising demand to retain all of Mexico, rammed the treaty through the Senate. Then this absolutely successful President—he also succeeded, where his predecessors had failed, in settling the banking and tariff questions according to hard-money, pro-planter principles—declared that his task was completed. Refusing to run for a second term, he stepped out of office to bequeath to his successor the task of attaching this ungainly new territory peaceably to a Union already perilously balanced between the slave states and the free.

III

Compromise of 1850
The Mexican War was hardly declared before the slavery issue was raised in Congress in the Wilmot Proviso to a bill to purchase additional land from Mexico. David Wilmot, an obscure Pennsylvania congressman motivated by obscure reasons, moved that slavery be excluded from all territory to be purchased from Mexico. The Proviso failed of passage and failed again the next year, but it introduced the issue which drove the nation to the verge of disunion in the next few years and dominated the sectional controversy down to the Civil War. Pending the election of 1848 leading politicians in both parties did what they could to ignore the issue, for it was disrupting to both parties, especially to the Democratic party, divided between antislavery "Barburners" and conservative "Hunkers." The Democrats, nominating the antiproviso Lewis Cass of Michigan, ignored the question in their platform. The Whigs, where the main antislavery strength lay, in order to win the election, passed over the party regulars to nominate the war hero Taylor, who was incidentally a slaveholding Southern planter. With nothing to choose between these parties, antislavery Northerners organized the Free Soil party and nominated Van Buren, who polled 10 per cent of the popular vote, most of it in New York and New England.

Taylor, who seems to have accepted the Presidency at first ceremonially as an honor bestowed upon him by a grateful country, was hurried to his death in the next two years, during one of the stormiest controversies in the history of the Federal government. Taylor, like Polk both a Southerner and a nationalist, wanted to see the new territory organized without worrying about the slavery issue. By the time he assumed the Presidency the gold rush was on in California, which within months attracted a population of about 100,000 from around the world, and when this happened, the President invited California to draw up a state constitution, which it did. He then ordered Congress to vote it into the Union. His commands were drowned out, however, by howls of Southern anguish and threats of Southern secession.

South Carolina's ruling group was ready to leave the Union, and the only issue it thought worth discussing was whether to go it alone or to wait for the forming of a Southern confederation. Calhoun, favoring a Southern nationalist movement, was unobtrusively instrumental in the calling of a state convention in Mississippi, which in turn called for a convention of the Southern states at Nashville. The Nashville Convention met while debates were raging in Congress and, amid the rebel yells of the fire-eaters, drew up a set of relatively moderate resolutions, chief among which was the insistence upon the extension of the Missouri Compromise line of 36°30′ to the Pacific Coast.

The fire-eaters at Nashville failed twice over, for they failed even to catch the attention of the nation. More momentous discussions were being carried on in the United States Senate, where a debate was proceeding which was in somber contrast to the mainly forensic contest of Webster and Hayne a generation earlier. Hayne by 1850 was dead, and the reigning titans of the Senate were all of them dying; Webster and Clay within two years; Calhoun within the month. These three men, each of whom had striven repeatedly for the Presidency, were past all personal ambition except to make a fitting resting place for themselves in the history of the nation. Calhoun made his final testament in the name of Southern nationalism, threatening Southern secession if the North did not submit comprehensively to Southern demands. Against him Clay and Webster appealed for a last compromise which would secure the Southern states in their slaveholding rights, while permitting the free westward development of the nation. For Webster it was a stand which placed him for the first time in his career under severe condemnation by the most eloquent and literate members of his party in New England, notably Emerson and John Greenleaf Whittier.

It was Clay, the Great Compromiser, who pieced together, from various bills thrown up by the controversy, a series of measures derisively labeled by President Taylor the "Omnibus Bill," whereby California would be admitted as a free state, the Southwest would be organized as a territory on the basis of "popular sovereignty" without mention of slavery, Texas would be compensated in specie for territory lost to New Mexico (which was attractive to politically influential holders of Texas bonds), the slave trade would be abolished in the District of Columbia, and a fugitive slave law would be passed which would guarantee to Southerners effective support in the capture of runaway slaves in the free states. Then, exhausted by the struggle, Clay turned his leadership over to the young Stephen A. Douglas of Illinois, who took Clay's main points one by one and steered them through the Senate.

The moderates won, as the nation plainly wished them to do,

and the nation turned to innumerable other more pleasant ways of achieving its manifest destiny than that of fighting an abolitionist war. There remained many in the North who were not abolitionist; yet who refused to accept the fugitive slave law as the law of the land; while Southern fire-eaters continued their agitation for secession. Furthermore the younger generation of senators, joining in the debate, had on the whole demonstrated a distinctly less conciliatory attitude than had the men from whom they were assuming power, Seward of New York speaking about a "higher law" which was above the Constitution. And the problem still remained of actually settling the vast expanse of territory under those compromises of 1820 and 1850.

IV

Sectionalism   National conditions during the debates over the Compromise of 1820 may have been such as to have invited the hope among conciliatory statesmen that a stable, long range solution to the slavery question could be achieved; this was no longer the case in 1850. Society in the 1850s was in motion in a way that could not have been predicted a generation earlier. That decade saw the greatest relative increase in urban population and in immigration of any in the nation's history before or since. It experienced a railroad boom which eclipsed all that had gone before, and, in addition to the settlement of the Far West, it experienced an ever accelerating westward expansion of the farming frontier across the Mississippi into Iowa, Kansas, Arkansas, and Texas and into the Great Lakes region of Michigan, Wisconsin, and Minnesota. All of these states entered the Union during the fifteen years before the Civil War, in addition to Florida, California, and Oregon.

The changes of the fifties intensified the differences between the slave and free states, for they revolutionized the North while leaving the expanding South, by comparison, unchanged. Although many immigrants entered the port of New Orleans, immigration left the South largely untouched. Urbanization altered the South only on its periphery, in New Orleans, St. Louis, Baltimore, Cincinnati, and Charleston. Five Southern states in 1860 did not have a single town with a population of 10,000. The beginnings of industrial development were to be seen in Southern cities in the fifties, most notably the iron industry in Richmond, Virginia, while the manufacture of textiles was spreading even into the rural areas. Even so, at the time the war broke out the entire Confederacy did not possess as much machinery for a textile industry as was operating in the one town of Lowell, Massachusetts.

The Old South remained a rural, largely frontier, and westward moving region producing staple commodities of hemp and tobacco in the upper South, sugar in Louisiana, rice in pockets along the coastal region from South Carolina to Texas, but mainly cotton. Of the 3.5 million slaves in the Confederate states, the majority were engaged in the raising of cotton, and it was the expansion of cotton which continually raised the price of slaves in the prewar years. In many areas of the South virtually no slaves existed, and even in the areas of their concentration the large majority of the white population owned none. Of those who did own slaves, about half were more or less well-to-do yeoman farmers, working side by side with their bondsmen, hopeful for a turn of fortune which would raise them to gentlemanly station and anxious lest some turn of ill luck drop them to the status of the slaves about them. More than half of all the slaves were owned by 12 per cent of the white population, the owners of twenty or more slaves. And from this select squirearchy there rose the still more select planter aristocracy, the ten thousand families of the South which were supported by a force of fifty or more slaves.

These were the groups—the squirearchy and the aristocracy— which absorbed the advantages of slavery; all other major classes in the South suffered from the system, economically as well as socially and politically. Yet slavery established the patterns of aspiration for Southerners generally. The yeoman farmer with no slaves of his own could observe about him no other standard of success than that of accumulation of land and of slaves. The poorer white could find reason for pride of position only in his whiteness and freedom, since his station in life might otherwise differ little from that of the slave.

Southerners like Cassius M. Clay of Kentucky and Hinton R. Helper of North Carolina, who argued that the average Southerner was damaged by slavery, inspired either indifference or violence among their nonslaveholding audiences. These men had at least a social stake in the system which was isolating and impoverishing them, and their approval of slavery in turn committed them to regard the slaveholders as the special, aristocratic custodians of Southern society, however recently the slaves had been acquired by the upstart "cotton snobs." Cotton, meanwhile, in addition to providing livings for many and fortunes for few, comprised two-thirds of the total value of American exports by the eve of the war, leading Southerners to suppose that economically cotton was king in the nation and that "The wealth of the South is permanent and real, that of the North fugitive and fictitious," and fundamentally dependent, taking the world view, on the Southern cotton crop.

In fact the agricultural wealth of the North was increasing much more rapidly than that of the South, not to speak of the prodigious advances in Northern industrial development. American farmers naturally had been reluctant to move from the forest areas to which they were accustomed, but in the forties and fifties they and the more numerous new immigrants from northern Europe were finding the prairie lands to be wonderfully fertile. They were further encouraged by the novel environment to adopt new farming methods. The generation before the Civil War saw a significant conversion to mechanized farming techniques, with the application of the McCormick reaper, of wheat binders, seed drills, and threshers to the new areas. Those who worked their own land were in a better position to appreciate the value of laborsaving devices than were planters who raised crops by the sweat of the brows of slaves. Consequently Northern farmers had reason to be more receptive to new contraptions than the Southern planters.

The transportation revolution also benefited the North disproportionately. The South shared in the railroad boom of the fifties, but it was in the Northwest that the main development took place, and the main result of this development, in conjunction with the Erie Canal, was to free the Northwest from its old reliance on the Mississippi River and on the port of New Orleans and to attach it to New York and Philadelphia instead. Southern leaders were aware of the fact that they were losing ground to the North in the railroad age, and they worked to regain the loss by seeking congressional authorization to build along a southern route the first transcontinental railroad to California and the Orient. Spokesmen for the other regions of the nation naturally had other ideas on the subject, and it was this competition for the first route to the Far West which unleashed a series of events leading directly to the Civil War.

Presiding over this onrushing competitive nation was an old-fashioned Jeffersonian Democrat, Franklin Pierce, from, of all places, New Hampshire. A dark horse candidate whose nomination had been made possible only by factional splits between Douglas of Illinois, Cass of Michigan, and Buchanan of Pennsylvania, Pierce had comfortably defeated the better known but less well-liked Whig candidate, General Winfield Scott of Virginia, in the election of 1852. In domestic politics Pierce pronounced himself a strict constructionist, committed to the Compromise of 1850 and to a permanent truce with regard to the slavery question. He intended to compensate for this negative, colorless domestic program, however, by stirring things up somewhat overseas.

Pierce represented the "Young America" element which saw America's "manifest destiny" as but imperfectly fulfilled by Polk's conquests. Canada remained shackled to the British monarchy and Cuba to the Spanish, while farther abroad private Americans were involving themselves in honorable responsibilities which the American government ought, in good conscience, to make its own. American missionaries, shippers, and pineapple planters had for a generation been active in Hawaii, and it appeared that American annexation would now be necessary to prevent the Hawaiians from coming under the dominion of a foreign power. In 1854 Pierce's Secretary of State, William L. Marcy, arranged a treaty of annexation. The Hawaiian insistence on statehood made it impossible so far as the Senate was concerned, however, and the matter was dropped. More successful was the opening of the Hermit Kingdom of Japan to American trade by the naval force of Commodore Matthew Perry in the same year. Additionally American ships, following in the wake of the British, had earlier gained trading rights in China and Siam. Despite these gains, however, Americans were disappointed in their exotic dream of capturing the trade of the Orient from their new position on the Pacific Coast.

There appeared to be even better prospects than these closer to home. Canada was not one at the moment, since America was, for the time being, on reasonably good terms with England, and under any circumstances any efforts to acquire Canada would have been fatal to Pierce's Southern-dominated party. To the south, however, there was Mexico, which, it was supposed, could certainly be induced, one way or another, to relinquish more territory. Better than that, there were heady prospects of a tropical empire extend-

ing from Florida to Nicaragua, the latter of which was briefly occupied by the American filibusterer, William Walker. As these
possibilities received thoughtful attention from the administration,
the point could hardly have been missed by his fellow Northerners
that Pierce was being drawn consistently toward the equator in his
expansionist aims.

The most dramatic incident in foreign affairs, and the one which
marked the effective end to serious manifest destiny activity for
two generations, was the Ostend Manifesto, delivered in 1854 by
the Minister to Spain, the Southern expansionist from Louisiana,
Pierre Soule, who was joined by the Minister to Great Britain,
Buchanan, and the Minister to France, John Y. Mason. The Manifesto requested Spain to sell slave-ridden Cuba to the United
States and added that if Spain did not do so, and if in the American view Spanish possession of the island constituted a threat to
American peace and union, "then, by every law, human and divine,
we shall be justified in wresting it from Spain if we possess the
power." Intended as a confidential dispatch, the Manifesto was
made public. Amid hue and cry Soule was recalled and his views
were disavowed by Secretary of State Marcy. Damage had nevertheless been done to an administration which was otherwise suffering at home from a reopening of the slavery issue, haplessly
brought on by sectional competition for the first railroad route
west to the Pacific.

V

Coming of the Civil War The great symbol of this heroic age of enterprise, the transcontinental railroad, awaited only
congressional authorization for its swift construction through Indian country, across the Great Plains, over the Rockies and the
Sierras down to the Pacific Ocean. As to the touchy matter of
choosing the route, the Deep South had its most powerful advocate
in Jefferson Davis, who as Secretary of War directed the Corps of
Army Engineers, which in turn was responsible for surveying the
possible routes and recommending the best alternatives. Under the
circumstances the extreme southern route seemed to the army engineers to be the most favorable of routes, which, from a purely
engineering standpoint, it probably was. It was the possibility of

this route which persuaded Congress in 1853 to approve the Gadsden Purchase, a barren stretch of Mexican desert, thus rounding out, as things happened, the permanent continental boundaries of the United States.

The Middle West had its own resourceful advocate in Senator Douglas of Illinois. Douglas, however, faced the difficulty that his route would cross through areas as yet unorganized territorially. But Douglas was chairman of the Senate committee on territories, and he was among the most nation-minded politicians in that time of sectional politics. He was impatient to see the continental nation take form and, in his view, the opening up of the great "Platte country" to settlement was overdue under any circumstances. In 1854, therefore, he presented a congressional bill to organize the territories of Kansas and Nebraska. Then, to placate Southern votes necessary for passage of the measure, Douglas in his bill opened up the possibility of slavery in the territory in an ambiguously worded provision which at least partially invalidated the supposedly perpetual Missouri Compromise of 1820. The ambiguity did not remain to create its own difficulties, however, for Southern pressure obliged Douglas explicitly to set aside the compromise.

The resulting measure was supported by the Pierce administration and passed into law after months of acrimonious debate. Douglas defended the measure as following the principle of popular sovereignty laid down by the Compromise of 1850. He further reasoned that under any circumstances slavery would be excluded from the territories when they became states, since the environment was not suited to a slave economy. Repeal of the Missouri Compromise would therefore be but a nominal concession, which, he must have supposed, would seriously disturb none but the doctrinaires and fanatics among antislavery Northerners. The event proved this line of reasoning to be the cataclysmic miscalculation which overwhelmed the nation in sectional controversy and rushed it into Civil War.

The Kansas-Nebraska Act presented antislavery men with the issue which brought the Northern majority to their side: the issue, not of slavery itself, but of the extension of slavery into territories where it did not yet exist, in violation of the Missouri Compromise. Throughout the North anti-Nebraska parties organized themselves immediately on this issue and joined together to form the Republican party, dedicated to preventing the extension of slavery. Created largely out of the disintegrating Whig party and representing a variety of Northern and also border state opinion, the Republican party was ready for action in the congressional elections of 1854, and Kansas Territory was opened for settlement at once to provide them with a bloody dramatization of their issue.

There would have been troubles enough in Kansas without the slavery issue, since the government opened the territory before extinguishing Indian titles or making surveys, but the Kansas-Nebraska Bill ensured that the troubles would be bloody. A month before the territory was opened, the Massachusetts Emigrant Aid Company—later the New England Emigrant Aid Company—was formed to rush free-state settlers into the area and to arm them with Sharp's rifles. Against settlers from free states, meanwhile, "border ruffians" poured in from Missouri and to some extent from the Deep South. By the time the first governor arrived, the Missourians had the upper hand, and they formed a government which limited office holding to proslavery men. The antislavery men later retaliated by establishing their own rival government.

Remarkably enough under a succession of ineffectual governors, hardly anybody was killed for two years. Then John Brown, a New England fanatic, after a lifetime of unfulfillment in various dubious and unsuccessful business enterprises, achieved a measure of national notoriety by leading a small band to Pottowatomie, Kansas, removing five proslavery men from their beds, and murdering and mutilating them. After a subsequent brush with proslavery men, Brown went East, where the Republican press had suppressed information concerning the "Pottawatomie Massacre." There he was warmly welcomed, Emerson and Thoreau hailing him as the true transcendental hero come at last. In the Senate, meanwhile, a congressman from South Carolina, Preston Brooks, had caned Senator Charles Sumner of Massachusetts on the floor of the Senate in retaliation against a speech in which Sumner had denounced Senator Butler of South Carolina. Amid the noisy adulation accorded Sumner and even Brown in New England and Brooks in the South, the sectional dispute underwent an emotional transformation, and a good many men on both sides became eager for war.

The Democratic convention of 1856 met this situation as it had

in the previous campaign, by nominating a "doughface" candidate
—a Northerner who could be counted on to follow the dictation of
the Southern wing of the party—James Buchanan of Pennsylvania.
The Whig party had already destroyed itself by attempting to
ignore the slavery question, and two rival parties were trying to
succeed it: the American, or Know-Nothing party, opposing itself
to Catholicism and immigration, and the Republican party, opposing itself to the extension of slavery into the territories. The one
nominated former President Fillmore, and the other nominated
John C. Fremont. Fremont, "the pathfinder," was famous for his
book, largely written for him by his wife, about his California explorations, led by Kit Carson and other experienced mountain
men. His lack of a political record made him an available candidate
for the new Republican party seeking a new political following in
a confused situation. In the election, with the American party running a poor third, Buchanan won 45.34 per cent of the votes and
was elected, the first candidate since John Quincy Adams to become President against the wishes of the majority of the voters.

Two days after Buchanan took office the Supreme Court
rendered a momentous decision in the Dred Scott case. Scott was
a slave whose master had taken him to a free state and later to
Federal territory where slavery was forbidden by the Missouri
Compromise, and then back to Missouri. Scott sued for his freedom in the Missouri courts on the grounds of his residence in a
free state and in free Federal territory. In the course of the suit
a New Yorker gained ownership of Scott. The case thereupon
entered the Federal jurisdiction and went to the Supreme Court.

The Court might have decided the case against Scott on various
narrow legal grounds which would have avoided major constitutional issues. Urged by the extremely doughface Buchanan to set
aside the Missouri Compromise, however, the Court took the occasion to declare a Federal law unconstitutional for the second
time in the nation's history. In nine separate decisions the majority
of the Court upheld the ruling of Chief Justice Taney that the
descendant of a slave could not become an American citizen, even
though he might become the citizen of a state, and that Congress
could not prohibit slavery in Federal territory.

The Court had thus needlessly set aside a Federal law, the Missouri Compromise, which Congress had in fact already specifically
invalidated in the Kansas-Nebraska Bill, and which almost every-

one was certain would itself have no practical effect so far as the extention of slavery was concerned. In "bleeding Kansas" six years after its first settlement only two slaves were discovered by the census takers, but it was a decade since David Wilmot had invented the rules of the game—for what reason, nobody has ever found out —and by then almost everybody was standing on principle.

In Illinois in 1858 Abraham Lincoln and Stephen A. Douglas, contending for a seat in the United States Senate, took part in a series of public debates turning mainly on the issue of the extension of slavery into the territories. Without challenging the authority of the Supreme Court, Lincoln nevertheless contended that the government had the right to exclude slavery from the territories, and in a debate at Freeport, Illinois, Lincoln challenged Douglas to defend his doctrine of popular sovereignty in the light of the Dred Scott decision. Douglas replied that slavery could not exist for a day without local police regulations to support it, and that a territorial legislature could therefore prohibit slavery simply by failing to pass such laws. This common sense "Freeport doctrine" alienated Southern Democrats, widened the breach in the Democratic party, and did much to keep Douglas from becoming President in 1860.

In October, 1859, John Brown led an attack on the Federal arsenal at Harpers Ferry, Virginia, for the purpose of arming Southern Negroes and organizing them into a force which would terrorize the South into emancipating the slaves. Captured by United States Marines, Brown was tried and executed for treason against the state of Virginia. Brown's raid struck a raw nerve: obsessive Southern fear of slave insurrection such as had made a holocaust of Santo Domingan slaveholders. Meanwhile, from quiet Concord, Massachusetts, Ralph Waldo Emerson could be heard by Southerners to remark that Brown's execution would make the gallows glorious like the cross. Actually few words in defense of Brown came out of the North at the time, even William Lloyd Garrison hesitating to support him. Democratic politicians were quick to implicate the whole Republican party, however, and Southerners were quick to implicate the entire North. Brown had drawn the first blood in the oncoming war.

Faced with the candidacy of Douglas for President in 1860, the radical Southern Democrats bolted the convention to nominate John C. Breckinridge of Kentucky; while a Constitutional Union party appeared for the occasion, founded for prosperous and contented old Whigs on the proposition that the crisis should be ignored by both sides and thereby avoided. The Republican party, meanwhile, passed over its leading politicians for the less prominent, and therefore less vulnerable, Abraham Lincoln of Illinois, who had made a national reputation in his debates with Douglas and who had won Eastern support with his moderate Cooper Union speech in New York. In the election Lincoln won every free state except for a split vote in New Jersey and lost every slave state, receiving not a single vote in ten of them. Receiving 40 per cent of the total vote, he won an absolute majority in the electoral college, by virtue of the concentration of his votes in the populous states.

Upon news of Lincoln's election, South Carolina called a convention which voted that state out of the Union, and this time South Carolina's lead was followed by the six other states of the lower South, to form the Confederate States of America, all before Lincoln had taken office. Refusing to relinquish Federal claims to sovereignty over the Southern states, Lincoln moved carefully to avoid alienating either the upper South or indecisive Northern opinion. Determined to retain at least some token of sovereignty, he finally decided to hold the Federal Fort Sumter in Charleston harbor, sending supply ships with food to maintain the garrison. South Carolina countered by shelling Fort Sumter and, by firing the first shot, rallied most Northerners enthusiastically to the Federal cause. The upper South, however, viewed Lincoln's decision to retain Fort Sumter as a constitutional violation of states' rights, and when Lincoln issued a call for Northern troops, they followed Virginia into the Confederacy, except for the border states of Delaware, Maryland, Kentucky, and Missouri. In July, 1861, the Civil War was launched, with high confidence on both sides, in the First Battle of Bull Run.

The cannon at Fort Sumter blasted through the entanglements of legal and constitutional argument and opened the way for a rush of Northern idealism. Ralph Waldo Emerson, for instance, crammed his journal with thoughts on war, heroism, morality, and freedom. "If the abundance of heaven only sends us a fair share of light and conscience," he wrote a friend, "we shall redeem America for all its sinful years since the century began." His literary colleague, Nathaniel Hawthorne, who believed in original sin as Emerson did not, took a more pessimistic and, as it proved, more realistic view of the struggle. No human effort on the grand scale, he wrote of the war, "has ever yet resulted according to the purposes of its projectors. The advantages are always incidental. Man's accidents are God's purposes. We miss the good we sought and do the good we little cared for." The war preserved the Union and rid the nation of slavery, but in a manner and at a cost which could hardly have been conceived of. It proved to be a brutal four-year bloodletting, and it ushered in sinful years such as had never been dreamed of in Emerson's philosophy.

The Civil War, the cataclysmic break in the nation's past, has remained inevitably the greatest source of controversy in American history. Northern writers, during and after the war, argued the existence of a conspiracy by an aggressive slavocracy to dominate the nation and to extend slavery throughout the North and West. Amid the war's bitter aftermath, spokesmen for the "lost cause," notably President Jefferson Davis and Vice President Alexander Stephens, presented the more or less official Confederate interpretation in constitutional terms. Slavery, they argued, had been the "main exciting proximate cause" but "not the real cause." Basically the war had been a defense of the sovereign rights of the Southern states against unconstitutional Federal coercion. Late nineteenth-century Northern historians, including John W. Burgess, attacked the Southern constitutionalists on their own grounds. Twentieth-century historians have tended to treat the constitutional controversy as a rather tiresome splitting of hairs. Most historians are agreed that Arthur Mier Schlesinger, Sr., in his article "The States-Rights Fetish," put to its final rest the contention that the South was really fighting, first of all, in defense of a constitutional theory.

Following the Civil War, two generations of Northern historians, led by James Ford Rhodes, while avoiding entire commitment to the Southern conspiracy idea, interpreted the war as an "irrepressible conflict" between freedom and slavery. In this view the war was a righteous crusade against an evil institution which, because of Southern intransigence, could have been eradicated only by force. This explanation of the war on moral grounds continued to be accepted by many Northern historians in the twentieth century, and it received strong support in the 1930s from Gilbert H. Barnes and Dwight L. Dumond, in their writings on the abolitionist movement. They found the abolitionists to represent, not a small band of irresponsible fanatics, but the conscience of the

North, expressing itself through many of the Northern Protestant churches.

In the meantime, two schools of thought had established themselves in opposition to the view that the war had been brought on by the moral issue of slavery: the frontier school, led by Frederick Jackson Turner, and the economic determinist school, led by Charles and Mary Beard, in their enormously influential *Rise of American Civilization*. Both schools saw the war as the result of an imbalance within the nation. To Turner's followers, the war was brought on, not by the issue of slavery, but by the issue of the extension of slavery into the territories and by the crises arising from the admission of new Western states to the Union. To the economic determinists, on the other hand, the war was fundamentally a struggle between "social groupings founded on differences in climate, soil, industries, and labor systems." In 1860, at a time when Northern business was fast extending its dominion over the national economy, the "planter interest" was consolidating its control over national politics. The war was a "second American Revolution" by which the economically dominant business classes grasped national political authority.

Few historians would deny that the westward movement, and the issue of the extension of slavery which it presented, was basic to the coming of the Civil War. Most, however, would probably find the Turnerian interpretation arbitrary in its emphasis upon the West rather than upon slavery. But it is the economic interpretation that has drawn the heavier fire from critics. It has been pointed out that, of all major economic groups in the North, the business community—to the extent that such a thing can be isolated and identified—fearing a disruption of its economic ties with the South, was the most conciliatory toward Southern demands. It has been further objected that the economic determinists, here, as in other crises in American history, treat the "business community" as a unified faction, when, in fact, it was a heterogeneous complex of often conflicting interests.

More recently, two additional schools of interpretation have opposed themselves to the main interpretations which have gone before: those who see the war as brought on by a "blundering generation" of politicians and those who see the war as the culmination of Southern nationalism. Spoken for principally by Avery Craven and James C. Randall, the "blundering generation" historians argued that, as Craven wrote, the Civil War represented "a complete breakdown of the democratic process in the handling of national problems. Men ceased to reason together." The politicians of the age, sectional in outlook, created symbols which oversimplified the issues and made men willing to fight, where more practically capable politicians would have arranged compromises. Against this interpretation, other writers have objected that the nation's political leadership was not demonstrably lower in caliber during the prewar generation than at other times in the nation's history. Allan Nevins, in his multivolume study of mid-nineteenth century America, has returned substantially to the Rhodes thesis, that the Civil War was basically the result of a failure in race adjustment, the relative scarcity of Negroes in the anti-Negro North permitting many to take an uncompromisingly righteous attitude toward the race question.

Akin to the "blundering generation" interpretation, in its emphasis upon psychological influences, is the Southern nationalism interpretation. The South, in the course of more than two centuries, had developed its own unique institutions in harmony with the "peculiar institution" of slavery. By the time of Lincoln's election, it had developed a national self-consciousness which created among many a positive desire for independence. The North, on the other hand, intolerant of what was, from the Northern point of view, an alien society, was determined, as W. J. Cash wrote, to achieve "the satisfaction of the instinctive urge of men in the mass to put down whatever differs from themselves—the will to make over the South in the prevailing American image and to sweep it into the main current of the nation." The controversy continues in ever-increasing volume, as the centennial years of the Civil War run their course, with a good deal of concurrence in the view that the war was brought about by a "multiple causation" but with less agreement in the adding up of the causes.

VI

Civil War The apparently overwhelming Northern military advantage diminished greatly upon examination of the military problems confronting the North, and it seemed to vanish altogether with the Battle of Bull Run, where the Confederate troops, had they pressed their advantage, might well have captured Washington and brought the war to an early conclusion. Southern whites were outnumbered four to one by Northerners, and in material strength their disadvantage was even greater. The South contained but one major iron works, at Richmond, and in all other important respects it was industrially a world apart from the enterprising North. Its comparatively backward railroad system compounded this disadvantage, confronting Confederate generals with tactical problems which Union generals did not face. The primitive state of Southern commerce was reflected in the lack of either a merchant marine or a potential navy. The North was in a position to move almost at will to close Southern ports against the enemy. In fine, the Confederacy would have been doomed to swift annihilation in a machine-age war.

That was not the sort of war that was fought, however. The Civil War was a small arms struggle for which the South was fairly amply equipped from start to conclusion. For the South it was a defensive war fought from interior lines. Against the defensive strength of the Southern position, overwhelming numerical superiority was indeed necessary, and the far-flung, motley North —much of its population strongly pro-Southern—could not command its manpower as effectively as could the beleaguered South. Nor, during the first three years of the war, was it able to utilize as skillfully the manpower it did muster. In the South, unlike the North, a strong military tradition had drawn some of the most capable Southerners to military service. Competently staffed from the first, the Southern armies faced opponents commanded by men of inferior ability, often quite untrained for their military duties. A more aggressive and able leadership might have brought Northern victory out of the Battle of Antietam in 1862 or Gettysburg a year later, but the Union commanders in both cases failed to press their advantages.

The North had had the advantage of an established government, as opposed to the ramshackle Confederacy of the Deep South, organized first at Montgomery, Alabama, and reorganized at Richmond following the secession of the upper South. The President of the Confederacy, Jefferson Davis, directed a nation always caught in the painful cross-purposes of waging an effectively unified war to the end of preserving the divided sovereignties of the individual states. Sensitivity to violation of states' rights was especially strong in the older Atlantic states. North and South Carolina and Georgia resisted Confederate control to the bloody end, although they had agreed initially to a Confederate constitution which departed from the Federal pattern only in minor states-rights details.

Davis, a West Point graduate who would rather have been general than President, presided over a shifting Cabinet of indifferently able men, who varied in views from extreme states-rights to downright unionist. The one most able and reliable member, Judah P. Benjamin, aroused anti-Semitic hatreds in the Congress which worked to the great disadvantage of the administration. The discordant Congress itself grew increasingly violent during the course of the war, members going around heavily armed against possible attack from each other.

The Confederate Congress passed the first conscription act in American history, to the principled fury of the states-righters and to the personal fury of those who could not qualify for one of the clutch of exemptions given to slaveholders, ministers, civil servants, professors, all of those who could afford to purchase a substitute and other privileged people. Desperately short of specie and of international credit, the Confederacy resorted to issuing currency which fell to one-fiftieth of its face value before the close of the war. It went on to levy one-tenth of the annual produce of the nation. So far did the war strain the South from its original aims, that the Confederate government by the desperate last days was contemplating the emancipation of the slaves, in the hope that this would move England and perhaps France to intervene on the Confederate side.

Lincoln suffered the same abuse from his Congress and from the public that the unhappily stiff-necked Davis did, but he absorbed it better, and, while he also suffered a good deal of disloyalty from his Cabinet, he appointed more capable men and got better service out of them. His Secretary of State, William H. Seward—until the nomination the leading figure in the party—had thought that he would become "premier" during the Presidency of this unprepossessing, informally educated, provincial politician, but Seward came to learn as did others that "The President is the best of us." Those associated with Lincoln discovered, unless, as in the case of Secretary of the Treasury Salmon P. Chase, they were wholly self-deceived, that he combined a lofty purpose and almost infinite forbearance with a most crafty dexterity in the smaller arts of politics.

Central to Lincoln's strength as President was the fixed purpose which guided his flexible politics. When the Southern states seceded, much of Northern opinion favored permitting them to depart in peace, but Lincoln did not waver in his determination to preserve the Union. When the war came, many Northerners were eager to conduct it as a righteous crusade to eradicate slavery. Horace Greeley, with many others, successively adopted both of these positions. It was to Greeley, the advocate of an abolitionist war, that Lincoln addressed his famous declaration of policy. "If I could save the Union without freeing any slave, I would do it; and if I could save it by freeing all the slaves, I would do it. . . . What I do about slavery and the colored race, I do because I believe it helps to save the Union; and what I forbear, I forbear because I do not believe it would help to save the Union," to which he added his personal, as opposed to his official, wish "that all men, everywhere, could be free."

Lincoln directed a war which was fought in order "that this nation, under God, shall have a new birth of freedom; and that government of the people, by the people, for the people, shall not perish from the earth." Like Bismarck and other European national leaders, as Bertrand Russell has written, "he stood for national unity, and like most nationalists he found his justification in the association of his nation with a moral idea. But unlike most others he was justified in making this association. America *had* been 'dedicated to the proposition that all men were created equal.' "

Following Sumter, Lincoln moved aggressively to save the border states of Delaware, Maryland, Kentucky, and Missouri, which remained doubtful, calling up additional troops, appropriating money on doubtful constitutional authority, and invading Maryland to place it under martial law. Following a more cautious policy toward Kentucky, he waited until Confederate troops had first invaded that state and then won it to the Union side. In Missouri, its government Confederate in sympathy, the local Federal forces, with strong support of the local German population, defeated the state forces in the first sizable fight of the war, and Missouri was largely saved for the Union. Northwestern Virginia was detached from the parent state and was admitted to the Union as West Virginia in 1863.

To the problems of financing, supplying, and manning the war effort the Union brought incomparably greater resources than did the Confederacy, and it brought correspondingly better results.

A highly successful bond drive under the leading financier Jay Cooke raised 400 million dollars in 1862, and in the last year of the war bonds began to sell well again. In addition 432 million dollars worth of paper "Greenbacks" were issued, which, while they declined to less than half their face value at one time, nevertheless always remained usable currency. The supplying of the war was marked by ubiquitous corruption, but the materials were available, and the government was in a position to get them. In 1863 the government instituted a draft, a year after the Confederacy had resorted to it. There followed draft riots and widespread violations, especially in New York City and in the upper Mississippi Valley, where there was much pro-Southern "copperhead" sentiment. Desertions were on a much larger scale in the Union than in the Confederate army, but so were enlistments, whether voluntary or enforced.

At the outset Confederate confidence had been strengthened by the belief that England and France would inevitably intervene, should the war continue to the point where their textile industries were deprived of American cotton. The leadership of both of these nations was sympathetic to the aristocratic Confederacy, as opposed to the democratic Union. Both nations had hopefully recognized the Confederacy as a belligerent and had opened their ports to rebel ships. However, cotton happened to be in long supply in Europe, and pro-Union sentiment was strong among the English people generally, especially after Lincoln's Emancipation Proclamation of January 1863. Shortly after that Proclamation the Confederate representative in England was recalled and the British consuls in Richmond ordered home. The British in the meantime had permitted the construction of large ships, built for the purpose of breaking the Union blockade, a matter which troubled Anglo-American relations in the postwar period.

From the Union point of view military strategy was determined by naval supremacy, which invited not only the blockading of the Confederacy but also the dividing of it through control of the Mississippi. Strategy was determined also by the Appalachian Mountains, which divided the conflict into two main theaters. The close proximity of Washington, D. C. to the Confederate capital at Richmond was a controlling factor also; for the defense of each capital was viewed as a matter of high importance to politicians on both sides, irrespective of military considerations. This point was clearly made in July, 1861, at the first major engagement, the Battle of Bull Run, when Washington was so nearly taken. Thereafter all was quiet on the Potomac for almost a year and only a little less so in the Western theater, as the main Union effort was restricted to naval operations which captured key points along the coast and in the spring of 1862 captured New Orleans.

The year 1862 saw victories by Gen. Ulysses S. Grant in the West at Fort Henry and Fort Donelson, which were balanced against McClellan's failure to exploit his numerical advantage against Gen. Robert E. Lee in the East. McClellan, for his lack of enterprise, was replaced by Gen. John Pope who promptly suffered defeat in the Second Battle of Bull Run. McClellan was thereupon returned to lead the Army of the Potomac to a disheartening draw at the Battle of Antietam against Confederate troops which McClellan's forces outnumbered two to one. Lincoln therefore replaced him with Gen. Ambrose E. Burnside, who, following his fiasco at Fredericksburg, was replaced in turn by Gen. Joseph Hooker. Hooker, following a shattering defeat at Chancellorsville in April, 1863, turned over his command to Gen. George Meade. Chancellorsville, where Lee's most brilliant general, Stonewall Jackson, was killed, proved the high point of Confederate success in a war where numbers were counting increasingly on the Union side and where a general was discovered who could make use of this advantage.

The turning point in the war came in July, 1863, with major Union victories in both the Eastern and Western theaters of action. In the West General Grant completed the conquest of the Mississippi with the capture of Vicksburg, followed up by the taking of the other remaining Confederate strong point on the Mississippi, Port Hudson, Louisiana. Thus Texas, Louisiana, and Arkansas were severed from the rest of the Confederacy. In the East, meanwhile, Lee launched his most aggressive attack on Union soil at Gettysburg, Pennsylvania and was repulsed. Lee was able to retire in good order, but the South was never again able to mount a major offensive. Five months later in the West the Battle of Chattanooga cleared the way for the invasion of Georgia, and Gen. William T. Sherman launched on his march to Atlanta, from Atlanta to the sea and from Savannah northward, the march which, more than anything else, broke the Southern will to resist.

Transferred East and appointed supreme commander, Grant

launched the Battle of the Wilderness against Lee in northern Virginia in May, 1864, and despite the indecisiveness of the battle, pressed ahead along Lee's right flank, clashing again at Spotsylvania Court House, and again at Cold Harbor and slipping south of Richmond to Petersburg. In April, 1865, with Sherman moving against the army of Gen. Joe Johnston and with Grant forcing Lee to evacuate Richmond, the war came to an end, after four years of fighting and at a cost in lives of more than 250,000 Confederate and more than 350,000 Union soldiers, among them, the Commander in Chief of the armies, shot to death in Ford's Theater eleven days after the conclusion of hostilities.

VII

Reconstruction "They have killed him, the Forgiver. . . .", wrote Herman Melville in *The Martyr*, "The Avenger takes his place. . . ." Lincoln had narrowly avoided repudiation by his own party in 1864. Saved mainly by Sherman's timely victory at Atlanta, he was renominated and returned to office to deliver his second inaugural address a month before his assassination:

> With malice toward none; with charity for all; with firmness in the right, as God gives us to see the right, let us strive on to finish the work we are in; to bind up the nation's wounds; to care for him who shall have borne the battle, and for his widow, and his orphan —to do all which may achieve and cherish a just and a lasting peace among ourselves, and with all nations.

Throughout the conflict Lincoln had opposed himself to the abolitionists in his war to restore the nation conceived in liberty to "a new birth of freedom . . . that government of the people, by the people, for the people, shall not perish from the earth." Against those who would make the war primarily one to free the slave and punish the slaveholder he had steadily lost ground. Powerful from the first in Republican councils, the abolitionists rapidly gained strength with the war. All the damage they were capable of doing to the Union had by then been done, and the war brought to Northerners generally the militant spirit of the abolitionists toward the South. The abolitionists argued the military advantage of emancipating the slaves, who provided the labor force for the Confederate home front. More important, the vindictive spirit of the evangelistic North, which wished to crush the serpent with its heel, spread readily among others, who came to abhor the thought of rebels enjoying the voluptuous luxury of slavery.

Idealism, religious faith, vengefulness, military advantage, and party advantage swelled the cause of abolition against Lincoln's moderate Unionist policy of so conducting the war as to win, not only victory, but afterwards also a true Southern reconciliation. A more immediately practical consideration for Lincoln was the volatile sentiment in the loyal border slave states, which naturally reacted against the antislavery Republicans. Then, overborne by radical power, and fearful of possible armed foreign intervention, Lincoln issued his Emancipation Proclamation on January 1, 1863, freeing those slaves which were in unconquered Confederate territory and thus transfiguring the struggle from a war to save the Union to a war to make men free; gaining for himself in the bargain the unsought title of Great Emancipator.

As the war drew to a close Lincoln and the radical Republicans again divided, this time over the terms of the peace. The Lincoln plan would have readmitted Confederate states to full participation in the Union as soon as one-tenth of the voters as of 1860 had sworn Federal allegiance. Against this plan the Radicals brought the Wade-Davis bill, requiring the loyalty of a majority of voters for statehood and imposing additional limitations. The struggle was thus well advanced when the assassination of Lincoln placed upon Vice President Andrew Johnson the responsibility of administering the process of reunion.

Nominated for Vice President in 1864 as a War Democrat from Tennessee in an effort to unite the North, Johnson was outside the Republican—or Union—party, he now nominally led, and he was therefore without effective organizational support. A contentious stump speaker and stubborn defender of what he thought to be right, Johnson did not have the political skill to persuade Congress to follow him in Lincoln's conciliatory course and, under excruciatingly disadvantageous conditions, he was unable through his oratorical gifts to bring the nation to the support of his program. Contemptuous of this self-educated former tailor, the radical Republicans in Congress moved ruthlessly and with wild disregard for constitutional limitations to demolish the executive reconstruction plan and then to demolish the nation's President in the bargain.

Although still a minority in Congress, the radicals had the advantage of a clear-cut, aggressively vengeful program and of an aggressively vengeful leadership. Their leader in the House of Representatives was Thaddeus Stevens, misshapen and formidable in appearance and terror-provoking in action. "His conversation," reported his fellow-radical Carl Schurz, "carried on with a hollow voice devoid of music, easily disclosed a well-informed mind, but also a certain absolutism of opinion with contemptuous scorn for adverse argument. . . . What he himself seemed to enjoy most in his talk was his sardonic humor, which he made play upon men and things like lurid freaks of lightning." In the Senate the radical leadership was divided among a number of righteous and vindic- tive men: Sumner of Massachusetts, Wade of Ohio, and Chandler of Michigan, to name the leading figures. Against these men there was no chance for the pigheaded Johnson's reasonable program.

The radicals were aided by the oppressive policies which the reformed Southern governments devised to control the freed Negroes, who were placed under special "black codes" designed to reduce them to a permanently subordinate position in Southern society. The black codes included vagrancy laws which, in their practical operation, might have returned a large part of the Negro population to slavery in all but name. And the laws were evidently intended, not as emergency measures, but as the permanent new dispensation. Strengthened by the Northern reaction to the black codes, the radicals passed the Freedman's Bureau bill, extending indefinitely the life of an earlier created emergency agency and au- thorizing it to use military force throughout the South to defend the rights of Negroes. Johnson successfully vetoed the bill. It was the last success he enjoyed. There followed the Civil Rights Act, passed over his veto, which transferred the duty of protecting the South- ern Negro from the Bureau to the Federal courts and transferred to the courts also the authority to call on military force.

The showdown between Johnson and the radicals came in the congressional elections of 1866. Johnson made a "swing around the circle" speaking for his candidates in the election. He was followed by radicals, who heckled him into vituperative statements, and then he was reported by a radical press which slandered him wildly. An atmosphere was created which gave the Radicals two- thirds control of both houses of Congress, and they moved at once to put their reconstruction program into effect. Abolishing the re- constituted Southern state governments, Congress divided the

South into five military districts. It created, under the supervision of the military, new reconstruction governments based upon Negro and limited white suffrage and composed of freedmen and Northern "carpetbaggers" in cooperation with those Southern "scalawags" who were willing to join the new dispensations. These reconstruction governments were responsible for some creditable reforms, especially in the areas of education and internal improvements. They were responsible also for an orgy of corruption, confusion, and state indebtednesses, and they aroused a new rebel recalcitrance, which showed itself most startlingly in the Ku Klux Klan and in similar secret organizations, created to terrorize the freed Negroes into submission and perhaps created also to work off rebel fury.

In 1868 congressional radicals moved to capture the executive branch by impeaching Johnson on an elaborately contrived technicality. The Senate failed by one vote to convict the impeached President, but Johnson nevertheless was effectively destroyed, and congressional supremacy was established. Against the Ku Klux Klan, Congress passed special force acts, and for the moment it appeared that military occupation might be indefinitely lengthened; but Northern lust for vengeance was waning, and with it waned the power of the Radicals. Thaddeus Stevens died in 1868, and no one could be found to take his place. Charles Sumner in the meantime began to slip from power, and in 1871 he was deposed as chairman of the Foreign Relations Committee. By that time congressional leadership had been won by practical "bloody shirt" politicians, notably Roscoe Conkling of New York and James G. Blaine of Maine, purely practical politicians interested in retaining reconstruction chiefly as a political device to maintain the Republican party in power by use of Negro votes.

This partnership of well-to-do Northern businessmen and impoverished Southern freedmen was an uncomfortable, illogical alliance which roused no real enthusiasm among Northern Republicans. The cause of the Southern Negro did not stir the North to stop the successful overturn of the carpetbag government in Tennessee in 1869, and during the next two years North Carolina, Virginia, and Georgia returned to white rule as well. Arkansas, Alabama, and Texas followed in 1874 and Mississippi in 1876. Federal troops were finally withdrawn from the South altogether in 1877, when the last reconstruction governments collapsed in

Florida, South Carolina, and Louisiana. Thereafter the South received tacit Northern consent to deal with the Negro problem as it saw fit.

Northern writers who saw the Civil War as a moral crusade against slavery took a less exalted view of its consequences than they did of its causes. The first important scholar of the reconstruction period, James Ford Rhodes, found the reconstruction governments to have been thoroughly corrupt jobberies by Northern "carpetbaggers" maintained in power by the votes of ignorant and gullible freedmen. Quite generally concurred in by Northern as well as Southern historians, this interpretation received comprehensive documentation in the twentieth century in the writings of William A. Dunning and in those of a number of Dunning's students.

Unchallenged for thirty years, these statewide studies of reconstruction have been reexamined during the past generation, and, in some respects, drastically revised. While not denying the prevalance of corruption in the reconstruction governments, recent writers, a number of Southerners among them, have pointed out that this was an aspect of the general history of the nation in the postwar period. Beyond that, they have pointed to genuine reforms accomplished by these governments in adjusting the South to a new labor system which proved at least a workable arrangement for the freed Negro, in the development of industry and internal improvements, and in education and organized religion, especially among the Negroes. The point has further been made that the historians of reconstruction, concentrating their attention upon the dramatic aspects, have ignored the quiet and orderly continuance of customary ways in times of crisis. James Bryce long ago wrote in his *American Commonwealth* that "there was never a civil war or rebellion . . . followed by so few severities." It has been toward this generalization that the revisionists have been tending.

In retrospect it nevertheless appeared that the Southern Negro had been poorly served by his Northern champions. This was in part due to the strong otherworldly religious character of abolition. The worst sin of slavery had been the sin of denying the slave the freedom to work out his own salvation and so prepare himself for an everlasting future life. The physical freeing of the slave answered this objection and largely accomplished this mission in the minds of many abolitionists. There remained only the establishment of educational and religious facilities among the Southern

Negroes to bring them within range of salvation, and, indeed, impressive and important Northern missionary work was done in both of these fields.

Other abolitionists, concerned to secure the Negro in his position of independence, put a heavy reliance upon purely political rights which proved misplaced. The Thirteenth Amendment to the Constitution abolished slavery, the fourteenth enacted guarantees of civil rights for Negroes, and the Fifteenth extended the vote to them. The assumption was that, together, these would place the Negro in a position of political equality with the White, despite the utter economic dependence of the Negro upon his former master. There was some talk about starting the freedman out with forty acres and a mule—a project which would have been favored by the cheapness of land in the South of reconstruction—but to many Northern idealists this seemed not only unnecessary but downright subversive of sound social and political principles.

The result was that the Negro farmer found himself economically dependent upon the white property owner, whose land he was allowed to farm in exchange for a share of the crop he raised. Politically innocuous to the new order, he was widely allowed to continue in his voting privileges until, toward the close of the century, competition for the Negro vote threatened to endow it with decisive political power. When that happened the Negro was by one means or another disenfranchised in state after state, and in other ways as well he was relegated to an enforced position of inferiority. Not until the 1930s did the Federal government begin to stir itself again to assist the Negro toward some of the benefits of freedom.

The Fourteenth Amendment to the Constitution, ratified shortly after the close of the Civil War, provided that "No State shall make or enforce any law which shall abridge the privileges or immunities of citizens of the United States; nor shall any State deprive any person of life, liberty or property, without due process of law. . . . " For a generation the Supreme Court understood this statement to refer to human beings, and most particularly to the emancipated bondmen. But by 1890 the court had found that, while the amendment could not be used effectively to protect the rights of Negroes, it did protect business corporations as legal "persons" against unfavorable state legislation. The Fourteenth Amendment, as its legal meaning changed, reflected one of the most fundamental, and unlooked for, consequences of secession and Civil War.

The war at its outset had been generally opposed by the business community for business reasons, and the war itself had diverted more than it had promoted industrial enterprise. Secession of the planting states, however, had surrendered the government to the business community. By the act of secession the South had ushered the nation politically into the industrial era.

BIBLIOGRAPHY FOR CHAPTER SEVEN

Ray Billington, *The Far Western Frontier, 1830–1860* (1956) is a survey of the subject by a leading authority. Its "flavor, or style, provides a rather familiar theme with a new and refreshing aura . . . with a very generous sprinkling of colorful contemporary quips, epithets, and Western jargon. . . . Students . . . will like the format, be aided by excellent maps, edified by the illustrations and informed and delighted by the text. . . ." Bernard DeVoto, *The Year of Decision, 1846* (1943) is a fast-moving account of a climax of American expansion. Joseph Baldwin, *Flush Times of Alabama and Mississippi* (1853) is a colorful account of frontier days in the South. C. A. Singletary, *The Mexican War* (1960) is "in brief compass a sound, readable, even provocative account of the Mexican War." Marquis James, *The Raven* (1929) is the well-written biography of the truly incredible Sam Houston.

There are two studies which examine those divisions in the Democratic party which preceded the Civil War. J. C. N. Paul, *Rift in the Democracy* (1951), is "an excellent account of the contest for the Democratic presidential nomination in 1884. The author's central thesis is that the acceptance by the Democratic party of the demand for Texas annexation was the Trojan horse of the Democracy that produced 'rift' in 1844 and disruption in 1860." R. F. Nichols, *The Disruption of American Democracy* (1948) is "a historical magnifying glass through which one can take an uncustomary look at Democratic party politics the five years before the Civil War. . . ." D. L. Dumond, *Anti-Slavery Origins of the Civil War in the United States* (1939) is a brief and persuasive account. Louis Filler, *Crusade against Slavery, 1830–1860* (1960) is a discussion which centers around William Lloyd Garrison. Harvey Wish, ed., *Ante-Bellum: Writings of George Fitzhugh and Hinton Rowan Helper on Slavery* presents extensively the arguments of the main Southern intellectual supporter of slavery and the main Southern opponent of the institution. H. B. Stowe, *Uncle Tom's Cabin* (1852) possesses a literary merit which has been obscured by its political importance. Harvey Wish, ed., Frederick Law Olmsted, *The Slave States* presents the descriptions of an accurate and remarkably perceptive Northern reporter. C. G. Post, ed., J. C. Calhoun, *Disquisition on Government and Selections from the Discourse* presents the main basis for Calhoun's reputation as a political theorist. There are two good collections of conflicting points of view concerning the origins of the conflict: E. C. Rozwenc, ed., *The Causes of the Civil War* and Kenneth Stampp, ed., *Causes of the American Civil War*.

Fletcher Pratt, *A Short History of the Civil War* is a rather slight summary. Bruce Catton's eloquent trilogy of the war, *Mr. Lincoln's Army* (1951), *Glory Road* (1952), and *A Stillness at Appomattox* (1954) are in paperback, as well as his *This Hallowed Ground: The Story of the Union Side of the Civil War* (1956). "To Catton war is much more than the relatively short time spent in combat. It is, in large part, the myriad experiences of hundreds of thousands of men in a strange society called an army, where so much time is spent in nothing resembling combat. These experiences are recaptured by the hundreds . . . inspired writing. . . ." Carl Sandburg's famous six-volume biography of Abraham Lincoln is available, as well as a carefully abridged three-volume version. David Donald, *Lincoln Reconsidered* (1956) is a series of essays "consisting of articles by the author which have appeared in various journals . . . a solid work, in many ways a brilliant one. Its ranging opinions deserve to be pondered by all scholars in the field." See also P. M. Angle, ed., *The Lincoln Reader* (1947). Margaret Leech, *Reveille in Washington, 1860–1865* (1941) "is done in technicolor . . . The book's impact is upon the senses; its impressions consist of noise and clatter, panoramas, alarms, panics, excitements— in short, the feelings, rumors, sensations, intrigues, and odors of Washington in Lincoln's day. . . . In the popular literature concerning the Civil War the book deserves its high place."

Clement Eaton, in *A History of the Southern Confederacy* (1954) "has written a well-balanced book and has compressed in a compact style a great deal of information. . . . His clear and restrained treatment of the war itself is an admirable feature of the book." B. I. Wiley, *Life of Billy Yank*, B. I. Wiley, *Life of Johnny Reb* and A. D. Kirwan, *The Confederacy* are collections of contemporary writings.

A good introduction to the controversy concerning the character of reconstruction is E. C. Rozwenc, ed., *Reconstruction in the South*. The account by the leading spokesman for the older Southern school, W. A. Dunning, *Reconstruction, Political and Economic* (1907) may be balanced against that of the Marxist supporter of the Black Republicans, W. E. B. Dubois in *Black Reconstruction* (1935). A recent brief survey, J. H. Franklin, *Reconstruction after the Civil War* (1961) is a scholarly rebuttal of Dunning. C. V. Woodward, *Reunion and Reaction: The Compromise of 1877 and the End of Reconstruction* (revised edition 1956) is a model monograph, neatly presenting and proving an original thesis concerning the nature of that compromise. Claude Bowers, *The Tragic Era* (1929) is an engrossing account of the reconstruction period sympathetic to President Johnson.

THE TRIUMPH OF INDUSTRY 8

I

Pre-Civil War Industry The Cinderella story of American industry took place in 1851 at the Crystal Palace in London. There, to celebrate its material magnificence, Great Britain held the Great Exhibition, placing on display the best of its industrial arts and inviting the rest of the world to contribute their own offerings. In the United States the invitation was gingerly received. Many warned that America would only expose itself to ridicule, and Congress withheld appropriations. In the absence of government support individual initiative was nevertheless able to collect

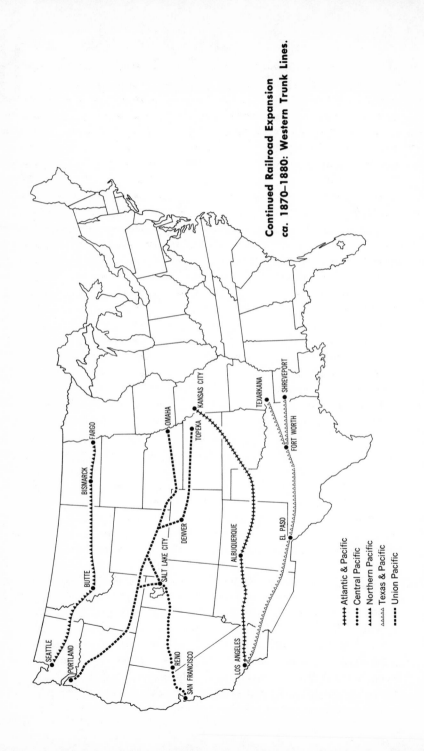

Continued Railroad Expansion ca. 1870–1880: Western Trunk Lines.

+++ Atlantic & Pacific
•••• Central Pacific
▲▲▲ Northern Pacific
△△△ Texas & Pacific
---- Union Pacific

SEATTLE
PORTLAND
BUTTE
FARGO
BISMARCK
OMAHA
SALT LAKE CITY
DENVER
TOPEKA
KANSAS CITY
RENO
SAN FRANCISCO
LOS ANGELES
ALBUQUERQUE
EL PASO
FORT WORTH
TEXARKANA
SHREVEPORT

a substantial number of American contrivances and ship them to London. The American minister to England put himself $15,000 out of pocket, so that the exhibit would not remain bare of decoration and be in homely contrast to the exhibits of other nations, all of which, naturally, were financed by their governments. The American exhibit proved too meager for the space allotted to it in the Palace. It brought little attention from visitors and a good deal of belittling notice from the British press.

Then came the competition for prizes, and the grubby American display transformed itself into the wonder of the day. The outstanding stars of the show were the awkward-appearing reapers of Obed Hussey and Cyrus McCormick, which "chewed up wheat" with a speed and efficiency amazing to Europeans. It was the farm equipment generally which made the most profound impression. The draft plows did not find serious competitors, and other agricultural contraptions and garden variety tools were of an order of excellence and ingenuity not known and perhaps not conceived of by non-American farmers. But the Americans took the prizes in other areas as well. American weapons were unrivaled. Colt revolvers and Lawrence rifles, with "the various parts made to interchange," were without competition. The sewing machines of Isaac M. Singer and others, though viewed as novelties, were enthusiastically admired as wonderfully ingenious contrivances. The vulcanized rubber of Charles Goodyear was on display, and something of its possibilities was seen at once. A chorus of praise for the American display issued from the press, and a parliamentary committee pursued the task of investigating the sources of American ingenuity and discovering ways in which England might benefit from the American example. "Great Britain," concluded one observer, "has received more useful ideas, and more ingenious inventions from the United States, through the exhibition, than from all other countries."

As the parliamentary committee correctly reasoned, America, rich in resources and poor in manpower, had found it expedient to do nothing by hand that a machine could do. In England scarcity of labor had earlier inspired revolutionary changes in the textile industry during the mid-eighteenth century; then population increases had seemed to remove the necessity for further laborsaving inventions. In America, despite heavy immigration, labor remained in comparatively short supply, and inventors and entrepreneurs never ceased wrestling with the problem of labor shortages. The absence of feudal exemptions, privileges, and traditions opened a fair field for material success in America and made of it the main basis there for achievement and recognition. The Americans, according to a greenly envious French observer, had "atrophied all the artistic part of human nature in order to concentrate on agriculture, industry, and commerce."

The first great step in the Americanization of industry was taken by weapons manufacturers—on the advice of the redoubtably agrarian Thomas Jefferson—in the organization of factories where standard parts were mass-produced so that they could be "made to interchange." There was a military advantage to this, and the French government, as Jefferson noted, while Minister to France, had earlier attempted such a method unsuccessfully. In America there was an economic advantage as well, in the saving of labor, and the principle of mass production was quite readily applied to the manufacture of clocks, watches, shoes, carpets, and numerous other items. The McCormick reaper, among other articles of farm machinery, was manufactured on a mass production basis. A trifling but impressive example of American ingenuity in the area of pre-Civil War mass production was a factory which produced a paper of pins from first to last by mechanical means, without the touch of human hands. Waltham watches, mass-produced and cheaply priced, were superior to all but the most expensive handmade watches. Necessity had in many lines of goods been turned to amazing advantage. The development was noted abroad with interest, but it was not emulated.

By the eve of the Civil War, the immensity of America's natural wealth had been revealed, but the industrial superiority which it would give to the nation was not yet clearly realized. California gold had made its impression, and discoveries of gold and silver in Colorado, Nevada, and elsewhere were creating fevers of excitement as war came. But the importance of the iron ranges at the western shores of Lake Superior were by no means yet understood, and the first drillings for oil in western Pennsylvania seemed to promise little more than novelty and excitement. Americans had not yet comprehended what became entirely clear in the first decade after the Civil War, that in the world-wide competition for industrial supremacy the United States possessed geographical advantages which far exceeded those of any competing nation. The big advantage consisted of those ranges of iron connected to the equally rich Appalachian coalfields by cheap water transportation on the Great Lakes. Beyond that the United States found itself to be possessed of unrivaled wealth in other industrial minerals. In the industrial age, economic geography provided the new Gospel for the old American faith that America was the especial favorite of divine providence.

The United States by 1851 had outstripped the old mother country in population, but despite its distinctive industrial achievements and its discoveries of vast mineral resources, it lagged far behind England industrially. In this the best index was heavy industry, where the American iron manufacturing remained small-scale, dispersed, to a considerable extent charcoal-fueled, and wholly inadequate to American needs. American railroad construction, greater than that of any other nation by far, was made possible by large-scale, coke-operated British furnaces, and little was being contemplated in America to meet this competition. Except for New England factory towns, American society was still basically agrarian, and the industrial revolution was still a troublesome disturbance, unsettling to what were thought to be normal conditions. In 1860 the economy was converting to industry at an annually accelerating pace, but America remained farm-minded, and the government was in agrarian hands. Clearest proof of this was the tariff of 1857, reducing protection for industry to the lowest point since the War of 1812 and advancing the nation toward the agrarian ideal of free trade. Lincoln won in 1860 on a platform containing a tariff protection plank, but both houses of Congress remained in safe, agrarian, low-tariff hands.

II

Wartime Legislation Then eleven planting states withdrew from the Union, and Northern industry tumbled into power. Congress in 1861 passed the Morrill Tariff, revising rates upward, and no session of Congress again met during the Civil War without adding further upward revisions. Excise taxes were levied also, which business did not like, but at the close of the war these were removed while the tariffs remained.

In 1862, with the South no longer present to contest the route, Congress passed railroad acts providing for the construction of a railroad from Omaha to Sacramento. It authorized the Union

Pacific to build the eastern section and the Central Pacific to build the western one. It made enormous grants of land to which it added loans ranging from $16,000 to $48,000 per mile. The companies, formed for the purpose by men of moderate means, found it even then impossible to raise the capital. Consequently the land grant was doubled and the government loans were converted to second mortgages, permitting the companies to acquire their private loans on the basis of first mortgages. No provision was made for a government-chartered construction company to build the roads. The controllers of the companies were therefore able to create their own companies and, with no government supervision or legislative limitations, to make what profit they liked.

In 1864 the Northern Pacific Railroad was chartered to run from Lake Superior to Puget Sound and given even more generous grants of land than those accorded both the Central Pacific and Union Pacific together. A similar charter and land grant was given to the Atlantic and Pacific in 1866 and to the Texas and Pacific in 1871 for southern transcontinental routes to San Diego and Los Angeles. The latter two were almost immediately acquired by the operators of the Central Pacific along with the land grants, and the roads never reached the West Coast. By that time more than 130 million acres of Federal land had been distributed to railroad companies since 1862, although one-third of it was eventually forfeited by companies for not meeting Federal terms. On a smaller scale private interests gained from government largess in timber and mineral lands during this period. Then with the panic of 1873 and revelations of national political scandals, the period of gargantuan government handouts came to a close.

Free land was given to the small farmer also in the Homestead Act of 1862, granting settlers farms free of charge in lots of 160 acres after five years occupation. This represented the final acceptance by the Federal government of the farmers' argument, older than the republic, that the vacant land of the nation belonged to those who settled it and improved it. By the time the act was passed, however, the best lands suited to the one-family farm, which the supporters of the act had had in mind, had been largely taken up. Homesteading the plains regions proved too expensive for most, who found they were better served by purchasing lands which the government had given to the railroads. A further act popular with the farmers, the Morrill Land Grant Act of 1862, distributed public lands among the states according to congressional representation—30,000 acres for each senator and representative—for the purpose of financing agricultural and mechanical colleges. The main result of the act was the large-scale advancement of public higher education, especially in the West where the best advantage was taken of the law. It served also, however, as another means whereby large areas of public land were eventually placed at the disposal of politically influential private interests.

The National Banking Act was passed in 1863 and largely revised the next year. In part this was to bring order to a formerly chaotic system in which banks operated under the miscellaneous regulations of the various state charters. In part it was a device to market government bonds issued to help finance the war. Provision was made under the act for the establishment of banking associations under national charters. One-third of the capital of these associations was to be invested in government bonds on which the government, in addition to paying interest on the bonds, would issue to the banks Federal notes worth 90 per cent of the cost of the bonds. The banks were to maintain reserves against both deposits and banknotes, and these were to be held in certain reserve cities. Then in 1865 Congress placed a tax on state banknote issues which drove them out of existence.

Originally the banking acts were not designed to favor any special group or region, but the reserve requirement enabled New York to establish itself as the main center for bankers' funds, and as the act was administered it discriminated heavily in favor of the Northeast. All the New England and middle states received banknotes in excess of their quotas at the expense of the rest of the nation. Another important means by which the war was financed was through the issue of 432 million dollars in greenbacks, paper money which was not redeemable in specie. Reluctantly resorted to at the time, the greenbacks remained after the war to create political as well as economic problems.

The war turned the Federal government into a buyer of goods and services on a scale for which the government had neither the experience nor the administrative organization, and every possible advantage was taken of its vulnerability. A "shoddy aristocracy" sprang up in the North on profits made from the necessities of the nation, the term deriving from the practice of selling shoddy material for army uniforms, which disintegrated under the first heavy use. The greatest scandal and the greatest profit was to be enjoyed in the illicit cotton trade. Southern cotton could be sold in New

England at almost 1,000 per cent profit, and the cotton trade, while bringing the Confederacy valuable specie, made many fortunes in the North.

Nor was it necessary to wallow in corruption in order to do well financially during wartime. To a remarkable extent the vast industrial enterprises of the late nineteenth century had their origins in Civil War opportunities, when young men like Andrew Carnegie and John D. Rockefeller emerged from it with the capital accumulation which enabled them to rise swiftly to economic power. During the Civil War the number of millionaires in America increased many times over.

It was one of the tragedies of the Civil War that it came at the critical period in American history when the nation was making the transition from an agrarian to an industrial society. No nation in the nineteenth century which passed through the experience of the industrial revolution was as ill equipped to cope with it politically as the American federal republic. England, France, Germany, and Japan, by contrast, all were administered by centralized governments at the time the industrial revolution centralized their economies. During the crucial period of this transition the American nation was distracted by the slavery crisis, civil war, and reconstruction, with the result that many of the basic problems of the industrial age did not receive serious concentrated nationwide attention until the twentieth century.

III

The Gilded Age   By the election of 1868 the transition had already taken place in the Republican party leadership from the abolitionist idealists like Sumner and Stevens to those like Simon Cameron of Pennsylvania and Roscoe Conkling of New York whose chief interest was in securing the wartime tariff, banking and railroad legislation against an agrarian counterattack and, more than that, in securing Republican political control against a reunited Democratic party. The Republican party had always been a minority party, and there was no reason to suppose that it could win an election in 1868 on the basis of those economic interests in the nation which its program attracted. In order to win the election, therefore, the Republicans nominated the war's leading hero, Gen. Ulysses S. Grant, and campaigned on the "bloody shirt" issue, that a vote for the Democratic party was a vote for the party of rebellion.

Grant himself had always been associated with the Democratic party, so far as he had interested himself in politics at all. He had broken with the Democratic Johnson, however, and he submitted unenthusiastically to the nomination, placing himself in the hands of the party managers. The Democrats in their convention nominated the governor of New York, Horatio Seymour, and went down to defeat by a margin of 310,000 votes. Crucial to the Republican victory was the activity in the South of the Union League clubs in organizing the Negro vote, which provided the narrow margin of victory. To strengthen this support Congress, when it met in 1869 initiated the Fifteenth Amendment, declared ratified a year later, which provided that, "The right of citizens of the United States to vote shall not be denied or abridged by the United States or by any State on account of race, color, or previous condition of servitude."

Hailed as the savior of the nation and as a second George Washington, Grant proved sadly incompetent to cope with the problems confronting him. He failed to familiarize himself with the duties of his office, placing responsibility instead in the hands of friends who over and over again betrayed his confidence. An unsuccessful businessman during much of his prewar career, Grant held successful businessmen in unbounded admiration, a confidence which was betrayed frequently during his administrations and again in later life when he was financially ruined by embezzling business associates. During his eight years in office he made an unusually large number of Cabinet appointments, many of whom were incompetent and corrupt, and of the few who were neither, only one, Secretary of State Hamilton Fish, survived to the end. Before coming to the Presidency, Grant had indicated by his acts a policy of moderation toward the South, but as President he accepted the program of the Radicals without question.

The Grant administration inherited from the war a maze of administrative confusion and corruption, which in the Lincoln and Johnson administrations had been obscured by war and reconstruction. During the Grant administrations corruption reached its full-bellied climax. Even before the election of 1872 the nation knew of what was going on. Most spectacularly in 1869 Jay Gould and Jim Fisk had attempted, through connivance with government officials, to corner the national gold market and so to force those who needed gold for business transactions to pay the monopoly price for it. The scheme went awry on "Black Friday" when the treasury threw gold on the market, ruining many innocent dealers. Fisk and Gould escaped loss by repudiating their contracts.

The President was more directly implicated the next year in a scheme to annex Santo Domingo in the interest of his private secretary Orville Babcock and others who hoped to acquire a large portion of the island's wealth. Bypassing the State Department, Grant arranged a treaty of annexation which, despite Grant's strong support, failed to pass the Senate. Senator Sumner, who led the fight against the treaty, lost his place as chairman of the Foreign Relations Committee shortly thereafter.

The extent of government corruption was not known during the Presidential campaign of 1872, but it was suspected by many, including a number of disenchanted Republicans. In Missouri Grant's trusted political boss was the leader of the "Whiskey Ring," which was systematically defrauding the government of millions of dollars in excise taxes and retaining its political power through the continued disenfranchisement of former Missouri Confederates. In 1868 Carl Schurz, Civil War general and idealistic refugee from the German Revolution of '48, was elected to the Senate from Missouri. In the election of 1870 Schurz and other Republicans in Missouri joined the Democrats and defeated the machine, capturing both the legislature and the governorship. In the Senate Schurz became the leader of a Liberal Republican movement to remove Grant by the same means, and he was joined in this by influential Republicans such as editor of the New York *Tribune*, Horace Greeley, editor of the *Nation*, E. L. Godkin, and former minister to England, Charles Francis Adams.

An alliance with the Democrats in itself seemed certain to assure victory, but there were additional discontented groups which might well be drawn in. There was discontent among the farmers, and an organization known as the Grange had developed through which they increasingly expressed their discontent. Formed in 1867 as a social organization, the Grange was beginning by 1872 to become a vehicle for political reform. The farmers, however, were less concerned about tariff reform and clean government than they were about railroad regulation and managed currency, both of which represented communistical departures from true Americanism, from the point of view of the Britisher Godkin and the German Schurz and other Liberal Republicans. Apparently more promising was the new National Labor Reform party. This party was an outgrowth of the National Labor Union, which, in turn, had been formed in 1866 under the leadership of William H. Sylvis, presdent of the Iron Molders Union, out of a heterogeneous collection of craft unions and general reform associations.

The National Labor Reform party disappointed the Liberal Republicans by nominating a not especially liberal Supreme Court justice, David Davis, but it was nothing to the disappointment the Liberals experienced in the candidate which their own convention nominated. The most promising candidate had seemed to be Charles Francis Adams, whose father and grandfather had both won the office. However, Adams did nothing for his own candidacy, the convention got out of hand, and the nomination went to Horace Greeley, eccentric faddist, former abolitionist, and formerly vituperative foe of the Democratic party. The Democrats met, swallowed Greeley in order to win liberal support, and went down with him to defeat, Grant winning by more than twice his previous plurality.

By the eve of the election the scandal of the Grant administration was all seeping into the open. Construction of the Union Pacific Railroad had been carried out by a company, Credit Mobilier, which had siphoned off huge profits above the actual cost of the road, leaving the company to languish for more than a generation with a crippling debt and a faulty roadbed. The management of Central Pacific had been guilty of an identical swindle, and both companies had bribed congressmen generously (prior to Grant's coming to office) in order to win government approval for their projects. Representative Oakes Ames of Massachusetts as the head of Credit Mobilier had, as he himself explained, handed out stock to congressmen "where they will do the most good to us." Important members of the administration, including Cabinet members, were found to be busy with a multitude of dishonest schemes, selling franchises to collect taxes for profit, selling rights in Indian trading posts, and defrauding the government of excise taxes on whiskey.

The act which aroused public indignation most of all perhaps was the legally honest but unbecomingly greedy "salary grab," by which congressmen voted themselves large retroactive pay raises. These they later rescinded in the face of public indignation. There was from this time forward a general concurrence with Ambrose

Bierce's definition of a congressman, in his *Devil's Dictionary*, as a member of the lower house in this world with little hope for promotion in the next.

But corruption in Federal places paled beside state and local corruption. The votes of state legislatures and state judges were busily bought and sold. Gould and Fisk, in company with Daniel Drew, had gained notoriety before their Gold Conspiracy exploit by their perpetration of the most outrageous and swashbuckling example of this practice. The struggles of these men with Cornelius Vanderbilt to control the Erie Railroad between 1866 and 1868, involved state judiciaries and legislatures of New York and New Jersey in an orgy of corruption and favoritism. The blatant speculations which marked the reconstruction governments in the South received more publicity than did the Northern statewide corruption, but these robberies in the South were on a much smaller scale than those of the North, mainly because there was less to rob.

The richest loot of all was to be found in the cities, where corruption was practiced most openly and systematically and where such political machines as the Gas ring in Philadelphia and the Tweed ring in New York raked in millions of dollars in their takes from bribery, shakedowns, inflated building contracts, and control of franchises. Every large city in the nation was under the control of a similarly corrupt political machine operating with apparently absolute immunity. It was one of the remarkable events of the age when Samuel J. Tilden managed to send Boss Tweed of Tammany Hall to the penitentiary, and it won Tilden the fame which helped to bring him the Democratic presidential nomination in 1876. Nationally the corruption of the "Gilded Age" was associated with the Republican party, because the administration was of that party, but in fact it was completely bipartisan, Democrats rooting and hogging right along with Republicans.

IV

Compromise of 1877

The Republicans by hook and by crook remained in the Presidency until 1885, and throughout that period a dominant theme of American political life was the three-cornered struggle within the Republican party between the Liberals, the "Half-Breeds," and the "Stalwarts." The major issue dividing these factions was political corruption; the Liberals, led by Senator Schurz, disapproving of it on moral and ideological grounds, the Half-Breeds, led by Senator James G. Blaine of Maine, holding to the view that rampant robbery was bad for the party, and the Stalwarts, to the extent that they were spoken for by their leader, Senator Roscoe Conkling of New York, convinced that the party could survive such scandals if the party machinery continued in good operating order and if the party kept on renominating Grant. The intraparty differences turned to a considerable extent on a personal enmity which existed between Conkling and Blaine, national politics during this period being controlled, with little regard for political issues, by the principles of personal loyalty and party regularity.

Blaine would probably have received the Republican nomination in 1876 had he not been discovered at the last minute to have been involved in an indiscretion, minor by the standards of the day, in connection with the Union Pacific Railroad. His Republican rival Conkling was able to defeat Blaine's candidacy by throwing his support to Governor Rutherford B. Hayes of Ohio. Hayes brought a momentary unity to the party, for he was an honest man whom the Liberals were willing to support, while the Half-Breeds had no alternative. Thus the thieves fell out and still won the election, but not without a subsequent series of ingenious dodges unparalleled in the history of presidential elections.

In the popular vote Tilden won by a plurality of 250,000 over Hayes. The count of the electoral vote was complicated, however, by the fact that three southern states, South Carolina, Florida, and Louisiana, were still under reconstruction governments, and these states each returned two sets of electoral votes, one for each candidate. Even without these contested votes Tilden would have won exactly the necessary 185, had it not been that a Republican elector in Oregon was disqualified by a technicality and arbitrarily replaced by a Democrat. To judge between the disputed returns, Congress, after several months of violent indecision, appointed a commission of five senators, five representatives and five Supreme Court justices. By party affiliation the commission stood eight to seven Republican, and by that margin it voted to uphold the Republican returns of each of the three Southern states, thereby electing Hayes by a margin of one electoral vote.

Throughout the four months between the election and the inauguration the threat of a new civil war was never absent. On the other hand, the dominant economic interests in both the North and the South were opposed to war no matter who got the Presidency. Negotiations were carried on among these groups outside political channels before and after the decision of the commission, successfully arriving at the compromise which resulted in the peaceful inauguration of Hayes. On the one hand Southern conservatives, who found their forced connection with the Democrats distasteful, had many of them argued in favor of joining the Republican party on the grounds that it represented their interests. Furthermore they wanted Federal support for internal improvements, which had been so lavishly handed out in the North and West while the South was out of the Union, and which the Northern Democrats opposed, following the revelations of the Grant administration scandals. Northern business, on the other hand, had opposed radical reconstruction as being bad for business and had looked favorably upon a restoration of the Whig alliance of pre-Civil War years.

Between these groups an informal bargain was arranged. Southern acquiescence in Hayes's election was exchanged for Hayes's removal of Federal troops from the South and his appointment of a Southerner to a Cabinet post. The compromise called also for Republican votes in favor of federally financed Southern rivers and harbors improvements and for passage of the Texas Pacific Railroad Bill, to give the South its own transcontinental line. The Southerners, on their part, in addition to accepting Hayes, were to help the Republicans organize the Democratic-dominated house and so enable them to nominate the Republican Garfield as speaker. These were not signed agreements, and none were carried out except the removal of troops from the Southern states and the making of a Southern Cabinet appointment, both of which might have taken place under any circumstances. The compromise nevertheless marked a fundamental political realignment, ending reconstruction on terms which renewed the prewar Whig alliance of Southern planters and Northern business, an alliance which has continued, with occasional interruptions, to dominate Congress down to the present.

To the disgust of the Stalwarts, Hayes proved throughout his administration to be a Liberal Republican with a vengeance. Indeed his major Cabinet appointments represented so many personified repudiations of leading tenets that had guided his party over the previous decade. He named a former Confederate, David M. Key of Tennessee, as Postmaster General, as had been agreed to in the compromise which secured his peaceable inauguration. Beyond that, however, he appointed as Secretary of State W. M. Evarts, the lawyer who had served successfully as President Johnson's chief counsel at the impeachment trial before the radical Republican-dominated Senate, while for Secretary of the Interior he appointed the civil service reformer and idol of the Liberals, Carl Schurz.

Viciously harried by Democrats on grounds of the disputable legitimacy of his election, Hayes immediately upon taking office invited the wrath of the Stalwarts in his party by pressing for civil service reform and by attacking Conkling directly through the New York Customs House which, under Conkling's direction, was the very model of smoothly operating political corruption. Momentarily defeated, Conkling managed to rally the faithful and put his customhouse substantially back in order, but Hayes in turn was successful, with Democratic support, in winning Senate approval for his customhouse appointments. The struggle marked the beginning of Conkling's fall from power. More importantly, it checked the tendency of the ruling group in the Senate to assume positive executive authority, in patent disregard of the Constitution, a tendency which from the time of President Johnson seemed to be altering drastically and perhaps permanently the nation's form of government.

Hayes had explicitly disqualified himself for renomination at the outset and had furthermore failed to create organizational strength for Liberal Republicanism. The Stalwarts and the Half-Breeds therefore had a free field in the nominating convention of 1880, and, with Grant once more available, Conkling apparently possessed the winning candidate. Out of a long deadlock between Grant and Blaine, however, the Half-Breeds emerged victorious with a dark horse candidate, Congressman James A. Garfield of Ohio. Then, in the interests of party harmony, the vice presidential nomination was given to a Conkling man, Chester A. Arthur. The Democrats in their turn, in order to remove as far as possible the taint of treason, nominated a Civil War hero named after a Mexican War hero, Winfield Scott Hancock of Pennsylvania. Hancock was a political novice who has been most famously described as "a good man weighing 250 pounds."

Garfield won with a plurality of 9,464 votes out of 9,000,000 cast

and immediately attacked Conkling's empire by appointing an anti-
Conkling man to Vice President Arthur's former post, that of Collector of the Port of New York. In the struggle which ensued, the
enormously arrogant Conkling sought to strengthen his position by
resigning his Senate seat, in company with his colleague the junior
Senator from New York Thomas Platt, and applying to the state
legislature for reappointment. It proved to be an ill-judged move,
for the legislature declined to reelect the two men, and Conkling
was abruptly and permanently dropped out of political life. It
would be too much to say that Conkling's defeat marked the end
of an era. It did to some extent, however, mark a transition in
American politics from the era of robber politicians, who acquired
wealth through politics, to the era of the robber barons, who gained
political power through wealth. In the years to come the Senate
was to be known as the "Millionaire's Club," where independent
spirits such as Conkling no longer dominated.

Five months after taking office, Garfield was shot in the back by
a disappointed office seeker, who shouted as he fired, "I am a Stalwart and Arthur is President now." Arthur as Collector of the Port
of New York certainly had been one of the spoilsmen, but now he
was President. He did not say to his former Stalwart comrades, "I
know you not, old men"; in fact, a number of them joined him in
his Cabinet. But he vetoed a major pork barrel bill and cleaned up
the mess in the Post Office Department, and in 1883 he signed the
Pendleton Civil Service Bill.

Civil Service reform from the end of the Civil War had been the
main panacea of the Liberal Republicans, who truly believed that
it would lead American politics out of a gilded age into a golden
one. Grant had put these men off by appointing a Civil Service
Commission with no authority, and the reform had advanced little
since then, despite Hayes's efforts. Then Garfield's death created a
martyr for the cause, and the Pendleton Act was passed, which provided for a system of civil service based on merit and protected
from political reprisal. The act put more than 10 per cent of government workers under its provisions immediately, and the percentage increased rapidly thereafter, due chiefly to the desire of
politicians, when turned out of office, to give incoming rival administrations the use of as little patronage as possible. Within a
generation, more than half of all government employees were clas-
sified, with the unforeseen consequence that party coffers no longer

could be filled by the postman's mite, and so the two major political parties became dependent as never before upon men of great wealth.

V

Labor and Farm Protest During the administration of President Hayes, unprecedented violent industrial warfare broke out across the nation, while agrarian radicalism for a time presented a real threat to the political balance of the nation. Within a few months of his coming to office, Hayes faced the Great Strike of '77, which began with the B. & O. Railroad, following the second of two 10 per cent wage cuts to trainmen. The strike spread to the four main eastern trunk lines and then swiftly throughout the nation, paralyzing transportation and erupting in mob violence in every major railroad city from Baltimore to San Francisco. There had never been anything like it before in American history, and thoughtful Americans could only suppose that it was the work of foreign agitators, "anarchists," who, from that time until the rise of the American Communist party, generally got the blame for each economic discontent which produced violence.

In response to desperate calls from state governors, President Hayes sent out Federal troops to suppress the rioting, reluctantly establishing a Federal precedent in labor disputes which was immediately and self-righteously followed by each of his successors to the end of the nineteenth century. The violence of the Great Strike resulted from the desperate condition of the railroad workers and from the absence of any effective labor organization to assert discipline. The National Labor Union had been so hopeful as to organize a labor party and field a presidential candidate in 1872, but it had been destroyed in the depression of '73, and few of its component craft unions had survived in any strength.

The problem of agrarian radicalism—the Granger movement—so far as it came within the purview of President Hayes, was the money problem. This concerned the question of whether precious metals provide the only reliable basis for a monetary system or whether a government can manage its currency according to the economic needs of the nation. Specifically, the monetary radicals wished to print paper money without gold or silver backing.

Hayes, a hard-money man, faced during his administration the familiar greenback issue and in addition the entirely new silver issue, which was to divide the nation fiercely fifteen years hence.

Since the Civil War, when the government had guiltily issued those 432 million dollars worth of inflationary greenbacks, unsupported by specie, the question of what to do with them had repeatedly vexed the nation. To bankers, to proprietors of old established businesses—especially in New England—and to merchants dealing in international trade, they were the means by which debtors defrauded creditors and by which a nation defaulted on its obligations to its bondholders and to its foreign customers. To farmers, on the other hand, they were a means by which more dollars were received for wheat, while for rapidly developing industries such as steel they were a means by which money was made available for capital investment. Congress passed various enactments with regard to the greenbacks and the Supreme Court handed down two decisions, one declaring legal tender unbacked by specie to be illegal and the other reversing the first decision. The Resumption Act was further passed in 1875 providing that the Treasury, beginning in 1879, would redeem greenbacks in coin. Hayes's Secretary of the Treasury John Sherman, the original author of the Resumption Act, built up a gold reserve to pay for the greenbacks, with such success that nobody bothered to redeem them when the time came.

The period from the panic of '73 to the Spanish-American War was a period of generally declining prices in America, as it was in Europe, and in American society the farmer, who still made up the largest element of the population, was hard hit by this tendency. Under these circumstances, the price of his mortgage and the debts owed on his farm machinery stayed up, while the returns from his produce, with which he had to repay the debts and mortgage, went down. Beyond that, railroad rates tended to stay up, where the railroad enjoyed a monopolistic position, and the price of farm machinery and other manufactured goods tended to stay up also, protected by tariffs. Tariffs had been placed on farm products also, but they were of no use to farmers selling on the world market.

Working through the Granges, the farm states met the problem of the railroads by establishing state railroad commissions, empowered to set rates and regulate operating conditions. The railroads refused to cooperate and, further, took the matter to the

Supreme Court. In 1877, the Court upheld the Granger laws in the case of Munn *v.* Illinois, on the ground that "When private property is devoted to public use, it is subject to public regulation." Thereafter the Supreme Court became more considerate of the rights of property, and it did not again decide so comprehensively in the public interest for more than sixty years, but even by the time that the Munn decision had been handed down, the Granger regulatory laws had been found disappointingly unenforceable.

The transcontinental railroads, which in many cases were worth more than the total wealth of the entire state through which they passed, bought out commissioners and confused the ones they could not bribe. Against the railroad lawyers, the state commissioners were in no good position to command the information necessary to fix fair rates or determine minimum safety conditions. The Granger laws served only to prove that railroads had clearly passed the bounds of state regulation. The farmers' cooperatives which had been formed to supplant those thieving middlemen, meanwhile, were going out of business. The one permanent such business to emerge from the movement was a private enterprise, the mail-order house of Montgomery Ward, established in 1872 in response to the needs of the farmers as expressed by the Grangers.

There remained the possibility of dealing with falling farm prices through controlled inflation. Out of the failure of the Granger experiments there emerged the Greenback party, nominating the New York industrialist Peter Cooper for President in 1876, on the main plank of withdrawing the specie backing for greenbacks. The party only polled 81,000 votes, but amid worsening conditions two years later it elected fourteen congressmen, by casting more than one million votes. Then good times returned to the American farm temporarily and ruined the party, which secured only 308,000 votes for the highly respected Gen. James B. Weaver of Iowa in the presidential election of 1880.

Bad times were presently to return to the farms, and with them returned the same agrarian radicalism. By the time that had happened, however, silver had supplanted greenbacks as the central solution to submerged farm prices, a development which was already getting under way as the Greenback party was reaching its peak of success. Since before the Civil War the nation had been on the bimetallic standard with the ratio of silver to gold set legally at 16 to 1. By 1873, however, silver was no longer available for minting, since its value on the open market was more than sixteen times that of gold, and Congress, in adopting a new coinage law, failed to provide for the minting of silver. In the same year the Big Bonanza was discovered on the Comstock Lode in Nevada, yielding millions of dollars worth of silver, while other nations of the world by ceasing to mint silver also, depressed the world price.

"Silver Dick" Bland of Missouri introduced a bill into Congress calling for the unlimited minting of silver once again at the ratio of 16 to 1. In the Senate, William Allison of Iowa substituted "limited" for "unlimited," and the resulting Bland-Allison Act, passed again over Hayes's veto in 1878, called for the minting of between 2 and 4 million dollars worth of silver each month, to be purchased at no fixed ratio to gold but at the current world price. The bill was passed at the behest of politically powerful silver miners, and it had no observable inflationary effect. When hard times came again to the farms of the nation, however, the free silver issue served to rally a host, which was able to capture the Democratic party in 1896 and, from that platform, raise issues which were to bedevil American politics for most of the next generation.

VI

The Far Western Frontier　The death struggle of the nation in civil war and the arduous aftermath of reconstruction had little observable effect on the accelerating settlement and exploitation of the Far West. Completion of the first continental railroad—the combined Union Pacific and Central Pacific systems—was delayed by the war until 1869, but, at the news of gold out West, horses, mules and oxen were kept in a lather, as settlements appeared throughout the region extending from the Rocky Mountains to the Pacific. Discovery of gold in California converted that quiet Mexican outpost in two years into a state of the Union, supporting a population of more than ninety thousand, or seven times the population of agrarian Oregon, where settlement had gone on for a decade. Unlike most of the Western mining areas, that of California was set amid potentially rich farming land. The gold rush was virtually over by 1852, but the population of California quadrupled during the decade of the fifties, based on agriculture and on the port facilities of San Francisco Bay.

Gold and silver were discovered at Pikes Peak in the territory of Colorado in 1858 and again the next year on the Comstock Lode in what became Nevada. During the Civil War, further mining discoveries opened up areas in what became Washington, Idaho, and Montana, and in the seventies the final major strike occurred in the Black Hills of Dakota Territory. These mining areas, unlike those of California, required large-scale operations, involving heavy capitalization, with the result that, almost from the beginning, the areas came into the control of a relatively few companies, generally financed by Eastern interests or by those from San Francisco. In the wake of the gold rushes there remained forsaken ghost towns and remnants of the original population staying on to farm or to work the declining yields from the consolidated mines or to work on the railroad. Within a generation, in most of these areas, the railroads had become the dominant economic interest and the controlling political agent.

The age of the open-range cattle kingdom came into existence almost as suddenly as that of the mining frontier, and it dropped even more abruptly into the past. Cattle, which had ranged Texas in Spanish times, were first demonstrated to be marketable on a large scale in 1866, when the first "long drive" was made to the railroad town of Sedalia, Missouri. During the next twenty years, cattle by the million were driven annually to the new railroad towns, notably Dodge City and Wichita in Kansas and Cheyenne and Laramie in Wyoming. Cattle soon came to dominate the economy of Wyoming to the same extent that mining had dominated that of Nevada. This was the era of the cattlemen's wars with the "nesters"—single-family farmers breaking up the open range—and with the sheep ranchers. Then in 1885 to 1887 two bitter winters and a scorching summer destroyed hundreds of thousands of cattle and drove the cattle ranchers to more modest and methodical cattle enterprises.

This was the era also of the wars with the plains Indians, the Arapaho, the Cheyenne, the Apaches and, above all, the Sioux, an era climaxed by the slaughter of George A. Custer and all his men at the Battle of the Little Bighorn in 1876, an era which was mainly concluded with the capture of the Apache leader Geronimo in 1886. Thus there came to a close the age which produced such colorful figures as Wild Bill Hickock, Wyatt Earp, Calamity Jane, and Billy the Kid, and with them produced an American tradition which is apparently an inexhaustible source of fascination to Europeans as well as to Americans.

The farmer's frontier, by the time of the Civil War, extended to the first tier of states west of the Mississippi and, with the main exception of Mormon Utah, then leaped across what was known as the "Great American Desert," to the inland valley of California and the Willamette Valley of Oregon. Americans had naturally been reluctant to move out of the forest areas into the grassy plains region. There they faced the problems of inadequate water supply, lack of building materials, and lack of protection against ranging cattle. These were to some extent remedied by the invention of barbed wire, the use of windmills, and the development of extensive—as opposed to intensive—farming techniques, supported by the use of farm machinery.

Heavily capitalized, huge "bonanza farms" in many cases paid rich returns on the investment. For the average single-family farmer, however, the life on the high plains was a hard and dreary and often unsuccessful one. Settlement in this area was encouraged during the Civil War by high wartime farm prices, by a decade of exceptionally heavy rainfall, and by the advertising campaigns of the railroads. It was the later drought conditions of the "sod house frontier" which kindled some of the most fiery leadership in the farm protest movement at the close of the century.

VII

Industrial Expansion   Temporarily diverted by the war from normal development, American industry at war's end expanded uncontrollably to the depression of 1873, checked itself, reorganized into larger units and expanded again at a redoubled rate to the depression of 1893. Deeper than the earlier depression, the panic of '93 was the occasion for correspondingly more thoroughgoing consolidation and for the rapid conquest of the economy by finance capitalism at the turn of the century. Politically triumphant over the agrarians with the Civil War, the businessmen prowled fearfully through the jungle of free enterprise, destroying one another and being destroyed, until the titans of Wall Street at the turn of the twentieth century managed to bring a semblance of order to the economy and a semblance of security to the business community. And out of this violent process of boom, bust, bankruptcy, receivership, and consolidation, the United States emerged at century's end the undisputed industrial leader of the world.

Basic to this industrial growth and consolidation was the railroad industry, huge beyond comparison to that of any other nation in the world and the main basis for the rise of heavy industry in the United States. By the time of the panic of '73 there were about 70,000 miles of railroad in the nation; by the panic of '93 there were about 170,000. In 1914, at the dawn of the gasoline age, the climax was reached with 256,000 miles of railroad. By 1860 the American railroads consumed more than half the iron produced in the nation, despite the heavy importations from Great Britain. Still in its infancy at the time of the war, the American iron and steel industry remained concentrated along the eastern seaboard and relatively small scale. With the high tariffs on iron and steel following the war this condition rapidly changed. With the large-scale development of the iron ranges of Minnesota and the coalfields of the Appalachians came the rise to industrial world leadership in the next generation.

Out of the commotion of civil war, reconstruction, and westward expansion there emerged a railroad barony which towered over the formerly mighty merchant princelings and wallowed in violence and corruption. Union Pacific had been gutted by Credit Mobilier, and except for speculative purposes it remained a losing venture for more than a generation. Central Pacific, however, similarly gutted by its operators, remained in the hands of the big four, Leland Stanford, Collis P. Huntington, Charles Crocker, and Mark Hopkins, who had been unable to unload it at a good price. Making the best of a bad thing, these men absorbed the CP into Southern Pacific and became themselves the political as well as economic rulers of a half dozen Western states. Cornelius Vanderbilt, an old man by the eve of the Civil War, capped one of the most successful business careers of his day by entering the railroad business and gaining control of the New York Central. These men, and others like them, became rich almost beyond belief and apparently powerful beyond control.

Yet to be the master of one of the nation's great trunk lines was to be astride a monster which was never entirely submissive to control and never out of danger from its fellow monsters. Railroad managers sought ceaselessly for escape from the struggle for survival. They organized together in railroad pools, attempting to stabilize prices, to divide the traffic equitably among themselves, and to operate in safety from one another. Public hostility and Federal laws attacked such agreements, however, while mutual suspicion and company violations of the pooling agreements even more effectively destroyed them. The managers were captives of their own companies, and their companies were caught up in the powerful centralizing tendencies of the day.

Terrified of one another, the railroads were at the same time forced to submit to the dictates of their major customers, on pain of being destroyed by the loss of trade to a rival. Rebates from published traffic rates were demanded by heavy users of the railroads, and these, in turn, helped those favored producers to destroy competitors in their own field. The leading example of this practice, and the classic case history of an American monopoly, was the Standard Oil Company.

The first commercial oil well in American history was drilled in western Pennsylvania in 1859, and into this fiercely competitive field, less than a decade later, stepped the greatest of the captains of industry, John D. Rockefeller. Concentrating on one phase of the industry, oil refining, Rockefeller successfully organized a local pooling arrangement which placed his company in control of a major portion of the industry in Cleveland. On the basis of its large volume of trade, the Standard Oil Company demanded and received rebates from railroads competing with each other for the Cleveland traffic. For a time the company received, not only rebates, but an equal rebate for every barrel of oil shipped by a competitor.

In the following years, Rockefeller bought out or drove out all of his important competitors, while extending this monopoly of the refining industry to control of the oil fields, rails, pipelines, and distributing agencies. The depression of 1873 ruined many competitors, some of whom had overextended themselves in the attempt to compete with Standard Oil. By 1879 Rockefeller controlled 95 per cent of the American refining capacity and virtually the entire world market. Reorganized in 1879, Standard Oil was ordered to dissolve thirteen years later by the Ohio State Supreme Court. In 1899, the company reappeared as the Standard Oil Company of New Jersey, availing itself of that state's lax corporation laws to remain a legal monopoly until dissolved by the United States Supreme Court in 1911. And where Rockefeller had shown the way, other industries—steel, copper, sugar, tobacco, rubber, leather, and so forth—soon followed.

The American iron industry, although it had a history as long as that of the nation, enjoyed a spectacular development rivaling that of the newborn oil industry in the postwar years, a development associated with Andrew Carnegie much as the oil industry was associated with Rockefeller. Carnegie concentrated his resources in the iron industry in 1873, behind the newly raised iron and steel tariffs, and, relying for markets on his close associations with leading railroad men, ignored the depression conditions to build the largest steel mill in the world. Without attempting to monopolize the field, he developed efficient methods which gave him the advantage of his competition as had, indeed, been the main basis of Rockefeller's original success. He then proceeded to make himself independent, so far as possible, of all outside sources. Buying vast holdings in the Mesabi iron ranges and in the Pennsylvania coalfields, Carnegie also acquired his own railroads and ore boats. By the close of the century, despite rising competition, Carnegie remained independent and the most important figure in the industry.

On the one hand, the triumph of American industry was characterized by a ruthless disregard for general welfare. On the other hand, it brought greater wealth to America and a higher general standard of living than was known elsewhere in the world. It is understandable, therefore, that the national attitude toward those early captains of industry should have been fiercely ambivalent. In the 1850s the *New York Times* applied the phrase "robber baron" to Cornelius Vanderbilt, and, to many American writers, the term remains the most fitting one available. During the Populist and Progressive eras, the exposures of corrupt business practices by "muckraking" journalists served to intensify opposition to the great industrialists, and the greatest of them, Rockefeller, became, to many, the incarnation of an evil system. In 1894, Henry Demarest Lloyd eloquently exposed the practices of Standard Oil in *Wealth against Commonwealth,* and Ida Tarbell followed some years later with an equally severe appraisal in *The History of the Standard Oil Company,* based upon even more thoroughgoing research. These, and similar exposures of other businesses, remained generally unchallenged by historians until about a generation ago. Two of the most influential and devastating of these attacks appeared during the period of the New Deal: Matthew Josephson's *Robber Barons* and Gustavus Myers's *History of the Great American Fortunes,* both written from a socialist, rather than from the old Populist point of view.

World War II ushered in an age of "new conservatism," when a new school of historians emerged which was more impressed by the creative accomplishments of American business leaders than by the corrupt practices alleged against them. These writers identified themselves as entrepreneurial historians, to point up the positive, creative quality of American business leadership. In 1948, a Center for Research in Entrepreneurial History was established at Harvard, and similar centers have been instituted elsewhere, fostering research in the histories of innumerable businesses.

As Rockefeller and Standard Oil had borne the main brunt of the earlier attack, so they received the most extensive and influential attention upon the part of the revisionists. Allan Nevins's *John D. Rockefeller* (1940), presented its protagonist as an industrial statesman who, without violating the accepted business practices of his day, brought combination and order to a bloated, lawless, and chaotic industry. In 1955 Ralph W. and Muriel E. Hidy's *Pioneering in Big Business* presented the history of Standard Oil similarly, as primarily a managerial triumph. Other influential works written from this generally sympathetic point of view include William Miller (ed.), *Men in Business* (1952), Thomas C. Cochran, *Railroad Leaders, 1845–1890* (1953), and various writings of Edward C. Kirkland.

Americans active in political life during the generation which followed the Civil War had dedicated themselves to the task of binding up the wounds of the nation and then reopening them periodically during election campaigns. Consequently, one very bad effect of the war had been this, that it had persistently directed the attention of the nation to the immediate past, at a time of industrial expansion, when things were changing so fast that, even with the undivided attention of its people, the United States could hardly have prepared itself for the immediate future. The captains of industry, who were rapidly supplanting the politicians as the leaders of the nation, were happy in the confidence that all was working out for the best. "The consumption of iron," wrote the iron manu-

facturer and politician Abram S. Hewitt, "is the social barometer
by which to estimate the relative height of civilization among nations." By that social barometer the American people, as they approached the election of 1884, were being civilized so rapidly that
they had no time to learn how to behave themselves properly in
the new society.

BIBLIOGRAPHY FOR CHAPTER EIGHT

Except for the Reconstruction controversy, the post-Civil
War period has attracted historians as little as any period
in American history, and this is reflected in a paucity of
paperback literature on the subject. The most recent, and
perhaps the best, general account of main economic developments is E. C. Kirkland, *Industry Comes of Age: Business,
Labor and Public Policy, 1860–1897* (1961), written by one
of the modern entrepreneurial school of historians and by one
of the most literate among them. T. C. Cochran and William
Miller, *The Age of Enterprise: A Social History of Industrial
America* (1942), covering a broader range of history, deals
extensively with this period. Against these mainly partisan
interpretations, Matthew Josepheson, *The Robber Barons*
(1935) is, as the title indicates, a spirited exposition of the
adversely critical view which dominated the field until the
present generation. H. D. Lloyd, *Wealth against Commonwealth* (1894) is the classic, and still controversial, exposé of
that classic monopoly, Standard Oil.

While business historians have come ardently to the rescue
of the reputation of the businessman in the Gilded Age, the
contemporary politician has been left to languish. For a generally accepted brief portrait of the politician of the period
read the chapter on "The Spoilsmen" in Richard Hofstadter,
The American Political Tradition. C. F. Adams, Jr., and Henry
Adams, *Chapters of Erie* is a fast-paced pioneer work in the
muckraking school, recounting in careful detail a series of
piratical financial operations which were carried on during
the Gilded Age in a milieu of rampant political corruption.
James Bryce, *American Commonwealth,* 2 vols., is a study
of American politics during the Gilded Age by a distinguished
English statesman-historian, a study which ranks with Tocqueville's as a masterpiece of analysis and description.

W. P. Webb, *The Great Plains* (1931), a study of the
means by which settlers subdued an alien and dangerous
region, has enjoyed, deservedly, more than a generation of

undiminished popularity. For the history of the cattle kingdom see J. F. Dobie, *The Longhorns* (1941) and E. S. Osgood, *The Day of the Cattlemen* (1929). For an absorbing account of the explorations of John Wesley Powell read Wallace Stegner, *Beyond the Hundredth Meridian* (1954).

I

Complacent Politics The Democratic party of "rum, Romanism, and rebellion" met the high standards of Liberal Republicanism five out of seven times, during the post-Civil War generation, in its selection of presidential candidates. The Republican party during that period nominated only one man, Hayes, who was entirely acceptable by Liberal Republican criterion. The Republicans Garfield and Arthur, on coming to the Presidency, tried to be good, but they had both been recruited from the ranks of the spoilsmen. Then, in 1884, James G. Blaine—"the continental liar from Maine," as he was called because of untruths he told in connection with certain of his under-the-counter dealings—won the

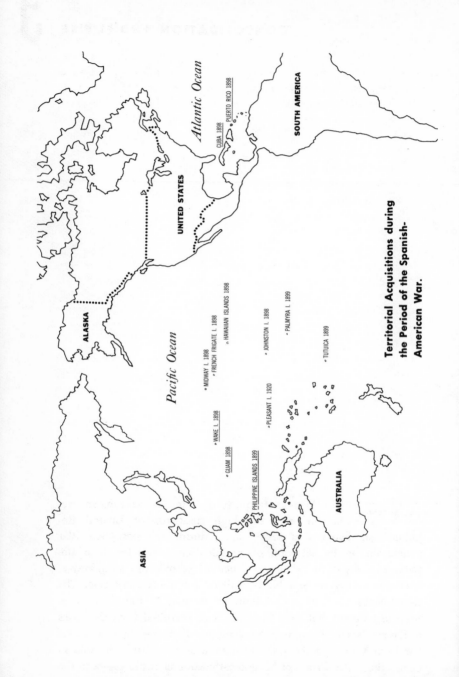

Territorial Acquisitions during the Period of the Spanish-American War.

ALASKA

UNITED STATES

Atlantic Ocean

CUBA 1898

PUERTO RICO 1898

SOUTH AMERICA

Pacific Ocean

MIDWAY I. 1898

FRENCH FRIGATE I. 1898

HAWAIIAN ISLANDS 1898

JOHNSTON I. 1898

PALMYRA I. 1899

TUTUICA 1899

WAKE I. 1899

PLEASANT I. 1920

GUAM 1898

PHILIPPINE ISLANDS 1899

ASIA

AUSTRALIA

Republican nomination. By contrast, Grover Cleveland, the stoutly upright reform governor of New York, won the Democratic one. Under those circumstances the Liberal Republicans—or Mugwumps as they came to be called—that year decided to "follow a noble impulse," as the comfortably righteous Carl Schurz put it, and go for Cleveland. The campaign that followed was the dirtiest one in American history, with the exception of the Adams-Jackson campaign of 1828. Cleveland won with a plurality of 23,000 votes, and the Democratic party returned to power for the first time in twenty-four years.

Cleveland represented the conservative Eastern wing of the Democratic party, as had the Democratic candidates Seymour and Tilden before him, and his views coincided with those of the responsible conservative element on Wall Street. He had been in politics for only four years by the time he entered the White House, and his mind was not yet made up on all matters. Where it was made up, however, it was pure Liberal Republicanism, and where he was in doubt, Cleveland went to Schurz and his colleagues for the answers. In common with them, Cleveland conceived of the President as the impartial umpire of a society which was basically governed by the immutable, God-given, self-operating law of supply and demand. Governments were instituted for the purpose of protecting life, liberty and property, and beyond this responsibility it was immorally wrong of them to go. A man of exceptionally strong character, Cleveland won the fight with the Senate which Hayes had begun, and firmly reestablished the President's appointive power which the Senate had wrested from Johnson. Beyond that, he made his force felt negatively through the use of the veto against veterans' pensions and pork barrel bills. During his term he vetoed or pocket-vetoed 413 bills.

Cleveland had not given the tariff question any systematic consideration at the time he assumed office, but he soon came to the Liberal Republican view that tariff reduction and extension of the merit system were the two basic reforms which would cure the ills of the nation. These nineteenth-century liberals were shocked, both by the spread of poverty beneath them and by the accumulations of great fortunes above them. The typical spokesman for this brand of liberalism was a member of the well-to-do part of the community, who was able to live graciously on his own moderate wealth and who therefore had reason to think that that was about as high as a fortune ought to go. Society was operating in a faulty manner when it resulted in such a grossly unequal distribution of the national wealth as had come to be the case. In the view of the liberals, monopoly and plutocracy were the results of governmental interference with the natural order, in erecting tariff barriers and in bestowing government subsidies. Under conditions of free trade, liberals were sure, monopoly would be broken by international competition, and the bloated fortunes of the new rich would be punctured.

Cleveland devoted his third annual message to Congress entirely to the tariff question, and the second half of his administration was devoted to lowering duties. The House of Representatives responded in December, 1887, with the Mills Bill, providing for those moderate beginnings to tariff reduction which Cleveland had in mind. Faced with the congressional elections of 1888, the House passed the bill, secure in the certainty that it would never pass the Senate, which kept debating it until the elections were over.

The one significant measure passed during the first Cleveland administration, the Interstate Commerce Act, was a congressional response to popular antirailroad feeling which Cleveland signed with considerable reluctance. The inability of the state regulatory commissions to exert any effective control over the interstate railroads in the seventies had been followed by increasing demands for federal regulation. The House and the Senate had each passed such bills, and they were ironing out their differences in 1886, when the Supreme Court rendered a decision in the case of Wabash, St. Louis, and Pacific Railroad v. Illinois denying to the states altogether the authority of regulating railroads which crossed interstate lines. Hastened by the Wabash decision, Congress passed the Interstate Commerce Act, which prohibited all discriminatory practices, including rebates, pools, and charging less for a long haul between major cities, where competition existed, than for a shorter intermediate haul, where monopolistic practices prevailed. It provided that all charges should be "reasonable and just," and it established the Interstate Commerce Commission, the first Federal agency of its kind, to administer the law, which would be enforced by the courts.

The act was greeted with popular approval, but it was at the same time supported by the railroads, which realized that some regulatory law was inevitable and, under those circumstances, liked the loopholes they saw in the one that was passed. The law insisted on "reasonable and just rates" without defining what the phrase meant, and it prohibited long-short haul discrimination only under "similar circumstances and conditions," which from the point of the railroads proved promisingly vague. The provision for judicial review generally gave the railroads a four-year period of grace, while the case was traveling to the Supreme Court, and, as it turned out, the railroads received favorable decisions from the archly conservative court in almost every instance.

In 1888 the Democratic convention nominated Cleveland, without thought of anybody else. The Republicans got Blaine out of the way, and then they were faced with the fact that they could decide on no other candidate who was well known and at the same time presidential timber. In the absence of an available candidate, the convention nominated the ghost of a former President. They nominated Benjamin Harrison, the grandson of William Henry Harrison, who had fought that Battle of Tippecanoe in 1811 with Tecumseh's Indians. Then the Republicans set out in dead earnest to secure the election of the right candidate by buying votes and by using money effectively in other ways. They were helped, free of charge, by the British Minister to America, who advised an English-born American, in a subsequently much published letter, to vote for Cleveland. And the result of it all was that, while Cleveland quadrupled his plurality of 1884, he nevertheless lost the election to "young Tippecanoe" by sixty-five electoral votes, a handful of votes in New York State deciding the issue in this as in so many nineteenth-century elections.

Harrison did not know much about politics and did not really attempt to learn how to be President. Everything was arranged for him, including a Cabinet in which Blaine was Secretary of State and John Wanamaker, the rich department store owner, was Postmaster General. There was the usual furious rotation in office (which had also occurred when the politically pristine Cleveland had entered the executive mansion), and then the administration settled down to the main business of distributing favors among special interests. The liveliest figure in the Harrison administration was Corporal Tanner, Commissioner of Pensions, who promised to raise all veterans' pensions and who contributed to history the one memorable statement of the Harrison administration: "God help the surplus."

The year 1890 was a red-letter year for legislation, the Sherman Antitrust Act, the Sherman Silver Purchase Act and the McKinley Tariff all being passed together. The Antitrust Act in its final version was intended by many who voted for it simply as something to appease the popular feeling against monopoly without doing anything to imperil the interests of the monopolists. It passed the Senate 51 to 1. The law prohibited all combinations in restraint of trade, using words such as conspiracy, monopoly, and trust, without defining the terms. It thus shifted to the courts the responsibility of deciding what the law meant, and, from the point of view of big business, the Supreme Court in 1890 was in good hands.

Neither the Harrison nor the Cleveland administration was enthusiastic in its prosecution of the new law, but within five years several antitrust suits had been brought to the Supreme Court and had been lost by the government. In 1895, in the case of United States v. E. C. Knight and Company, the government attempted to dissolve the sugar trust, which controlled 98 per cent of the sugar refined in the nation. The Court held that this control did not constitute a combination in restraint of trade, since the sugar trust was a manufacturing monopoly to which the monopoly of trade was incidental. The decision met with the complete satisfaction of Cleveland's Attorney General, who wrote a friend that he had never believed in the law anyway. Until the twentieth century, the law was applied in earnest mainly against labor unions, a purpose for which, of course, it had not been designed at all. Commenting on the Antitrust Act the political humorist Peter Finley Dunne observed that "What looks like a stone wall to a layman, is a triumphal arch to a corporation lawyer."

The Sherman Silver Purchase Act and the McKinley Tariff, also passed in 1890, were companion measures, Eastern Republicans reluctantly supplying votes for the one in exchange for Western support for the other. The Silver Purchase Act provided for the monthly purchase by the government of four and one-half million ounces of silver bullion, against which the government would issue silver certificates, redeemable in gold as well as silver. The value of silver was not fixed at a ratio of 16 to 1 with gold as the inflationists demanded, and the measure failed to check the deflationary trend. In the view of many conservatives, however, it was a wicked bill, fraught with potential dangers to the financial system. On the other hand, many spokesmen for this point of view were apt to find much to please them in the McKinley Tariff, which once again raised rates on imports all along the line. The purpose of the tariff, according to the author, Representative William McKinley of Ohio, was to secure "the great comforts to the masses," and to assure "the safety and purity and permanency of our political system."

In the election of 1892 the Democrats, who had captured the House two years earlier, renominated Cleveland, while the Republicans renominated Harrison. There followed a quiet campaign, disturbed only by the farmers, who organized their own indignant Populist party. Cleveland won by almost 400,000 votes, the largest plurality since Grant ran against poor Greeley. With what apparently amounted to a mandate, Cleveland returned triumphantly to office. He was plunged almost at once into the depression of 1893 to 1899—by far the worst depression in the history of the nation up to that time. Faced with problems which he had hardly considered he was soon rendering dogmatic decisions which split the party he led and crippled it for more than a generation.

II

Labor

The depression, which was already five years old for the farmers, struck the business community at the time Cleveland returned to office. It was brought on mainly by too rapid railroad construction, by the decline in the purchasing power of the farmer, and by depression conditions abroad, which resulted in the selling of American securities by foreigners. There was a run of bank failures through the South and West, and, in the summer of 1893, the Erie Railroad, Union Pacific, Northern Pacific, and the Santa Fe all went into bankruptcy. Within a year, the number of unemployed had risen to four million, while workers who held their jobs were subjected to sharp successive wage cuts.

The whole nation agreed that the money system was at the root of the trouble, but there was diametric difference of opinion as to how the money system was at fault. For the farmers, struggling under the depressed prices for farm products, the problem lay in the insufficiency of currency, to be remedied by the unlimited coinage of silver at 16 to 1. For Cleveland and the other "gold bugs," the fault lay with the Silver Purchase Act, which caused the hoarding of gold and weakened business confidence. To check the run on the gold surplus, which accompanied the depression, Cleveland called an emergency session of Congress and pushed through the repeal of the Silver Purchase Act. When the run on the government gold reserve continued, Cleveland arranged through a banking syndicate, directed by J. P. Morgan, for a loan of 65 million, half of it from abroad. This helped to end the crisis, at great political cost to Cleveland, who was charged with being the lackey of Wall Street, most loudly, of course, by the silverites. Cleveland sustained a further political defeat in 1894, when, in response to his call for a lowering of the tariff, the Wilson-Gorman Tariff was passed, without his signature, providing for no significant reductions in duties.

Massive labor violence, to which the nation had first been introduced in the Great Strike of '77, broke out with redoubled fury and met with harsh government-supported suppression. Following the collapse of the National Labor Union, the Noble Order of the Knights of Labor had emerged as a major attempt to unite American labor in a single union. Under the leadership of a Philadelphia tailor, Uriah S. Stephens, and later more effectively under Terence V. Powderly, it opened its ranks to unskilled as well as skilled labor—in fact to everybody except professional gamblers, bankers, liquor dealers, and lawyers. After fifteen years of slow beginnings, the Knights of Labor won a major railroad strike against Jay Gould. Its membership leapt abruptly thereafter to 700,000, and it became a powerful pressure group, successfully agitating for a law in 1885 prohibiting the importation of contract labor.

Then in 1886, amid a campaign by the Knights and others for an eight-hour day, a labor meeting at Haymarket Square in Chicago was broken up by police. Someone threw a murderous bomb, and a riot followed. In the absence of any good suspects to charge with the bombing, eight anarchists were accused of murder, on the grounds that they had used incendiary language which, it was charged, incited the deed. Four were executed, one committed suicide, and the other three were pardoned six years later, when Governor John P. Altgeld came to office in Illinois. In the meantime, amid the nationwide wave of antilabor sentiment following the Haymarket riot, the Knights of Labor gradually declined and disappeared, its place to be taken by the American Federation of Labor.

Formed in the 1880s of skilled craft unions under the leadership of Samuel Gompers, the AFL set itself against both the utopianism and the indiscriminate admissions policy of the Knights of Labor. It sought membership primarily among the craft unions, which could command a degree of bargaining power, and it limited itself to short-range nonpolitical objectives of shorter hours, better pay, better working conditions, and the closed shop. It organized as a federation of national unions, each of which enjoyed autonomy within the federation. It won its first major victory in 1890, when it secured a labor contract with the Carnegie Steel Company, and it suffered its first main setback two years later, when it lost its first main strike at Carnegie's Homestead plant in Pennsylvania. Victorious against a small army of Pinkerton private detectives, the strikers were beaten by the state militia and the courts. At first they had the support of some public sympathy, but the attempt of an anarchist to assassinate the president of the Carnegie Steel Company, Henry C. Frick, proved sufficient again to associate the strike with foreign radicalism in the public mind and so weaken the strength of organized labor as the depression of 1893 set in.

In that first year of the depression, Eugene V. Debs organized the American Railway Union, which, unlike the older Railroad Brotherhoods, was open to all railroad workers and not just the skilled elite. In 1894, the Pullman Company near Chicago discharged a third of its workers and cut the wages of the rest by as much as 40 per cent. Debs' Railway Union joined the strike, providing money and cutting the Pullman cars off trains. The railroads naturally wanted government intervention but were not inclined to go to the prolabor Governor Altgeld for it. Constitutionally the Federal government had no authority to intervene with troops except upon the request of the governor, but Cleveland intervened on the pretext of insuring the continued functioning of the Federal postal system. In the process the strike was put down and Debs was jailed. In the course of suppressing the strike the courts played a new role, issuing an injunction against the strike on the grounds that it involved a conspiracy in restraint of trade under the terms of the Sherman Antitrust Act. Under depression conditions and under continuing government hostility, the unions did well to retain their organizations and survive until better times after the turn of the century. That they survived the depression intact, however, was of far greater significance than were their temporary bloody defeats.

III

Populist Revolt The farmers suffered a longer depression than did any other major segment of the population, and they held a disproportionately heavy voting power over any other segment under the American representative system, especially in the Senate. They were also able to look upon themselves, in a way the workingmen were not, as representing the traditional American values. As a result of all these factors, they developed steadily in power during the depression, at the time when the unions did well to remain on the defensive.

The new wave of farm discontent arose this time not so much in the Middle West, where the Granger movement had been strongest, but in the cotton country of the South and in the wheat region of the Great Plains. The Middle West, with a more stabilized railroad system, increasingly diversified agriculture, and growing urban markets close at hand, tended to stay Republican through the whole period of agitation. In the South and in the plains region, meanwhile, farm organizations of protest emerged in the 1880s, which joined together in the Southern Alliance on the one hand and the National (Northern) Alliance on the other, supported by a smaller Colored Alliance. Various differences of opinion, enforced by old Civil War animosities, kept these alliances separate, but they drew up similar reform programs and worked in cooperation with each other. In 1890 the alliances entered politics, and, in 1892, they joined together at Omaha to found the People's (or Populist) party.

The Populists launched their program with a fiery preamble, written by Ignatius Donnelly of Minnesota, condemning the ubiquitous corruption of the two major parties. It went on to denounce the system by which "The fruits of the toil of millions are boldly stolen to build up colossal fortunes for the few," breeding from "the same prolific womb of governmental injustice" the "two great classes—tramps and millionaires." It asserted that "A vast conspiracy against mankind has been organized on two continents," by which silver was systematically being demonitized around the world, in order to enrich the international bankers at the expense of the rest of society.

The platform called for government ownership of the railroads, for the immediate increase in the national currency, and for the unlimited coinage of silver at the ratio of 16 to 1 with gold. Additional planks included political reforms: the secret ballot, direct election of senators, and the initiative and referendum by which voters could petition for special legislation. In an effort to attract labor votes, the platform endorsed the eight-hour day for government workers, immigration restriction, and enforcement of the law against imported contract labor. The party nominated Gen. James B. Weaver of Iowa, for President, supporting him with more than a million popular and twenty-two electoral votes in the election, and raising up a lively group of leaders including "Sockless Jerry" Simpson and "Bloody Bridles" Waite.

The Populist attack, although launched along such broad areas of reform, tended for various reasons, to concentrate its force, over the next four years, on the one overriding objective of currency reform. One reason for this was that the one important source of wealth for the party was the silver mining interests, which were enthusiastic contributors to the party in proportion to the importance the party placed on the silver issue. Repeal of the Silver Purchase Act in 1893 served also to focus attention on the money issue, and in 1894 there appeared the immensely influential William H. Harvey's *Coin's Financial School,* exposing the "Crime of '73" by which silver had been demonitized at the direction of the international bankers, in order to increase the value of their capital at the expense of the value of everybody else's property and product. To those who argued that silver would drive out gold and leave the United States without the necessary medium for international trade, Harvey argued that America could force the world to accept its system. If England refused to cooperate, he continued, the United States would be justified in going to war for the cause of humanity.

The Populists found villains aplenty, but with the repeal of the Silver Purchase Act the attack came to center on President Cleveland. "Cleveland might be honest," supposed William Jennings Bryan, "but so were the mothers who threw their children in the Ganges." The attack spread within the Democratic party, dividing its Southern and Western wings against their party's Eastern leader. The Republican party, when it held its nominating convention in 1896, therefore, had good reason to be optimistic about the forthcoming election. The Republican party, it is true, had its own silverite faction, which bolted the convention following the convention's acceptance of a "sound-money" plank, but it was not so severely damaged by the issue as was the Democratic party.

In the Democratic convention the radicals gained control and made of the platform a blanket repudiation of Cleveland's administration. The debate over the money plank produced the most famous speech in convention history, when the young William Jennings Bryan spoke "in the defense of our homes, our families, and posterity" against the gold standard, concluding with his famous injunction, "You shall not press down upon the brow of labor this crown of thorns, you shall not crucify mankind upon a cross of gold." The young Nebraska politician won the nomination and thereafter received the endorsement of the Populist convention, and this "Cross of Gold" speech set the keynote for the first campaign since before the Civil War when the contest revolved around major national issues.

The Republican party in 1896 was in the hands of a politically astute, candidly honest, and engagingly reasonable new national political boss, the Ohio industrialist Mark Hanna. Looked rather down upon by the genteel as a "diamond in the rough," Hanna was a kindly realist who saw beyond the simple certitudes of Liberal Republicanism, to an industrial America where the rich would rule, in part by their great power and in part by giving to the people an increasing share of the increasing wealth which their labor was creating. Hanna was not altogether successful in persuading his friends in the Union League Club that everybody ought to have a fair share, but he had greater success in the task of organizing his colleagues for the purpose of seeing to it that the rich should rule. In the nominating convention, he secured the candidacy of his protege William McKinley, and then he directed a campaign, which was remarkable for its high degree of organization and its unprecedented expensiveness.

For the impoverished Democratic party, on the other hand, the campaign was by contrast the personal effort of Bryan, who traveled continually through the nation delivering more than six hundred speeches. And the result was that, carrying the Solid

South, the plains states, and the silver states, Bryan lost every state in the Northwest and Northeast, as well as California and Oregon, and went down to defeat by a margin of 600,000 votes. It was the worst defeat of a major presidential candidate since 1872. The defeat and the divisions it created damaged the Democratic party for years to come. The Populist party, meanwhile, was destroyed by its support of the Democratic Bryan, by the return of farm prosperity and by discoveries of gold in South Africa, Australia, and Alaska, which brought to the farmers the inflation they had wished to achieve through silver. By the time the nation went officially on the gold standard, with the Currency Act of 1900, the farmers had lost their interest in the money question, and for a generation thereafter, until hard times came again in the 1920s, they remained correspondingly less concerned about reform politics.

The election of McKinley was a victory for a Republican party in which control had been won from the spoilsmen by the big business interests, organized by Hanna. It was therefore appropriate that, under McKinley's Presidency, industrial consolidation should proceed at a faster pace than at any other period in American history, the way having been prepared for the conquest of finance capitalism by the depression of 1893. As in the case of previous depressions, bankruptcies facilitated consolidation, and this was most evidently true in the case of the railroads. The novelty of the new consolidations was the centering of control, not finally in the hands of the railroad men themselves, but beyond them in the hands of the Wall Street financial giants. Railroad men remained to operate the roads, but control was centralized over major areas and competition so far as possible eliminated. The same process took place in all major areas of American industry.

There were two main centers of financial control on Wall Street: J. P. Morgan and Company and the rival firm of the Rockefeller interests: Kuhn, Loeb, and Company. These were the only two American financial houses with extensive European connections. The Morgan group, working through the National Bank of Commerce and the First National Bank of New York, controlled the operations of banks throughout the nation and influenced the policies of major corporations. Among these, U.S. Steel was famous as the nation's first "billion dollar corporation," created by Morgan out of Carnegie's former holdings, combined with other steel companies and subsidiary businesses, and accounting for the greater part of the nation's steel-producing capacity. The Rockefeller group, working through the National City Bank, the Hanover City Bank, and the Farmers Loan and Trust Company, and driven by the pressure of finding outlets for the ever-increasing volume of profits from Standard Oil, similarly created its network of rail-roads under the control of Edward H. Harriman and similarly arranged combinations in other industries. Industrial combinations to emerge, aside from U.S. Steel and Standard Oil, included American Tobacco Company, Amalgamated Copper, American Sugar Refining Company, International Harvester, and General Electric, among the larger ones.

To big business the McKinley administration contributed the Dingley Tariff, which once again raised duties to the highest point in history. The main service of the administration, however, was in appointing sympathetic men to the Interstate Commerce Commission and to the Attorney General's Office and then permitting the masters of capital to do as they wished. In 1904 John Moody in his *The Truth about the Trusts* found that two-fifths of the manufacturing capital of the nation was concentrated in 318 companies, these in turn largely controlled by the Morgan and Rockefeller groups. The study concluded that "These two mammouth groups jointly . . . constitute the heart of the business and commercial life of the nation."

Men were to go on into the twentieth century talking about competition and free enterprise as though it were the rule of American life, but the revolution away from free enterprise had substantially taken place by the coming of the Progressive movement. The conquests of the finance capitalists in turn did much to create the atmosphere which made the Progressive movement possible. The climax of consolidation was the occasion for a brief labor-management honeymoon, which saw Hanna and Morgan co-operating cordially with Gompers in various enterprises, and which saw also the rapid increase in AFL membership. During the United Mine Workers strike of 1902 it was Mark Hanna and J. P. Morgan who were instrumental in helping Theodore Roosevelt settle the strike favorably for the workers. The new-found sense of security on Wall Street was demonstrated in the presidential campaign of 1904 by the willingness of Rockefeller and Morgan to support Roosevelt during the heyday of his reputation as a trustbuster. The Republican party was their party, and they were apparently not greatly disturbed by Roosevelt's denunciations of "bad" trusts. Progressivism bloomed in the quieter time of the early twentieth century, when the struggling, recalcitrant robber baron had been effectively supplanted by consolidated and comparatively cooperative management.

IV

Diplomacy   The United States during the thirty years following the Civil War remained more densely isolationist than at any other period in its history. During the 1880s, Africa was divided between the frantically scrambling European nations, at a time when these same nations were gaining additional protectorates, colonies, and concessions in Asia, but the United States was comparatively immune from the fevers of imperialism. Whereas the slavery controversy had checked the manifest destiny tendencies in the fifties, the Civil War apparently had supplied the generation which passed through it with as much martial adventure as it cared to experience. Then, during the reconstruction era, economic development of the South and West had provided American capital with its own colonial exploitations within the national boundaries. Northern bankers found more profitable and safer outlets in Southern railroads and textile mills and in the iron industry of Birmingham, Alabama, than would have been available to them outside continental United States, and the mining and cattle frontiers of the West and the bonanza ranches of the Great Plains provided colonial opportunities for which American capital competed vigorously with that of Britain and Europe. It was only after the cattle lands had been fenced in and the mining regions had settled down to methodical, consolidated enterprises of declining productivity that Americans began to look beyond the nation's boundaries in the spirit of the "new imperialism" of the age.

The fixed principles of American foreign policy before the Civil War had consisted of the Monroe Doctrine and freedom of the seas, but the war, itself, had presented European nations with opportunities for large-scale violations of the Monroe Doctrine, which Spain took advantage of in Santo Domingo, and France in Mexico. Chaotic Mexican conditions in the late fifties, which had moved Buchanan to think of the fruitful possibilities of another

Mexican war, gave an opening to European nations, which the French took advantage of. Acting originally in concert with Spain and England against Mexican suspension of its international obligations, the French invaded unilaterally, occupied Mexico City, and, in 1863, invited Archduke Maximilian to form a monarchy under French protection.

Maximilian's Mexican Empire received general European recognition, and Maximilian was filling his mind with thoughts of extending his conquests into South America, when the American Civil War came to an end and with it an end to Maximilian's bright prospects. Departing from the wartime policy of neutrality toward Maximilian's Mexico, President Johnson's Secretary of State Seward became increasingly aggressive toward the Mexican Empire, demanding that the French set a time limit to their evacuation. Since Seward's demands were backed up by 50,000 troops in Texas, Napoleon III of France withdrew his troops, and Maximilian met his fate before a Mexican firing squad, in February, 1867.

Spanish attempts to reannex Santo Domingo, meanwhile, had collapsed prior to the close of the Civil War. At war's end Seward was ambitious to use the nation's great war-created military and naval power to resume the expansion which the slavery controversy had interrupted. He hoped to acquire Caribbean possessions, the Hawaiian Islands, and, in time, Canada. Unsupported by public sentiment he was successful only in the purchase of Alaska from Russia and the occupation of Midway Islands in 1867, but in none of his other promising schemes extending from Santo Domingo to Pago Pago.

More popular for the moment among the American people was the project of wresting Canada from England in retaliation for British hostility during the war and as payment for the damages done by Confederate blockade runners, including the *Alabama,* which the British government had permitted to be constructed in Scottish shipyards. Senator Sumner as chairman of the Senate Foreign Relations Committee was the leading spokesman for the view that Britain should be charged in these so-called *Alabama* claims with half the cost of the war. These huge claims against England were used by expansionists to justify the United States in annexing Canada, at a time when it had the military force to accomplish the feat.

The Grant administration, including Secretary of State Hamilton

Fish, at first accepted Sumner's estimate of claims against Britain, but Grant became offended with Sumner for other reasons, while Fish came to look upon such exorbitant claims as unreasonable and futile. The British government, for its part, came to regret having permitted the construction of blockade runners, partly because it had, in so doing, established a precedent which might in the future be used against it by other neutral nations in time of war. In 1871, the Washington Treaty was arranged between England and the United States, providing for submission of the *Alabama* claims and also certain fishing disputes to international arbitration. The treaty contained a British expression of regret for having permitted the escape of the blockade runners. This expression of regret, from the American point of view, ensured that the American claims for direct damages would be met, since they implied British admission of culpability. From the British point of view, meanwhile, it served to establish the inadmissibility in international law of such a practice in the future. The treaty, which contained settlement of a number of additional smaller disputes, passed the Senate overwhelmingly, being voted for by even Senator Sumner.

The treaty quieted Anglo-American relations for a generation, but the British ruling classes had not come to like the American democracy any better, while Americans, especially Irish-Americans, continued to look upon England with varying shades of hostility. And, as the century drew to a close, developments in Latin America placed the two nations once again increasingly in conflict. As the United States industrialized, its interest in Latin-American markets and raw materials naturally increased. The American government, especially under Secretary of State James G. Blaine in 1881 and 1889 to 1892, responded to this growing interest with attempts to achieve closer economic ties with the nations of South America. Blaine failed in his attempts to create a Pan-American customs union, but he did win advantageous individual commercial treaties.

European interests, especially English, were no less attracted than the Americans by the Latin-American possibilities. In 1893, British and German business interests endorsed a rebellion in Brazil, which, for a time, threatened America's favored economic position in that nation. In 1895, Britain blockaded the Nicaraguan port of Corinto and occupied the island of Trinidad, off the coast of Brazil. France, meanwhile, made threatening advances against

Santo Domingo and attempted to occupy an area in Brazil which it had previously claimed but never governed. It was against the background of these events that the Cleveland administration precipitated the Venezuela crisis in 1895.

At issue was a long-standing boundary dispute between Venezuela and British Guiana, which had been made critical during Cleveland's first administration by the discovery of gold in the disputed territory. Britain had maintained her position against Venezuelan protests, and the Cleveland administration, its offer to arbitrate being declined by Britain, had done nothing more in the matter. The situation remained much the same when Cleveland returned to office, but the President on that occasion made up his mind to do something different. In the only widely popular act of his distressing second administration, he directed his Secretary of State, Richard Olney, to deliver a message to the British government announcing that the United States intended to intervene in the dispute and make final settlement. That it had the power as well as the right to do so, was apparently not to be doubted. "The United States," the note declared, "is practically sovereign on this continent and its fiat is law upon the subjects to which it confines its interposition. Why? It is not because of the pure friendship or good-will felt for it. . . . It is because in addition to all other grounds its infinite resources combined with its isolated position render it master of the situation and practically invulnerable against any and all other nations."

At the time of that note, the entire American Army stood at about 28,000 men. Dispersed in small numbers for Indian patrols, this force was without either the training or the organization to fight a coordinated battle. There was, in addition to the Army, a national guard of about one hundred thousand men, divided under the commands of the state governors and largely untrained except for some close order drill. The guard officers, elected by the guardsmen, were without any special military training. The Navy, neglected since the Civil War, was without a single modern battleship, although plans for naval expansion were in the designing stage and construction was in progress. Britain, by contrast, maintained a large, well-trained army and possessed the most powerful navy in the world. For the United States to have intervened by force in the Venezuela dispute would have been out of the question. In a showdown with England, it is true, the United States might have invaded Canada, but in 1895 the circumstances were hardly more favorable for such a venture than they had been in the ill-starred venture of 1812.

It is impossible to know how Cleveland and the United States would have worked their way out of their difficulties had England remained firm in its rejection of arbitration, which it undoubtedly intended to do originally. As it happened, England found herself suddenly in serious trouble in Europe and South Africa, and, wishing for American friendship, bowed to the demands for arbitration. The United States was therefore able to continue unchallenged in its easy assumption, that an isolated and lightly armed nation could, as a practical matter, stand guard over one of the world's two hemispheres. The results of World War I only confirmed the nation in this view. On the eve of World War II, therefore, the American attitude toward military affairs had in important respects not yet emerged from the eighteenth century.

V

Spanish-American War   The immense American enthusiasm for Cleveland's assertive attitude toward the Venezuela dispute heralded the arrival of that new spirit of imperialism which reached its climax three years later, in 1898, in the Spanish-American War. A new generation of Americans had arisen, which had had no share in the Civil War, and some of its more red-blooded members were spoiling for some kind of fight of their own, so long as it was in a good cause. These men were imbued with the spirit of the new imperialism, which still raged abroad, and, for a brief span of years at least, Americans generally joined in with the spirit of the times. The new imperialism differed from the old of the seventeenth and eighteenth centuries in the great power the industrial revolution had given the colonizing nations to dominate the "lesser breeds," as the colonized peoples came to be known. The emphasis was no longer on strategic trading posts but on control of the whole territory in order that it might be best exploited by Western methods.

Chauvinism, lacking in the old imperialism, was a driving force in the new, supported by the growing conviction, alien to eighteenth-century America, even in slave areas, that superior races existed whose duty it was to rule. The division of Africa in the 1880s between fiercely competitive European powers had taken place in large measure without any indication of the possibility of economic gain, but simply to enhance the glory of the conquering nation. Missionary zeal, which had played an important part in the old imperialism, played an equally important one in the new and was an especially strong motive so far as America was concerned.

In 1885, Josiah Strong, a Congregational minister, published an influential book, *Our Country,* in which he called America to its duty to "dispossess many weaker races, assimilate others, and mold the remainder, until, in a very true and important sense, it has Anglo-Saxonized mankind," and at the same time has established a "Christian stewardship" throughout the world. In 1895, the national enthusiasm aroused by Cleveland's threatened intervention on behalf of the Venezuelans was an indication that the American people were tending toward the point of view of the Reverend Mr. Strong.

Several months before the Venezuela note, the second Cuban insurrection within the generation broke out against the feeble, inefficient, and corrupt Spanish colonial regime. The earlier insurrection, 1868 to 1878, had been met with the same harsh methods which characterized the attempts to suppress the second, and, in the course of it, the American ship *Virginius* had been captured by the Spanish and fifty-three of her crew summarily executed. Nevertheless, despite the natural burst of outrage in America, relations with Spain had not been severed as a consequence. In 1895, however, the new insurrection, as a dramatic distraction from the wretched domestic conditions of the depression, was taken up by the newspapers and eagerly followed by the public. The most enterprising coverage was given to it by the two leading New York rivals, Joseph Pulitzer's New York *World* and William Randolph Hearst's New York *Journal,* and their accounts were avidly copied by other newspapers throughout the country, as they presented lurid and dramatic accounts of the guerilla warfare, the Spanish concentration camps, methods of Spanish torture, the cruelty of General "Butcher" Weyler, and, best of all, the incarceration of the heroine Evangelina Cisneros by the Black Spaniards.

A Cuban junta established itself in New York at the outset to work for "Cuba Libre," while American investors, who had increased their properties in Cuba since the previous insurrection, were early calling for American intervention. When a Spanish gunboat fired on the American ship *Alliance*, talk about going in and taking over became quite widespread, but it had no effect whatever on President Cleveland, who declared American neutrality and stood pat. Cleveland's successor McKinley at first was similarly disinclined to meddle. Despite America's Cuban investments, which were not very large, American business interests generally were opposed to engaging in any international adventures which might unsettle business conditions, at a time when they were improving rapidly and when the delicate and all-important process of business consolidation was under way.

A war party did exist in the Republican party, however, and events played into its hands. The New York *Journal* obtained a letter sent by the Spanish minister to America, Dupuy de Lome, to a friend, commenting disparagingly upon McKinley. Thus dishonored the American nation had not yet recovered from the insult, when the new American battleship, the *Maine*, at anchor in Havana harbor on a mission of "friendly courtesy," exploded and sank, with the loss of more than 250 lives. Cause of the disaster was never discovered. A naval inquiry followed which could find no shred of evidence connecting the Spanish with the explosion, and, naturally not wishing to put the blame on the Navy itself, it was left with lame speculations about the possibility of the existence of Spanish mines. It did not matter to the "yellow press," which reported that the Spanish undoubtedly did it, or to the American people who demanded war. Driven by popular pressure and by influential men within his party, McKinley made stern demands on the Spanish government, which, being in enough trouble as it was, capitulated to them. Himself a man of peace, McKinley faced a bellicose Congress which now demanded war no matter what the Spanish government did. Unwilling to disrupt his party, McKinley thereupon responded to the Spanish capitulation with a previously written war message to Congress, lamely adding the information that the Spanish government already had agreed to all of the American demands.

What followed was a sorry little struggle in Cuba to which the incompetent Cuban Governor General with six weeks warning could muster but 1,700 men at Santiago. Incompetence and confusion on the American side were also scandalous, but 17,000 American troops were nevertheless landed in Cuba, unopposed. The brief battle at Santiago, featuring Theodore Roosevelt's celebrated charge up San Juan Hill, sufficed to bring to an end four centuries of Spanish rule. Two days later the defective Spanish fleet, bottled up in Santiago harbor, received orders to be destroyed rather than surrender, and in broad daylight Admiral Cervera sent his wooden ships to their destruction at a cost in dead and wounded of 474 Spaniards. The entire war cost the United States less than four hundred fatalities in combat and more than five thousand through disease and food poisoning.

To most Americans, including apparently the President, the war, at the outset, was purely one to free Cuba. There were some, however, who from the first had had larger ideas, and among these was Assistant Secretary of the Navy Roosevelt. Roosevelt shared with others of his generation, such as Senator Henry Cabot Lodge and Admiral Alfred T. Mahan, a Darwinistic view of the power struggle among nations which was rather more European than it was American. In this view, nations became great through the fitness of their people, the willingness of their people to express themselves in war, and the spiritually strengthening experience of war itself. "When great nations fear to expand," Roosevelt declared, "shrink from expansion, it is because their greatness is coming to an end." He further believed that "No triumph of peace is quite so great as the supreme triumphs of war."

To this doctrine, Admiral Mahan contributed an internationally important theory concerning the relationship of sea power to national power. Historically, Mahan found, naval power had been the key to national power. Naval power in turn required far-flung naval bases. American national power, Mahan argued, depended upon a powerful navy, provided with naval bases in the Caribbean and in the Pacific. Mahan's arguments influenced British and German naval construction more than American, but it was having its effect on an expanded American Navy also, and in 1898 Roosevelt was in a position to do something about Mahan's demand for those naval bases.

With the Spanish war in prospect, Roosevelt as Assistant Secretary of the Navy, took advantage of the absence of his superior to send orders to Commodore George Dewey, in charge of America's Pacific squadron at Hong Kong, ordering him to keep in readiness for offensive operations in the Philippine Islands. Accordingly Dewey, upon receiving word of war, sailed into Manila Bay and sank the small, helpless Spanish fleet. He was without troops to occupy Manila, but within three months he was rescued from this anomalous position by 11,000 American soldiers, supported by Philippine insurrectionists under the Philippine patriot leader Emilio Aguinaldo. Taking Manila proved an easy matter, but thereafter for more than three years the Americans fought a much longer and bloodier struggle than the Spanish-American episode, against Aguinaldo and his guerilla fighters. The Americans, furthermore, found themselves, in the course of that struggle, resorting to the concentration camp horrors and to the methods of torture which, in the beginning, had aroused American sentiment against the Spanish in Cuba. The Americans were not yet in entire possession of their new empire before they had reason to regret its acquisition.

VI

Imperial America — The war had been launched in a chivalrous spirit with no thought of conquest, and Congress had written that spirit into law with the amendment to the declaration of war, put forward by Senator H. M. Teller of Colorado, pledging Cuban independence. Once in the war, however, America was swept by imperial ambitions, to which Congress gave vent during the week of Roosevelt's charge up San Juan Hill with a joint resolution annexing Hawaii. Two weeks later McKinley had so far freed himself of his earlier anti-imperialist inhibitions as to demand Puerto Rico and Guam as the price of an armistice.

Then people began to think about taking the Philippines; first Manila, then Luzon, and then all of them. By the time of the treaty negotiations McKinley had become convinced that "There was nothing left for us to do but to take them all, and to educate the Filipinos and to uplift and civilize and Christianize them, and by God's grace do the very best we could by them as our fellow men for whom Christ also died." The United States accordingly dictated the terms. Cuba was to become independent, Guam and Puerto Rico were to be taken outright, and the Philippine Islands were to be purchased for 20 million. In February, 1899, the treaty passed the Senate after a sharp debate by the necessary two-thirds majority, with but two votes to spare, and the government faced the unprecedented problem of absorbing into the American democratic system subject peoples in noncontiguous territories extending halfway around the world.

The organizing of the empire was embarrassed by a rising bipartisan opposition to the conquests, expressing itself through the Anti-Imperialist League and urging all the difficulties and inconsistencies and apparent unconstitutionalities involved in the maintenance of an imperial government by a federal democracy. In the face of this opposition, the government moved diffidently, establishing no "Secretary of the Empire" to administer the new acquisitions, but instead taking them one at a time and tucking them under other departments, such as Navy and Interior. Cuba, to the surprise of the rest of the world (and to the regret of the people of the United States sixty years later), did receive her independence, but only under the restrictions of the Platt amendment to an army appropriations bill of 1901. By these terms, the United States asserted its authority over Cuban diplomatic and financial affairs as well as over various other internal Cuban matters, reserving the right to occupy Cuba militarily and reserving also the right to buy or lease Cuban land for the purpose of establishing naval stations. Cuba received its limited independence only after incorporating the terms of the Platt amendment into its constitution.

Annexation of the Philippines and Puerto Rico raised constitutional problems, since it was not the American intention, as it was in Hawaii and Alaska, eventually to admit these territories to statehood. These perplexities, however, were wafted away by the Supreme Court in a series of "Insular Cases," which found that Congress had the right to keep a territory "like a disembodied shade, in an intermediate state of ambiguous existence for an indefinite period," which was to say, among other things, that it could simultaneously retain the territory as American soil and raise up tariff barriers against it. As to the rights of the natives of these "unincorporated" territories of Puerto Rico and the Philippines, the Court found that they had "fundamental" rights to life, liberty, and property but not "procedural" rights, which the Court never defined comprehensively. Nevertheless, it must be said for the American masters that they did not avail themselves by any means of all of these sovereign advantages. Representative institutions were established at the outset, and in 1917 American citizenship was extended to the Puerto Ricans, being denied the Filipinos because eventual independence was contemplated for them. American governments encouraged economic imperialism unself-consciously, but with political imperialism they had as little to do as possible.

The Caribbean conquests caused no major diplomatic complications, for the United States was in a position to assert itself effectively against the challenge of any potential foreign enemy, and Roosevelt as President was able to apply an unrestrained "big stick" diplomacy to this area. Faced with the fact that Caribbean nations were repudiating European debts and that European powers might make this a pretext for conquest, Roosevelt in 1904 enunciated the Roosevelt Corollary to the Monroe Doctrine: Since the United States would not tolerate European intervention in America, it must therefore assume the responsibility for upholding legitimate European interests, by occupying the defaulting nations and administering the repayment of their honest debts. Beginning with the occupation of the Dominican Republic in 1905, this policy was followed by Roosevelt and his successors—including Wilson, who had denounced it as immoral before taking office—until the coming of the New Deal.

The new American position in the Caribbean, as well as the two-ocean naval requirements which the war had dramatized, served to revive interest in an isthmian canal in Central America. In 1901, treaty negotiations freed the United States from diplomatic commitments to England regarding canal construction, and Roosevelt on taking office moved vigorously to accomplish the task. Of two alternative routes the one through Colombia was chosen, partly because of the lobbying of the successors to a bankrupt French canal company who saw their opportunity to snatch profits from disaster by selling out to America. When the reluctance of the Colombian government to come to terms threatened the Panamanian enterprise, company officials, with American naval support, staged a little revolution and established the Republic of Panama, which elected a government of canal company officials and quickly came to terms with the United States. Construction proceeded at once, and the Panama Canal was opened in 1914, leaving disagreeable Latin-American feelings toward the United States which Congress in 1921 did something to assuage by a 25 million dollar grant to Colombia.

Acquisition of the Philippines, on the other hand, presented the

United States with problems which were not so easily disposed of. There the United States found itself in the midst of English, French, German, and Japanese colonial rivals, and, amid this fast company, it was committed to the defense of a gigantic archipelago for which it had nothing like the requisite naval and military resources. McKinley's Secretary of State, John Hay, exhibited America's fundamental weakness in the Orient by issuing "Open Door" notes to imperial rivals in the Far East, inviting them to agree to equal privileges and equal trading rights for all nationals in all "spheres of influence" which these nations had wrested from China. Despite the fact that no nation agreed to his terms unequivocally, Hay remarkably enough announced that they had done so and that the Open Door policy was in effect. There followed upon this the rising of the Chinese nationalist Boxers against the extraterritorial foreign communities in China, which was put down by an international force and made the pretext for further dismemberment of China. Hay met this with a second note, calling for the imperial powers to guarantee "Chinese territorial and administrative entity," with no better success.

Roosevelt, while not overtly repudiating the Open Door idea, developed a policy of his own, upon coming to office, which depended fundamentally upon maintaining a balance of power between the two leading Asiatic nations, Japan and Russia. Following his mediation of the Russo-Japanese War in 1905, Roosevelt was faced with a Japanese resentment, which incidentally was increased by Japanese segregation in San Francisco schools. Roosevelt persuaded the San Francisco city schools to integrate and gained from the Japanese a "Gentleman's Agreement" not to issue further American passports to Japanese, if the United States did not pass a humiliating Japanese exclusion law. Then he sent the American fleet around the world as a salutary demonstration of American power. In 1908 the Root-Takahira Agreement was signed by which Roosevelt recognized Japan's special interest in Manchuria, where he was happy to see Japan and Russia contesting each other, Open Door morality aside.

This balance-of-power diplomacy, however, was reversed by the "dollar diplomacy" of Roosevelt's successor, President Taft, whose policy was that of strengthening America's position in the Caribbean and the Far East through the expansion of private American investments. So far as the Caribbean was concerned, this policy worked well enough, at the cost of stirring up more anti-Yankee feeling than Roosevelt's taking of Panama ever had done. In the Far East, however, it was disastrous. When Taft urged American financiers into Manchurian enterprises, Japan and Russia were quick to smooth over their mutual differences, in order to unite against the United States. Under any circumstances, however, possession of the Philippines placed the United States in a damagingly weak position. Just as Canada throughout the nineteenth century remained diplomatically a British hostage in American hands, so the Philippine Islands became an American hostage in the hands of Japan, serving to weaken America's bargaining position with Japan from the first Open Door note down to Pearl Harbor.

BIBLIOGRAPHY FOR CHAPTER NINE

Most of the bibliography for the preceding chapter is relevant for this one, and the generalization concerning the relative lack of historical writings applies to this period also. The best introduction to this period is the brief Samuel Hays, *The Response to Industrialism, 1885–1914* (1957), which contains an essay on the literature dealing with the period. "Within its area of predominantly economic, political, urban, and international developments, the volume has pronounced advantages. For one thing the time span is a sound one. . . . For another thing Professor Hays has dropped the conventional framework. . . . His chapters on 'Organize or Perish' and 'The Individual in an Impersonal Society' are exceptionally perceptive and suggestive. Elsewhere the old commonplaces are repeated." H. U. Faulkner, *Politics, Reform and Expansion, 1890–1900* (1959)is a mainly economic and political account.

F. L. Allen's uncritical *The Great Pierpont Morgan* (1949), "a 282-page essay by historian-journalist . . . Allen represents the only scholarly . . . interpretation of Morgan's career . . . a series of episodes rather than an account of continuing activities . . . brightly executed from the literary standpoint. . . ." For the main study of the climax of the farm protest movement see J. D. Hicks, *The Populist Revolt* (1931), an exhaustive and still generally valid study written from a sympathetic point of view. Among subsequent cityminded second thoughts concerning Populism, the most provocative, perhaps, are to be found in the early chapters of Richard Hofstadter, *The Age of Reform* (1955). Still more recent studies, however, have repudiated some of Hofstadter's main conclusions.

Frank Freidel, *The Splendid Little War* (1958) is "a first-rate pictorial history of the war with Spain." A more important study is H. K. Beale, *Theodore Roosevelt and the Rise of America to World Power* (1956). "Perhaps the first feature of this study to impress the critical reader is the vast amount of source material that has gone into its composition. . . . Roosevelt's impact upon world affairs and upon the course of American foreign policy Professor Beale regards as for the most part unfortunate, or at best negative." George Kennan, *American Diplomacy, 1900–1950* (1951) is a series of critical commentaries on American foreign policy from the Spanish-American War to the cold war. Engagingly written by a former leading State Department policy-maker, it contains a good, highly critical chapter on the origins of the Open Door policy. The controversy concerning the origins and consequences of the war are aired in T. P. Greene, ed., *American Imperialism in 1898.* F. R. Dulles, *America's Rise to World Power, 1898–1954* (1955) is "a convenient, well-written summary . . . a narrative rather than analytical book. . . ." It covers the subject somewhat more briefly than do the relevant sections in the leading textbooks on American diplomacy, and, with its good bibliographical discussion, it is probably the best available introduction to the subject.

I

Urbanization   In 1900, the population of the United States stood at
seventy-six million. It had increased from five million
in 1800 and from somewhat less than thirty-two million on the
eve of the Civil War. It was of course the cities which assumed
the main burden of the population increase, including the overwhelming majority of the new immigrant population. New York
had grown from somewhat more than a million on the eve of the
Civil War to somewhat less than four million, while Philadelphia
was approaching a million and a half. The greatest urban growth
had taken place in the Midwest, where Chicago passed Philadelphia to become the nation's second largest city, and St. Louis

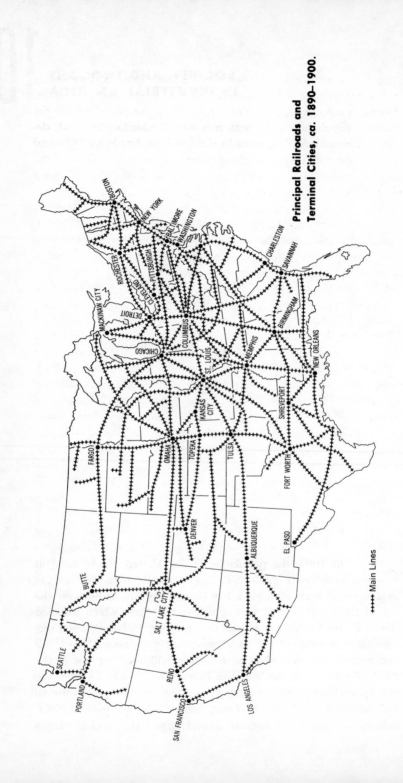

Principal Railroads and
Terminal Cities, ca. 1890–1900.

+++ Main Lines

rose to rank fourth. The countryside had become measurably urbanized as well, the number of communities of more than 2,500 having quadrupled since 1860, to account for one-third of the nation's population. The South remained predominantly rural, despite important developments in the Southern textile industry and despite the conversion of Birmingham from a cotton field to the second largest iron-producing region in the nation. New Orleans had dropped to fifteenth among the nation's cities.

The cities were, of course, sinks of sin and of political corruption, each with its ruling political ring and wide open red-light district. The rate of growth had been accompanied by no effective control over housing conditions, and, in all major cities, thousands lived in cellars and many thousands more were crowded into airless, windowless rooms. A board of health was created in New York City in 1866, with powers to establish housing controls, but an investigating commission in 1900 concluded that conditions were even worse than they had been a half century before. The congestion of humanity upon Manhattan Island was very likely worse than in any other community in the world. The density of its slum population was estimated to be twice that of the London slums. Disease naturally spread readily through these areas, the death rate in the slums of Mulberry Bend being about twice that of the national average. Individual reformers and various municipal commissions did what they could, but until the twentieth century the city conditions continued to get the best of their efforts.

The cities also wore their happier aspects. To J. P. Morgan, according to his son, "New York was still a friendly, neighborly city and was a pleasant place in which to live. . . ." It was in the cities that the great and growing disparity between the rich and the poor revealed itself most dramatically. The average workingman earned a maximum of about $500 a year, which had a purchasing power of about $1,500 in modern terms. This, however, was well above the average earnings of the slum dweller, eking out an existence rolling cigars or doing piecework for the garment industry. On the other end of the scale, Andrew Carnegie's earnings for the year 1900 were 23 million dollars, and, since the Supreme Court had declared the income tax to be unconstitutional, Carnegie could do with his money as he pleased. He chose to devote his earnings mainly to philanthropic enterprises, notably the building of public libraries, and other rich men such as Stanford and Rockefeller to some extent followed this example. But for those who had climbed to the top of the heap the money rolled in faster than it could be spent, even given the enormous opportunities for philanthropy.

One way by which these men tried to spend their money was in the building of numbers of palatial residences—the huge "cottages" in Newport, as well as the vast town houses in New York, Chicago and elsewhere. It has been estimated that the cost of the seven Vanderbilt houses in New York, in terms of today's money, was more than 36 million dollars. In 1900 the occupants of these houses still had to do, to a considerable extent, without modern conveniences, although electricity was taking the place of gas lighting in the best homes. They compensated for this, however, with the assistance of a retinue of from one hundred to three hundred servants, available at wages of from $3.50 a week and up. Some rich men, including Rockefeller, Carnegie, and Morgan, while they lived magnificently, did not choose to live in a constant state of competitive ostentation. For most of the new rich, however, life was an endless exertion to keep up with the Vanderbilts, and an important status index was provided by the number of servants in one's employ.

There remained the middle class, which was soon to assert itself in the Progressive era. The professional people, the middling businessmen, and the rising class of salaried executives lived modestly and respectably in good brownstone houses with the aid of from two to four servants. They considered themselves the backbone of American society, and the future proved them right. The twentieth century was to see a great broadening of the middle-class element in American society, but in 1900 it appeared to many of these people that they were in the process of being ground out between the rich above and the poor below.

The move to the city was predominantly an immigrant movement, and by 1900 it was part of what was coming to be known and worried about as the "new immigration." Down to 1890 the majority of immigrants continued to come from the British Isles and Germany, as had always been the case. Beginning in the 1880s, however, a rapid shift in the place of origin occurred from this area to that of Russia, Italy, and Austria-Hungary. Of somewhat more than eight million immigrants during the first decade of the twentieth century, more than five and one-half million came from these three areas of Southern and Eastern Europe. Their movement to the cities was made necessary in part by the great general population increases of the nineteenth century and in part by the breakup of the manorial system and of the institution of serfdom. The serfs had formerly been bound to the land. They were now not only free to go, but they were forced off the land by owners who wished to be freed of the burden of supporting more people than was necessary for the working of their lands. Once forced from the land, the peasant might go to New York or Chicago almost as easily as to Vienna or Naples, for the cost of trans-Atlantic transportation had dropped sharply, and steamship company agents were busy everywhere in Europe recruiting customers. In addition, unscrupulous immigrant "bankers" made good profits from arranging passage for their countrymen, on terms which amounted to temporary slavery.

Except for the one and a half million Jews who came to America, mainly from the urban areas of Eastern Europe, the overwhelming majority of the new immigrants were Catholics from the European countryside. Raised in an isolated peasant atmosphere, many of them had never seen a city before the move from the land which brought them to Ellis Island, and many of them never saw the countryside again. As had formerly been the case with the Irish, they arrived penniless and under obligations which required them to take the first job offered them. They moved into slum tenements, where they were among people of their own culture who spoke their own language, and there they remained, kept in debt to landlords, grocerymen, and saloon-keepers and kept from advancement by language difficulties and illiteracy.

For second generation immigrants the prospects were a good deal brighter, despite the slum environment. Brought up to speak English, they might have the opportunity to receive as good or better an education as the average American child of older stock, who still lived mainly in the country, where the farmers still didn't see much sense in taxing themselves heavily for the schooling of their children, especially when there were plenty of chores to be done around the farm. The Americanization of second-generation immigrants was at the cost of an alienation from the old-country parents, which remained a cruel theme of the social history of the new immigration. It was an Americanization, furthermore, in which the neighborhood gangs were apt to play a more important role than the city schools. Of these murderous gangs of the American-born sons of immigrants, Jacob Riis wrote, "The 'assimilation' of Europe's oppressed hordes, upon which our Fourth of July orators are so fond of dwelling, is perfect. The product is our own."

It was by the sweated labor of the new immigrants that modern American industry was created, just as the labor of the Chinese and the Irish had created the railroads of an earlier generation, and as, before them, the Germans and the Scotch-Irish had cut back the frontier and guarded the native American colonists against the Indian menace, not to mention the burdens placed on the slaves and afterwards upon the freed Negroes. Native white Americans have had the luck, during most of their history, to have somebody always coming along to do their hardest and most dangerous work for them.

II

Religion

The Catholic Church, to which most of these immigrants belonged, had become numerically significant for the first time in the thirties and forties, with the coming of the Germans and the Irish. It had rapidly developed into the largest denomination in the nation, and by World War I it accounted for about one-third of the nation's church members. Deeply suspected by the older Protestant Americans and forced to adjust itself to American laws, the Catholic Church was rent with internal dissensions throughout the nineteenth and early twentieth centuries. An early issue, which divided the Church, was the question of whether Church property should be owned by the Church hierarchy, as was the case in Europe, or by the members, as was the case with American Protestant churches. By the eve of the Civil War, this battle had been largely won by the hierarchy.

There was, at the same time, the more bitter struggle between the originally Spanish and French hierarchy and the German and Irish majority, a struggle which had resulted, by the eve of the Civil War, in the capture of the Church leadership by the Irish. Then, with the new immigration, this struggle was resumed by Italian and Polish Catholics against Irish priests. The native American Catholics, for their part, shared with American Protestants a nativist prejudice against the new arrivals, strengthened by the realization that the new immigration was reawakening the anti-Catholic sentiment which had subsided with the Civil War.

The Church hierarchy was itself divided between those who

wished to "Americanize" the Church and those who wished to isolate Catholics from an American society which they considered to be subversively Protestant. The urban environment was subversive of the Catholic Church, probably to a greater extent than was true of the Protestant churches, since the European orientation of Catholicism was more thoroughly rural than was the case with most Protestant sects. At the same time, the Church was continually strengthened in numbers and strengthened also by the attacks made against it by nativist organizations such as the American Protective Association. This persecution, without rising to the anti-Catholic fury of the fifties, tended to unify the Church and strengthen the hand of the clergy.

As a result of the new immigration, the Jewish population rose from 23,000 in 1877 to 3,000,000 in 1914. Arriving largely from the urban centers of Europe, especially from Russia, where they fled from anti-Semitic pogroms, the Jews were better prepared to adjust to city life than were the Catholics. In American society, the Jews were subjected to a rather folkish anti-Semitism, but their lack of a hierarchy exempted them from some of the opposition directed against the Catholics. It also relieved them from the organizational stresses which plagued the Catholic Church. The large majority of Jews remained thoroughly orthodox, but a movement developed under the leadership of Isaac M. Wise, which, while accepting the moral laws of the Mosaic code, rejected ceremonial and rabbinical regulations. This school of "modernism" founded Hebrew Union College in Cincinnati in 1875.

With the rising tide of the new immigration came a rising tide of opposition in America to unlimited immigration. The opposition was directed earliest against Oriental immigration, Chinese laborers being excluded in 1882 and Japanese by the Gentlemen's Agreement of 1907. The association of foreign radicalism with labor violence, in the late nineteenth century, encouraged immigration restriction. In 1897, Congress passed a literacy test, which would have effectively barred the large majority of the new immigrants, but the bill was vetoed by Cleveland. Similar bills were subsequently vetoed by Taft and Wilson, but, in 1917, a literacy test bill was finally passed over Wilson's veto. The high tide of anti-immigrant sentiment was reached following the First World War, and, in 1921, amid the rising power of the nativist Ku Klux Klan, the Immigration Act was passed, establishing an annual quota of 3 per cent of the number of persons of each nationality living in

America in 1910. In 1924, under the National Origins Act, the quota was reduced to 2 per cent and the base year put back to 1890, when the new immigration was in its early stages. In 1929 the national origins provisions went into effect within the confines of an absolute annual limit of 150,000 immigrants.

Protestant churches in America, triumphant during the first half of the nineteenth century, found themselves increasingly on the defensive in the years following the Civil War. The Civil War proved a massively demoralizing influence, and Protestant churches were further confronted by the fact that many of their members, when they left the farm, left the church as well. Family-centered and small-town-centered American Protestantism faced problems of adjustment to the city which it was not altogether successful in resolving. The city provided a host of diversions with which the churches had to compete and also an impersonality which provided former farm dwellers with a new freedom from clerical supervision. And in the cities, Protestantism became a minority religion to the predominant Catholic Church.

One important reason for the apparent decline in faith among the masses of urban Protestants was the Protestant social philosophy, which continued faithfully to reflect the old American faith in self-help, both for the achieving of salvation, so far as the next world was concerned, and for the making of one's own way in this world. This doctrine did not translate readily from the self-sufficient farm to the interdependent city. Protestant theology and classical economics, at the close of the Civil War, had been inseparable in the sermons of the American ministry, sanctifying the most antisocial abuses of individualistic free enterprise and explaining poverty and slum conditions as God's judgment upon the sinful. The high cost of church property in the cities made the churches dependent upon their well-to-do parishioners and thus further contributed to their conservatism. The consequence was a growing hostility to churches on the part of the urban working classes.

One effort to win the allegiance of urban Protestants was made with the establishment by Mary Baker Eddy of the Church of Christ, Scientist, first chartered in Boston in 1879. Preaching the unreality of sin and of disease and the ability of the good Christian to overcome these errors, Christian Science was successful in winning converts among the middle classes, but it had little impact upon the lower economic groups.

During the last two decades of the century, however, there

emerged in the churches of America, preachers of a new Social
Gospel, arguing that the salvation of society, itself, was necessary
to the saving of individual souls. Leaders of this movement tended
to come from an urban background in which the social doctrines of
the churches had, from the first, appeared irrevelant to urban circumstances. Slums, they argued, were not caused by the sinfulness
of slum dwellers, as many ministers continued to assert, but were
themselves the cause of evil. Works such as Washington Gladden's
Applied Christianity preached that Christian solutions existed for
social problems. The standard for politics and for business practice
should be the Golden Rule.

Preaching a simple, undoctrinaire, righteous message, the Social
Gospelers, together with reformers and scholars of strong religious
leanings, formulated the new ethic for the industrial age. In so
doing, they prepared the way for the reform movements of the
Progressive era and gave to that era the strong moral tone which
was its chief quality. Prominent among the formulators of this new
doctrine was a new school of economists, socially conscious and
strongly moralistic in tone. Its organization was the American Economic Association, founded in 1885 on the proposition that the
purpose of economics was to reform society rather than to defend
the *status quo,* and in this view of the reforming role of scholarship,
it was joined by an increasing number of scholars in other of the
social sciences.

The assistance which Protestantism received from the social sciences, however, was outweighed by the damage it sustained from
the physical sciences. In 1859, Charles Darwin's *Origin of Species*
appeared, and, despite the national absorption with the slavery
controversy, it received immediate and widespread attention, including widespread condemnation on religious grounds. Until the
appearance of this work, literal belief in the word of the Bible had
been unqualified, so far as most American church members were
concerned. It is true that findings in geology, in the late eighteenth
and early nineteenth centuries, had contradicted the Book of Genesis in asserting that the earth had been created, not in six days, but
in the course of many millions of years. This new idea had had a
disturbing impact within college classrooms, but it had not
achieved general currency.

Darwin's work, however, bristling with factual evidence and immediately and loudly acclaimed by many distinguished scientists,
presented religious literalism with a challenge which it was unable

to combat effectively. Sides were taken at once, and the issue was argued out fiercely during the next generation. The debate did not find the scientists lined up against the religionists altogether, for distinguished scientists, such as Louis Agassiz, continued to denounce the theory, while distinguished ministers, such as Henry Ward Beecher, insisted that religious belief be adjusted to the new knowledge. In the rural areas of the nation and especially in the South, the fundamentalist churches held firm against a theory which declared man to have been created, not by God, in His own image, but by a process of natural selection from lower forms of animal life.

For them, the climax of the struggle came in 1925, in the Scopes trial, when a Tennessee school teacher was tried for violating the state law against teaching evolution in public schools. Attracting avid nationwide attention, the trial featured William Jennings Bryan for the prosecution and Clarence Darrow, Dudley Field Malone, and Arthur Garfield Hays for the defense. Bryan was driven to concede that he did not believe the earth to have been created in six days, but the prosecution won its case, the teacher being fined $100, later rescinded, and the state law upheld. It was a victory, however, which brought a unity to the modernists and placed fundamentalism decisively on the defensive. Meanwhile, evolution had long since been accepted by most Americans and with its acceptance had come an irreversible decline in religious faith, at least on the old grounds. Less widely noted, but also destructive of Biblical literalism, was the new Bible scholarship, which, through archaeology and textual comparison, discounted older ideas concerning the origins of the Bible. These new ideas were vigorously combatted by Catholics as well as by Protestants and Jews, but the challenge to Protestantism and Judaism was the greater, because of the greater importance placed by these religions upon the word of the Bible.

III

Intellectual Currents   It was in the field of religion that the issues raised by Darwinism were most hotly contested, but evolutionary science also exerted a profound influence on all areas of thought, in America as elsewhere. Darwin had, himself, been brought to his theory by his observance of social conditions in industrial England, where evolutionary change, through the process of survival of the fittest, was so abundantly apparent. It was this same obvious evolutionary change of the industrial revolution which provided Darwin with an immediately receptive audience in America. The generation which fought the Revolution and formed the Constitution had assumed that the world and human society were pretty much as they had always been and as they always would remain. That generation, and those which followed it down to the Civil War, had believed in progress, but they had thought of progress in terms of the perfectibility of a society which would retain substantially its existing outlines. This idea of a changeless world had gained support from Newtonian science, with its revelation of a rationally ordered, changeless, mechanistic universe. The age of Emerson had tended to envelop itself in a mysticism which would have been alien to Jefferson or Franklin; nevertheless it had inherited its ideas from the age of the Enlightenment, including the assumption of a basically changeless universe ordered according to immutable laws.

The industrial revolution introduced the new intellectual experience of a fundamental material progress, raising up great cities, spanning the nation with railroads, and, year by year, visibly altering the character of the world and of society. Material progress was the most striking phenomenon of the age, and the process by which it was being achieved, in America especially, was the one of ruthless, uncontrolled competition. To account for this striking phenomenon, a new theory of society developed, a social Darwinism which applied to society the evolutionary laws of biology. The most persuasive spokesman for social Darwinism was William Graham Sumner of Yale, who originally had trained for the ministry, but who had been won to sociology by the new scientific findings of the age.

Sumner was, in politics, a Republican of the liberal school, who subscribed to the view that the purpose of government was to protect the life, liberty, and property of the individual and nothing more. In effect, therefore, he was Jeffersonian in his views, opposing any artificial regulation of society by government. At the same time, he was thoroughly scornful of Jefferson and of the natural rights philosophy. In his view, man had no God-given natural rights. The law of society was the law of the jungle, where every man got what he deserved by fighting for it, and where society advanced through the process of struggle and through the resulting survival of the fittest.

The two main purposes for which governments were formed were to protect private property and to defend the virtue of women. Sumner arrived at this conclusion, not from the natural rights philosophy, but from his anthropological investigations. His signal disapproval of robbery and rape was based upon his anthropological conclusion that the two great pervading institutions running through human history were those of private property and of marriage and the family. No matter what changes society went through, Sumner concluded, these were the institutions to which man continued to cling. Government should therefore restrict itself to the defense of these, allowing all else to change itself through the natural process of survival of the fittest. Government controls would only disrupt the natural process and encourage the survival of the unfittest.

This brand of social Darwinism won the support of businessmen who wished to remain free of government regulation, although, at the same time, Sumner's logical opposition to the protective tariff resulted, on several occasions, in pressure being brought against Yale by businessmen to fire him. Against Sumner's contention, other social scientists, notably Lester Ward, argued that the biological analogy was a false one, as applied to society, and that the very measure of excellence in any society was the degree to which it protected its citizens from the dangers and uncertainties of the natural state. Society, Ward argued, should be improved by the process of artificial selection by government planning, just as man improved breeds of animals and forms of plant life for his own purposes by the process of artificial selection.

The most influential American social theorist of the age was Henry George, whose most important work, *Progress and Poverty*, appeared in 1879. With but little formal education, George formed his ideas, in great measure, from his experiences, but also very much within the Darwinian evolutionary scheme. The fact of American life which continued to strike him as most remarkable was the paradox of increasing poverty in a nation, which, at the same time, was rapidly increasing in wealth. "This association of poverty with progress," he wrote, "is the great enigma of our times. . . . So long as all the increased wealth which modern progress brings goes but to build up great fortunes, to increase luxury and make sharper the contrast between the House of Have and the House of Want, progress is not real and cannot be permanent."

Like Sumner, George rejected the traditional natural rights philosophy, but unlike Sumner he rejected, especially, the traditional belief in the natural right to property. The earth, he argued, rightfully belonged to all of humanity, and from it wealth was created by labor. Those who labored, therefore, should receive the rewards of the labor, rather than those who owned the land that was thereby being improved. George's solution was the "single tax." All taxes would be abolished except the land tax, that is, the total rent on land exclusive of improvements and rent-collecting fees. This would bring economic justice without requiring any revolutionary changes such as the expropriation of private property by the government.

Another reforming theorist, Edward Bellamy, wrote a utopian novel, *Looking Backward, 2000–1887*, which depicted America of the year 2000 as a model communistic state, arrived at, not through Marxian revolution, but through the continuation of the process of consolidation. Neither Bellamy nor George persuaded many people to follow any specific programs they advocated, but both of them, in calling popular attention to the cruel absurdities of the existing system, did much to prepare the way for the reforms of the Progressive era. They were abetted in this by the muckrakers—journalistic exposers of political and business corruption—who became especially active after the turn of the century. The misdeeds of Standard Oil were documented by Henry Demarest Lloyd in 1894 in *Wealth against Commonwealth* and by Ida Tarbell in *The History of the Standard Oil Company* (1902–1904). Lincoln Steffens exposed the political corruption of the times in his *Shame of the Cities*. These muckrakers presented themselves in the guise of scientists, not pleading for reform but simply illustrating the laws by which society worked. Their revelations were, nevertheless, powerful influences for reform.

Whichever way Darwinism might be argued, either as a defense of *laissez faire* or as a defense of political reform, those it influenced shared the idea of a constantly evolving society in a constantly evolving universe. In philosophy, a school of idealism emerged in the post-Civil War period, dominated by Josiah Royce of the University of California and Harvard, which attempted to reconcile evolutionary change with an immutable God. Idealism dominated academic philosophical thought to the end of the century, when it declined in influence and was supplanted partly by pragmatism.

The pragmatists, led by William James of Harvard and John Dewey of the University of Chicago, were completely converted to the Darwinistic view of life, asserting that truth was not absolute and unchanging, but, rather, relative to changing circumstances. As a practical matter, "truth" could be only provisionally established in terms of the results that followed from a belief in it. James was characteristically individualistic in his application of pragmatism, concerning himself especially with religion and with the impact of religious beliefs upon individuals. Dewey was concerned, rather, with the changing course of society and with developing in the individual the ability to adjust to social change and to help create a society which would serve the highest possible human purposes.

In science, itself, the United States was able to provide abundant evidence in support of Darwinian evolution from its wealth of natural phenomena. Asa Gray, the leading American botanist at the time of the appearance of Darwin's work, was an acquaintance of Darwin's who supplied Darwin with valuable material for his work and then became his leading champion in America, attempting to reconcile, so far as possible, Darwinian evolution with orthodox Protestant Christianity. The importance of science generally to American thought was rapidly increasing at the turn of the twentieth century, encouraged by the beginnings of graduate schools, but much more by the growing importance of science to industry. The patronage of science by men like Rockefeller and Carnegie gave it a solid and practical respectability, which it had not enjoyed in the days of Joseph Henry, and the relevance of scientific investigations to material progress, especially in the field of electricity, added support to sciences generally. By the turn of the century, industrial laboratories were being established, notably those of General Electric, Du Pont and, somewhat later, Bell Telephone.

Science also was revolutionizing higher education in America at the turn of the century. Until the third quarter of the nineteenth century, college presidents had been recruited from the ranks of the ministry, and colleges had served the purpose of training Christian gentlemen, whose knowledge of the classics and of moral philosophy would equip them to conduct themselves properly in refined society. State colleges had been created in a more democratic and practical spirit, but they had been, generally speaking, poorly supported by state legislatures in their early stages. The Land-grant Act of 1862, however, gave the states the means to improve their institutions, and state colleges and universities enjoyed a rapid growth in the postwar period.

The state legislatures would have nothing to do with the old formula of education, which had been retained from seventeenth-century England, and, in the state colleges, modern languages, modern history, and the practical mechanical and agricultural sciences were made the main basis of the curriculum. Colleges had been able to remain so nearly unchanged for more than two centuries, because they had had almost no relevance to social and economic conditions on the outside. With the growing educational needs of an industrial society, however, this ceased to be true. Johns Hopkins, the first American graduate school to be established on European standards, was founded in 1876 and became the pattern, during the next generation, for graduate schools organized by the older institutions.

A key date in the shift from the religious to the scientific orientation in higher education is 1869, when the scientist Charles W. Eliot became president of Harvard. Eliot made comprehensive changes in the curriculum and in the faculty, causing the greatest commotion by introducing the elective system, against the traditional belief in that basic core of information which should comprise the mental equipment of the cultivated gentleman. This elective system had been previously introduced at other colleges, including William and Mary and the University of Michigan, but it was introduced at Harvard on a more thoroughgoing basis than elsewhere, and its institution there exerted a profound influence on other colleges throughout the nation.

The shift from the religious to the scientific point of view was perhaps most rapid in those new private colleges and universities established by large private fortunes at the close of the century, notably the University of Chicago, financed mainly by John D. Rockefeller, and Stanford University, financed mainly by the California railroad man, Leland Stanford. A further main development of the period was the increased opportunities for higher education for women. Most of the state universities admitted them from the outset on an equal basis with men, and a number of women's colleges, such as Smith and Wellesley, were created from private fortunes in the generation after the Civil War. The specialization and professionalization of knowledge in America was marked by the organization of a series of learned societies, the American Historical Association in 1884, The American Economic Association in 1885, the American Academy of Political and Social Science in 1889, The American Political Science Association in 1903, and The American Sociological Society in 1905.

For those who did not have the opportunity for a college education, opportunities were presented through the Chautauqua movement, which began in the 1870s in New York as a training program for Sunday school teachers and spread throughout the nation. It was similar to the earlier lyceum movement, which had sent lecturers throughout the nation in the pre-Civil War period and had provided intellectuals, such as Emerson, with their main means of subsistence. The Chautauqua movement similarly enlisted the services of intellectuals, such as William James, and orators, such as William Jennings Bryan, for the benefit of Americans bent upon mental improvement. In addition, there were available such culturally elevated magazines as *Atlantic Monthly, Harper's, Nation,* and *Forum.* Technological advances in printing as well as increasing literacy served to make the American public better informed than the pre-Civil War generation had been, or, at least, more familiar with the world as it was presented in Hearst's *Journal* and in Pulitzer's *World.*

IV

Realism and Naturalism — The literary richness of the 1850s was destroyed by the Civil War and the Gilded Age. Longfellow published *Tales of a Wayside Inn* from 1863 to 1874. Whitman's *Drum-Taps* appeared in 1865, and Whittier's *Snow-Bound,* in 1866. These were the last major literary efforts of the old generation, except for *Billy Budd* by Melville and for *Democratic Vistas* by Walt Whitman, in which Whitman inveighed against soulless American materialism, in a strain which contrasted with his hugely optimistic and patriotic *Leaves of Grass.* Lowell had declared that he hated science as an Indian hated writing, because he feared it would hurt him, and so it did. In the new age of science, Lowell and all of his literary generation were lost. Many of them, Whitman, Lowell, Longfellow, Melville, Whittier, and Emerson, lived on into the eighties and nineties, but they remained largely silent amid the new America.

The most influential American literary figure of the postwar generation, and the one whose reputation probably stood highest among his contemporaries, was William Dean Howells of Ohio, who served as editor of *The Atlantic Monthly* in Boston during the seventies, and as contributing editor to *Harper's* in New York during the eighties. Howells, himself an extremely prolific writer as well as critic, established himself as the leading spokesman for the realistic school, against the genteel writers of such courtly and sentimental works as Thomas Nelson Page's *In Ole Virginia* and Henry Harland's *Grey Roses*. He urged his fellow writers to create a fiction which would "portray men and women as they are, actuated by the motives and passions in the measure that we all know," and to "leave off painting dolls and working them by springs and wires." His own contributions to a realistic portrayal of life in industrializing America, widely popular in his own day, have, for the time at least, gone out of fashion. The one work of his which continues to be read is *The Rise of Silas Lapham,* dealing with the moral problem of business ethics and the social problems of rising in a changing society. From the present vantage point, Howells's contributions as a writer appear less noteworthy than his contributions as guide and defender for the new generation of writers.

The writers who most nearly conformed to Howells's definition of realism were the local colorists such as Edward Eggleston, in *The Hoosier Schoolmaster,* Sarah Orne Jewett, in *The Country of the Pointed Firs,* and Edgar W. Howe, in *The Story of a Country Town.* These realistic writings, however much they varied in quality, shared the virtues and also the limitations which Howells himself placed upon realism, by meeting his requirement that writers should create only what it would be proper for pure maidens to read. That this involved the avoidance of much that went on in life, Howells conceded, but he urged that life in America was, on the whole, purer and more "smiling" than life in Europe, and that purity and realism, to that extent, found a greater opportunity to go hand in hand in America.

That writers so diverse as Howells's close friends, Mark Twain and Henry James, should appear together as the two greatest practitioners of the art of realism, indicates again how difficult it is to fit writers into any one school. Mark Twain met the requirements of the local color school of realism in the works upon which his reputation is chiefly based. *Huckleberry Finn, Tom Sawyer,* and *Life on the Mississippi* were descriptive of the area and the society he had known in his youth, while *The Gilded Age,* which he coauthored with Charles Dudley Warner, was the description of materialistic postwar American society which gave the period its name. Beyond that, Twain succeeded better than any of his contemporaries in capturing, in the conversations of his characters, the tone of the society about which he wrote. Yet, if the realist were held to Howells's requirement that he concern himself with the commonplace, Twain's writings, with their extravagant situations and humor of exaggeration, would not do at all. An increasingly mordant critic of American society, Twain appeared, to his contemporaries, as a leading humorist but not as an outstanding literary figure. It was only in the generation following his death that his high literary reputation was achieved.

While Mark Twain left his native West to settle, somewhat uneasily, among the genteel and dying literary group of New England, Henry James, brought up in the most intellectually sophisticated circles of the East, removed himself from America altogether, eventually becoming an English citizen. From the European vantage point, James dealt, in his writings, with the contrast between Americans and Europeans—between innocence and experience—and with the impact of Europe upon Americans. His realism, a world apart from that of either Howells or Twain, was psychological realism. His concern was not with the events in which his characters are involved, but with the impact of the events upon the thought and the consciences of his characters, as these are revealed in drawing room conversations. Although there is no general critical agreement as to what constitutes the greatest of James's voluminous writings, included among them would certainly be *The Portrait of a Lady,* dealing with the moral problem of an American girl, who, through her own misjudgment, has made herself the part of an evil and decadent European situation. *The Ambassadors, The Wings of the Dove,* and *The Golden Bowl* figure prominently among the writings of James which deal with this theme of the American in Europe.

Toward the close of the century, a group of writers, most of them associated with Howells, moved away from the school of realism to that of naturalism. Again, a term which includes such diverse writers as Stephen Crane and Theodore Dreiser is not one which is susceptible of exact application. The attribute which mainly served to distinguish the naturalists from the realists, however, was their acceptance of the Darwinian view of life as an endless, amoral struggle with the blind forces of nature. For the realists, there had remained objective standards by which conduct might be judged, and there had existed, beyond that, the free moral will of the individual to choose between right and wrong. Thus, Silas Lapham is able to make the right moral decision at the cost of business success, Huckleberry Finn is able to make the right moral decision not to return Jim to slavery, and Isabel Archer, in *The Portrait of a Lady*, is able to make the right moral decision to accept the responsibilities she has incurred by the bad marriage she has made.

By contrast the heroes and the heroines in the writings of the naturalists are not confronted by moral issues of right and wrong, and they would not have the freedom of will to make their own decisions if they had been. They are created by the environment in which they live. They do what they have to do, and their success or failure depends partly on accident and partly upon their degree of natural fitness for survival. Stephen Crane pioneered in the American school of naturalism with the publication, at his own expense, in 1893, of *Maggie, A Girl of the Streets,* dealing with a girl driven by her slum environment, first to prostitution, and then to suicide. Crane's reputation was largely achieved, and continues to rest, upon *The Red Badge of Courage,* dealing with a boy caught in the blind forces of battle, and *The Open Boat,* concerning the struggle of shipwrecked men with the ocean. But while Crane's themes were thus naturalistic, his style, poetic and filled with imagery, was in clear contrast to that of his naturalistic colleagues. Hamlin Garland remains best known for his early accounts, in *Main-traveled Roads,* of the dispiriting impact of the prairie farming region on the farmers, who are helpless in their environment, "like a fly in a pan of molasses."

Frank Norris, who rejected Howells's realism of the commonplace because it wasted its time on "the tragedy of the broken tea cup," dealt, in his best writings, with the Darwinistic struggles of industrializing America. In *The Octopus,* he wrote of the inexorable conquest of the California wheat growers by the Southern Pacific Railroad, while in *The Pit,* he depicted the struggles between the operators on the Chicago wheat market. Jack London wrote of struggles in nature in *The Call of the Wild* and of similarly savage conflicts among men in *The Sea Wolf.* Perhaps the most thorough-going of the naturalists, and certainly the most prolific among them, was Theodore Dreiser, whose *Sister Carrie* became a cele-brated cause when it was removed from the market by its publisher in 1900, on the moral grounds that its heroine sinned and never-theless succeeded. Often drawing his accounts, as in the case of *An American Tragedy,* from actual newspaper files, Dreiser wrote with a disregard for stylistic matters which, on the whole, tended to increase as his career progressed. Dreiser, like some, although not all, other naturalistic writers, apparently looked upon stylistic excellence as involving the risk of falsifying life.

It is significant that the schools of realism and naturalism drew as heavily as they did from the background of the newspaper office. Twain and Howells both received their early training as newspapermen, as, to a greater or lesser extent, did Norris, Crane, London, and Dreiser. The dearth of poetry is also a noteworthy characteristic of the period. The one poet of the period to achieve critical recognition, Emily Dickinson, was virtually unpublished and unknown during her own lifetime, achieving her recognition amid the great renaissance of American poetry which occurred be-ginning early in the twentieth century.

BIBLIOGRAPHY FOR CHAPTER TEN

Historians have left the rise of the modern city largely to the urban sociologists, while tending not entirely to approve of what these scholars have done. None of the few general historical studies of American cities is in paperback. Two contemporary exposés, however, remain significant and vivid. Jacob Riis, *How the Other Half Lives* (1890) is the descrip-tion of slum life by an urban immigrant journalist. Lincoln Steffens, *Shame of the Cities* (1904) deals with various cities mainly in terms of systems of political corruption. Jane Addams, *Twenty Years at Hull House* (1910) is the reminis-cence of the most famous American social worker of the day.

For the new immigration, which largely populated these cities, the most eloquent study is Oscar Handlin, *The Up-*

rooted (1951), which "sketches the disintegration of the time-honored Old World village society which drove thousands upon thousands to take refuge in emigration . . . describes the miseries of the crossing, the cold welcome and disillusionment . . . in the city slums . . . pictured with the emotional warmth and psychological insight of one who has been close to the newcomers . . . a study of those immigrants only who came from the village background of central and southern Europe and were stranded in our eastern cities." Oscar Handlin, *Race and Nationality in American Life* (1957) is a collection of articles in much the same vein. Carl Wittke, *We Who Built America* (1939) is a more conventional historical account of immigration.

John Higham, *Strangers in the Land: Patterns in American Nativism, 1860–1925* (1955) "is essentially a study of the opinion of one segment of the population about another—and of the impact of political, social, economic, and organizational pressures upon nativist thought and action . . . tempered handling of a passionate theme. . . ."

J. T. Ellis, *American Catholicism* (1956) is an "attractive little volume by one of America's outstanding Catholic historians, . . . a brief survey of Catholicism in America from colonial times to the present. The unifying thread is the significance of immigration in the history of the Church . . . the account is straightforward, well-documented, calm, and reasonable even where controversy exists." Nathan Glazer, *American Judaism* (1957) "moves chronologically from the Sephardic synagogue to German Reform to the Orthodox and Conservative Judaism of the Eastern European immigrants and their descendants. His conclusion . . . is that most Jews today care less about religion than retaining their identity as a historic people . . . not a definitive history but an always interesting and intelligent exploratory essay. . . ."

On the impact of biological science combined with industrial and population changes upon social thought, see Richard Hofstadter, *Social Darwinism in American Thought* (1944). "If ideas are truly weapons of change and implements of action, this volume could hardly fail to captivate a generation of scholars who seek to understand the one and to direct the other. . . . Dr. Hofstadter essays to illustrate how social theories inferred from biology were reflected in human motivations and how the prevailing 'intellectual climate' provided an environment favorable to their acceptance . . . there is far too little conceptual discrimination. . . . Yet . . . what he has done, he has done well." M. G. White, *Social Thought in*

America: The Revolt against Formalism (1949) also deals with the theme of relativism in early twentieth-century thought. H. S. Commager, *The American Mind* (1950), covering much the same period, sees the 1890s as an intellectual watershed, where significant currents of modern thought had their main origins. Perry Miller, ed., *American Thought, Civil War to World War I*, although not very helpfully edited, presents an excellent selection of essays by leading intellectuals. Merle Curti, *Social Ideas of American Educators* (1935) is an important study. Richard Hofstadter, *Academic Freedom in the Age of the College* (1955) and W. P. Metzger, *Academic Freedom in the Age of the University* (1955) together offer a good deal more than the titles promise. "The real subject is the development of higher education, and the authors make a fresh contribution of the highest scholarly order to intellectual history."

Thomas Beer, *The Mauve Decade: Life at the End of the Nineteenth Century* (1926) is a provocative and highly readable account, as is Lewis Mumford, *The Brown Decades: A Study of the Arts in America, 1865–1895* (1931). Alfred Kazin, *On Native Grounds* (1941) is an account of modern American literature which begins with the 1890s. Edmund Wilson, ed., *The Shock of Recognition*, vol. II, is an anthology of essays and letters of writers about other writers. Most notably it includes W. D. Howells's memoir of Mark Twain which captures so well the moribund world of letters in post-Civil War America. Henry Adams, *The Education of Henry Adams* (1918), a surfeit of delicious self-pity, measures the Gilded Age against Adams and finds it wanting. Wallace Stegner, ed., *Selected American Prose, 1841–1900* is a useful anthology.

I

Origins of Progressivism Reform was a cloud no larger than a man's hand in 1900, when McKinley was reelected to the Presidency. The contestants in that election were the same as those in the election of 1896, but the contest was wholly different. Good times had come again in the intervening four years, and as a consequence Bryan had been deprived of any good political issue upon which to campaign. For want of anything else he campaigned on the issue of imperialism. He himself had abetted the acquisition of the Philippines, however, and under any circumstances, two years after the "splendid little war" too many Americans were still exhilarated by the event and still in a mood to want

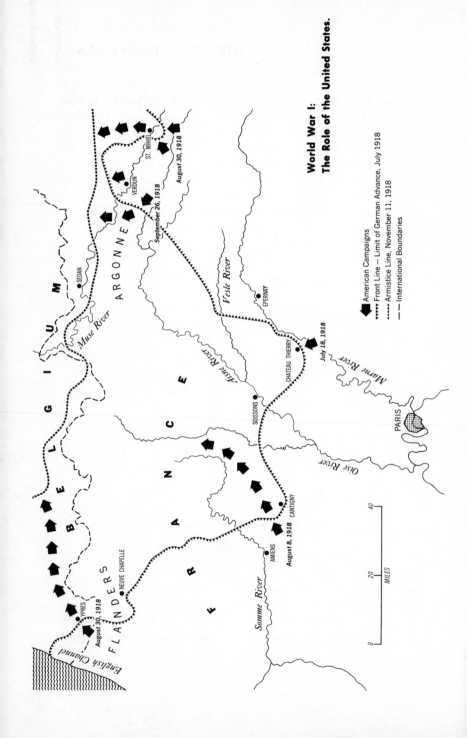

World War I:
The Role of the United States.

American Campaigns
Front Line – Limit of German Advance, July 1918
Armistice Line, November 11, 1918
International Boundaries

BELGIUM

SEDAN

Muse River

ARGONNE

VERDUN

September 26, 1918

ST. MIHIEL

August 30, 1918

FLANDERS

YPRES

August 30, 1918

NEUVE CHAPELLE

Vesle River

EPERNAY

Aisne River

SOISSONS

CHATEAU THIERRY

July 18, 1918

Marne River

Oise River

PARIS

CANTIGNY

August 8, 1918

AMIENS

Somme River

FRANCE

English Channel

0   20   40
MILES

the sun never to set upon the American empire. Consequently Mc-Kinley won by a considerably wider margin than he had in 1896 on the slogan of the "full dinner pail."

Going in with a sure winner, the Republicans gained further political advantage from the election by nominating Theodore Roosevelt as vice president and thereby removing him from New York politics, where his reforming activities as governor had disturbed the Republican political machine of Boss Platt. Everything seemed to be going right for the Grand Old Party and its business-minded backers when, seven months after his return to office, McKinley was assassinated and, as Mark Hanna bitterly complained to his colleagues on the funeral train, "that damned cowboy" Roosevelt was plucked from the oblivion of the vice presidency and put into the White House.

Descending upon the nation with flashing teeth, blazing pince-nez glasses, and a high, shrill voice of righteousness, Teddy Roosevelt dominated the political scene as had no previous President since Andrew Jackson. Like the Democratic Roosevelt who was to follow him, he combined a vivid impression of stormy radicalism with an ingrained patrician conservatism. Like F.D.R. he was, in his own age, the incomparable political animal. He sensed the amorphous will of the people, and he gave voice to it forcefully and amorphously. By no means the radical reformer that many of his fellow Republicans feared him to be, Roosevelt tried to quiet fears on coming to office, announcing that he would be guided in his acts by the realization that it was McKinley and not he whom the American people had elected as their President. But this irrepressibly rambunctious political leader immediately and dramatically altered the tone of the nation's politics. He rallied the scattered forces of reform, and the country swiftly passed over into the Progressive era.

The Democratic party had already gone Progressive with its capture by Bryan in 1896, and reformers continued to dominate its councils. That victory however had been at the cost of reducing the party to minority status in national politics, where it remained except briefly under Wilson down to the Depression. It was the conversion of the majority Republican party to reform, therefore, which marked the arrival of the new era. And this conversion, in times of prosperity, is harder to account for than the Democratic conversion in times of depression, since Roosevelt drew his following in large measure from those who had voted contentedly in 1900 for McKinley Republicanism and who four years earlier had voted fearfully against Bryan Democratic-Populism.

The immediate reason, certainly, was Roosevelt's forceful personality, for he was able to change people's minds almost overnight. A case in point was William Allen White, the famous and politically influential editor of the Emporia *Gazette* in Kansas. White had first gained national fame in an editorial attack against the Populists. "We have," he had then written, "an old moss-back Jacksonian who snorts and howls because there is a bathtub in the State House: we are running that old jay for Governor. . . . Put the lazy, greasy fizzle who can't pay his debts on the altar, and bow down and worship him. . . . What we need is not the respect of our fellow-men, but the chance to get something for nothing." Then Roosevelt came along like a shining knight and won White, with millions of others, to the cause. "I was a young arrogant protagonist of the divine rule of the plutocracy," White later remembered, when Roosevelt "shattered the foundations of my political ideals. As they crumbled then and there, politically, I put his heel on my neck, and I became his man."

Roosevelt Progressivism had been prepared for in many ways during the preceding generation. Faced with the continuing and increasing problem of poverty in an industrializing nation, the old self-righteous humanitarianism of the pre-Civil War period was giving way to the new scientific philanthropy which viewed poverty less as a moral problem than as a social one, for which the community as a whole was directly responsible. The last quarter of the nineteenth century had seen the establishment of various sorts of state commissions which, while they may have achieved little actual reform, had gathered many statistics revealing to the respectable citizenry the horrors of the system which they were tolerating.

And muckrakers were beginning to rub the noses of these people into those conditions of corruption, sin, and squalor of which they were already painfully aware. Most effectively of all the Social Gospel was exerting itself powerfully to mold the thinking of the new generation. The Social Gospel had by no means made a general conquest of Protestantism, even in the Northern cities where its strength lay, but its influence had been concentrated upon those middle- and upper-middle-class citizens who were to become the heart and soul of the Progressive movement.

Everybody had known all along that the cities were sinfully bad, and good-government groups, or "goo-goos" as they were called, were being organized in the eighties and nineties to do what they could about the situation. It was a discouragingly Augean task, but Tammany Hall was temporarily unseated in 1894, and Chicago was under a reform government by the end of the century. In 1901 Tom Johnson, the industrialist, converted to reform by Henry George's *Progress and Poverty*, became mayor of Cleveland, and during the next generation Johnson made Cleveland the model for municipal reform nationally.

Urban reformers tended to find that the trail of corruption led to the statehouse, and sentiment for statewide reform was strong when Roosevelt took office. In that year Robert M. La Follette became Governor of Wisconsin, and he launched upon the most ambitious program of state reform to be undertaken during the Progressive era. It included tax reforms, railroad controls, conservation measures, factory inspection procedures, a workman's compensation law, and various purely political measures such as the direct primary election for senators, the purpose of which was to take politics out of the hands of the "interests" and place it in the hands of the "people." La Follette was followed, during the next decade, by Hiram Johnson in California, Charles Evans Hughes in New York, Woodrow Wilson in New Jersey, "Alfalfa Bill" Murray in Oklahoma, and by additional Progressive reform governors in state after state.

Wisconsin Progressivism, in the extent of the state intervention which it entailed, represented the movement in its most radical form. Progressives actually were by no means united in their programs. They were united rather by a common background, which was mainly urban, middle-class, Protestant, and older-generation American, and by a common mood which was righteously moral.

Governments should be returned to the people, and the most popular devices by which it was hoped that this would be achieved were: the direct election of senators—in the place of their election by state legislatures—and initiative and referendum measures—by which private citizens by petition could place reform measures on the ballot and vote them into law. During the first decade of the century, laws such as these were passed in dozens of states, and in 1913 the Seventeenth Amendment to the Constitution was passed, providing for the direct election of senators in all states.

Some Progressives hoped that these purely political reforms would be sufficient to reform the nation; others saw the need for social reforms to protect the individual against exploitation. Laws limiting child labor had already been passed in almost half the states by the end of the century, and they were rapidly adopted in others in the years thereafter. Laws limiting the number of working hours for women were passed by most states during the Progressive era, and fifteen states had passed minimum-wage as well as maximum-hours laws for women by the time the Supreme Court declared such laws to be unconstitutional in 1923 in the case of Adkins *v.* Children's Hospital. During the same period most states passed accident insurance laws, providing the protection for workingmen and their families which had been altogether lacking under common law.

Progressives were brought to the support of these social reforms partly out of a sense of Christian duty and partly out of a fear of the alternative consequences of proletarian discontent. The Socialist party under the leadership of Eugene Debs was rising in popularity, receiving 6 per cent of the national vote in the election of 1912. Meanwhile, socialists were actually winning municipal elections in various parts of the country. It was a relatively moderate form of Christian socialism which won in these local elections, rather than the class-warfare socialism of the revolutionary Marxians, but it frightened responsible citizens into doing something for the lower classes.

At the other end of the scale the plutocracy must be held to its responsibilities by the national government, and it must be deprived of the political control which it had wrested from the people. Still, the Progressive movement occurred during times of prosperity, and the Progressives themselves wished to do nothing to disturb a system which was in good operating order. That the new order of finance capitalism was here to stay was conceded by many Progressives, including Roosevelt, but the directors of the great combinations must not say, "The public be damned," as William Vanderbilt had done. It was high time for the will of the people to assert itself through its government and place these giant corporations to some extent under public control in the interest of the general welfare.

When Roosevelt gave voice to this indignantly righteous, but temperately middle-class, point of view, he rallied the nation behind him and behind those Progressive tenets which were rather vaguely understood but most fervently believed in, "the principles of Theodore Roosevelt."

II

Roosevelt Progressivism During his second year in office T. R. made two dramatically original demonstrations of executive power: one in support of organized labor and the other in opposition to those two giants of Wall Street, Morgan and Rockefeller. In May, 1902, the United Mine Workers struck for shorter hours and higher wages against the coal mine owners. Comparatively weak and divided, the coal industry was unhappily spoken for by the president of the Reading Railroad, George F. Baer. Baer brought the scorn of the nation upon all of the owners by declaring that the miners would be protected "not by the labor agitators but by the Christian men to whom God in His infinite wisdom, has given control of the property interests of the country."

Against such a man, and with no anarchists blowing anything up for the moment, the sober Bible-quoting president of the UMW, John Mitchell, was in a position, unprecedented in American labor history, to win the sympathy of the nation and thereby win the strike. As the strike lengthened toward winter, and as the mine operators refused to arbitrate, Roosevelt prepared to seize the mines and operate them. With the aid of Morgan and Hanna he then persuaded the operators to submit to a commission of arbitration, which decided in favor of a substantial wage increase and shortening of hours.

It was the first time the American government had intervened on the side of labor, and it was therefore a highly significant event in American history. Roosevelt never again intervened in such a manner; nevertheless his handling of that strike, and the support of public opinion which he won for his novel prounion stand, constituted a major event in the rise to power of organized labor in America.

Roosevelt simultaneously defeated the Wall Street behemoths in the Northern Securities Case, successfully carrying through the courts an antitrust suit against a railroad combination arranged by the Morgan and Rockefeller groups. Exultant that "the most powerful men in this country were held to accountability before the law," Roosevelt went on to bring similar suits against other trusts, including Standard Oil and American Tobacco Company, both of which were ordered dissolved during his successor's administration. Although victory in the Northern Securities Case won for Roosevelt the title of "trustbuster," it did not seriously alienate the bankers whose trusts he was busting. Morgan was sufficiently worried to make a trip to Washington, to the delight of Teddy and the nation, but he went away apparently satisfied that the President would do nothing seriously to disarrange the establishment.

Roosevelt's attack on Northern Securities has been criticized on the diverse grounds that, on the one hand, in selecting railroad trunk lines for his test case, he chose a form of industrial combination which was most obviously defensible as contributing to a smoothly operating transportation system, and, on the other hand, that the victory was nearly meaningless, since the combination was thereafter effectively achieved by other means. Indeed throughout both of his administrations Roosevelt's attitude toward the trusts was thoroughly ambivalent.

The political humorist Finley Peter Dunne described this attitude exactly when his Mr. Dooley said of Roosevelt, " 'Th' thrusts' says he, 'are heejous monsthers built up by th' inlightened intherprise of th' men that have done so much to advance progress in our beloved counthry,' he says. 'On wan hand I wud stamp them undher fut; on th' other hand, not so fast.' " T.R. was torn between his highly popular public image as a trustbuster and his private conviction that these consolidations, though they should submit to a degree of government control, were inevitable and, on the whole, beneficial to society.

In 1904 Roosevelt ran for the Presidency against the conservative colorless Democrat, Judge Alton B. Parker, and won by a landslide. Having resuscitated the Sherman Antitrust Act in his first administration, Roosevelt brought the Interstate Commerce Act to life in his second. In 1903 the Elkins Act had been passed prohibiting the railroads from making rebates to customers and providing punishment for violations, an act which was both in the public interest and in the interest of the railroads themselves. In 1906 the Hepburn Act was passed empowering the ICC to set maximum rates and placing the burden of proof on the railroads themselves, when they appealed the decision to the courts. Some objected that the act failed to place the commission in command of sufficient facts, but thousands of cases were quickly brought before it, and many rate reductions resulted.

In 1906 the Pure Food and Drug Act was passed providing modest beginnings to a system of Federal inspection. More important than any of these acts, probably, were Roosevelt's conservation activities. Acting under a Forest Reserve Act of 1891, he set aside many millions of acres of land as national forest areas and checked the encroachments upon public lands which until that time had continued against only the most haphazard Federal opposition.

Still at the height of his popularity in 1908, Roosevelt honored an earlier pledge not to run for a third term and selected his friend, Secretary of War William Howard Taft, to succeed him. Taft defeated Bryan, running for the third and last time, and launched his administration as the appointed caretaker of Roosevelt Progressivism. Things went wrong for him from the beginning, however. Taking upon himself the responsibility for tariff reform, which Roosevelt had successfully avoided, he called Congress into special session to reduce tariffs. Lobbyists and Old Guard Republicans succeeded in blocking any major downward revisions, and when Taft signed the resulting Payne-Aldrich Tariff he broke with congressional Progressives, before he had been in office for six months.

The rift was widened in the course of the successful fight of the insurgents, as the Progressive Republicans were called, against the conservative and dictatorial Speaker of the House, "Uncle Joe" Cannon. It was felt by the insurgents that Taft, who had expressed the wish that Cannon's powers be reduced, had deserted them in the fight. Then, amid the fight against Cannon in 1910 the disgruntled Progressives found a cause upon which they could rally against the President. Gifford Pinchot, who had been closely associated with Roosevelt's conservation policies, brought charges against Taft's Secretary of the Interior Richard A. Ballinger of having agreed to the transfer of reserved Alaskan coalfields to private hands. Pinchot's dismissal from the Department of Agriculture was followed by a congressional investigation which, while exonerating Ballinger of the charges, revealed him to have no real interest in protecting the public domain against private exploitation. Taft's continued support of Ballinger served to keep the issue alive until the presidential election of 1912.

Taft had come to office with a distinguished record as a lawyer and public administrator, but he had never before run for political office. His lack of political experience was an evident weakness in his dealings with Congress, and his position was further weakened by his legalistic and sharply limited conception of the Presidency. Initiative, which had been so vigorously asserted from the White House in Roosevelt's time, shifted to Congress, in part because that was where Taft thought it belonged constitutionally.

A friendly 350-pounder, Taft was personally offended by the "yelping and snorting" of the insurgents, and though he did not approve of the objectives of the Old Guard, he found their company more pleasant. As the attack against him mounted he found their support necessary. He nevertheless demonstrated a Progressivism which angered the Old Guard by supporting the Sixteenth Amendment to the Constitution, the income tax amendment. Passed by Congress during his first year in office, and ratified by the states in his last, the income tax amendment proved in time to be one of the most momentous reforms of the entire era. Although not going far enough to please the insurgents, he brought the displeasure of the Old Guard upon him further by advocating greater government controls over the railroads. And he incurred their displeasure most greatly by instituting twice as many anti-trust suits in his one administration as Roosevelt had done in two.

But even this failed to win him insurgent support, for it was seen that the dissolved companies retained their unified control by appointing the same members to the boards of direction of the technically competing companies. As the election of 1912 approached, the open organization against him of the insurgent opposition dictated the not entirely comfortable alliance between Taft and the Old Guard.

III

Wilsonian Progressivism The overwhelming choice of the Progressives, once they had broken with Taft, was undoubtedly Roosevelt. Although T.R. had gone to Africa and Europe upon leaving office, to hunt lions and emperors and stay out of "Big Bill" Taft's way, he had continued to crowd the President out of the news with the accounts of his day-to-day activities. Upon his return to the United States he soon joined the attack on the Taft administration, speaking in strong support of antiadministration measures. He showed no disposition to attempt a third term, however, and Progressive support began to gather behind Senator La Follette—rather hesitantly, for La Follette was thought by many insurgents to be rather too much on the radical side. When Roosevelt indicated his willingness to run early in 1912, therefore, the main body of La Follette's support took the first opportunity to desert him; when La Follette collapsed during a speech he was conveniently accounted too ill to run.

The Republican convention of 1912 found the Taft supporters in control of the party machinery and in a position to win a majority through rulings involving more than 250 contested delegation seats. Defeated by the machine the Roosevelt supporters bolted the convention and formed their own "Bull Moose" Progressive party as a vehicle for their hero. The Democrats nominated a political newcomer, Governor Woodrow Wilson of New Jersey.

In the campaign that followed Taft was largely ignored by the other two candidates, both of them running on distinctly Progressive platforms. The main issue to develop during the campaign between these two Progressive candidates was that of the rival conceptions of Wilson's "new freedom" and Roosevelt's "new nationalism." Wilson argued that the trusts as they stood were too powerful to be controlled in the public interests and that therefore their dissolution was necessary for regulation. Roosevelt replied that the process of consolidation was beneficial to the people and, under any circumstances, irreversible, and that the need was for more effective government agencies to regulate them. These conflicting views were to divide reformers down through the New Deal. In the election of 1912, however, most of Roosevelt's supporters probably voted for the man while continuing to accept the more familiar antitrust argument as expressed by the Democratic opponent. The result of the election was that Wilson, receiving but 42 per cent of the popular vote, swept the electoral college and won the Presidency.

Like Taft, Wilson was a learned authority on the Constitution, but unlike Taft he had reached the conclusion that under the Constitution the President should provide Congress with forceful leadership. Like Taft also, except for his two years as governor of New Jersey, he was without political experience. His career had been that of a professor of political science at Princeton University

and later president of Princeton. Temperamentally he was restrained, diffident, dogmatic, and self-righteous. If politics is the art
of compromise, Wilson was as little suited to political life as any
man who ever entered the Presidency.

It might therefore be supposed that this administration would
have been marked by the same weaknesses which had marked the
administrations of such similarly touchy men as John Adams, John
Quincy Adams, and, in the Confederacy, Jefferson Davis. Wilson,
however, was a remarkably effective speaker with a gift for capturing national aspirations in striking phrases. In 1913, furthermore,
despite his minority status as President, he had the support of a
Democratic-controlled Congress backed by insurgent Republicans,
and he launched his administration with a dazzling display of
power in the field of tariff reform. Wilson appeared in person
before Congress to present his tariff message, the first time since the
eighteenth century that a President had done so. Congress responded with the Underwood bill, which passed the House only to
be altered past recognition under the influence of lobbyists in the
Senate. Against them Wilson directed an eloquent attack, which
Progressive senators supported with an inquiry into lobbying. The
result was the Underwood-Simmons Tariff, the first significant tariff
reduction since before the Civil War, and one which incorporated
a graduated income tax to compensate for the resulting losses in
revenue.

The new tariff was followed by the Federal Reserve Act, creating
the Federal Reserve Board, appointed by the President, with control over Federal Reserve Banks in twelve districts throughout the
nation. The Reserve Banks were owned by all nationally chartered
banks and by any state banks which chose to join by subscribing 6
per cent of their capital. The Reserve Banks did not themselves engage directly in banking but operated only as agents of the member
banks, to which they issued a new currency, Federal Reserve Bank
notes.

The act had been passed in response to appeals from the banking
community in part, following the "bankers" panic of 1907, when
inelasticity of credit had forced major banking institutions to close
down. An Aldrich-Vreeland Act of 1908 had been viewed as only
a temporary measure, and both parties had advocated further
reforms in their 1912 platforms. The Federal Reserve Act brought
heated attacks from bankers, mainly on the grounds that the Fed-

eral Reserve Board was placed in government hands instead of in private ones. Within a decade, however, more than two-thirds of the banking resources of the nation had placed themselves under the new system.

In 1914 an act was passed establishing the Federal Trade Commission, with the authority to investigate industries engaged in interstate commerce for violations of antitrust laws and for "unfair" trade practices. As with the ICC, the FTC could resort to the courts if its orders were not obeyed. This act was followed by the Clayton Antitrust Act, which attempted to make explicit what had been left so vague in the Sherman Act. It prohibited a number of specific business practices, notably the interlocking directorates by which Standard Oil had retained its unity after dissolution by the courts. It prohibited price discrimination leading to monopoly. The Clayton Act further exempted labor unions from its provisions, although in purposely vague terms, and went on to prohibit issuance by the courts of injunctions against strikers, except where protection of property was involved.

Wilson considered his program to have been largely completed with the creation of the FTC, and he failed to give active support to the Clayton Act. Furthermore, he appointed bankers and businessmen to the Reserve Board and conciliatory men to the FTC. The continued prodding of the insurgents in the Senate led to the La Follette Seamen's Act in 1915, abolishing the crime of desertion in the merchant marine, but Progressivism appeared to be drifting into the past, as signs of a coming depression in 1914 brought Wilson, as it had Roosevelt in 1907, cautiously to closer cooperation with Wall Street.

As the election of 1916 approached, however, Wilson moved noticeably to the left, at the urging of important advisers, notably Bryan and the distinguished lawyer Louis D. Brandeis. In that election year, Congress passed the Federal Farm Loan Act, authorizing loans to farmers through special Farm Loan Banks which accepted farm property as security. It passed also the Adamson Act, establishing an eight-hour day for workers on interstate railroads, the Keating-Owen Child-labor Act, government subsidies for various state programs, and the first major Federal highway construction program. All of these measures were passed with administration support. Beginning his first term as essentially a nineteenth-century liberal not very far removed from the Grover

Cleveland school, Wilson appeared at the time of his campaign for reelection to be moving to the vanguard of radical Progressivism, with its emphasis upon Federal responsibility for the general welfare. Whether he could have achieved further reforms against growing opposition in both parties and whether he would have wished to do so, however, are both open to question.

Running against the moderately progressive Supreme Court justice Charles Evans Hughes and a reunited Republican party, Wilson won reelection in 1916 by a large popular plurality, although barely winning in the electoral college. By that time, the issues of domestic reform had been overshadowed by those of neutrality and the world war, the peace vote going heavily for Wilson. Then a month after Wilson's second term began, America entered the war, and the Progressive era came to a close.

IV

Wilsonian Diplomacy "It would be the irony of fate," remarked Wilson, the scholarly authority on America's domestic politics, "if my administration had to deal chiefly with foreign affairs." His first experiences in the unfamiliar areas of diplomacy gave weight to his remark. Having denounced Roosevelt's policy of intervention in Latin America, he found himself soon doing the same. After extended and futile dealings with the Dominican Republic and with Haiti, he sent in the Marines as Roosevelt and Taft had done before him. And though he had also denounced Taft's dollar diplomacy, he acquired rights in Nicaragua, through his Secretary of State Bryan, which virtually reduced that country to an American protectorate in the interest of American business. Then Wilson, faced with the continual crisis of the Mexican Revolution throughout his administrations, involved himself more embarrassingly in the affairs of a Latin-American nation than Roosevelt or Taft ever had done.

The Mexican Revolution, beginning in 1910 under the leadership of the constitutional liberal Francisco Madero, succumbed to a counterrevolution and the assassination of Madero in 1913 by General Victoriano Huerta. Huerta was opposed by constitutionalists under the leadership of Venustiano Carranza, but his authority appeared established, and the nations of the world therefore extended recognition to his government. Wilson, however, against the demands of American business interests with a billion dollars worth of Mexican investments, withheld recognition on the grounds that the Huerta government did not rest upon law or upon the consent of the governed. In doing so he established the novel "moral diplomacy," unknown in international law, which has since frequently guided America—during the twenties in the case of Soviet Russia, during the thirties in the case of the Japanese puppet state of Manchoukuo, and at present in the case of Communist China—and which has remained a strange and annoying practice to other nations of the world.

When nonrecognition did not achieve a Mexican government of which Wilson approved, he made a minor incident the pretext for the occupation of Vera Cruz. This bloody reprisal united all factions in Mexico against him, and Wilson was happy to be rescued from his difficulty by the offer of Argentina, Brazil, and Chile to arbitrate the disputes between the United States and Mexico. Subsequent raids on American soil by the Mexican bandit Pancho Villa invoked American retaliation, and a punitive American expedition found itself three hundred miles inside Mexico. Formal recognition of the Carranza government in March, 1917, came in time to help avert a war which was being called for by many. Certainly Wilson's conduct toward Mexico had been high-handed. Nevertheless Wilson's acceptance of arbitration by the ABC powers did mark the beginning of the transition toward the Pan-Americanization of the Monroe Doctrine which was the central tenet of the Good Neighbor policy as it developed during the 1930s.

After 1914 Wilson was necessarily distracted from his Latin-American concerns by the war in Europe, which placed increasing strains on the simplicities of America's isolationist foreign policy and on the complexities of America's ethnic makeup. Americans knew little about the conditions leading up to the war, which broke out that summer, and news of it came as a surprise, but it did not seem, at the time, seriously likely to involve the United States. Europeans themselves assumed that it would be won by one side or the other within a matter of weeks or months, and Americans accepted that conclusion. As the war continued, however, it aroused increasingly disturbing loyalties and animosities in America and created increasingly perplexing problems concerning America's position as a neutral.

Although Wilson urged Americans to be impartial in thought as well as action, majority opinion in the United States tended to favor the Allies from the first, based upon the predominantly Anglo-Saxon origins of the nation and upon the fact that Germany had launched its main attack through neutral Belgium, in violation of treaty obligations. The British had a large measure of control over the means of communication to America, and they were much more skillful than the Germans in their propaganda activities. Their accounts of German atrocities in Belgium later proved largely false, but at the time they were widely believed in America. There remained millions of Americans of German descent and millions more of Irish descent, however, who naturally tended to oppose themselves to the Allied cause.

In the early stages of the war it was the English rather than the Germans who inspired official American protests, through their violations of the American conception of neutral rights. English and French naval power was early successful in laying down a blockade of the central powers against contraband, and Britain then extended the definition of contraband to include virtually all important items of commerce. Beyond that Britain asserted the right to take American and other neutral ships into Allied ports for examination, in violation of previous concepts of neutral rights under international law. These infringements on the rights of neutrals were met by repeated American protests, but trade with Germany in the meantime was dwindling to nearly nothing, while trade with the Allies was booming and was providing the means whereby the United States rapidly emerged from the recession of 1914. Dependent upon this growing trade for its continued prosperity, the United States was soon confronted with the fact that continuance of the trade could be made possible only by loans to the Allies, which would give them the capital to purchase from America. Faced with this prospect, the Wilson administration reversed its former policy and permitted the extension of private American loans to the Allies.

In 1915 the German government established a war area around the British Isles where enemy ships were destroyed by submarines without warning. Against Secretary of State Bryan's urging Wilson insisted that Americans were within their neutral rights to travel on passenger vessels of belligerent nations. In May, 1915, the British *Lusitania* was sunk with the loss of more than a thousand lives, including the lives of more than one hundred Americans. The American government sent notes of protest, one of which Bryan refused to sign on the grounds that it constituted virtually a threat of war. He was replaced by the pro-British Robert Lansing, and thereafter Wilson, to a greater extent than before, became his own Secretary of State.

American protests following further sinkings succeeded in altering the German policy of submarine warfare, and the elections of 1916 were held during a period of relative quiet in America's relations with the warring European nations. In January, 1917, however, Germany announced the intention of sinking all vessels within a prescribed war area, in the belief that, although America would probably enter the war as a consequence, Britain could be starved into submission before American force could save her. Wilson responded by breaking diplomatic relations and authorizing the arming of American merchantmen.

In February the British naval intelligence turned over to Wilson an intercepted message from the German Foreign Secretary Zimmerman to the German Minister in Mexico instructing him to offer the Southwestern portion of the United States to Mexico in exchange for a military alliance, in the event that the United States went to war with Germany. In March, Americans learned that Czarist Russia was overthrown by a provisional republican government. As a consequence of this the war thereafter presented itself to Americans as a struggle between the democracies, England, France, and Russia, on the one hand, against the autocracies, Germany and Austria-Hungary, on the other. On April 2, following the sinking of American merchant ships by the Germans, Wilson went before Congress and, urging that "The world must be made safe for democracy," asked for a declaration of war which was voted two days later by an overwhelming majority of both houses.

In the years of disillusionment following the war the argument raged for two decades as to why America entered the war and who was to blame for it. The widely held assumption was that it had been a disastrous error and a malign conspiracy. The trickery of the British was blamed by many, and then, in the mid-thirties, a Senate committee headed by Gerald Nye reached the conclusion, widely believed at the time, that the purpose of American entrance had been to save the investments of American bankers and munitions manufacturers.

The weakness of this accusation rested in the lack of evidence that these groups exerted any influence upon Wilson, and upon the fact that Wilson in his foreign policy had consistently resisted the appeals of American business men with Mexican investments. Writers since World War II have tended to agree that American entrance in the war was decided most basically on the narrow grounds of violation of traditional conceptions of neutral rights, especially where those violations resulted in loss of life, granted a general predisposition of the nation, and even more of the administration, in favor of the Allies.

V

World War I   It turned out that the Germans made two errors in their calculated risk of unrestricted submarine warfare in 1917. They destroyed shipping to England on schedule, but England did not starve into submission as soon as it should have, according to the German timetable. And the United States entered the war on schedule, but it armed itself and made its force felt much more rapidly than had been anticipated either by the Germans or by the Allies. The French high command had hoped that, at the most, 500,000 American troops would be raised and sent to Europe; yet four million were in uniform at war's end, and two million of these were in France. These two errors lost Germany the war at a time when victory seemed almost certainly in her grasp.

Upon declaring war the Congress of this mainly unarmed, polyglot, Federal democracy immediately conferred upon its President wartime powers exceeding those of any of the leaders of its new Allies. Wilson in turn delegated much of this new authority to the Council for National Defense, under which a series of boards were created which brought the national economy under dictatorial control. Chief among these agencies was the War Industries Board, directed by Bernard Baruch, which rationed materials, fixed prices and schedules, decided upon all governmental purchases, and directed the conversion of peacetime industries to wartime production.

The Railroad Administration under the direction of Secretary of the Treasury William Gibbs McAdoo assumed control of the railroads of the nation and operated them as one unified system. The Emergency Fleet Corporation supervised the expansion and operation of the merchant marine. The Food Administration under Herbert Hoover fixed the price of food and allocated priorities to such good effect that the United States, while continuing to eat well, trebled its exports of foodstuffs and meat.

Thought control was entered upon by the government in a similarly centralized, efficient, and thoroughgoing manner. The German assumption that the mongrel character of American society would divide it along old-country lines was to some extent shared by the American government, and against this possibility the Committee on Public Information launched a massive campaign to make Americans hate the "Hun." Mobilizing an army of sidewalk speakers and commandeering the audio-visual resources of the nation, this committee was immediately successful in converting the Germans in American eyes from a nation of home folks and music lovers to a depraved race of lustful killers. Beethoven and Mozart were banned for the duration. Sauerkraut became "liberty cabbage," wieners became "liberty sausage" and dachshunds became "liberty pups."

Congress passed the Espionage Act in 1917, making it a prison offense to discourage loyalty, and then passed the Sedition Act in 1918 providing imprisonment for people who spoke or wrote in an abusive way of any of a list of subjects, including the flag and the Constitution. About 1,500 persons were arrested under these laws, including the Socialist presidential candidate, Eugene Debs, and the Socialist congressman from Milwaukee, Victor Berger. The American Socialist party, on its side, increasingly dominated as it was by recent immigrants, had invited suppression by being the only major socialist party in the world, with the exception of the Russian Bolsheviks, not to support its own country in the war effort. In addition to these repressive acts on the part of the government, private groups throughout the nation did what they could to keep traitors under control and see that they bought their full share of Liberty Bonds.

The Wilson administration also appealed to the better nature of the American people. In this appeal Wilson himself was the incomparable spokesman for libertarian ideals. The Fourteen Points, which he announced in January, 1918, as the main goals of the war, made an enormous impression, not only upon the American people, but upon the entire world, strengthening the Allied sense of purpose while offering Germans and Austrians brilliant glimpses of the brighter side of their impending defeat. Beginning with "Open covenants openly arrived at," and ending with the creation of a league of nations, the Fourteen Points depicted a world lighted by the principles of peace, disarmament, free trade, and the national self-determination of all peoples.

The Allies desperately needed immediate naval and military support. America could do little for them at the moment on the battle line, but the American Navy, due mainly to the writings of Admiral Mahan and the activity of Roosevelt, was in good condition to attack German submarines and to open the sea-lanes once again to starving England. The later troop transportations were carried through by the British and American navies so effectively that no American troopship was torpedoed on its way to Europe during the course of the war.

The United States had learned enough from the pratfalls of the Spanish-American War to create a general staff for its army and to increase the Army in size. Then the bipartisan demand for "preparedness" during the presidential campaign of 1916 had brought further results. At the time America entered the war, however, the combined strength of the Army and the National Guard was still less than four hundred thousand. A selective service act was passed at once, which went quietly and effectively into operation, in contrast to the violence and evasion which had met the Civil War draft laws.

It was only after the nation had entered the war that the government became aware of how close the Allies were to defeat, and a year of further preparation was required before substantial assistance could be rendered. In the spring of 1918, Communists having taken power in Russia and withdrawn that country from the war, Germany mounted a massive attack on the West, and "the race for France" began barely in time to turn defeat into victory for the Allies. Initially distributed among English and French armies, the American forces were later united under Gen. John J. Pershing. American troops launched successful counterattacks at the Battle of Belleau Wood in June and the Second Battle of the Marne in July. In September they participated in force in the Meuse-Argonne sector of the final offensive which brought the war to a conclusion, at a cost in American lives of more than 100,000.

VI

The victors met at Versailles in January, 1919, and among the members of the Paris Peace Conference Wilson was the one dominating figure. He represented the one major nation which was rising in military strength, at a time when the will to fight had been all but destroyed among those who had undergone the full four years of war. Wilson's idealistic plans for the postwar world had fired the imagination of people throughout the world, and although the Allies were not committed to these plans, they were necessarily the basis for the discussion of peace terms.

There were weaknesses in Wilson's position, however, which he failed to take properly into account. In the congressional elections of 1918 he had called for a Democratic mandate to carry him through the conclusion of the war and the establishment of the peace. The result had been a sweep of both houses of Congress by the Republicans. Wilson's failure to curry Republican support or even to take any prominent member of the Republican party to Paris with him was, under these circumstances, a disastrous act of political thoughtlessness. He was also misled in supposing that the adulation accorded him in Europe gave him the strength to speak to the peoples of Europe over the heads of their national representatives at the peace table. Elections had been held in England and they had indicated a popular desire for revenge which the English Prime Minister Lloyd George was obliged to take into account.

The resulting treaty nevertheless was in a number of respects in accord with the Wilsonian proposals. An independent Poland was reconstituted, the Hapsburg monarchy was broken up into independent states, created, so far as was possible, on ethnic grounds, and boundaries were elsewhere rectified on the same basis. Above all else a League of Nations was created in response to what had been and to what remains a characteristically American ideal.

In return for these achievements Wilson naturally was forced to make compromises. His first point, concerning open covenants openly arrived at, was rashly made in the knowledge that secret covenants had already been made, which bound the Allies to violate certain of his Fourteen Points. Italy had been promised the non-Italian port of Fiume as part of the price for entering the war. When the Italian Prime Minister Vittorio Orlando insisted upon it, Wilson had the presumption to appeal to the Italian people against him, with adverse results, not only in Italy, but also among the Italian-American population.

Wilson won his point at the conference, but Italy withdrew as a consequence, and at that point in the proceedings Japan came forward with proposals which similarly violated Wilson's principle of self-determination. Unwilling to see the departure from the peace table of a second major power, Wilson acquiesced in the Japanese designs on Chinese territory. The most blatant violation of the principle of self-determination was the establishment of an independent Austria, against the desire of its German-speaking people to annex themselves to Germany. But it was, after all, unthinkable that the price of defeat for Germany should have been the considerable increase of its size and power in Europe.

Wilson made other concessions to the European desire for revenge, including the huge reparations which Germany was forced to pay France and England into the indefinite future. These reparations were justified, furthermore, on the grounds, which German scholars were quick to prove historically untenable, that Germany had been responsible for the coming of the war. As he made one concession after another, Wilson came to place greater and greater importance upon the League of Nations, where the United States would be a leading member and where, when passions cooled, rectifications would be made of the injustices of the Paris conference.

Sentiment in the United States was apparently in favor of such a league, and, more importantly, sentiment in the United States Senate was also favorable. There were senators who were bitterly opposed, however, and they represented a growing host of Americans who disapproved of the treaty for various reasons. Americans of German, Irish, and Italian descent did not like it, and traditional isolationists, strong in the Midwest especially, wanted no part of the League of Nations.

In the Senate the fight against the treaty was led by the vindictive Henry Cabot Lodge, whose old friend Colonel Roosevelt had been deprived of the war leadership by Professor Wilson, and who had, himself, lost the chance for the Presidency to which he had given much thought. Returning from Europe to fight for the treaty, Wilson was stricken with illness and sequestered in the White House. Isolated from the changing events, he insisted that the treaty be accepted by the Senate without the reservations demanded by Lodge and others. He succeeded in defeating the Lodge reservations, but the Senate, which certainly would have joined the League under some terms, failed to provide him with the two-thirds vote necessary to ratify the peace treaty. By a wide margin the treaty was defeated, and the United States was set upon the isolationist course which it maintained with the blindest of stubbornness for the next two decades.

In later years World War II and the conditions of the world that survived it naturally changed the past in the minds of American scholars, and gave rise to new criticisms of Wilson's foreign policy. It is argued that America's reason for entering the war was too narrow, on the one hand, and that its objectives, once it was in the war, were too broad on the other. America entered the war on the grounds that Germany, through submarine warfare, had violated a conception of neutral rights which, while held by many Americans and other people, had no provable validity in international law. Then, once in the war, the United States made it a war "to make the world safe for democracy."

Critics have argued that American security before, during, and after the war depended upon the maintenance of a balance of power in Europe, and that this, therefore, should have been the reason for entering the war and also should have been the guiding consideration at the peace table. Wilson and other members of his administration were aware of this hard fact, but the American people were not. Wilson met this situation, therefore, first by the legalism which has always touched a responsive chord with the American people, and second by the visionary idealism of the Fourteen Points. The treaty itself was not such a harsh one, given the circumstances, but it disappointed millennial expectations in America and invited a national repudiation of Wilson and of Wilsonian internationalism.

BIBLIOGRAPHY FOR CHAPTER ELEVEN

Two recent general studies together span the period of the Progressive era and provide a comprehensive bibliographical guide as well as a stimulating survey of the period. They are:

G. E. Mowry, *The Era of Theodore Roosevelt and the Birth of Modern America, 1900–1912* (1958) and A. S. Link, *Woodrow Wilson and the Progressive Era, 1910–1917* (1954). "The high standards of Mowry's scholarship, the ease of his prose, and the unfailing good humor of his argument make this book a memorable contribution to the literature of American history." Link's history of the Wilsonian era is "an able study . . . focusing on the Progressive movement and the reasons why America was drawn into World War I. . . . Teachers will find this book extremely useful. It provides students and the general reader with a well-written, intelligent analysis of those meaningful years. . . ."

Two histories of reform politics, giving extended attention to this period, are in interesting contrast to each other. They are E. P. Goldman, *Rendezvous with Destiny: A History of Modern American Reform* (1956) and Richard Hofstadter, *The Age of Reform* (1955). Goldman gives sophisticated expression to what is essentially the well-worked-over interpretation of American history as a struggle between the dollar and the man. At the same time he has uncovered new information and "has not hesitated to raise provocative questions; every page invites a quarrel and a self-examination, but he secures attention." Hofstadter for his part draws upon sociology and social psychology to interpret the Progressive movement in terms of the urge of the middle classes to regain lost status. "What Mr. Hofstadter has done is to write the history of recent reform groups in terms of both their perceptions and feelings as they moved up and down relative to other competitive units in the power and prestige complex of American life . . . a brilliant foray into the psychology of reform groups . . . full of sparkling new viewpoints, insightful remarks, lively quotations, and sharply etched characterizations."

Among the studies of Roosevelt, W. H. Harbaugh, *The Life and Times of Theodore Roosevelt* (1961) "has performed a distinct service to the profession by reviewing and analyzing Roosevelt historiography. . . ." Beyond that he has written the most authoritative one-volume biography of the man. An older, rather hostile and highly readable biography of high merit is H. F. Pringle, *Theodore Roosevelt* (1931). J. M. Blum, *The Republican Roosevelt* (1954) is a "penetrating analysis of the man, his motives, his thinking, and his actions, which attains in 161 pages an understanding that full biographies only rarely succeed in reaching." Blum has also written *Woodrow Wilson and the Politics of Morality* (1956), "a review of Wilson's career, with emphasis on his disposition to measure every act by his standards of right and wrong. . . . The study is well-conceived and the book well-written." Of exceptional interest, because of its authorship by one of twentieth-century America's line of scholar-Presidents, is Herbert Hoover, *The Ordeal of Woodrow Wilson* (1958), "a work of rare importance. . . . The outstanding significance of this volume lies in the chapters dealing with the economic problems of the Peace Conference, the relief and reconstruction of Europe, and the difficulties that arose from the continuation of the blockade." Daniel Aaron, *Men of Good Hope: A Story of American Progressives* (1951) is a series of biographical essays.

Louis Filler, *Crusaders for American Liberalism: The Story of the Muckrakers* (1950) is "a good and very readable general survey of the muckraking movement from 1900–1917." R. M. Bremner, *American Philanthropy* (1960) "In less than 200 pages . . . traces American philanthropy from Squanto to the Ford Foundation. His book abounds in little-known facts . . . well written and highly informative—an achievement all the more remarkable because so little in the way of scholarly monographs was available to lighten his task."

Discussions of the literature of Progressive diplomacy, World War I, and the peace negotiations may be found in Mowry and Link and in F. R. Dulles, *America's Rise to World Power* (1955). For the war itself see P. G. Fredericks, *Great Adventure: America in World War I* (1960).

12

I

The Great Red Scare — "Once lead this people into war," Wilson predicted on the eve of his war message to Congress, "and they'll forget there ever was such a thing as tolerance." Conformity would be the only virtue, and every man who refused to conform would have to pay the penalty. Wilson then proceeded to carry out his prophecy with the Committee on Public Information and enforcement of the Sedition and Espionage Acts. The administration mobilized public opinion all too effectively for the good of the nation; for when the war came to an end, the reconversion of public opinion to peacetime purposes was not so readily achieved. The Wilson administration, which had begun with the new freedom, ended with the Great Red Scare.

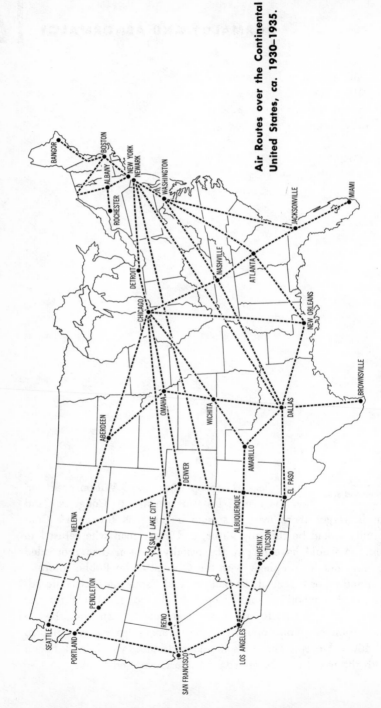

Air Routes over the Continental
United States, ca. 1930–1935.

----- Air Routes (Mail, Express, and Passenger)

The democratic Russian revolution of the spring of 1917 gave way to the Bolshevik revolution in the fall, and the triumph of communism in Russia was followed by the call for world revolution and by the organization of the American Communist party. In 1919 a series of mysterious bombings took place. Postal clerks discovered three dozen bombs addressed to important persons in business and political life, and in 1920 a bomb was exploded on Wall Street, killing thirty-eight persons. The persons responsible for most of these bombings were never discovered, and there was no evidence of Communist complicity. Nevertheless to many Americans it appeared that the proletarian revolution was at hand and that the most stringent measures should be taken to defend Americanism.

The main sufferers from the Great Red Scare were the labor unions, strengthened in membership during the war and awaiting peace to strike for better terms. During the war Samuel Gompers, serving as a member of the Council of National Defense, had pledged labor not to strike if the war were not made the means by which labor was exploited. Collective bargaining was assured labor in return, and various war labor boards were created to settle disputes. The result was that organized labor did make substantial gains in real wages and even greater gains in membership. AFL membership rose from two million in 1915 to more than four million in 1919. The gains in real wages had lagged behind the gains received by industry and agriculture, however, and in 1919, with the wartime restraints removed, the unions went out on strike. More than 3,500 strikes took place that year, the biggest ones being those called by United Mine Workers and by nonunion U.S. Steel workers. Half of the steelworkers at the time still worked a twelve-hour day and a seven-day week.

The strikes and the bombings occurred during the same period, and businessmen, while genuinely fearing a Red insurrection, saw that the Red scare might well be worked to their own advantage. Their ideal was the "American plan," by which they meant either the open shop or the substitution of management-controlled company unions for independent labor unions. The Wilson administration had been by far the most prolabor administration in the nation's history, but in Wilson's formerly prolabor Attorney General A. Mitchell Palmer, the businessmen had a doughty supporter.

Abetted by Palmer, the steel industry was able to associate the steel strike with Red radicalism in the public mind and defeat it absolutely. Management in the coal industry followed, against the UMW strike, with the charge that the conservative John L. Lewis and his United Mine Workers were being directed by Moscow, and Palmer halted the strike by an injunction. The strikers ignored the injunction and eventually received substantial raises in pay. The times were against the unions, however. AFL membership dropped by more than a million during the next three years, and the company unions gained in membership throughout the twenties, aided by open support from government agencies such as the Railroad Labor Board.

Palmer then went after the Reds themselves, rounding up thousands of suspects and establishing himself momentarily as a national hero. His hopes for the Democratic nomination were defeated, however, when many of his arrests proved to be on false grounds and when his warnings of a May Day rising were followed by nothing. The Red Scare was over by the election of 1920. There remained the celebrated cause of Nicola Sacco and Bartolomeo Vanzetti, anarchists who were sentenced to death in 1921 for murder on the most specious of evidence. After many delays the two men were executed in 1927, amid international protests. Their case served to discredit the Red baiters rather than to inflame fears of radicalism.

Although fears of a Communist revolution soon subsided, the old suspicion of foreigners, which the war had whipped to a fury, continued on, achieving its most powerful expression in the new Ku Klux Klan. Borrowing its title from the southern post-Civil War organizations, the Klan was originated in 1915, and in the postwar period it mushroomed to about 4½ million members. Under the hooded protection of secrecy, Klansmen terrorized Negroes, Jews, Catholics, foreigners, radicals, and persons who in one way or another were deemed to be violating the code of the community.

The Klan expressed itself in floggings, mutilations, and the burning of homes and churches. Drawing its membership from the rural Protestant native stock, rapidly dwindling in national importance, it was a desperate, blindly self-righteous fight for what this group thought to be Americanism. At the same time the secrecy of the Klan provided opportunities for robbery and for the working off of personal spites which were widely taken advantage of. A rising political power in several states, especially Indiana, the Klan collapsed following revelations of corruption and immorality among some of its leaders in 1925, but more basically, perhaps, it collapsed because of the passage of immigration restriction laws, beginning in 1921 which quieted the antiforeign sentiment.

Prohibition, which became a part of the Constitution in 1919, was in large measure an expression of the same nativist sentiment which the Klan embodied, directed primarily against the vino, bier, and schnapps of the recent immigrants in the cities. During the Progressive era, antiliquor sentiment had been more broadly supported on the basis of Progressive opposition to the saloon as a center for political as well as moral corruption. The Anti-Saloon League, founded at the close of the nineteenth century and supported by all of the evangelical churches, had used this nonprohibitionist opposition to the saloon with great shrewdness to convert drinking Progressives gradually, by way of local option and statewide prohibition, to national prohibition.

The League had won major advantages from the war by denouncing the brewing industry as German-owned and by achieving wartime prohibition for the wartime purpose of conserving grain. Finally, in the fight for the Eighteenth Amendment, the drys had had the advantage of a constitutional amending process which gave disproportionate influence to the rural and older American segments of the nation especially in the state legislatures. Prohibition represented the last futile effort of evangelical America to reassert the dominion which it had held over the nation in the mid-nineteenth century and which by 1920 it had irretrievably lost.

Far from achieving the millennium as its supporters anticipated, prohibition, and the Volstead Act which provided for its enforcement, made of the twenties an age of speakeasies, bootleggers, and bathtub gin. The maintenance of a national law which a major part of the population refused to accept resulted in a climate of opinion which supported the bootlegger in order to get the booze, and beyond that hailed the racketeers as upholders of personal liberty. Organized crime had existed in America before the Eighteenth Amendment, but the nationwide crime syndicates of modern times are substantially a product of the era of "Scarface" Al Capone. The attempt on the part of the churches, especially through the Anti-Saloon League, to enforce the law through cafe raids and hip flask raids and other such niggling forms of repression meanwhile introduced a widespread anticlericalism which remained after prohibition had been repealed.

II

The handsome and affable Warren G. Harding was an enormous relief to the American people after eight years under the Presidency of the Puritan professor. Wilson had wished to make the League of Nations the main issue in the election of 1920, but the ailing President had lost control of his party, and the American people were concerned about other matters such as prohibition, immigration restriction, and the Chicago White Sox scandals. The Democrats nominated Governor James M. Cox of Ohio, who, though favoring the League, was the choice of the machine politicians rather than of Wilson. Cox's running mate was Franklin D. Roosevelt. The Republican party bosses selected the little-known Senator Harding of Ohio and, avoiding all issues, carried him to the most resounding victory in the history of popular presidential elections up to that time. For vice president the Republicans nominated the Governor of Massachusetts, Calvin Coolidge.

The election of 1920 was the first one to be held under the Nineteenth Amendment to the Constitution, passed the year previously, extending the vote to women. Success had come to the women suffrage movement, after three quarters of a century of struggle, largely on the basis of the growing support it received from reform and church groups. These groups had been impressed by the effectiveness of women, especially through the Women's Christian Temperance Union, in the campaign for prohibition, and they had reasoned that if women were given the vote they would bring virtue to American political life. It was therefore ironic that the first administration to be voted for by the women should have been one of the most corrupt in American history.

Historians, most of whom are men, have generally concluded that the women's suffrage amendment has had little effect on politics. The presidential election statistics, however, do not bear this out. Down to 1920 the landslide elections of Jackson and Roosevelt were unusual, the vote generally being rather evenly distributed between the two major parties. From 1920 on, however, it has been the landslide election which has been normal, and it appears that women suffrage is mainly responsible for this. Women are apparently less controlled by party loyalty than men and more apt to vote for the individual candidate regardless of party considerations. This was especially evident in the 1950s in the defection from the Democratic party of the wives of labor union men to vote for Dwight D. Eisenhower.

Harding caught the spirit of the times and contributed a new word to the language when he declared that "America's present need is not heroics but healing; not nostrums but normalcy; not revolution but restoration." It was evidently Harding's intention to return the nation politically to the by then golden age of William McKinley in the days before the reformers had taken over, and in this wish Harding already had been overtaken by events. The war had gone beyond a nullification of the Progressive reforms to place big business more thoroughly in control of the nation than had ever before been the case. It had been the businessmen who had directed the War Industries Board and the other wartime agencies, and the politics followed had necessarily been those which served the interests of the most powerful elements within the various industries.

As Wilson himself had predicted, the war had placed the government at the mercy of the business community, and advantage had naturally been taken of this situation. During the four years of the war the number of Americans with annual incomes in excess of $50,000 had more than doubled, while industrial consolidation was afforded government assistance for the purpose of creating more effective war machinery. Farmers also had profited greatly from wartime markets, with the bad result in their case, however, that they had overextended themselves and prepared the way for relatively depressed farm conditions in the twenties.

Harding made some distinguished appointments to this Cabinet, including Herbert Hoover as Secretary of Commerce, Andrew Mellon as Secretary of the Treasury, Charles Evans Hughes as Secretary of State, and Henry C. Wallace as Secretary of Agriculture. Other appointments, however, were handed out to what came to be known as the "Ohio gang" of boon friends whom Harding liked to bum around with in the White House. Harding was from the outset audibly baffled by his duties, and his friends set out at once to capitalize on his incompetence.

His political manager, Harry Daugherty, was made Attorney General and allegedly set forth to feather his nest by fixing cases involving the Department of Justice. Charles Forbes, a former army deserter, was made head of the Veterans' Bureau, and he cost the government about a quarter of a billion dollars in thefts.

The Secretary of the Interior Albert B. Fall, in what became known as the Teapot Dome scandal, made hundreds of thousands of dollars leasing government oil lands in Wyoming and California on the sly. Increasingly aware of the corruption which surrounded him and borne down by the burdens of office, Harding died in August, 1923, before the scandals had become known to the nation, and Vice President Calvin Coolidge became the Chief Executive.

An honest, shrewd, thrifty, narrow-minded Yankee, President Coolidge said and did little. He was at his most active in issuing vetoes of legislation passed by Congress. Under Coolidge the able and honest members of the Cabinet were retained to give the administration as much luster as it wanted; the dishonest ones went out, some of them to jail. As a consequence, to the chagrin of the Democrats, by the election year of 1924 the Republican party was standing in a perfect posture of probity. Coolidge, who had come to symbolize prosperity and the American Way, won the Republican nomination as a matter of course, and the Democrats, who had depended on the corruption issue, could think of no good alternate issue—at least none upon which the party itself could agree.

The Democratic party, normally the more unruly of the two parties, was worse split in 1924 than at any time since the silver campaign in 1896. Two issues, prohibition and Catholicism, divided the party: the rural, old-American Democrats standing behind William Gibbs McAdoo and the urban, recent-immigrant Democrats behind Governor Al Smith of New York. The struggle between the Protestant dry McAdoo and the Catholic wet Smith went for 103 ballots, and then the party compromised on a J. P. Morgan lawyer, John W. Davis.

There were many in the country who did not like what the Republican administration stood for and who at the same time had the sense to see that the Democrats that year stood for nothing. These malcontents included farmers, who were not sharing well in the prosperity, labor union men, who did not fit quite anywhere in the American Way, and old line Progressives, yearning for the old campaigns. These people created a new Progressive party, nominated fighting Bob La Follette of Wisconsin, and ran on a platform of farm-labor reform, although labor union support weakened as the election approached. The result was a landslide for Coolidge over Davis, with La Follette gaining 16.5 per cent of the vote.

In 1928 the Democrats returned with the same sorry division in the ranks, but with the determination on the part of Smith's followers that the Irish immigrant's son from the sidewalks of New York this time should not be denied. The Protestant-dry faction succumbed, rather than repeat the previous performance, and, with little hope of victory under any circumstances, it permitted the nomination to go to Smith. The Republicans for their part still had prosperity on their side and, beyond that, Secretary of Commerce Hoover as their tremendously popular candidate.

The result was a foregone conclusion. Amid a bitter campaign waged over the religious issue, Hoover won by a landslide. He broke the Solid South for the first time since the Civil War. At the same time, Smith's candidacy brought the major cities of the North to the side of the Democratic party, also for the first time since the Civil War. In that respect Smith's campaign was an important step in the process whereby the Democratic party emerged once again, after three quarters of a century, as the indisputably dominant party in the nation.

III

Hooverism

It was Harding who had given the most famous statement of Republican policy in 1920, when he had declared that "What we want in America is less government in business and more business in government." It expressed a conviction, however, which was held more fervently by Coolidge than it had been by Harding. During the Coolidge administrations, it became a clearly formulated ideology, and Secretary of Commerce Hoover became its chief philosopher.

The post of Secretary of Commerce had been hardly more than an honorary one until Hoover took it over, but during his tenure it became the most active and formative of all the Cabinet positions. Indeed it is probably true to say that Hoover did more to direct the course of the nation as Secretary of Commerce than Coolidge did as President. At the center of Hoover's program was the trade association movement, wherein the firms within an industry would use the Commerce Department as a central clearing office to pool ideas and patents, standardize and simplify production methods and articles of manufacture, and indirectly—although this was not Hoover's intention altogether—reach agreements concerning markets, wages, and prices.

Competition, Hoover believed, was wasteful and ought, in many of its aspects, to be abolished. In Hoover's mind, however, it was of the utmost importance that these associations be voluntary and self-directed. Government coercion, in his view, would have meant an end to liberty, whereas "industrial self-government" was the model of free government. The result was a continuation of the process which the war had encouraged of ever-increasing industrial consolidations, benignly assisted by those commissions, the ICC and the FTC, which had been created to defend the nation against them. The creation of circumstances which would be favorable to the small businessman was one of Hoover's prime intentions, but one of the most basic results of the trade association movement was the increased authority of big business over its smaller competitors.

As Secretary of the Treasury, Harding had appointed one of the three or four richest men in the country, Andrew Mellon of the aluminum monopoly, who won the unstinted admiration of Coolidge and Hoover and who devoted his career in office to the freeing of the rich from the tyranny of taxation. Initially Mellon was checked by insurgents in the Senate, but some reductions were made in 1921 and 1924, and then in 1926 the Revenue Act was passed slashing taxes. In 1928 further tax reductions virtually nullified the tax system of the Wilson administration.

The Supreme Court, meanwhile, worked to obliterate remnants of Progressivism which could not be reached by congressional enactment or by presidential appointment. Against labor unions, the Court had upheld the yellow-dog contract in 1915, making the promise not to join a union the condition of employment. Then, in a series of decisions, the Court stripped unions of protection they thought they had received in the Clayton Act. In Hammer v. Dagenhart in 1918 the Court had declared the child-labor law to be an unconstitutional extension of the commerce clause, and in 1923 in Adkins v. Children's Hospital it outlawed a minimum-wage law for women in Washington, D.C.

The farmers retained strength in the state legislatures and in Congress, and they did battle throughout the twenties with the business governments. Wilson's farm program had created the conditions out of which there had emerged the Farm Bureau Federa-

tion, which in turn during 1921 helped to organize the "farm
bloc" of senators from rural states and congressmen from rural
areas. With farm acreage actually declining and with the farmers'
share of the national income dwindling rapidly, the agrarians
came at last to see themselves as a special interest group rather
than as the true representatives of the American majority. Organizing on this basis they were able to achieve much by their congressional strength.

The farmers had gained heavily during the Wilson administration and during the war, but they suffered during the recession of
1921. Corn, wheat, and cotton farming remained in a markedly
depressed state throughout the twenties. And the farmers generally
did not share in the rapid economic progress of the industrial areas,
nor did farm prices rise behind tariff barriers as did the manufactured goods which the farmers, in common with others, wanted.
To meet the farmers' problems, the farm bloc pressed successfully
for a series of enactments in the early twenties, increasing their
credit facilities, exempting farm cooperatives from antitrust suits,
and placing the middleman with whom the farmer dealt under
governmental scrutiny.

The farm bloc failed, however, in its major effort to achieve
the McNary-Haugen plan, whereby the government would raise
farm prices by purchasing at home and dumping abroad. Coolidge
vetoed this measure twice following its passage through Congress.
Defective in its failure to provide for production controls, the
McNary-Haugen bill developed some of the ideas and the leadership which finally triumphed with the agricultural program of the
New Deal. Two days after Coolidge vetoed the McNary-Haugen
bill, he increased the pig iron tariff by 50 per cent, thereby permitting a price rise of 50 cents per ton. In the view of his administration, government would take care of business alone, and business
would take care of the nation.

IV

Isolation   In foreign affairs Harding settled the League question to
the satisfaction of most people in his first message to Congress, by declaring that the United States would have nothing
to do with it, and Secretary of State Hughes, a few years later,

explained why. "The League of Nations," Hughes said, "by its constitution presupposed that peace could be maintained by economic pressure and military force." This, he said, was a dangerous error. The one true "Pathway of Peace" was through the uniting of the will of the peoples of the world in its favor and the maintaining of it through the process of agreement. There remained, throughout the twenties, dedicated champions of the League in America, but the argument of Hughes was generally acceptable, and the United States, signing a separate peace with Germany, went it alone.

The return with a vengeance to traditional isolation after the brief internationalist interlude was hurried along by America's emotional reaction to the war and to the terms of the Peace of Versailles. The postwar disillusionment, which expressed itself in American politics and literature as well as diplomacy, has remained something of a puzzlement to European observers, because the reaction appears disproportionate to the experience. In terms of actual war, of battle casualties and of spiritual exhaustion, the United States got off comparatively lightly; yet the revulsion against war was more universal and more deeply felt in the United States, perhaps, than in the European nations which were ravaged by it.

Americans were convinced that they had been duped into joining a war which was no affair of theirs, and then had been hornswoggled by their erstwhile allies at the peace table. They accepted as martyred prophets that "little band of willful men" who had held out, first against entering the war and last against joining the League. Among these, Senator William E. Borah of Idaho became the most forceful and influential spokesman for the new isolationism. Beyond refusing to meddle with the League, the United States refused also to join the World Court. Rather it put forward its own peace plans in the Washington Conference of 1921 and the Kellogg-Briand Pact of 1928, both of them undertaken upon the insistence of Senator Borah.

The Washington Conference was called to meet the problem of a naval arms race among nations who at the moment could not well afford one. So far as the United States was concerned, the main problem was presented by Japan, emerging more powerful than ever following the war, in the region of America's unarmed Philippine Islands. To the surprise of the delegates, Hughes, instead of opening the meeting with a formal observance of the amenities, launched at once into a detailed plan for the destruction of capital ships already built or in the process of construction by the major naval powers.

Naming the specific ships he had in mind to a total of sixty-six foreign and thirty American, Hughes won a disarmament victory unique in diplomatic history, whereby a ratio of 5 to 5 to 3 would be maintained between the United States, Britain, and Japan, in addition to smaller ratios by Italy and France. Japan and other nations further agreed to abide by the Open Door policy of respecting the administrative and territorial integrity of China, the agreement which Hay had failed to obtain at the opening of the century. A separate treaty between the United States, Britain, Japan, and France provided for consultation in the case of future Far Eastern disputes. It was a diplomatic success upon which Hughes might well preen himself, for the United States gave away nothing it wanted, but events were to prove that it was something less than the permanent solution to Asiatic affairs which Americans assumed it to be.

The Kellogg-Briand Pact of 1928 was entered into without enthusiasm by the French Premier Aristide Briand, who really wanted binding military commitments from the United States against a resurgent Germany. What developed from it was the signing, eventually, by most of the nations of the world, of the promise to renounce war as an instrument of national policy, except in the case of self-defense. And that, in the minds of Americans, settled that problem.

More seriously damaging to international relations than the American faith in a "parchment peace" was the American unwillingness to adjust to its new role as the financial center of the world. Through its entire history down to World War I, American economic development had been financed by foreign investments, which America had paid for by exporting more than it imported. The war reversed this situation to turn the United States into a creditor nation, faced with the necessity of importing more than it exported, in order to export the dollars necessary for the repayment of debts owed to it by other nations.

It would have been difficult enough for Americans—especially American farmers—to have made the wrenching adjustments necessary to meet this new situation, but the government refused even to acknowledge that the situation existed. Instead of inviting greater imports, it passed the Fordney-McCumber Tariff in 1922, substantially reenacting the Payne-Aldrich Tariff of 1909 with a number of additions. In 1930 the climax was reached in American tariff history with the Hawley-Smoot Act, passed over the protests of thirty-four nations. In 1924, with the allies unable to pay their American debts and with the Germans unable to pay their reparations to the allies, the Dawes Plan was instituted, whereby the United States loaned money to Germany with which Germany paid reparations to the allies with which the allies paid interest on their American debts. American capital, meanwhile, was colonizing Europe as well as most of the rest of the world, helping to prepare the way for world depression when Americans withdrew their foreign investments following the crash of 1929.

V

Fordismus — From the days when the Puritans first established a New Zion in the wilderness Americans have always had a message for the world, and the profane world of postwar America was no exception. Turning from the crusade to create a pure Christian democracy, the twenties preached the gospel of the American Way. Probably most Americans in that decade were convinced that the chief contribution of the United States to civilization lay in its achievements in the field of business enterprise. Nor were Americans by any means alone in this thought. Teams of experts came from the corners of the earth to see how this miracle had been achieved. The Germans coined a word for it, "Fordismus." In Russia, it was said, Henry Ford was honored above all other foreigners. Of all America's messages this was the one which has been most eagerly received by the world.

Mass production was the key to the American Way. Ford said much too much for himself when he claimed to have invented mass production, but certainly he ranks as one of its master creators. The distinct contribution generally credited to Ford is the moving assembly line, with its revolutionary change of factory organization. Beyond that, Ford was a tireless tinkerer, searching for improved methods, whether in minor details or on such a scale as would require the scrapping of a factory. And it was Ford who possessed the democratic vision of a nation of car owners and who devoted his life to producing this automobile for the masses.

Scientific management, or Taylorism as it was called for its chief apostle, Frederick W. Taylor, established itself in the twenties and worked production miracles for American business. Taylor, a shop foreman during the late nineteenth century, had been struck by the tremendous losses which factories sustained, owing to the settled opposition which existed between labor and management and to the tendency of the worker to do as little as possible for his pay. The fault, Taylor argued, rested with management. It was the responsibility of management to know plant operations to the last detail, so that it could instruct each worker on the most efficient method of carrying out his task and then could measure his work by exact standards. Beyond that, incentive pay would encourage the worker to increase his productivity. Scientific management might well double the value of a factory, or of the industry of a nation, and all might benefit accordingly.

Like Ford a tireless tinkerer, Taylor put his system into effect at Bethlehem Steel Company with spectacular success; yet he was slow in gaining support from industry as a whole. His tinkering upset routine. Labor was suspicious of Taylorism and rightly so. During the twenties, scientific management resulted in great increases in the national income, but it was the stockholders and executives who benefited from the speed-up systems much more than the working force. And an important aspect of scientific management, as it was understood in the twenties, was the company union, which was on the verge of overtaking the declining AFL in total membership when the Great Depression struck.

Basic to the new prosperity, which exceeded anything that had ever been known anywhere in the world, was the increasing use of gasoline and electricity in place of steam power and the development of new articles of manufacture based upon these sources of energy. The rapid supplanting of the railroad for many purposes by automobiles, trucks and buses further vastly improved the transportation system, facilitating the distribution of the new massproduced goods. And protected by high tariffs American business enjoyed a protected market which was not remotely rivaled elsewhere in the world. In 1929 the national income of the United States was far greater than that of all of the other major industrial nations of the world combined.

Of all the new industries the automobile was most important to the material progress of the twenties. From an annual production of 4,000 in 1900, the output of automobiles had increased to more than four million annually by the close of the twenties. At the opening of the century the automobile had been the rich man's plaything, which Wilson thought was doing more than anything else to stir socialistic discontent among the masses. In 1914, however, Ford, driven by the vision of the common man's car, was assembling Model T Fords in the space of an hour and a half, at a cost within the reach of the average American skilled workman.

Where Ford led, General Motors followed in the twenties with the Chevrolet, while the more expensive cars came to be similarly mass produced. The automobile was the symbol of America, and the factory parking lot filled with workingmen's cars was among the most startling attractions which America offered to foreign visitors. In the meantime, the production of oil increased sixteen times and that of iron and steel five times during the first three decades of the century.

The decade saw, with the rapid increase in the use of electricity, the first popular use of electrical appliances: stoves, refrigerators, toasters, vacuum cleaners, irons, and radios. The number of telephones in the nation doubled between 1915 and 1930 to more than twenty million. The American chemical industry, a more recent development, experienced an even more rapid expansion. The war drove the government to producing potash, nitrates, and dyes which formerly had been imported from abroad, the most notable achievement being the construction of the chemical plant at Muscle Shoals in the Tennessee Valley. Synthetics became the basis for major new industries in the twenties including Bakelite, rayon, and cellophane.

The material progress of the twenties was a profoundly democratizing force from a social point of view. Although the rich got richer faster, it was the increased wealth of the working classes which resulted in the much more momentous alterations in the character of society. American workers, whose real wages had remained almost unchanged during the Progressive era, saw their purchasing power rise rapidly in the twenties while their work week tended to decline. U. S. Steel reduced its working day from twelve to eight hours in 1923, and Ford introduced the five-day week in 1926.

There was also introduced the equalitarianism of mass production and standard brands. Differences in wealth were not so clearly distinguishable in different grades of machine-made clothing as had been the difference between the tailor-made and the homespun. The average man could have his own car and his own radio, even though he could not afford the custom-made possessions of the rich man. And the new inventions and production methods brought to society as a whole inexpensive forms of diversion in the radio, the phonograph, and the movies.

This tendency toward social democratization owed much to the fact that immigration restriction took place at the same time that domestic laborsaving devices were first made widely available. The very rich might still be able to afford a retinue of servants at higher wages from the declining supply, but the middling groups in society, even though they were improving themselves economically, found, on the one hand that they no longer could afford a staff of three or four servants, and on the other that all but perhaps one servant could be very handily supplanted by the introduction of household appliances and by the move to smaller houses or to apartments.

Wars have tended to improve the position of women in American society, and World War I was no exception. Just as the Civil War was the occasion for the entrance of women into teaching on a large scale, so World War I was the occasion for their invasion of secretarial jobs, and the twenties provided ever widening opportunities for women in a variety of fields of work.

VI

Emancipation of the Women During the two decades between 1910 and 1930 the urban population of the nation rose from 46 per cent to 56 per cent, and women's skirts rose from the ankle to the knee. The number of inches between the hemline and the ankle was rightly taken as the index of the revolutionary change in morals and manners which accompanied and followed World War I, and responsible elements moved to check the revolution by putting women back into their old clothes. Fashion writers warned that the American woman had "lifted her skirts beyond any modest limitation," and they decreed that she should drop them the next year. The YWCA issued a national "Modesty Appeal," and reported that it was getting good results. Bills were introduced in the Utah Legislature fixing skirts at three inches above the ankle and in the Virginia Legislature fixing necklines to within three inches of the upper part of the throat.

In April, 1920, some Americans were diverted from the Great

Red Scare by the publication of F. Scott Fitzgerald's *This Side of Paradise,* which told of "one vast juvenile intrigue" against the old moral order. The thing had apparently been going on even before the war, and year by year it was getting worse. Girls who would not have thought of entering a saloon in the days of legal drinking were bellying up to the bar in the illegal speakeasies with skirts short, stockings rolled below the knees, and lips and cheeks daubed with lipstick and rouge which formerly had been the trademark of the streetwalker.

Nineteenth-century American society in all but the "degraded" classes had, by all available evidence, been Victorian through and through. Victorian Englishmen visiting America had had occasion to express their shocked surprise that Americans went beyond the forms of Victorianism to the very substance of it. The lavish parties of the gilded aristocracy had been wholesome, decorous affairs. The chaperone had played an indispensable role in upper society. Somewhat lower down on the social scale, they had not been present in person, perhaps, but they had been present in spirit in youthful gatherings—at least if one can believe that W. D. Howells really knew what was going on in his day. Then it all changed. The younger generation suddenly rebelled, and the older generation, unable to lick them, joined them. By the mid-twenties the waltz had given way to the Black Bottom and the Charleston, and except for the blue-nosed drys and the "Bible belters," it could almost be said that "Everybody's doin' it now."

That this most non-Wilsonian new freedom was not simply a postwar phenomenon is evident from an examination of prewar Greenwich Village, where the horn already had been blown brassily for the moral as well as intellectual revolt against traditional America. The Progressive movement, which had achieved the perfect society for its generation, evidently left the younger generation with the uneasy feeling that there must be something better. The Progressive movement had striven for changes which would reestablish the old values amid new circumstances; the younger generation rejected the older values on the grounds that they had no relevance to current circumstances.

The Lost Generation found plenty of intellectual arguments to defend their new emancipation, but the revolution in morals was not primarily a cerebral development. Darwinism convinced many intellectuals that there were no eternal verities in religion or in morals; that Dreiser's Sister Carrie was to be admired as one who adjusted to circumstances and not to be condemned as a fallen woman. For most Americans, however, Darwin and the theory of natural selection probably contributed less to the new social conduct than did Thomas Alva Edison and the electric light. Material and technological progress represented a triumph not only over nature, but also over nature's God. Liberal churches responded to this urbane attitude by adding on game rooms and coffee rooms and toning down the otherworldly aspect of religion.

The decline of the family as the basic unit of society can be dimly seen even in earliest colonial times, when a public school system was established to perform a duty which the heads of households were found not to be performing adequately. In the early nineteenth century the further breakdown of the family as an integrated unit took place in New England when farmers' daughters, ceasing to make homespun, bought manufactured cloth with money they had earned at the textile mill.

Then the move to the city converted the large family from an economic asset to an economic liability, and a decline in the birthrate rapidly took place. The father, away at work during the day, necessarily left the upbringing of the children to a large extent to the mother, who, if she wanted, could leave it up to the maid, freeing mother, father, and child from the continuous association which circumstances formerly had forced upon them. The general tendency was to lose old values and gain new freedom, and when the children showed the uses that could be made of the freedom, their elders proved quick to learn from them.

Sexual restraint had given cohesion to the old order, and sexual freedom was the most explosive force in its demolition. Sex became the stock in trade of the movies and also of the tabloid newspapers, which made their appearance in the postwar period. The "petting" question became the topic of the day. On the level of theory the American psychiatrist A. A. Brill began translating the work of Sigmund Freud into English in 1908, and Freud himself was agreeably surprised to notice how well his ideas were known "even in prudish America." As popularized in America in the twenties, Freud was understood to prove that life was sex-centered and that human and social ills stemmed from sexual repression. Some came to look upon uninhibited sexual expression as the universal panacea, much as Sylvester Graham had viewed dietary reform in the mid-nineteenth century.

Sexual liberty was especially a declaration of independence for women; for even Howells conceded that the boys he grew up with, although models of deportment with nice girls, nevertheless felt free to stray across the tracks. That the women did not know quite where to go with their new freedom was indicated in the styles, which combined short skirts and makeup with bobbed hair and boyish figures. Nevertheless the flapper was the symbol of the Jazz Age. Compared to her the American male could offer no more meaningful symbol for whatever freedom he had won than that of the arctic raccoon coat combined with the Hawaiian ukelele. It was clearly the women rather than the men who in the twenties increased their freedom, winning political rights, legal rights, broader economic opportunities, liberation from household drudgery, and largely winning, in principle at least, social equality with men.

VII

The Lost Generation   In the field of the creative arts, as in the world of manners and morals, every day of the 1920s was Fourth of July. In poetry, the novel, the essay, and the drama, American writers wrote their independence of Europe, of their Puritan American past and of their Philistine American present. The twenties was a decade of crashing triumph in American cultural history, when what Frost, Eliot, Hemingway, Faulkner, O'Neill, and a crowd of others had to say was exciting and important to Europe as well as to America. A climax of world recognition came in 1930, when the novelist Sinclair Lewis became the first American to win the Nobel Prize for literature.

In his acceptance speech, entitled, "The American Fear of Literature," Lewis lamented the failure of his homeland to support its serious writers. This was the same Sinclair Lewis whose *Main Street* ten years earlier had sold 400,000 copies, to rival *The Sheik* as the best seller of the year, and whose subsequent novels had all gone briskly. Lewis here spoke for the "Lost Generation," which had had the luck to have its cake and eat it too. This was the generation cordially welcomed and well paid by the world against which it breathed its defiance; which, if it wished, escaped abroad from the vulgarity of the American marketplace, on steady remittances from indulgent businessmen-fathers. And the result of it all, in retrospect, appears to have been an output of creative writing unrivaled for excellence and diversity by any other decade in American history, including the productive 1850s.

The origins of the Lost Generation may be at least faintly traced to the 1890s, when little magazines appeared in the big cities, attempting, with little success, to persuade Americans out of their genteel provincialism. The most influential early critic was James Gibbons Huneker, learned and enthusiastic, who wanted his fellow Americans to see that there were a lot of things going on abroad in music, art, and literature, which they ought to know about.

In 1902 Gertrude Stein expatriated herself to Paris, where she remained for forty years, keeping an influential salon for temporary expatriates including O'Neill, Hemingway, and Sherwood Anderson. In 1908 the drama critic, George Jean Nathan, and the universal critic, Henry L. Mencken, joined the *Smart Set* magazine, where they quickly established themselves as the literary and intellectual arbiters of the generation. Equipped with a superb vocabulary of invective, Mencken rained shattering blows upon the genteel literary tradition and against the old shibboleths of American culture.

The first main stirrings of revolt came during the high noon of Progressivism. In 1911 the *Masses* was started, employing the services of Max Eastman and John Reed and advocating a political radicalism not quite thinkable to the Progressive temper. It was followed in a few years by the *New Republic*, less radical but a little impatient with mere Progressivism.

In 1912 *Poetry: A Magazine of Verse* appeared in Chicago, followed by the *Little Review*, signaling the advent of a new age of American poetry, after a hiatus of a half century. By 1913 Greenwich Village was becoming an artistic and literary center, and in that year the Armory Show was held in New York revealing to American audiences the cubist and postimpressionist art of France. The show traveled to other major cities, and, despite some loud catcalls, was a resounding success. In 1913 the Provincetown Players organized, and three years later they produced their first O'Neill play, *Bound East for Cardiff*. In 1915 appeared Van Wyck Brooks' *America's Coming-of-Age*, greeted as a rallying cry for the new generation. The war and its aftermath brought its disillusionment with past as well as present, but the artistic and literary rebellion of the twenties seems to have been less a postwar movement than it was a post-Progressive one.

The rise of American drama during and after the war was the more impressive for the fact that America had previously contributed virtually nothing original to the theater except minstrel shows and burlesque. O'Neill was early recognized as the towering genius of the new American theater, with an experience and skill which enabled him to create marvelous impressions and moods from inarticulate dialogue combined with impressionistic settings and unerring stage directions.

Other plays appeared in rich variety, including the comedies of Philip Barry, S. N. Behrman, and George Kelly; the verse dramas of Maxwell Anderson and the tragic dramas of Robert Sherwood. The thirties produced Clifford Odets, Thornton Wilder, and William Saroyan, and the theater has continued to the present, with Tennessee Williams, Arthur Miller, and William Inge, among many others, to hold its place in the forefront of the international theater. Since World War II it has furthermore developed a form of musical drama which remains a distinctively American art form.

The poetry of the period was remarkable for its diversity and profusion. From Chicago came the powerful, shaggy, Whitman-esque poetry of Carl Sandburg, the heavy rhythms of Vachel Lindsay, and the small town epitaphs of Edgar Lee Masters. From New England came the polished verse of Edwin Arlington Robinson and the extensive works of Robert Frost, considered by many to be the greatest poet of his age. Frost, best known for his rather folksy poems such as *Mending Wall*, developed a remarkable range of poetic style and the ability to universalize from the New England of his experience. From the South, centering around Vanderbilt University, came a group headed by Allen Tate and John Crowe Ransom; from California, the violent celebrations of the Pacific Coast and the hatred for humanity by Robinson Jeffers.

Highly influential were the early brief poems of Ezra Pound, attempting to capture conceptions in fleeting images, but perhaps most influential of all American poets was T. S. Eliot, who, as did Pound, expatriated himself to Europe early in his career. Eliot's highly intellectualized *The Wasteland*, with its depth of classical, anthropological, and mythological allusion, has probably been the most influential poet's poem of the twentieth century. There were the experimentalists, the most ingenious and brightly amusing of whom, surely, has been E. E. Cummings, experimenting with startling word juxtapositions and surprising use of typography. Notable among other experimentalists are Marianne Moore and Wallace Stevens. The list of American poets of genius might be extended still further. If there was a quality common to them all, it was a seriousness of purpose—even if of a flippant purpose—a professionalism which was stiffened by an extensive literature of deadly serious poetry criticism.

The body of verse produced by Americans in the twentieth century, including Randall Jarrell, Theodore Roethke, Karl Shapiro, Richard Wilbur, Peter Viereck, and Delmore Schwartz, may well comprise America's most impressive modern contribution to the world's literature. Without question, however, the greatest world recognition has been accorded its writers of fiction, five of whom have been awarded the Nobel Prize in literature. Novelists of the 1920s manifested some of the diversity in style and subject matter which characterized the drama and poetry. They can, however, be more readily generalized upon.

In their subject matter they were characteristically attracted to the sordid, the seamy, and the animallike qualities in society, either stripping away the genteel covering from the "sunlit" middle-class world of W. D. Howells, or venturing into smelly, violent places that had been, until then, politely ignored by acceptable writers. Their warm European reception was surely enhanced by the fact that they said the worst about an America which had always exhibited a tendency to speak smugly of itself. They were self-consciously disillusioned, as with Hemingway and Dos Passos, or they were self-consciously without illusions from the beginning, as with Dreiser. Darwinian naturalism remained a powerful influence; while Freudian psychology arrived in the twenties to mix with it.

Sinclair Lewis was the most ubiquitous debunker of American society, moving from the small town in *Main Street* to the moderately large Midwestern city in *Babbitt*, to religious quackery in *Elmer Gantry* and to general criticism of America in *Arrowsmith* and *Dodsworth*. A satirist as well as a realist, Lewis leavened his debunking with a humor which no doubt made his writings more widely acceptable to the Americans he was attacking. Sherwood Anderson's *Winesburg, Ohio* exposed the constricting, deadly aspects of small-town life, and Dreiser, and later James T. Farrell in *Studs Lonnigan*, dealt with the struggle for survival in the big city.

Most of Dreiser's best writing appeared before World War I. His greatest financial, and perhaps his greatest critical, success, *An American Tragedy,* however, appeared in the mid-twenties. William Faulkner examined the society of Yoknapatawpha County, Mississippi, where the old decadent civilization was overrun by the brutish, animalistic Snopes clan. Faulkner's writings are marked by a technical facility and by the ability to alter his style to meet the needs of the narrative, probably the extreme example of this ingenuity being the section of *The Sound and The Fury* which is told as if seen through the eyes of an idiot.

Of all recent American novelists, Ernest Hemingway has probably had the greatest influence on other writers, in the simple, spare, and "nonliterary" yet poetic quality of his postwar novels, *A Farewell to Arms* and *The Sun Also Rises.* He went on to deal with the theme of courage and death in understated writing, seemingly naturalistic but more truly impressionistic in the economy of words and their artful arrangement. The opposite of Hemingway in this respect was the North Carolina writer, Thomas Wolfe, who in poetical language expressed his feelings in almost endless volumes.

The coming of the Depression changed much, though not all, of this. One sign that the end of a literary era had arrived with the Depression was the sudden loss of authority suffered by Mencken. Another was the adverse reception by the critics of one of F. Scott Fitzgerald's best novels, *Tender Is the Night,* in 1934. Fitzgerald had identified himself with the Jazz Age and especially with the high living of the irresponsible rich, in a spirit not so much of admiration as of fascination. Fitzgerald's great craftsmanship and poetic charm is exhibited in *Tender Is the Night* almost as well as it is in his best work, *The Great Gatsby,* but to the depression era this represented the flippant irresponsibility of a silly age. The allowances of the expatriates had been cut off and they were home. American society, broken and bleeding, was no longer something to laugh at. The New Deal became a hive for intellectuals and the Works Progress Administration's writers' project became a workhouse for literary talent.

There emerged in the thirties a flood of proletarian novels, earnestly, boringly Marxist. Some writers of a somewhat broader class of problem novels did better, notably John Steinbeck in a number of novels including *Grapes of Wrath.* John Dos Passos, whose career began with the beginning of the twenties, achieved critical acclaim with a panoramic trilogy of American society, part fictional, part historical, entitled *U.S.A.* Some other writers, especially Faulkner and Hemingway, succeeded in spanning the periods of prosperity and depression. On the whole, however, the literature of the depression period concerned itself most earnestly with "problems" where the twenties had concerned itself most earnestly with what Hemingway called his "craft," and the quality of literature declined.

In architecture there was taking place a break with the neo-classical and pseudo-Gothic past which was suggested by the new industrial possibilities. In the cities the lack of elevators had limited buildings to six stories until the final quarter of the nineteenth century. This limitation overcome, however, buildings were constructed of twelve stories and more, and American architecture was for the first time obliged to depart entirely from European models. In the age of steel and concrete the leading American pioneer was Louis Sullivan, who most successfully challenged orthodoxy, perhaps, with the Wainright Building constructed in St. Louis in 1891.

More than anyone else, Sullivan introduced America to the ideas of making use of the new industrial materials and of making function the basis for architectural design. His disciple, Frank Lloyd Wright, continued, through a long and contentious life, to attack the old shibboleths in the contruction of residential homes as well as office buildings. America, however, tended to resist breaks with tradition in this as in other fields.

BIBLIOGRAPHY FOR CHAPTER TWELVE

William Leuchtenburg, *Perils of Prosperity, 1914–1932* (1958) is "an informal history with substance . . . in a book that is a pleasure to read. . . . The omissions are not important, but the generalizations and interpretations often hit a new mark and are useful to historians for their fresh insights." John Hicks, *Republican Ascendancy, 1921–1933* (1960) "ranges primarily through political, economic, and diplomatic developments . . . a volume that is packed with factual information. . . ." A. M. Schlesinger, Jr., *The Crisis of the Old Order* (1957) is a history of the twenties which serves as a backround for Schlesinger's multivolume history of the New Deal, still in progress. Oscar Handlin, *Al Smith and His America* (1958) "illustrates the strengths and defects of impressionistic biographical history."

F. L. Allen, *Only Yesterday* (1931) is a vivid and often rollicking social history of America in the twenties, and at the same time a study which remains, in retrospect, solid and significant history. R. S. and H. M. Lynd, *Middletown* (1929) is an important sociological study of Midwestern America, based upon a detailed examination of Muncie, Indiana. T. C. Cochran, *The American Business System* (1957), "Despite limitations of space . . . has attempted an extensive narrative and analytical account of American business in the twentieth century. . . . The work, fortunately, is that of a literate, skeptical, and experienced student of the American system." Several brief biographies of Ford are available in paperback, among which Roger Burlingame, *Henry Ford* (1954) is an objective and readable treatment.

Alfred Kazin, *On Native Grounds* (1942) is an outstanding history of modern American literature. B. S. Oldsey and A. O. Lewis, Jr., eds., *Visions and Revisions in Modern American Literary Criticism* is a collection of essays. Alistair Cooke, *The Vintage Mencken* is one of several such collections.

THE GREAT DEPRESSION 13

1

The Crash   Almost as regular as clockwork the United States has plunged into a severe economic depression once every generation under peacetime conditions. The first one occurred in the Confederation period. Then, following the unstable economic conditions which accompanied the French Revolutionary and Napoleonic Wars, depression came again in 1819 and thereafter in 1837, in 1857, in 1873, and in 1893. A brief "bankers' panic" of 1907 did not unsettle the economy for long, but in 1914 signs pointed to another severe depression.

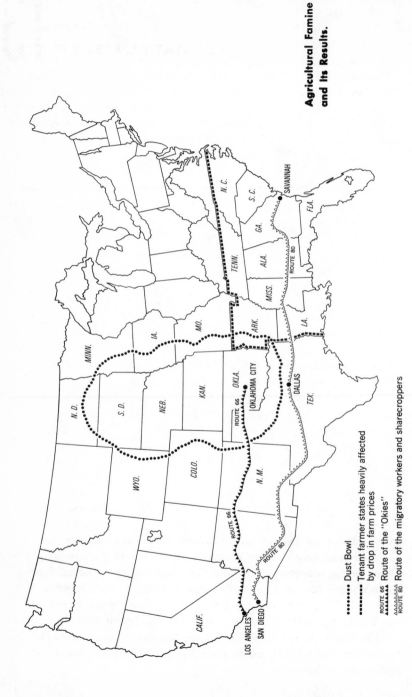

Agricultural Famine and Its Results.

•••••• Dust Bowl

━━━━ Tenant farmer states heavily affected by drop in farm prices

ROUTE 66 Route of the "Okies"

▲▲▲▲▲ Route of the migratory workers and sharecroppers
ROUTE 80

The nation was rescued on that occasion by World War I, and it recovered quickly, except for certain classifications of farmers and some other smaller economic groups, from the recession of 1921. Then in 1929 it suffered a depression deeper and more enduring than any it had yet experienced. Brought out of the Great Depression by World War II, the nation in 1949 drifted again into depression, despite defense and Marshall Plan spending. This trend checked itself, however, and with the Korean conflict the next year and the prodigious subsequent defense spending, the national economy, while falling far short of the ideal of full employment, has managed to stave off a further major depression.

The depressions of the nineteenth century had been preceded by reckless land speculation and heavy expenditures on internal improvements, especially on railroads. Irresponsible banking practices followed by bank failures had been part of the pattern. Furthermore America, as a prime field for foreign investment, had been sensitive to economic conditions in Europe, especially in Britain. European business panics, followed by an unloading of American investments, had periodically weakened the American economy. In 1929, however, the United States was the world's creditor, and it was the withdrawal of American investments on that occasion which knocked the economic props from under other national economies and precipitated the world-wide depression.

Throughout American history these depressions, despite the regularity of their occurrences, have come as shocking surprises to the American business community and to American politicians, and in the case of 1929 the element of surprise was especially marked; for the belief was by then quite generally held, that America had at last discovered the secret of perpetual prosperity.

The perennial problem of maintaining a national credit which would be both flexible and sound had been solved, it was argued, through the Federal Reserve system. The evils of competition had been eliminated without fundamental damage to the saving principle of free enterprise; for business was working out its own problems without arbitrary governmental interference. The national product was increasing annually, and the nation as a whole was gaining. To be sure the distribution of the new wealth was far from equal, but this problem was understood and was being solved.

Broad-visioned businessmen were developing profit-sharing programs for their employees and were distributing company stock

378 THE GREAT DEPRESSION

among them. The day would come when the workers of America would own their own factories, not through the violent process of Communist revolution, but through the peaceful evolution of responsible, civic-minded free enterprise. "We in America," declared Herbert Hoover in 1928, "are nearer to the final triumph over poverty than ever before in the history of any land . . . given a chance to go forward with the policies of the last eight years, we shall soon with the help of God be in sight of the day when poverty will be banished from this nation."

The New York Stock Exchange, the most spectacular barometer of the nation's material progress by the late twenties, soared to new heights following Hoover's election. Enormous quick profits were made possible in stock speculation by buying on the margin, that is, putting up a small percentage of the purchase price with a broker. It was widely observed at the time that anybody could be rich who wished to be. The Federal Reserve Board, for its part, was concerned about the sudden expansion of bank loans, and it took steps to check them. The move, however, came too late.

The crash descended in October, and when the wild confidence turned to wild panic no means were found to check the rout. Within days the market values of stocks had dropped by one-third, and thereafter it was not found possible to check their downward course for the next three years. By the end of 1932 even the "blue chip" stocks had dropped to a quarter of their 1929 values. Millions of investors had been ruined, and that distrust of the business community and of the economic system had settled in, which was to remain as a stubborn impediment to improved conditions.

The wild rise and fall of the market, beyond heralding the coming of the Great Depression, did much to initiate it and to lengthen it, but behind the crash was a fatal weakness in the economy which had been largely overlooked at the time but which became evident once the Depression had set in. Henry Ford put his finger on the problem when he explained that the Depression had come because the buying power of the people was all used up. Although wages had risen wonderfully during the decade, they had not kept up with the increased value of the national product. That the nation was producing more than it could purchase was disguised for a time by the growing practice of buying on credit, but this in turn, while delaying the Depression, deepened it once it was upon the nation. The trade association system, furthermore, had facilitated price-fixing arrangements so effectively that prices did not respond to market conditions. As purchasing power declined, businesses resolutely priced themselves out of their markets.

It had never been supposed that it was the duty of the Federal government to intervene in economic matters, either to aid the victims of depressions or to return the nation to prosperity. Depressions had been viewed as deviations from the normal condition of prosperity, created by a temporary malfunctioning of the law of supply and demand. The problem, it was agreed, was essentially one of overproduction, and the solution was to permit nature to take its course. Unsound businesses would inevitably go to the wall, production would decline to the level of consumption, and there would thereafter be a steady return to normal conditions. Beyond cutting government expenses, reducing taxes, and maintaining the gold reserves there was nothing the Federal government could or should do in the matter.

Herbert Hoover, it is true, went beyond this negative conception of the government's role. It is also true that, in the face of unprecedented economic and personal catastrophe, he moved most reluctantly and slowly and most reluctantly of all where government assistance would benefit directly those people suffering most desperately from the Depression. A self-made millionaire who had experienced no serious depression since his college days, Hoover throughout his administration held to the optimistic view that prosperity was the normal condition and that during depressions, as well as during times of prosperity, the balanced budget should be the highest aim of the Federal government.

At the same time Hoover was early convinced that the Depression was a serious one, that its duration would be indefinite, and that as a practical matter the government would have to do something. His earliest major concern was for depressed farm conditions, and in June, before the crash, he supported a program under which the Federal Farm Board received 500 million dollars to grant loans to farm cooperatives which would work out programs to benefit their members. Working through these cooperatives and directly through its own corporations, the Board financed the purchase of wheat and cotton in order to remove surpluses. By the end of the first year of its experiment, however, it was forced to concede the futility of a program which did not enforce limitations upon production.

A second solution to the farm problem, in Hoover's view, was tariff protection, and his support of the Hawley-Smoot Tariff Act of 1930 was chiefly made on this basis. The tariff, however, proved no more effective for farmers producing for the world market than had previous ones, and it was made the occasion for sharp tariff increases upon industrial imports as well.

Hoover's most ambitious attack upon the Depression, recommended to Congress in December, 1931, was the establishment of the Reconstruction Finance Corporation "to make temporary advances upon proper securities to established industries, railways and financial institutions . . . where such advances will protect the credit structure and stimulate employment." Denounced as the rich man's dole, the RFC disbursed 1,500 million dollars during its first year of existence, mainly to banks and trust companies. It was defended by Hoover partly on the grounds that its intended beneficiaries were the smaller institutions and partly on the grounds that the benefits were in the form of loans which would be returned to the government. It remained true that he was notably less willing to extend to the indigent individual the government support which he extended to the indigent corporation.

In the face of rising unemployment, which eventually drove one-third of the nation's working force onto the streets, Hoover refused to use Federal funds to prevent mass misery until his final year in office. Then, while vetoing a more generous congressional relief program in July, 1932, he was moved to sign a bill extending Federal loans to the states of 300 million dollars, on the condition, which also applied to the activities of the Farm Board and the RFC, that the money should eventually be returned to the Federal government.

In these matters Hoover continued to be controlled by his original assumptions: that Federal handouts "would have injured the spiritual responses of the American people," presumably to a greater extent than those of private charities, that the end result of increased Federal authority would be the creation of an authoritarian state, and that, under any circumstances, economy remained the chief concern of the government. "The urgent question today," he told Congress in 1932, "is the prompt balancing of the budget. When that is accomplished I propose to support adequate measures for relief of distress and unemployment."

In June, 1932, the Republicans met in convention and without opposition or enthusiasm renominated Hoover as their candidate. In July the resolutely unpolitical Hoover opened his campaign for reelection by calling out the National Guard against the pathetic "bonus marchers:" World War I veterans who marched on Washington to demonstrate for immediate bonus benefits. Amid precipitously worsening conditions the Democrats held their convention and nominated as their candidate the Governor of New York, Franklin Delano Roosevelt.

A distant cousin of Teddy's, F.D.R. had indicated his vote-getting powers by winning the governorship in the Republican year of 1928 and then by winning a second term overwhelmingly two years later. His had been one of the most vigorous of the state administrations in combatting the Depression, but his record was not widely known nationally, and he did not especially campaign upon it. What he said during his campaign was largely noncommittal and by no means consistent, although one fighting speech before the Commonwealth Club in San Francisco gave some indications of the main directions the New Deal would take. Against the Hoover of that year, however, Roosevelt's brilliant personality and vague promises of reforms were sufficient to reverse the landslide of four years earlier and open the way for what Roosevelt, in his acceptance speech at the convention, had called "a new deal for the American people."

II

Coming of the New Deal Roosevelt, according to the ancient Supreme Court justice Oliver Wendell Holmes, Jr., was "A second-class intellect, but a first-class temperament." Unlike the intellectual Hoover, F.D.R. brought to his task no clearly formulated economic theory and no fixed idea of the role which the government should play in a depression economy. "The country needs," he declared, "and unless I mistake its temper, the country demands bold, persistent experimentation. It is common sense to take a method and try it. If it fails, admit it frankly and try another. But above all, try something." Unburdened by any association in the public mind with the national debacle, Roosevelt suddenly convinced the American people, as Hoover himself had been glumly determined to do, that they had "nothing to fear but

fear itself." The administration opened with a dramatic national
bank holiday followed by a merry outpouring of legalized 3.2 beer
made possible by congressional modification of the Volstead Act.
Momentarily, at least, in full command of the nation's confidence,
the Roosevelt administration, in an unprecedented hundred days
of administrative and legislative activity, dealt out new deals to
the clamoring, desperately needy economic interests of the nation.

Consistency was no New Deal criterion. Each major problem
was faced separately, with only passing concern for the effect that
each program might have on some other area of the economy. Most
sharply criticized in this respect was the program to destroy farm
produce in a time of starvation. There was, however, more food
being produced than the nation could consume, even in good times,
and, for the New Deal, relief for the starving was a distinct problem to be handled by other agencies. If the result of relief work
programs was government competition with struggling private enterprise, then business in its turn would benefit from separate programs designed to aid in its recovery.

Once the nation had lost the bright honeymoon happiness of the
Hundred Days, it fell once again into acrimonious dispute. The
New Deal, its enemies charged, was a revolutionary overthrow of
the democratic, federal, individualistic American system. In important respects, Hoover declared, it was "fascism, pure fascism."

The champions of the New Deal were notably more divided than
its critics. Many among them delighted in accepting the reforms as
constituting a revolutionary break with the dead and discredited
past. The more politic among them defended these reforms as the
heroic means by which an actual bloody revolution was averted,
and narrowly averted, in 1933. At the outset New Dealers tended
to treat somewhat casually the question as to whether desperate
emergency measures could be traced to an immaculately American
historical tradition. Increasingly, however, New Deal partisans
tended to defend it as the fulfillment of the reform tradition of
the Progressive era.

The answers to these questions were to be sought first of all in
the character and purposes of the President, for F.D.R. dominated
his age in a manner altogether unprecedented in American history.
Ruling always amid violently divided councils, he retained a generally flexible and undogmatic approach to the problems of the
Depression. In a famous reply to the question concerning his

ideological bent, he decided, after a moment's thought, that he was "a Christian and a democrat."

A patrician reformer in the line of Theodore Roosevelt and Samuel J. Tilden, he was, in the view of recent historians, fundamentally conservative, and, in the view of many reformers in his administration, downright old-fashioned. He might well have nationalized the banks and the railroads in 1933 with virtually no opposition, had he been so inclined, but then, as throughout the Depression, he thought in terms of restoration rather than revolution. A strong admirer of both Theodore Roosevelt and Woodrow Wilson, he had entered politics during the Progressive era and was himself basically Progressive in outlook.

Much old-time Progressive support, Republican as well as Democratic, flowed to the New Deal, which was permeated with the ideals of social justice of the earlier reform period. The Progressive movement had itself sharply divided on fundamental economic issues, however, and these divisions continued to split the New Deal. The spirit of the new freedom burned brightly in such New Dealers as Secretary of State Cordell Hull, who thought in terms of trust-busting and free trade. Against them, and in a commanding position at the outset, were old Bull Moosers such as Secretary of the Interior Harold L. Ickes, and younger converts to the new nationalism, who argued for extending government controls over a consolidated economy which was, itself, an inescapable fact of modern life.

This neo-new nationalism gained support from the widespread belief that the American economy had reached the stage of maturity and an end to fundamental economic advances. Its Western lands were now settled and its industrial complex essentially completed. Progress, henceforth, was to be achieved, not through the moving back of new frontiers, but through the wise husbanding and just distribution of the now limited national resources. This depression-born pessimism was generally shared by both friends and foes of the New Deal until they gained sudden new insights into the economic potentiality of the nation in the course of mobilizing the economy for World War II.

It had also been true that World War I had altered the nation's conception of its capabilities, and for the New Deal the precedents arising out of World War I proved of greater practical value in the battle for recovery than did those inherited from the prosperous

Progresive period. The New Deal attacked the Depression much in the manner of a nation-at-arms attacking an enemy. The National Industrial Recovery Act, initially the basic recovery program, was a vast scheme for government-directed industrial cooperation, developed somewhat along the lines of the War Industries Board of World War I. It was headed by Hugh S. Johnson, who had gained experience in the WIB as assistant to Bernard Baruch. Similarly George Peek's wartime experiences in mobilizing agricultural resources were made use of when he was placed at the head of the Agricultural Adjustment Administration.

The Tennessee Valley Authority had had its origins during the war in the dams constructed at Muscle Shoals, Tennessee, to furnish power for government industry. The Civilian Conservation Corps was operated on a semimilitary basis with assistance from the Army. Governmentally supervised labor arbitration had first been instituted during the war. The war had provided the precedent for the tax policy of the New Deal and, more important than that, for the efficacy and practicality of deficit spending. "Where we spent millions before the war," the English economist John Maynard Keynes had declared, "we have now learnt that we can spend hundreds of millions and apparently not suffer for it." Roosevelt never took an entire liking either to Keynes or to Keynesian economics, but deficit financing nevertheless became the main strategy in the war against the Depression.

As a social movement, the New Deal was in striking contrast to Protestant, middle-class, moralistic Progressivism. When Theodore Roosevelt invited the Negro leader Booker T. Washington to the White House, his "lily white" following, in the North as well as the South, protested so loudly that he was persuaded not to do such a thing again, and when Wilson appointed the Jew Louis Brandeis to the Supreme Court it was accounted a remarkable act of political bravery. By contrast Jews and Catholics provided the New Deal with leadership as well as with rank and file support, and Negroes became an object of concern, at least, to the government for the first time since Reconstruction. To this change the immigration restriction laws of the twenties had contributed much by converting the recent immigrants from the vanguard of an invading horde to a part of an exclusive community of Americans.

The moral certitudes of Progressives were largely discarded by New Dealers, many of whom shared the anticlerical outlook which

had been fostered in the twenties by the fight against fundamental-
ism and even more by the fight against prohibition. Roosevelt in his
speeches retained much of the moralistic and even Biblical tone of
the earlier age, but at the same time he cheerfully and openly accepted such unrespectable support as the Kelly-Nash machine in
Chicago and the Hague machine in Jersey City, where this support
advanced the interests of his party and his program.

Intellectuals, meanwhile, were welcomed unashamedly into the
administration and given seats of power from which they were able
to frustrate again and again the most modest designs of the
machine politicians who had engineered the victory. F. D. R. was
much less intellectual in his interests than had been T. R., Taft,
Wilson, or Hoover, but much more than even Wilson he provided
a leadership which won the loyalty of intellectuals and a government which gave them authority. During his terms as Governor of
New York he had acquired the services of a "brain trust," recruited
heavily from Columbia University, which he brought with him to
Washington.

A number of these brain trusters passed from the scene within
a few years, to be replaced, to an extent, by a new circle associated
with Harvard Law School and with Supreme Court Justice Felix
Frankfurter. The remarkably intellectual and apolitical character of
the administration remained however. The chief party political
boss, Postmaster James A. Farley, despite his enormous political
skills, found himself continually balked in his attempts to strengthen
the party machinery through distribution of the patronage.

No President in the nation's history was the superior of F.D.R.
in political skill, and it is not to be supposed that he under-
estimated the need for party machinery or party patronage. In
1932 he had demonstrated something of his political skill in knit-
ting together the badly split Democratic party. He remained somewhat distrustful of the machine politicians, however, and beyond
that he was aware that as long as the party remained an alliance
between Northern city bosses and Southern Democrats it would
remain a minority party. By shifting authority to political in-
dependents like Ickes and like Henry Wallace he helped to broaden
the appeal of the party, and in this he was assisted by the stand-
pat Republicanism of the opposition. By the time of the election of
1936, the Democratic party had transformed itself once again into
the party of the American majority.

III

F.D.R. took office in the midst of a banking crisis which was paralyzing the economy. Bank holidays had been declared, temporarily closing the banks in almost half the states, and Roosevelt at once closed all of the rest of them for a four-day period, and an emergency session of Congress passed the Emergency Banking Act legalizing the President's action and providing for the process whereby the sound banks would be reopened. Roosevelt delivered the first of his "fireside chats" over the radio, reassuring the nation of the soundness of the banks. Within the course of the next month most of the banks were reopened, and the crisis was over. The Glass-Stegall Banking act was passed instituting various reforms in banking procedures, including the creation of the Federal Deposit Insurance Corporation, insuring bank deposits. In 1935 the Banking Act gave the Federal Reserve Board power to regulate interest rates. The key to the victory, however, had been that first fireside chat by which, as Walter Lippmann wrote, "the nation, which had lost confidence in everything and everybody, has regained confidence in the government and in itself."

Currency manipulation accompanied the banking legislation in an effort to achieve the old Greenback and Populist aim of managed inflation. The President was empowered to issue 3 billion dollars worth of greenbacks. He was further authorized to reduce the gold content of the dollar up to 50 per cent and to provide for the unlimited coinage of gold and silver at whatever ratio he chose. Then, to win support of the silver bloc, Congress was obliged to add legislation enforcing government purchase of the national silver production at set rates, a monetarily meaningless addition to the existing currency legislation, which thereafter cost the nation about 100 million dollars annually. As it turned out, the currency reforms disappointed the expectations of everybody but silver interests by having no appreciable effect on the commodity prices, which, it had been assumed, would be forced up.

Government control over the New York Stock Exchange was extended through the Securities Act and the Securities Exchange Act, creating the Securities and Exchange Commission to regulate securities and insuring that information was published concerning the nature of the securities and of the corporations they represented. Later acts extended the authority of the commission, notably the Public Utility Holding Company Act of 1935, which placed holding companies under its supervision.

Relief from starvation for the 12 to 14 million unemployed and their dependents was, with the banking crisis, an obviously urgent matter when the new President took office. Congress established the Federal Emergency Relief Administration, whose director, the New York social worker Harry Hopkins, laid down the principles upon which relief would thereafter be administered. Hopkins determined that work would be performed for relief money. The principle was thereafter followed in the various relief programs, including the Civilian Conservation Corps, the Civil Works Administration, the Public Works Administration, and the Works Progress Administration.

The CCC, which provided conservation work for younger men—healthful and obviously useful work which was noncompetitive with private enterprise—escaped much of the criticism directed against other relief programs. The PWA provided big business with profitable contracts for heavy construction of such things as bridges, dams, and public buildings, in addition to providing work for the unemployed, and was therefore not looked upon as an unmixed evil by the business community.

The "make work" projects of the WPA, such as the raking of leaves and the digging of unneeded ditches, drew the heaviest fire from administration critics and introduced the word "boondoggling" into the language. WPA was probably the most controversial single measure of the whole New Deal. A poll of public opinion taken at the close of the Depression asked what had been the best thing and also what had been the worst thing that the New Deal had done, and the WPA received the highest number of votes in both categories.

The main hope for recovery from the Depression centered at the outset in the National Recovery Administration. Under the NRA businesses in each major industry were invited to draw up codes of fair trade, including the fixing of prices and production quotas, which, if approved by the government, would be permitted to regulate the industry in violation of the antitrust laws. As part of these codes, business was obliged to accept agreements concerning wages and working conditions which would be acceptable to labor, and it was obliged to guarantee labor the right of collective bargaining. Both management and labor would thereby receive the order and security necessary to advance them together into prosperity.

Initially the NRA probably had wider support in administration circles than any other enactment, but it soon proved to be the most disastrous failure among the New Deal enterprises. Labor, which at first had welcomed the act, soon found that loopholes existed in Section 7a which was to secure labor's collective bargaining rights. Price-fixing agreements resulted in an abrupt rise in the cost of living without a corresponding increase in the private incomes of consumers, and this naturally met with a howl of public outrage. Business was the chief beneficiary, but smaller businesses, if they were to cooperate, were obliged to operate under codes which had been drawn up by the major businesses in the field and which naturally tended to favor themselves against the smaller ones.

At the same time there were leaders of big business, most conspicuously Henry Ford, who simply refused to go along, and when this happened there was nothing to be done. Hoover's trade associational movement of the twenties had been the main forerunner of NRA, but to Hoover this new movement, because it involved a degree of government coercion, was un-American and totalitarian. The codes themselves were hastily drawn up and were officially approved by overworked government administrators, who were often in a poor position to judge the codes on their merits.

The successful operation of NRA required strong public support, and when this began to fall away adherence to the codes could not be enforced. The act had become an albatross around the neck of the administration, when, in 1935, it was invalidated by the Supreme Court and swept out of existence. Thereafter Congress passed various acts salvaging aspects of the NRA which had proved beneficial to small business and to labor.

Nowhere in the economy was the paradox of poverty amid plenty more dramatically evident than on the commercial farms of the nation, producing rich surpluses which were left rotting for the lack of a profitable market. Farm foreclosures followed upon the failure of the Agricultural Marketing Act. Foreclosures were in turn resisted by emergency state laws and by mob violence. Rural America was in a revolutionary mood when Roosevelt came to office, and Congress hurried to pass the Agriculture Adjustment Act. The one major novelty of the AAA was its provision for maintaining high prices through the controlled restriction of production. Farmers were to be paid to limit their output, the payments to be financed by excise taxes imposed upon food processors.

The eventual aim of the program was to raise farm prices to parity with those of the five good farm years preceding the outbreak of World War I. Seven commodities were initially placed under this program—cotton, wheat, field corn, hogs, rice, tobacco, and dairy products—to which a number of others were later added. The government, in addition, encouraged marketing agreements between farmers and processors and distributors whereby prices were raised and production limited in the case of numbers of other farm commodities.

The AAA got off to a spectacularly bad beginning in the opinion of the undernourished nation by the slaughtering of millions of pigs and by the plowing under of millions of acres of cotton. Once the programs were in operation, however, and scarcity was achieved simply through enforced limitations, public acceptance was won with the argument that the programs were doing no more for the farmer than industrial combinations had long been doing for themselves. More controversial was the question as to the effectiveness of the programs in maintaining high prices. In the case of tobacco and cotton it was evidently successful, aided by punitive taxes upon surplus production; in the case of wheat and corn it apparently was not. The bad weather conditions of the mid-thirties, however, imposed effective limitations on crops where the AAA failed to do so, and farm prices rose precipitously during the next three years.

The AAA assisted mainly the politically powerful farming minority which specialized in commercial crops. It largely ignored the subsistence farmer and severely injured tenant farmers and sharecroppers, who were moved off the land withdrawn from production. Various additional programs were therefore devised to alleviate the miserable conditions of the five million noncommercial farmers. Loan agencies and resettlement programs offered some assistance, as did the various relief agencies. These programs received continued opposition from landlords, however, and were never remotely equal to the problems they faced.

Loftiest in motivation among the programs of rural reforms was the Tennessee Valley Authority, established in 1933 to operate and extend the government power facilities at Muscle Shoals. Under its original chairman, Arthur E. Morgan, it was conceived of, not as simply a public power project, but as an idealistic social experiment. Society in the Tennessee Valley, which included areas from seven states, was to be comprehensively enriched through government aid and government planning.

Morgan faced the opposition of colleagues on TVA, notably David Lilienthal, who distrusted programs of comprehensive utopian dictation and who saw the need to fight vigorously against the private power companies, if TVA was to maintain itself. In a three-way struggle between Morgan, Lilienthal, and Wendell Willkie of the Commonwealth and Southern utilities holding company, Lilienthal emerged victorious. On the one hand TVA became a more aggressive producer of public power; on the other hand it moderated its social programs, deferring to the interests of the more prosperous farmers of the region.

Organized labor, reduced since the war from 12 per cent to 6 per cent of the national work force, moved hopefully in 1933 to take advantage of Section 7a of the NRA, guaranteeing its right to bargain collectively. Against these unions the employer organizations mobilized to defend the American Way, which they had fashioned so successfully during the twenties. In Minneapolis a clash between the Teamsters Union and the Citizens Alliance paralyzed the city, killing four and wounding many more. In San Francisco the struggle of the International Longshoremen's Association against the Industrial Association killed two and wounded many, before broadening into a general strike. In Toledo, National Guardsmen killed two and wounded many in the course of strikes.

In each of these cases union demands were generally met. Elsewhere, however, Section 7a, indifferently supported by the government and little implemented by the AFL, proved generally ineffective. In 1934 the National Labor Relations Board was created independently of NRA but with no power to enforce its opinion. F.D.R., while he thought of himself as a friend of labor, did not see the need for a powerful labor movement. His views were those of the Progressive era, which thought the rights of labor should be protected rather by governmental supervision than by independent labor action. The AFL under William Green, meanwhile, took a view that was hardly more militant than F.D.R.'s.

The dramatic change, both in administration policy and in the fortunes of organized labor, was, in its beginnings, very largely the work of one man, Senator Robert Wagner of New York. With little support and considerable opposition from administration officials, Wagner in 1935 introduced into Congress a bill to secure the collective bargaining provisions of Section 7a. The resulting National Labor Relations Act gave the bargaining representative of a majority of workers the right to represent all workers. It gave the National Labor Relations Board the right to supervise labor elections, and it placed limits upon the power of the employer to coerce his employees. There remained the bitter struggle to enforce acceptance of the Wagner Act by employers. Nevertheless it proved to be the great single turning point in the whole history of organized labor.

William Green had spoken wistfully of organizing 25 million workers, but since he, in common with most of the AFL leadership, fought any developments which would disturb the old craft relationships, little was accomplished. In the AFL convention of 1934 a compromise with the advocates of industrial unions was arrived at which actually left the old craft unions in undisturbed authority. In 1935, however, the break came. Led by John L. Lewis of the United Mine Workers, the industrial unionists formed the Committee for Industrial Organization—later the Congress of Industrial Organizations—which, in 1936, began to organize the steel industry in defiance of AFL.

In 1937 militant tactics such as the "sit-down strike" brought U.S. Steel, General Motors, and Chrysler Corporation to terms. Bloody fighting continued elsewhere in the steel and automotive industries throughout the rest of the thirties, while AFL and CIO remained bitterly divided. Nevertheless the new age of governmental support and labor militancy brought to the labor union movement a position of power within the nation which could hardly have been conceived of by labor leaders in former times. By 1941 total union membership had risen to 10.5 million, more than three times the membership at the outset of the New Deal.

IV

The Second New Deal The New Deal in 1934 was endorsed by hugely impressive victories in the congressional elections, but in 1935, as the administration approached another presidential election, resurgent social discontent threatened to raise up third parties which might wreck the Democratic chances for victory. Although business had been perhaps the chief beneficiary of the New Deal, it had already gone into angry opposition to "that man in the White House." Lower middle-class and mudsill America had failed to receive major consideration, and leaders were rising up to organize this massive discontent. In California the Socialist Upton Sinclair had captured the Democratic nomination for governor in 1934 and had nearly won the election on a thoroughly radical EPIC program of End Poverty in California. His fellow Californian, Dr. Francis E. Townsend, advocating old-age pensions of $200 a month, was gaining a fervent following among the old people of the country. In Detroit a Catholic priest, Father Charles E. Coughlin, built up an enormous radio following with his demand for an end to capitalism and a victory for his National Union for Social Justice. Increasingly a spokesman for racism and the corporate state, Coughlin, an early Roosevelt supporter, determined in 1936 to pit his own popularity against that of the President.

Most ominous of all was Senator Huey Long of Louisiana, whose Share the Wealth program appeared to be winning national support from unnumbered millions of voters. As Governor of Louisiana, with the support of the dirt farmers against the corrupt and entrenched vested interests, Long had gained a mastery over the state which he maintained through an extensive—and graft-ridden—public improvements program, on the one hand, and terrorism and police control on the other. Moving to the United States Senate, Long set out to nationalize his authoritarian system.

Never very explicit as to the details of the Share the Wealth program, the "Kingfish," as Long liked to call himself, promised a general redistribution of the wealth and a "homestead allowance" of at least $5,000 for every American family. He attracted Townsendites with promises of old-age pensions of an indeterminate amount. Ably assisted by the spellbinder Gerald L. K. Smith, Long moved, in 1935, to organize a party of the nation's discontented which he predicted would sweep the country.

The Marxist left, by contrast, offered the New Deal little competition. The Socialist party under the ministerial Norman Thomas had lost much of the appeal which it had enjoyed under Eugene Debs. Nor was the Communist party under Earl Browder, which had won only one quarter of 1 per cent of the popular vote in 1932, to be taken seriously as a political threat. Despite its success in acquiring the allegiance of a cluster of intellectuals, in broadening its support through Communist front organizations, and in infiltrating the government and the labor movement, the party was hopelessly incapable of presenting itself as an American political force. The threat to the New Deal was from native political radicalism.

While angry masses were rising up against the New Deal, the Supreme Court was coldly cutting it apart. Early in 1935 the Court declared the Railroad Retirement Act and the Frazier-Lemke Act, for the relief of farm mortgagors, unconstitutional and then, in a unanimous decision, went on to invalidate the entire NRA. In the Schecter Poultry Corporation case the Court found the NRA to entail both an unconstitutional delegation of authority by Congress to the President and an unconstitutional extension of Federal authority under the commerce clause of the Constitution. The Court decisions were so broadly and in some respects vaguely worded, furthermore, as to threaten other major New Deal programs, such as the AAA, which was, in fact, declared unconstitutional a year later in the case of United States v. Butler, et al., and the TVA, which the Court, as it turned out, upheld.

Roosevelt, in the face of these defeats, seemed, both to the public and to members of his administration, to have lost the power of leadership which he had until then so forcefully asserted, and as Roosevelt waited, administration officials argued heatedly among themselves. The main dispute was between those like Hugh S. Johnson of the NRA, who wished to seek new means to establish Federal control over the economy, and those like the "brain truster" Rexford G. Tugwell, who wished to strike out on new courses. By late spring of 1935, however, F.D.R. had regained the initiative and the government was launched upon the so-called second New Deal.

This second New Deal made itself the champion of the people and the enemy of privilege in a series of enactments, chief of which were the Wagner Labor Relations Act, the Social Security Act, the Wealth Tax Act, and the Public Utility Holding Company Act. Together this legislation broke the attempted New Deal alliance with big business and transformed the New Deal for the first time clearly into the champion of organized labor, of the aged and the unemployed, and generally of what Roosevelt called the "one-third of the nation ill-housed, ill-clad, and ill-nourished."

At the same time it shifted the orientation of the New Deal from the new nationalism of government control to the new freedom of enforced competition combined with enforced social justice. This shift was accompanied by a marked shift in government personnel.

With the Wealth Tax Act the income tax was employed for the first time, not simply as a revenue-producing measure, but as a social instrument, narrowing the gap between the extremes of wealth and poverty. The tax on the largest incomes was placed at 75 per cent, while corporate taxes reached an unprecedented height. The Public Utility Holding Company Act struck at the corporate device whereby a holding company, by controlling the stock in ostensibly competing businesses, could operate them in a monopolistic manner. Any holding company which could not demonstrate its economic value to the nation was to be dissolved. The Banking Act, in the meantime, increased Federal authority over the Federal Reserve system.

But it was the Social Security Act, more than any other, which cut the ground out from under the hopeful demagogues. In co-operation with the state governments it provided for unemployment insurance, pensions, and assistance to widows, dependent children, the blind, and the disabled. More, perhaps, than any other single New Deal enactment it marked a break with past Federal policy. On the state level such legislation had been attempted much less comprehensively. So far as the Federal government was concerned, however, it had been true, as Eleanor Roosevelt said, that "there was no recognition that the government owed an individual certain things as a right." Henceforth, she added, it would be accepted "that the government has an obligation to guard the rights of an individual so carefully that he never reaches a point at which he needs charity." It was during the 1935 congressional session that the WPA was created.

In the presidential campaign of 1936 everything went Roosevelt's way. Men of great wealth organized the Liberty League against him and, in a lavishly financed campaign, dramatized their own greedy and reactionary aims. The Republican party drew up a platform which comprehensively repudiated the New Deal, and the convention went on to select as its candidate the Governor of Kansas, Alfred M. Landon, a former Bull Mooser, who, as he said, had cooperated with the New Deal to the best of his ability. By no means a compelling campaigner, he was obliged to direct his fight against the party which, in many respects, more nearly expressed his convictions.

There remained the third-party threat. In the highly competent opinion of James Farley, a third party with Huey Long as its candidate would poll six million votes, despite the legislative enactments of the second New Deal. Then, in the fall of 1935, Long was assassinated, and his supporters fell to quarreling among themselves over the succession. As it turned out, William Lemke of North Dakota was chosen by the Union, Royal Oak, Third Party, National Union for Social Justice, and Independent parties. In the election Lemke gathered in less than 2 per cent of the vote. The Communists in their turn lost ground, while the Socialist votes declined by four-fifths. Roosevelt's was a massive victory, which brought every state but Maine and Vermont into the Democratic column and piled up overwhelming Democratic majorities in both houses of Congress. The second New Deal had received a mandate, it appeared, which gave Roosevelt an unprecedented popular authority to press for further reforms.

The event proved that the New Deal had largely played itself out. There were a few new enactments of reforms, it is true. A new housing act was passed authorizing long-term loans for the purpose of slum clearance. Tenant farmers received protective legislation, and a new food and drug act increased the power of the Food and Drug Administration. In only one area, however, was significant new ground broken: in the Fair Labor Standards Act, instituting minimum wages for many classifications of workers employed by firms engaged in interstate commerce. Passed in 1938, the act initially established a minimum of 25 cents an hour, which has periodically been increased since then. A year later Roosevelt, himself, announced the end of the New Deal, declaring that "We have now passed the period of internal conflict in the launching of our program of social reform."

The very magnitude of the 1936 victory apparently had weakened Roosevelt in his control over Congress by giving members a confidence in their political strength which emboldened them to oppose their popular leader. It was also true that in 1937 Roosevelt did not have the patronage at his disposal, which the change in administrations had given him in 1933. The election was followed by the recession of 1937, which served to cast discredit on the recovery and reform programs and to discourage their extension. As had been the case with previous depressions the President was forced to temporize with those who directed the nation's businesses. On the other hand, bad as they were, economic conditions in 1937 were by no means as desperate as they had been four years earlier, while political conditions were incomparably more stable. Most basically, perhaps, many who had been frightened into supporting changes in 1933 were no longer frightened.

And in 1937 Roosevelt committed the greatest political error of his career, when, with his "court-packing" scheme, he gave to his miscellaneous opponents a moral issue around which they could unite against him. Faced with the sweeping invalidation of New Deal legislation by the Supreme Court, he presented to Congress a measure authorizing him to appoint an additional judge to the bench for each of the existing six judges who were seventy years of age or older. The proposal was met with howls of outraged reverence for the highest Court in the land, and a number of former New Deal supporters joined in its defeat and made it the occasion to go over to the opposition. Roosevelt was able to claim a victory in the fight, even though the bill was overwhelmingly defeated, for the Court thereafter consistently upheld New Deal legislation. Beyond that, all but two of the justices retired during Roosevelt's second administration, to be replaced mainly by New Dealers. Meanwhile a conservative coalition in Congress had once again achieved its dominion.

By then a moderate revolution had taken place which permanently altered the character of American society and its government. The protected status under the government, which formerly had been limited largely to business, was extended to agriculture, labor, and to those in the nation who were not equipped to provide for themselves. The main outlines of capitalism were little disturbed, but the duty of the government to control capitalism in the public interest was for the first time clearly established. Nor, in retrospect, does the cost seem to have been unreasonably great, although to many contemporaries it seemed prohibitive. The national debt doubled, but so also did the national income, and New Deal spending came to be dwarfed, under the pressure of war and cold war, by the spending of subsequent Democratic and Republican administrations.

The most telling criticism of the New Deal has been that it failed in the main task of lifting the nation out of the Depression.

On the eve of World War II there remained nearly nine million unemployed, as compared with perhaps thirteen or fourteen million at the time of Roosevelt's first election. It was only when the war contracts began to come in that the Depression really lifted. This criticism is the more damaging when America is compared with the other industrial nations of the world, all of which were emerging from the Depression by the mid-thirties (all of them aided earlier than was the United States, however, by large military expenditures).

The great achievement of the New Deal, in the view of contemporaries throughout the Western World, was the maintenance and strengthening of the democratic process under the most challenging conditions the nation had suffered since the Civil War. Roosevelt's victory in 1936 was greeted throughout the democracies of Europe as a victory for themselves. "You have made yourself," John Maynard Keynes had written Roosevelt early in his first administration, "the trustee for those in every country who seek to mend the evils of our condition by reasoned experiment within the framework of the existing social system. If you fail, rational choice will be gravely prejudiced throughout the world, leaving orthodoxy and revolution to fight it out." The success of the New Deal in this was a truly worldwide triumph in what Roosevelt himself spoke of as "a war for the survival of democracy."

BIBLIOGRAPHY FOR CHAPTER THIRTEEN

J. K. Galbraith, *The Great Crash, 1929* (1954) is a straightforward history of the coming of the Depression by a witty and literate economist. It is a breezy account which, while presenting an admirably clear analysis of its subject, tends to treat the Depression rather puckishly as the well-deserved pratfall of the American Babbitt. That it was more than that is documented to the hilt in D. A. Shannon, ed., *The Great Depression* (1960). Memory being blessedly what it is, the stark miseries of the Depression are nearly impossible to recapture, but something of the extent of the nation's suffering is seen in Shannon's collection of newspaper and magazine articles and official reports.

W. E. Leuchtenburg, *Franklin Delano Roosevelt and the New Deal, 1932–1940* (1963) is a political account which manages well the extremely difficult feat of moving chronologically through this period. A considerably briefer account is Dexter

Perkins, *The New Age of Franklin Roosevelt, 1932–45* (1957), "a useful introduction to the Roosevelt era for those general readers who do not remember it." A. M. Schlesinger, Jr., *The Coming of the New Deal* (1959) is "concerned chiefly with the domestic aspects of the New Deal in 1933 and 1934 . . . a first-rate piece of historical writing, centering upon the President but skillfully developing the main themes topically." Schlesinger's subsequent volume, *The Politics of Upheaval* (1960), equally well written, carries the story through the election of 1936. It is especially good on "the theology of dissent," the splinter parties, and protest movements spawned by the Depression.

The New Deal produced a large literature of political reminiscences, of which the following are in paperback: Eleanor Roosevelt, *This I Remember* (1949), R. E. Sherwood, ed., *Roosevelt and Hopkins* (rev. ed. 1950) and John Gunther, *Roosevelt in Retrospect* (1950). For the writings of F.D.R. himself see Basil Rauch, ed., *F. D. Roosevelt, Speeches, Messages, Press Conferences and Letters.* David Lilienthal, *Big Business* (1953), and T. W. Arnold in the ingenious, amusing, and persuasive *The Folklore of Capitalism* (1937) present the thinking of two leading New Deal intellectuals of the neo-new freedom school of thought. Samuel Lubell, *The Future of American Politics* (1952) is a stimulating speculation on main changes in the course of American politics. F. L. Allen, *Since Yesterday* (1940) is a readable social history of the Depression, which, however, falls short of the mark of its predecessor.

GLOBAL WAR 14

I

Origins of World War II   In September, 1931, the Japanese invaded Manchuria. In March, 1935, Nazi Germany formally denounced the disarmament provisions of the Treaty of Versailles and increased its military forces. That September Fascist Italy invaded Ethiopia. In July, 1936, civil war broke out in Spain, the insurgents receiving support from Italy and Germany; the loyalists, from Communist Russia. In March, 1938, Germany annexed Austria. Seven months later, following the Munich agreement among the leaders of Germany, England, France, and Italy, Germany annexed the Sudetenland of Czechoslavakia, opening up that country to subsequent German occupation. In September, 1939, Germany invaded Poland.

World War II in Europe and the Pacific.

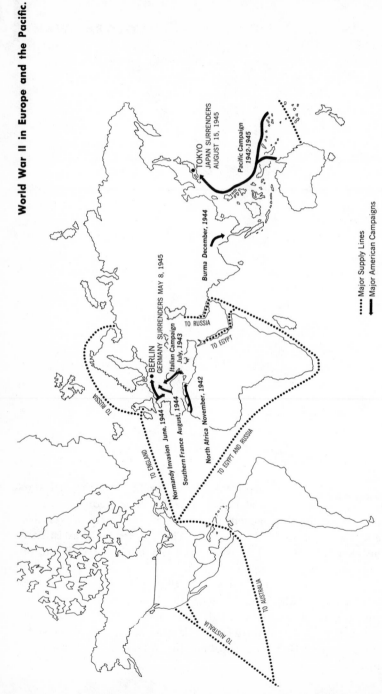

TOKYO

JAPAN SURRENDERS
AUGUST 15, 1945

Pacific Campaign
1942-1945

Burma December, 1944

TO RUSSIA

BERLIN
GERMANY SURRENDERS MAY 8, 1945

Italian Campaign
July, 1943

TO EGYPT

TO RUSSIA

Normandy Invasion June, 1944

Southern France August, 1944

North Africa November, 1942

TO ENGLAND

TO EGYPT AND RUSSIA

TO AUSTRALIA

TO AUSTRALIA

⋯⋯⋯ Major Supply Lines
⟶ Major American Campaigns

There followed in the West six months of inactive "phony war." Then, within the space of a few weeks, in the spring of 1940, the German blitzkrieg demolished all opposition on the continent. Remnants of the British and French armies escaped from Dunkerque in France, leaving their war materiel in the grasp of the all-conquering Nazis. After Dunkerque a militarily defeated, almost unarmed England remained alone against the apparently unbeatable Nazi war machine, defended from invasion only by the battered Royal Air Force. In June, 1941, the German armies invaded Russia, moving swiftly and at will into the Russian heartland. These were the events which increasingly borrowed the attention of the American people from the internal war they were waging against the Great Depression.

American foreign policy during the early years of the New Deal appeared to most Americans to have achieved no less than the final fulfillment of the century-old Monroe Doctrine. So far as its relations with Europe were concerned, America had never been stronger in its determination to stand apart. For the first time in American history, Congress passed neutrality legislation giving legal force to this isolationist sentiment. Toward Latin America, in the meantime, the United States was fashioning a "Good Neighbor" policy to make the protection of the Western Hemisphere a Pan-American, rather than a unilateral, responsibility.

The Good Neighbor policy had been faintly prefigured in Wilson's willingness to submit the Mexican-American controversy to arbitration in the hands of Argentina, Brazil, and Chile. Its main development, however, took place during the Coolidge and Hoover administrations. In the mid-twenties the United States was administering the finances of ten Latin-American nations, fighting a popular uprising in Nicaragua, and quarrelling with Mexico over expropriated American oil lands. Then in 1927 Coolidge named Dwight Morrow ambassador to Mexico; Morrow and the Mexicans became courteous toward each other, and, for the time at least, the disputes over the oil lands were settled. Hoover made a highly successful goodwill tour of Latin America, and during his administration the declaration was made that "The Monroe Doctrine was a declaration of the United States versus Europe—not of the United States versus Latin America."

The Roosevelt administration went beyond this to sign a convention, denying to itself the right to intervene in the affairs of other American nations. Accordingly American troops were withdrawn from Haiti, and the Platt Amendment, which had given the United States the right to intervene in Cuban affairs, was revoked. The good American intentions were severely tested in 1938 by the Mexican expropriation of American oil lands. Following more than three years of dispute, the American oil companies were offered but a fraction of the value of their properties, and, under pressure from the American government, they accepted.

In 1934 the Reciprocal Trade Agreements Act was passed authorizing the government to negotiate bilateral agreements with other nations, reducing tariffs up to 50 per cent. These arrangements were not limited to Latin America, but they were concentrated in that area. In some Latin-American countries—notably Argentina, where the economy was thoroughly competitive with that of the United States—nothing was accomplished. Elsewhere inter-American trade increased, and Latin-American nations came to look upon the United States as their means for emerging from the Depression. The substantial success of the Good Neighbor policy was demonstrated during World War II, when all American nations declared war on Germany and Japan, including eventually even Argentina.

Toward Europe, despite the Reciprocal Agreements Act, the New Deal policy was fundamentally one of economic isolation. It had been the view of Hoover that economic recovery was to be achieved largely through a stimulation of world trade and through the improvement of conditions abroad. To Roosevelt, on the contrary, the Depression was a domestic condition, best treated in isolation from disturbing world conditions. In this he received the strong support of a nation, indignant over the failure of its former allies to repay the debts incurred during World War I.

The debtors had argued that the American tariff kept out European goods and deprived Europe of the dollars with which to make their American payments. It remained true that the Allies were demanding reparations payments from Germany, which in turn were made possible by private American loans to Germany. Faced with the threatened loss of these loans as well, Hoover in 1931 had proposed a one-year moratorium on all intergovernmental debts. He had further agreed to send representatives to the London Economic Conference in 1933 to seek international agreements on a wide variety of economic matters.

To Roosevelt, however, the objective of international stabilization of currency conflicted with the New Deal program of managed currency. He therefore cabled his refusal to cooperate in this and so effectively disabled the conference. His action was met with protests from many American economists but with the general endorsement of the nation.

It was in this atmosphere of bitter distrust of Europe that a Senate investigating committee under Gerald P. Nye of North Dakota subjected to hostile scrutiny the vast wartime profits of bankers and munitions makers. It was the conclusion of the committee that these bankers had exerted powerful, perhaps decisive, influence to bring America into the war in order to protect their loans to the Allies. No evidence was produced to indicate that the Wilson administration had been affected by any such pressure. The conviction was nevertheless quite general among the American people that in entering the war, America had been duped by its bankers and that in the settlement of the peace it had been swindled by the wily diplomats of Europe.

In 1934 Congress passed a bill prohibiting private loans to defaulting nations—which was to say all of America's former Allies with the exception of Finland. Then in 1935, to prevent the recurrence of the neutral rights controversy which had preceded World War I, Congress passed the Neutrality Act, imposing an embargo of arms shipments upon all nations at war and charging American citizens to travel on belligerent vessels only at their own risk. Roosevelt signed the bill, although he would have preferred the embargo to have been limited to aggressors. A year later the neutrality legislation was reenacted in a stronger form.

Mussolini's conquest of Ethiopia in 1935 and Hitler's reoccupation of the Rhineland in 1936 strengthened isolationist convictions in the United States by demonstrating the impotence of the League of Nations. When Francisco Franco's Falangists rose up against the republican government in Spain, the United States joined England and France in denying aid to the government. On the other hand, when in 1937 Japan invaded China, Roosevelt refrained from invoking the Neutrality Act, in order that the Chinese might continue to receive American supplies. When in Chicago in 1937 Roosevelt very vaguely called upon the peace-loving nations of the world to "quarantine the aggressors," the hostile reaction in the nation deterred him from anything which would alarm isolationist sentiment further.

Japan and Italy were but lightly regarded in America as international threats. Germany, however, was a different matter. With the conquest of Austria and Czechoslovakia in 1938 the American mood commenced to change, and when the invasion of Poland brought England and France into war with Germany in September, 1939, the edifice of isolationism crumbled. A Gallup poll found 69 per cent of the American people favoring all aid to Britain and France, short of war. Against bitter opposition in the Senate the neutrality legislation was revised to permit the cash sale of arms to the allies.

The American mood nevertheless remained relatively complaisant, if partisan, following the swift fall of ramshackle Poland, a catastrophe which had been looked upon as a foregone conclusion. During the months of "phony war" which followed, Americans, confident in an eventual Allied victory, were distracted by the Russian invasion of Finland.

Then in the spring of 1940 the Nazis struck with a lightning speed which few had conceived of, through Norway and Denmark, Belgium and Holland and France. Within weeks the conquest of France and the defeat of the French and British armies was accomplished. Pinned to the English Channel at Dunkerque, the British and much of the French armies escaped, with heavy losses, to England, leaving their machinery of war on the beaches behind them. A week later Mussolini breathlessly brought Italy into the war, barely in time to precede the French armistice.

As the presidential campaign of 1940 approached, the American nation was in the throes of shocked, angry, and confused debate. There remained the hardcore isolationists, declining in number but highly financed and widely supported in the American press, notably in the Hearst newspapers. Isolationists organized the America First Committee to convince Americans that they had no stake in the conflict, and that, even if they did, they could not possibly win a war against Germany in Europe. Against the America Firsters, others, advocating all aid short of war, organized the Committee to Defend America by Aiding the Allies. In addition there were some who wished to commit American troops to the conflict, but down to the bombing of Pearl Harbor this represented a small minority of public opinion. American policy continued to be confused by the wishful thought that somehow an Allied victory could be achieved without American intervention.

That the Democratic nomination would go to Roosevelt was a

foregone conclusion by the time of the convention, despite sentiment against a third term. Roosevelt attempted to remove foreign policy from the campaign so far as possible by appointing Republicans to his Cabinet: Henry L. Stimson as Secretary of War and Frank Knox as Secretary of the Navy. At the same time he risked his popularity by giving Britain fifty overage American destroyers in exchange for ninety-nine-year leases on British naval bases in America.

It was in the Republican party that isolationist sentiment was strongest, and there the nomination was won by an internationalist, Wendell Willkie, a public utilities businessman who had gained his reputation fighting the TVA. Both Roosevelt and Willkie promised all aid to the Allies short of war, but the isolationist vote went predominantly to Willkie and the internationalist to Roosevelt, who won by a margin of five million votes.

As the German air force pounded Britain and while an invasion fleet stood in readiness to cross the channel, Roosevelt moved to bring aid more effectively to the English. In March, 1941, the "Lend-Lease" bill was passed authorizing the President to "sell, transfer title, exchange, lease, lend, or otherwise dispose of" materials to "any country whose defense the President deems vital to the defense of the United States." An initial seven billion dollars was appropriated for the purpose. In April, 1941, America assumed responsibility for the protection of Greenland and began patrolling the sea-lanes to that point in the name of hemispheric defense. Then, when German submarines sank American vessels, Congress in November authorized trade with belligerent ports and the arming of American merchant vessels.

In June, 1941, Hitler attacked Russia, and in November Roosevelt extended lend-lease aid to the Russians. Already directly involved in the conflict, America awaited momentarily the outbreak of formal war with Germany and Italy, when, in December, war came to the country from Asia.

With the outbreak of war in Europe, Japan had acted at once to gain advantages in the Southeast Asian possessions of foreign powers. The United States answered by giving notice that it was going to suspend its commercial treaty with Japan, vitally necessary to the Japanese in view of their lack of essential raw materials for war. Japan's answer was the forming of the Rome-Berlin-Tokyo Pact, pointedly directed against the United States. The United

States replied in turn by placing an embargo upon shipments to Japan of aviation gasoline, scrap iron, and steel.

In the spring of 1941 protracted negotiations with the Japanese were undertaken, beginning and ending with mutually irreconcilable terms. In July, 1941, Japan assumed authority over all of French Indo-China. Japanese assets in the United States were thereupon frozen. In November the Japanese made an unacceptable offer which the American government knew, from decoded Japanese messages, was their last one. An attack on American territory was not expected, but warnings were nevertheless sent to the Pacific commanders. The event proved that the warnings were not strong enough, and also that, such as they were, they were followed out negligently by the military and naval commanders in Hawaii and elsewhere. The result was the disaster of Pearl Harbor on December 7, which left the United States for the moment virtually defenseless in the Pacific, although it at once unified the nation in the war effort. On December 11, Germany and Italy followed Japan into war with the United States, as America mobilized to enter the conflict.

II

World War II   At the time the United States entered the war, a German invasion fleet was poised against Britain along the English Channel. The German armies, hundreds of miles inside Russia, fought at the gates of Leningrad to the north, Moscow at the center, and Stalingrad to the south. The German Wehrmacht continued to inflict prodigious casualties on the Red Army, and few in the West thought that Russia would hold out long. To the south, Germany ruled the Mediterranean, holding Italy and French North Africa in contemptuous control. Everywhere the German blitzkrieg tactics, based upon mechanization and air power, quickly annihilated opposition. It seemed to some of the best-informed Americans that Germany was invincible against all possible military combinations.

Britain, it was true, had withstood invasion through the exertions of the Royal Air Force, and the British Navy dominated the seas—but only on the surface of the seas. German submarines, more deadly by far than those of World War I, were to be hunted down by fleets of British and American destroyers far less adequate to the task than those of the earlier war. The German U-boats, busy along the American coastline as well as the British, were sinking merchant vessels more rapidly than they could be replaced by combined British and American construction.

In the Far East the disaster at Pearl Harbor had crippled America's Asiatic fleet and for the time being had reduced it to a strength far inferior to that of the Japanese. Militarily the American Army was hopeless to make more than a token resistance against the Japanese, who captured Wake Island and Guam immediately. The Philippine Islands were overrun at once, although American forces at Bataan continued to hold out for five months. In the meantime virtually all of Southeast Asia had fallen to Japanese forces, and the invasion of Australia was expected at any moment. Japan possessed one-sixth of the earth's surface and one-quarter of its population, and at the time no force existed which could challenge its control.

In relation to its military potential, the United States came but lightly armed into this global death struggle. Even at that, however, it was far better prepared than it had ever been at the beginning of any of its previous wars. Naval construction had been pressed by Roosevelt during the Depression partly as a recovery measure. Nor did the Pearl Harbor attack destroy this fleet; for much of the damage was rapidly repaired. Furthermore a massive naval construction program was in process, although more than a year would pass before the substantial effects of it would be felt. Japanese knowledge of this impending naval expansion had been a motive in hurrying the Japanese into war with the United States.

Congress in 1940 had passed the Selective Service Act, the first peacetime draft in American history, and at the time of Pearl Harbor a million and a half Americans were in the Army. The expansion from a standing army of 200,000 had taken place so rapidly, however, that effective fighting units had not yet been created. Basic military equipment was not yet available, and the leadership was, of course, inexperienced. Time, it was evident, would be needed to prepare for large-scale land engagements. The Navy was in a position to make its force felt earlier, supported by a rapidly augmenting air power.

And the longer the war lasted, the better were the American prospects; for the United States had never before entered a war in potentially so fit a condition. The national divisions, ethnic and ideological, which had disturbed the home front in 1917 were largely absent in 1941 with the coming of Pearl Harbor. More important than that, World War II was a kind of war which the United States was incomparably well-equipped to wage. The blitz-krieg war of mobility and firepower had astonished the world when Hitler unleashed it against Britain and France, but compared to the war machine created by America during the next two years, the Wehrmacht was a rather primitive and horse-drawn affair. Nothing in the world compared with Detroit as the production center for the new war machinery. Roosevelt's call, in 1940, for 50,000 airplanes a year was dismissed by business leaders as hopelessly unrealistic, but by the close of the war, planes were being produced at twice that rate, and war production generally was advancing on a similarly gigantic scale. Nor was this productivity at the expense of quality. American military equipment proved generally superior to that of the enemy. This was markedly true in the case of American airplanes.

Roosevelt brought to the task of mobilization both the American experience in World War I and its experience in fighting the Depression. As in the case of both of these experiences, numerous, confusing and conflicting agencies were created and reorganized and combined and superseded during the war, none of them being permitted by Roosevelt to lessen his authority as Commander in Chief and President. The War Production Board was created which assumed the main task of mobilizing industry, allocating materials, supervising conversion to wartime manufacture, and developing new, government-operated industries such as the synthetic rubber industry. Organized labor signed no-strike pledges and received favored treatment through the War Labor Board, which gave it the power to organize the newly developing wartime industries. A War Manpower Commission worked to redistribute labor to areas where the new industries were developing.

Congress, as in the case of previous wars, chose to finance the war largely through loans, only about 40 per cent being raised in taxes. In the meantime enormous profits were made in business, and a rapid rise in wages occurred. The Office of Price Administration was created, which placed price ceilings upon many consumer goods fairly effectively. Agriculture rapidly increased production, despite the wartime decline in farm population. Cost of the war was 350 billion dollars, or ten times that of World War I. Those who had warned that the doubling of the national debt to 48 bil-

lion dollars during the New Deal would be an intolerable burden
to the next generation saw the debt increase by an additional 200
billion dollars during the war.

World War I had been marked by widespread violations of civil
liberties, and the fact of this was in the mind of the Roosevelt
administration in the course of World War II. It was also true
that there were fewer incitements to the suppression of liberties,
since sentiment for the enemy was less widespread. On the score
of civil liberties, therefore, the record was better than that of any
other American war, with the one glaring exception of the Japa-
nese-Americans in California. Despite the fact that Japanese-
Americans in Hawaii, left to themselves, proved loyal to their
nation, and despite the fact of heroic contributions to the European
war made by Japanese-American troops, those on the West Coast
were moved from their homes to concentration camps (pronounced
"relocation centers") for the duration.

At the outset the British and American forces were united under
a single command into the Combined Chiefs of Staff, the Americans dominating its councils by virtue of the greater American
military contribution. Those among its members who mainly determined the strategy of the war were the American Chief of Staff,
Gen. George C. Marshall, and the American Chief of Naval operations, Adm. Ernest J. King. The then almost unknown Dwight D.
Eisenhower was selected by Marshall as Supreme Commander of
the European theater of operations, while Douglas MacArthur
commanded the military forces in Asia. Never before had the
United States entered a war under a military leadership as capable
as this one. One of the advantages which the United States enjoyed over both Germany and Japan was this superiority of its
military leadership.

From the outset it was agreed that Europe rather than Asia
would be the main theater of combat, since Germany was more
powerful than Japan and likely, if given time, to develop rocket
missiles and atomic weapons which would give it world mastery.
The American Army required another year to ready itself for a
major land engagement, however, and, in the meantime, American
force made itself felt mainly through naval actions in Asiatic
waters.

Two main objectives lay immediately before the Japanese in
1942: the conquest of Australia and the immobilization of the
Hawaiian Islands through the capture of Midway Island. In May

the first of these objectives was made impossible by the Battle of Coral Sea in the area of New Guinea. In June the second of these objectives was denied them when the Japanese were routed at the Battle of Midway with tremendous losses in pilots, airplanes, and aircraft carriers. These two battles, the first of their kind in the history of warfare, were fought out by airplanes between fleets out of sight of each other. This new form of naval warfare between aircraft carriers had had to be learned hastily, when it was found that the old reliance, the battleship, was all but helpless against air attack.

In August the United States followed up its advantage with an attack upon Guadalcanal Island, east of New Guinea, and from that point until the end of the war against Japan it continued to maintain the offensive.

In Europe, during the first year, the American forces remained primarily in a state of preparation. The Royal Air Force already had gained the advantage of the German Luftwaffe, and it hammered at continental industrial areas in massive night raids. In October, 1942, the American Air Force launched its first large-scale raid; unlike the British force it flew during daytime, depending for protection upon the heavy armor and armaments of its four-engine bombers. Then winter set in, and the heavy raids were not resumed until May of the next year. By then the United States had assumed the major burden, and by the end of the war it had rained a greater volume of destruction upon Germany than had England, even from the beginning of the Battle of Britain.

In November, 1942, American and British forces landed at Casablanca, Oran, and Algiers to crush the German Afrika Korps eastward against the British forces driving west from Egypt. After inauspicious beginnings, the battle surged back and forth across the desert until in May, 1943, the German forces were destroyed at Bizerte in Tunisia. The attack on Sicily, and then Italy, followed immediately upon the North African victory. Within a month Sicily was cleared of the Germans and in September Italy surrendered, proceeding thereupon to declare war upon Germany. In September, 1943, American troops landed at Salerno, and there followed the long, slow, discouraging, and rather unenterprising, campaign up the mountainous Italian peninsula.

On June 6, 1944—D-Day—the allied forces launched their all-out attack upon the German Wehrmacht. The German high command, faced with massive engagements against Russian forces following the holocaustal defeat at Stalingrad, chose to concentrate their western troops in the coastal cities, leaving the beaches relatively lightly guarded. It was upon the beaches of Normandy that the Allies, for that reason, landed, constructing their own harbors as they came, despite fearfully adverse weather conditions. Fighting from field to field through French hedgerows, the American Army captured the communications center of St. Lo in July and then unleashed a blitzkrieg the like of which the Germans had never achieved at the peak of their performance. Refusal of Hitler to withdraw his armies resulted in their substantial destruction, as the American Army drove northward to connect with the British and create the Falaise Pocket.

In August an American army invaded southern France, and within a month France was virtually cleared of the Germans, while Russian armies moved swiftly westward. The war was far from over, however. Retreating behind the fortified Siegfried Line, the Germans stalled the Anglo-American advance, and then, in December, in a desperate gamble which almost naid off, they launched the first German winter offensive since .ne day of Frederick the Great. Driving through the Ardennes Forest, in the Battle of the Bulge, they appeared for a time to be in a position to capture vast allied supplies of food and war materials and then to overrun France. Their attack stalled when they failed to capture the communications center of Bastogne, surrounded by them but defended successfully mainly by American paratroopers.

The final rout followed. In March, 1945, the Americans had the luck to capture a bridge across the Rhine River at Remagen, and during the following months, British and Americans swarmed eastward to make contact with the Russians. Hitler ordered the Germans to raze Germany and fight to the last man, but Hitler's death was announced on May 1, and on May 7 the commander of the German army signed an unconditional surrender.

In the Asiatic theater in November, 1942, American naval forces engaged the Japanese South Pacific Fleet in the area of the Solomon Islands. At stake was the island of Guadalcanal, but the Japanese lost much more than this. In a three-day naval battle their fleet was destroyed as an effective unit. Never again did the Japanese navy willingly oppose the American one. America held the initiative in Asian water and retained it from that time until the end of the war.

The task of undertaking an almost endless series of island engagements was lightened by the strategy of island-hopping toward Japan, capturing key positions and leaving intervening islands to wait out the war. It was a strategy which had been made possible by the winning of naval and air supremacy. Accordingly, in November, 1943, the Marines invaded Bougainville, the northernmost island in the Solomon chain. In February, 1944, Kwajalein, in the Marshall Island group, was taken. Saipan in the Marianas fell in June, and Guam was retaken a month later. The conquest of Guam was accompanied by a sea battle which wrecked much of a new Japanese navy, completely rebuilt since the disasters of 1942.

Up until that point in the war the island-hopping had been carried out by the Navy and the Marines, the Army under MacArthur concentrating on the reduction of the enemy forces in New Guinea. In October, 1944, the Army and Navy combined in the invasion of the Philippine Islands. The Battle of Leyte Gulf, the greatest naval battle in history, completed the destruction of the Japanese navy and prepared the way for the Army to invade the island of Leyte. In February, 1945, the Army won control of the main island of Luzon, while the Marines landed on Iwo Jima, on the direct route to Tokyo. Okinawa was invaded in April, and preparations for the invasion of the Japanese homeland were under way when, on August 6, the first atomic bomb was exploded over Hiroshima. Three days later a second atomic bomb destroyed the city of Nagasaki, and the Japanese government began to negotiate a surrender. On September 2, 1945, the terms of surrender were signed, and World War II was at an end, at a cost to America of more than one million casualties and 325,000 deaths.

Of the world's major nations, the United States suffered by far the least from the war. By contrast, the cost to Russia was about 20 million casualties. By the close of the war there were more than twelve and one-half million Americans in uniform, but, again, proportionately American men participated in the war on a smaller scale than those of any other major power involved. Where Germany maintained three hundred divisions, the United States created one hundred, despite its much larger population. The reason for placing these limits upon the American military force was to leave free a sufficient work force to create in the United States the "arsenal of democracy."

Man for man, however, the American soldiers and sailors undoubtedly counted for more than those of any other nation. The enemy infantryman, both Japanese and German, was far better trained than the American one, but in a war which depended upon fire power and mobility, the American was far more effective. Furthermore, although the Germans had devised the new form of warfare, their generals never grasped the full meaning of it as did the American high command. The high commands of both Germany and Japan continued to misplace their main reliance upon the foot soldier, in a war which had become first of all a logistical problem.

It was also true that in organization and orderly cooperation the democratic countries demonstrated a great superiority over the dictatorships. On the one hand, in Germany, the Nazi war machine was characterized by confusion, duplication, and often incredible mismanagement, directed overall by an irresponsible paranoid. On the other hand, in Japan, the war machine was rigidly directed by the top admirals and generals down to tactical details. When battles went amiss, the generals on the divisional level had no authority to alter their plans. To make matters worse, the Japanese code of military honor prohibited those in the chain of command from passing along the news of dishonorable defeats. As a consequence, the rigid authoritarians who were directing the war were often systematically misinformed by those serving underneath them.

In a war which depended so much upon scientific enterprise, the democracies had the decisive advantage. They gained enormously from the refugee scientists who had escaped to America and England from Germany, Italy, and Hungary. Beyond that they provided a climate conducive to scientific inquiry. Nazi Germany possessed its own abundance of brilliant scientists, but, as events proved, they were fatally mismanaged. At the outset of the war, German scientists were at least as advanced as those of any other nation in atomic science. They might well have created an atomic bomb in time to have won the war, but the ultimate decision rested with Hitler, and Hitler diverted the energies of the scientists to rocket warfare, resulting in the murderous but militarily indecisive "buzz bombs."

And finally the greater value which the democracies placed upon human life turned out to be an advantage rather than a disadvantage, militarily. The troops were better cared for, generally speaking, and proved to be correspondingly better fighters. This was a major factor especially against the Japanese, who often were defeated by malaria and beriberi before they came in contact with the enemy. In large measure, those democratic qualities which were despised as weaknesses by the overlords of Japan and Germany provided the conditions under which the United States converted itself into incomparably the greatest military power in the history of the world.

III

Peace Settlement Determined not to repeat the errors of Wilson, F.D.R. began to work out the terms of the peace even before the United States entered the war. In August, 1941, he met with Churchill on an American battleship to draw up an Atlantic Charter, outlining the principles which should underlie the postwar world: self-determination, self-government, international economic cooperation, disarmament, and a "permanent system of general security." Thereafter Roosevelt and Churchill, despite their disagreements, cooperated cordially, both in the conduct of the war and in planning for the peace. Russia, on the other hand, declined the offer to unite militarily, and Stalin remained suspicious and often resentful of the leaders of the democracies.

In January, 1943, Roosevelt and Churchill met again at Casablanca and worked out the main strategy to be followed in the immediate future. In August, 1943, they met at Quebec to plan the forthcoming invasion of Europe and the campaign in the Far East. In October, 1943, Secretary of State Hull met with the Foreign Ministers of England and Russia in Moscow to discuss the terms of settlement so far as Germany was concerned. At the Moscow meeting the ministers united in a declaration of the intention to create an international organization to keep the peace. In November, 1943, Roosevelt and Churchill met with Generalissimo Chiang Kai-shek at Cairo to discuss the war in Asia.

In December, 1943, at Teheran the first of the conferences was held in which Roosevelt and Churchill were joined by Stalin. There the three leaders discussed the coming second front, and Stalin agreed to enter the war against Japan following the defeat of Germany. In the course of those meetings the most basic difference of opinion to develop between Roosevelt and Churchill turned upon the question of the Second Front, Roosevelt favoring the channel crossing and Churchill favoring an attack on the "soft underbelly" of Europe, the Balkans.

In part this difference of opinion was based upon military considerations. As an Englishman, Churchill tended to think in naval terms, and the allied naval superiority would have counted for much in such an invasion. Roosevelt, on the other hand, appreciated better than Churchill, perhaps, the unparalleled productivity of the American arsenal. The Normandy invasion involved logistical problems which only the United States could have coped with. Churchill remained somewhat dubious about the channel venture, and some leading British military leaders continued to oppose it actively down to D-Day itself. Except for Eisenhower's fixed determination, D-Day would probably have been delayed and perhaps abandoned altogether.

Aside from military considerations, Roosevelt's and Churchill's differences were founded upon conflicting views as to the nature of the war and the character of the Russian ally. To Roosevelt and to the American people, the purpose in fighting the war was to win it in as short a time and at as small a cost as possible. Furthermore, F.D.R. felt that he was getting along well with Stalin and that at the conclusion of hostilities the Big Three would be able to work out terms of peace agreeable to all. Churchill did not share Roosevelt's optimism so far as Stalin was concerned, and he wished to pursue a strategy which would strengthen the Anglo-American position against Russia at the war's end. This the attack in the Balkans would obviously do, by leaving Central Europe in Anglo-American rather than Russian hands. England was the junior partner in the common war effort, however, and Roosevelt's views, and those of his generals, prevailed.

In February, 1945, with Germany moving rapidly to defeat, the Big Three met at Yalta and further worked out the terms by which Europe would be reconstructed. Germany was to pay reparations as directed by a reparations commission. The Polish boundaries were fixed, and Stalin agreed to the establishment of a Polish government based upon free elections.

Stalin promised "broadly representative governments" throughout Central Europe generally. Marshal Tito's government in Yugoslavia was recognized. The structure of the United Nations was agreed upon. Beyond these publicly announced decisions, the Big Three arrived at a secret agreement. Russia would declare war on Japan following the defeat of Germany, and, in exchange, the Western Allies would recognize the independence of Communist-dominated Outer Mongolia, and Russia would regain the Asiatic possessions and rights lost to Japan in the Russo-Japanese war of 1904 to 1905 and additional islands as well.

Later, when the cold war set in, the Yalta Agreement received harsh criticism in America as a betrayal of America's Chinese allies, as well as a betrayal of the peoples of Eastern Europe. Indeed the eastern settlement specifically violated promises which Roosevelt and Churchill had made to Chiang Kai-shek at Cairo. Indignation was the greater for the fact that the atomic bomb rendered Russian aid of vastly less importance to the United States. At the time of Yalta, however, the bomb had not yet been tested, and nobody knew whether or not it would ever work. It was further true that Roosevelt's advisers overestimated the Japanese determination to continue the war at all costs. Roosevelt was naturally influenced by the enormous estimated American casualties which an invasion of Japan would have entailed, when, in fact, Japan probably would have surrendered without either an invasion or an atomic attack, although not on the same terms.

But the strongest defense of the Yalta Agreement is the argument that Roosevelt and Churchill surrendered nothing to Stalin which Stalin could not have taken just as well without their consent. Russian arms either were or would soon be in possession of the territories involved, and Russian control could be contested only at the cost of a third world war, which would have been politically supportable nowhere in the West. It was also true, however, that the Red Army was permitted to penetrate farther west in the final days of the war than purely military considerations dictated. Had they wished to do so, the Western Powers might easily have won the race to Berlin.

In April, 1945, delegates from fifty nations met in San Francisco to draft the Charter of the United Nations Organization, which had been drawn up mainly during a conference in 1944 at Dumbarton Oaks, near Washington, D.C. The UN was a mainly American conception, just as the League of Nations had been before it, and the final draft was a primarily American document.

Stalin would have preferred to dispense with such a league and manage international affairs through conferences of the great powers. He agreed at Yalta to join such an organization only when it was decided—at least according to the Russian interpretation of the agreement—that each of the great powers, with permanent seats in the Security Council, should be able to veto the discussion, even, of all matters which might require the use of force. At San Francisco the Americans for a time threatened to withdraw from the UN if the veto on procedural questions were retained, as it of course was; yet it is not to be supposed that the American people would have accepted the UN for long if the United States had not had the veto power.

The UN Charter established a two-house legislature: the Security Council of eleven members, including five permanent and six temporary members, and the General Assembly, in which all member nations would be represented with one vote, except for Russia who received three. The General Assembly would discuss questions and make recommendations to the Security Council. The Security Council held the authority to make the actual decisions. To the UN were added a number of additional organizations, including the International Labor Organization and the United Nations Educational, Scientific, and Cultural Organization (UNESCO).

Throughout the long course of these drawn-out negotiations, Roosevelt, again remembering Wilson's difficulties, had worked in constant consultation with leaders in the Republican party. He had brought prominent Republicans into his Cabinet as Secretaries of War and Navy. Following his victory over Willkie in 1940, he had sent Willkie to England as his special representative. To the American delegation at San Francisco he had appointed Republican Senator Arthur H. Vandenberg of Michigan and the former Republican Governor of Minnesota, Harold E. Stassen.

When the United Nations Charter came before the Senate the administration received its reward for this solicitude. Where the Covenant of the League of Nations had been defeated after eight months of acrimonious debate, the Charter of the UN was approved within the week by a vote of 89 to 2. In 1946 the UN took up permanent headquarters in New York City. The United States had taken up its responsibilities as a world leader. It had as yet hardly the faintest inkling of what those responsibilities would entail.

IV

The Truman Administration It was not to be supposed that the unified war effort would result in the suspension of what politicians scornfully refer to as "politics." In 1940 the Republicans, officially accepting the New Deal at last in their party platform, had cut Roosevelt's margin of victory by half, and hope was in sight for victory in 1944; for "that man in the White House" would surely not run for a fourth term. To conservatives the war had presented itself as the opportunity to vanquish the New Deal at last; while to liberals it had presented itself as the opportunity to promote further economic reforms at home, during so vast an enlargement of Federal power, and beyond that, to carry their missionary work to the world.

From the first the conservatives had the best of it. The war brought the business community back into power at once; while military defeats and highly publicized episodes of military mismanagement gave the Republicans their first good political issue since the coming of the Depression. In the congressional elections of 1942, consequently, the Republican party made gains in both houses of Congress.

Congress had grown conservative even before Pearl Harbor, and throughout the war the congressional coalition of Republicans and Southern Democrats wrung concessions from Roosevelt in domestic matters, in exchange for its support of his war measures. Engrossed in the conduct of the war, Roosevelt no longer was able to concentrate upon national affairs, which, under any circumstances, would be bound to be shaped by the exigencies of war.

By the election year of 1944, however, final military victory seemed almost in sight, and "Dr. Win-the-War," as Roosevelt had referred to himself, automatically won the nomination for the fourth term. Having already broken the traditional two-term limitation for the Presidency, Roosevelt, in his campaign, was little threatened by the fourth-term issue. More serious was the issue of his advancing age and very apparent decline in health. There seemed every likelihood of his failing to survive a fourth term, and one result of this possibility was an unusually vigorous struggle in the convention over the nomination of a vice presidential candidate.

In 1940, against the wishes of conservative Democrats, Roosevelt had named as his running mate Secretary of Agriculture Henry Wallace. During the war Wallace had spoken for the wing of New Deal missionaries, who, their enemies complained, wished to deliver "a quart of milk for every Hottentot." Out of the struggle between the supporters of Wallace and those of James F. Byrnes of South Carolina there emerged a compromise candidate, Senator Harry S. Truman of Missouri, a relatively little-known figure, who, however, had gained some national recognition for his able chairmanship of the Senate war investigating committee.

Against Roosevelt the Republicans nominated Governor Thomas E. Dewey of New York, who had gained his main national reputa-

tion as the nation's leading gang-buster. Dewey's youth and vigor
was an added advantage in a campaign against the careworn President. Roosevelt, however, threw himself into the campaign in a
remarkable display of vitality which brought him his fourth victory
by the margin of 3.6 million votes. Thereafter Roosevelt's physical
condition visibly worsened. Awaiting the San Francisco United Nations meeting in April, 1945, he was stricken by a cerebral hem-
orrhage and died immediately.

For the third time in the nation's history the Commander in
Chief had been struck down at the moment of victory. When Truman came to office the American Armies, pouring into Germany,
had reached the Elbe, while the Russians were at the gates of
Berlin. In Asia the invasion of Okinawa was under way. The San
Francisco Conference met two weeks later. Germany capitulated
within a month of Truman's taking office, and Japan followed three
months after that. Truman came to office with little special knowledge of what the administration was doing. He was not even aware
that an atomic bomb was in preparation, the use of which would
be up to his discretion. "Boys," he told reporters the next day, "if
you ever pray, pray for me now."

Rising in politics in the scandalously corrupt Pendergast machine
of Kansas City, Truman had remained scrupulously honest. He had,
at the same time, prepared himself thoroughly in the art of politics,
however little he was prepared, at the time of assuming office, to
meet the world-shattering problems which abruptly rushed in upon
him. As little self-confident upon taking office, as any President in
the nation's history, he grasped his authority forcefully to make
some of the most momentous decisions in the nation's history.
Humble and cocky by turns, given to off-the-cuff blunders in small
matters and masterful achievements in large ones, he was a ward
politician who enlarged himself into the saving statesman of Western civilization.

For the immediate future, at least, a course of American foreign
policy had largely been set when Truman came to office. In
domestic affairs nothing had really been planned. The resources of
the nation were geared to the task of invading Japan, and production for military purposes continued to increase. Then it all ended.
The nation danced in the streets on V-J Day and hurried to get
back to what President Harding after World War I had called
normalcy.

"Reconversion," as the process came to be called, was a vastly greater operation in 1945 than it had been in 1919. There were more than three times as many Americans in uniform and correspondingly greater government involvement in the economy. For the United States the war had endured three times as long. For millions of Americans it had been by no means an altogether unhappy experience. It had brought full employment, rapid wage increases, and exorbitant profits, despite wage and price controls. It had also, of course, brought severe shortages of consumer goods, and at war's end the American people had accumulated 140 billion dollars in savings. These were the spoils of war which the people had created for themselves, and the people demanded the peacetime conditions which would allow them to enjoy their gains.

As to the matter of how the new wealth should be shared, there were differences of opinion. The loudest cry was for demobilization, and the military forces were reduced from twelve and one-half million to one million almost immediately, a national disaster as General Marshall said at the time. President Truman fought to no avail for a program of universal military training, against the peace-minded nation. Wartime construction had been mostly government-financed, and most of this construction was convertible to civilian uses. Its transfer to private hands, at wonderful bargain prices, went on at headlong speed, from the sale of large aluminum factories down to the sale of canteens and leggings at war surplus stores. These pleasant developments proceeded swiftly against the futile opposition of organized labor and of liberal groups.

Naturally not all of the fruits of victory were so sweet. Despite price and wage controls, inflation had accompanied the war, and at war's end, with virtually unlimited money and not much to buy, inflation continued apace. With it came also the demand for an end to controls. Organized labor, far more numerous than before, prepared for a trial of strength; while businessmen and farmers demanded an end to price ceilings. Old New Dealers called for a new era of reform, while conservatives sought for opportunities to sweep away the remaining New Deal restrictions along with the wartime ones. Everyone recalled the parallel postwar period which had begun in 1919, some with horror and some with hope.

Truman, by his voting record in the Senate, was a convinced New Dealer, and, during his first year in office, he indicated his reformist views in a series of recommendations to Congress. He called for an increase in the minimum wage, a Fair Employment Practices Act to defend against racial discrimination, extension of public works, a Federal housing and slum-clearance program, Federal aid to education, and a Federal health insurance program. Amid the distractions of reconversion, however, he won little, except the increase of the minimum wage from 40 to 75 cents per hour and the Maximum Employment Act establishing the Council of Economic Advisers. In the area of price controls, meanwhile, he followed a wobbly course against determined Republican opposition and amid black market conditions. In the area of labor relations his policy appeared, if anything, even more inconsistent.

As in 1919, organized labor did not intend to submit to the freezing of wages. The United Automobile Workers led with a strike against General Motors for a 30 per cent wage increase, and they were quickly followed by the United Steel Workers and by unions in other industries. These demands generally received a good measure of support from the White House until April, 1946, when John L. Lewis took his coal miners out on strike in defiance of government recommendations. Then in May the threat of a strike by the Brotherhoods of Locomotive Engineers and of Railway Trainmen inspired an unprecedented counterattack by Truman. To avert the paralysis of a nationwide railroad strike, he went before Congress to ask for a law empowering him to draft railroad strikers. Agreement was immediately reached between unions and management, however, and the proposed legislation was dropped.

By the time of the congressional elections of 1946 Truman had alienated conservatives by his New Deal program and alienated liberals by his failure to pursue the program. Reconversion had absorbed ten million returned members of the armed forces with unlooked-for facility, but unemployment was now increasing, and the coming postwar depression was widely predicted. International affairs were beginning to wear an ominous look, and people were beginning to speak of the coming war with Russia. Inflation was rampant. The honeymoon, traditionally accorded an incoming President, had been a short one for Truman, who was mercilessly derided in the press. In 1946 the Republicans needed only the slogan, "Had enough?" to win control of both houses of Congress for the first time since the coming of the Depression.

The Seventy-ninth Congress had simply ignored Truman's program. The Eightieth one came aggressively forward with one of its own. Most of the remaining price controls were lifted; while government appropriations were slashed under the direction of the chairman of the House Appropriations Committee, John Taber, making good his promise to apply a "meat-axe to government frills." A new tax bill, reducing income taxes on the highest incomes by 65 per cent, and on the lowest by 3 per cent, was vetoed by Truman. Also vetoed by Truman, but passed again over his veto, was the Taft-Hartley Act, the most contentious enactment of the Eightieth Congress.

Defended as necessary to restore a fair balance between labor and management, which the Wagner Act was accused of destroying, the Taft-Hartley Act outlawed the closed shop—the exclusive hiring of union men—while permitting the union shop—where the employee, once hired, was obligated to join the union. It required a "cooling-off" period, following the announced intention of a strike, before the strike could be held. It prohibited various practices such as jurisdictional strikes and secondary boycotts, and it extended certain new legal rights to employers in their dealings with the National Labor Relations Board. The act did not break the labor unions, as was widely predicted at the time, but it did return them solidly to the Democratic ranks. Having thus unequivocally declared themselves, the Republicans renominated the moderately liberal Governor Thomas E. Dewey of New York and moved confidently toward a presidential victory in 1948.

The postwar trend toward conservatism alone seemed sufficient to secure a Republican victory. It also appeared to be true that President Truman was wrecking the great Democratic coalition which his predecessor had created, simultaneously driving away Northern liberals and Southern conservatives. Truman won the nomination against the bitter opposition of many party leaders, who were convinced the party could not win with him. Beyond that he faced the opposition of two new parties, which would draw their support mainly from Democratic ranks: the Wallace Progressives and the Dixiecrats. Henry A. Wallace, dismissed from Truman's Cabinet for his loudly spoken soft line toward Russia, headed a party which was made up of discontented New Dealers and other critics of Truman's hard policy toward the Communists. The Dixiecrats, on the other hand, alienated by the demands for Negro equality on the part of Truman and of the Democratic platform, organized behind Governor J. Strom Thurmond of South Carolina as the States' Rights Democratic Party.

Absolutely assured of victory by the public opinion polls, Dewey campaigned mildly on the issue of the need for unity, in order to arouse as few antagonisms as possible against his coming administration. Truman, for his part, largely ignored his opponent, who differed with him little on either foreign or domestic policy. He turned his attack instead on the Republican Eightieth Congress, in a "whistle-stop" campaign, covering more than 30,000 miles and delivering more than three hundred speeches.

Against this vulnerable Congress he successfully focused many of the same postwar discontents which had been directed against his own administration. The result was that with strong support from labor and Northern Negroes and from generally Republican, but momentarily unhappy, farmers he won by a margin of somewhat more than two million votes. The Dixiecrats, with somewhat more than a million votes, won in South Carolina, Alabama, Louisiana, and Mississippi. The Wallace Progressives, with an approximately equal popular vote, failed to win in any state. The Democrats regained control of both houses of Congress.

An enormous personal triumph for Truman, the election was a victory also for Franklin Roosevelt and the New Deal. Prior to the election it had been widely assumed that the American people were of a mind to accept a general conservative reform of existing New Deal legislation. Truman's victorious campaign on his "Fair Deal" platform, was as generally viewed as a fundamentally significant mandate at least for retaining the existing programs.

Leading from strength for the time, Truman set out vigorously to press for the broad range of legislation which Congress had until then largely ignored. No sooner had he returned to office, however, than international storms broke upon the American political scene, tangling and disfiguring domestic political issues and interfering with the processes of orderly, constitutional government. Fast upon Truman's reelection the nation moved suddenly and violently into the era of Joseph McCarthy, as in foreign affairs the nation moved from the successes of the Marshall Plan to the defeats of the Korean conflict.

V

The Cold War   At the time of Roosevelt's death, as Winston Churchill wrote, "Every question about the future was unsettled. . . . The agreements and understandings at Yalta, such as they were, had already been broken or brushed aside by the triumphant Kremlin. New perils, perhaps as terrible as those we had surmounted, loomed and glared upon the torn and harassed world." The period from Yalta in February, 1945, to Potsdam in July was the time of awakening for the American government— though not the American people—to some realization of the bitter meaning of the victory.

General Eisenhower had voiced the almost unanimous American view when, following a trip to Moscow, he had declared that "nothing guides Russian policy so much as a desire for friendship with the United States." Roosevelt was confident that the United States and Russia would get along very well indeed after the war, although his last days were darkened by the beginnings of doubt. Truman, on the contrary, suspected Stalin's intentions from the first, but he could bring himself to do no more than protest angrily against the Russian subjugation of Poland.

On the advice of Eisenhower and over the protests of Churchill, Truman voluntarily relinquished enormous bargaining power to Stalin by withdrawing American troops from the Elbe River, back more than one hundred miles to the American line agreed upon at Yalta. At Potsdam the Western Allies accepted the accomplished fact of the bloody and dictatorial Russian solution in Poland and arranged for the division of Germany into the four military zones. A Council of Foreign Ministers was created to conclude treaties with Germany's European allies, and Truman returned to America, determined to avoid such bleak summit conferences in the future.

In March, 1946, Winston Churchill snapped up the offer of the presumptuous president of little Westminster college in Fulton, Missouri, to deliver an address there, and he spoke his mind. "From Stettin in the Baltic to Trieste in the Adriatic, an iron curtain has descended across the Continent. . . . I do not believe that the Soviet Russia desires war. What they desire is the fruits of war and the indefinite expansion of their power and doctrines. . . . I am convinced that there is nothing they admire so much as strength, and there is nothing for which they have less respect than weakness, especially military weakness." He announced the cold war to an American people who were still far from willing to admit its existence.

In September, 1946, Henry Wallace, then Secretary of Commerce, delivered a speech implicitly denouncing the administration's foreign policy for its harshness toward Russia. "I realize," he declared, "that the danger of war is much less from communism than it is from imperialism." Secretary of State James F. Byrnes, negotiating with Russia in Paris at the time, threatened to resign immediately, and Wallace was dismissed from his Cabinet post. Two months after Wallace's speech the Republicans won control of both houses of Congress, and Senator Robert A. Taft, the nation's most powerful isolationist, became the leader of the Senate.

At this critical moment in world affairs, when America was moving reluctantly into the cold war, Senator Arthur M. Vandenberg of Michigan emerged as the key figure in American, and therefore world, diplomacy. The leading presidential candidate of the Republican isolationists in 1940, Vandenberg had gradually abandoned the old certitudes under the impact of the war. In 1945 he finally declared his new position in a Senate speech. " . . . I do not believe that any nation hereafter can immunize itself by its own exclusive action. . . . I want maximum American cooperation." It was the notorious Eightieth Congress, dominated by former isolationist diehards, which legislated America into the cold war, and it was preeminently the political skill and reputation of Vandenberg which made this possible.

In February, 1947, the British government sent a note informing the American government that Great Britain was no longer capable of maintaining its support of the Greek government. Unless the United States took Britain's place, the note continued, Greece would no doubt become Communist, Turkey would come under Russian control, and the whole of the Middle East might be swept into the Russian orbit. That the United States must act, despite hostile public opinion, was agreed upon by Truman, Vandenberg, and the new Secretary of State, Gen. George C. Marshall. Truman took Vandenberg's advice "to make a personal appearance before Congress and scare hell out of the country." There he declared what became known as the Truman doctrine "that it must be the policy of the United States to support free peoples who are resisting attempted subjugation by armed minorities or by outside pressures." He asked for, and received, 400 million dollars to aid Greece and Turkey. A century and a quarter after Monroe stated his isolationist doctrine the United States finally officially turned its back on the historic policy.

But even worse news was coming from Western Europe, which, in Churchill's words, had become a "rubble-heap, a charnel house, a breeding-ground of pestilence and hate." Communism was fanning out through Western Europe, threatening to capture the

governments of France and Italy. Against this threatened catastrophe, General Marshall, in June, 1947, announced the momentous
forthcoming American action in a commencement address at Harvard. The nations of Europe, Communist and non-Communist,
were to draw up their own program of recovery. The United
States, if it approved the program, would underwrite it to the extent of billions of dollars.

Western Europe went to work at once. Indeed British Foreign
Minister Ernest Bevin leaped out of bed at the news to put his
department staff to work. "This is the turning point," he told
them. Within the month representatives of the nations of Western
Europe were assembled in Paris to draw up the plan. Soviet
Russia, meanwhile, had made the whole thing politically possible,
so far as the United States was concerned, by prohibiting Communist nations from participating. The resulting Marshall Plan,
or Economic Recovery Program, following nominal congressional
modifications, received overwhelming endorsement from Congress.

Again Vandenberg was the key figure in the administration victory, and he was aided by the organization of private committees
throughout the country, stirring up national sentiment in favor
of Marshall aid. Most helpful of all was Stalin. In the midst of the
congressional debate Soviet Russia overthrew the democratic
Czechoslovakian government and placed that country behind the
Iron Curtain. When the roll was called in the Senate, even Taft
voted in favor of the program. All told, the program cost 13 billion
dollars, much less than had been anticipated. Altogether, however,
the United States in the first decade after the war spent 50 billion dollars in foreign aid of all kinds.

In June, 1948, the American, British, and French governments
announced the unification of their three sectors of occupation in
Germany into an independent united West German government
with membership in the Economic Recovery Program. Russia retaliated by ordering the Western Allies out of Berlin and sealing
off access to the city. The United States and Britain countered
with the airlift, which for almost a year flew in sufficient supplies
to support a population of more than two million.

In April, 1949, the North Atlantic Treaty Organization was
created, joining the United States to the nations of western Europe
in a military alliance and creating a unified international military
force under the supreme command of General Eisenhower. Militarily weak by comparison to the Red Army, the forces of NATO

possessed the great equalizer, the atomic bomb. Russia shattered this basis for confidence five months later with a successful atomic explosion of its own. In the meantime, the main pressures of communism had shifted dramatically from the West to the Far East.

Americans had traditionally felt a missionary concern for the Far East, which was in contrast to their isolationist rejection of Europe. This sentiment had been especially strong among the Midwestern isolationists, who during the war had opposed the policy of concentrating the main military effort in the European theater. In response to this "China First" sentiment Roosevelt, throughout the war, had insisted upon what Churchill called the "absolute farce" of treating Chiang Kai-shek's Nationalist China as a major power. Politically and militarily weak, the Chinese Nationalists at the conclusion of hostilities were faced with the threat from a growing army of Chinese Communists. American attempts to reconcile the two forces were fruitless, and in 1947 all-out civil war erupted.

The American-supplied Nationalists proved powerless against the more dedicated Communists. Following a year of successive victories the Communists overran all of China by the end of 1949, driving Chiang and the Nationalists to the island of Formosa. Its Far Eastern ally thus overwhelmingly defeated, the United States did what it could to redress the balance of power in Asia, as in Europe, by turning to its former enemy. In 1949 it reversed its policy of breaking up the industrial combinations in Japan, and in 1950 it began to negotiate a peace treaty, which was ratified two years later by the United States Senate. By that time events in the Far East were driving America toward a military alliance with a reluctantly rearming Japan.

During the last frantic days of the war, with the Russians hurrying—two days before victory—to win the spoils of victory in Asia, the United States agreed that in Korea the Russians might have the honor of accepting the Japanese surrender in the northern half, as far south as the 38th parallel. Once in control of the richest area of the nation, the Russians created a Communist government of North Korea and thereafter naturally refused to consider unification except on their own terms. Faced with this accomplished fact, the United States, after assisting in the establishment of the government of South Korea, withdrew its forces. One year later, in June, 1950, North Korea went on the attack.

The attack found the American military largely dismantled, and it took place in an area strategically most difficult for the United States to defend. The American government, indeed, had encouraged the attack by explicitly placing Korea outside the American defense perimeter. It remained true, however, that a Far Eastern repetition of the unopposed Communist conquest of Czechoslovakia would have been, for the United States, a diplomatic disaster throughout the world. With this in mind, President Truman summoned a meeting of the UN Security Council to act against North Korea, and he simultaneously ordered American naval and air forces into the conflict. The absence of the Soviet representative, in protest, from the Security Council enabled the United States to achieve UN authorization, without threat of Soviet veto, and made possible the creation of a United Nations army.

Placed under the command of General MacArthur, the UN forces, including contingents from various nations, were composed mainly of American and South Korean troops. Hopelessly unprepared at the outset, these were necessarily thrown to the slaughter in the opening weeks of the conflict, in order to slow the advance and maintain at least a foothold on the peninsula. This objective was successfully achieved in the securing of a fortified bridgehead around the port of Pusan. For five weeks the UN forces held, while reinforcements continued to arrive. Then, with a surprise amphibious attack at Inchon, north of the 38th parallel, UN forces snatched victory from apparent defeat almost overnight. Within a few days the capital city of Seoul was recaptured, and the harried North Korean army was fleeing for the border.

Faced with this swift reversal of fortune, the United Nations authorized pursuit into North Korea with the objective of creating a united democratic nation. This authorization was given in the face of Chinese Communist threats to intervene, and MacArthur eagerly implemented it. Moving rapidly northward, the UN army launched the attack late in November which was to bring the conflict to an immediate close. Two days later Communist China attacked with a force of 200,000 troops, overrunning the UN forces and recapturing Seoul. Then the UN forces held and moved slowly on the offensive. By the end of March, 1951, Seoul had been once again retaken, the opposing armies faced each other across approximately the original boundaries of North and South Korea, and Truman, with the United Nations, was prepared to negotiate for peace.

Truman was determined to negotiate, because for him the main theater of the cold war was Europe and not Asia. Culturally America was part of the European community, and militarily America had much more to hope for from allied, industrial Western Europe than from pro-Soviet, underdeveloped China. MacArthur, however, his long military career associated with the Far East, disagreed, and he went over the head of his Commander in Chief to make his point. In a letter to Joseph Martin, the Republican minority leader of the House of Representatives, he called for a full-scale attack on China, beginning with the bombing of bases within China. His argument that "There is no substitute for victory" struck a powerful chord with an American public baffled and outraged by the bloody and inconclusive struggle. It also struck a powerful chord with President Truman, who relieved MacArthur of his command and ordered him home.

MacArthur, upon his return to the United States, received a hero's welcome which made his trip to Washington a triumphal march. His sentimental "old soldiers never die" address to both houses of Congress highlighted the dramatic Korean issue, which remained to liven the presidential campaign of 1952. As a practical matter, however, Truman's decision had settled the issue. In June, 1951, Soviet Russia proposed a truce, and negotiations began shortly thereafter, although they were destined to drag on through the next two years. The result, when all was over, was a return to the original stalemate, at a cost to America of 157,000 casualties, including 53,000 dead. The gains were not as clearly apparent as the losses. They included, however, the return of the American nation to a position of military strength and the beginning of a general realization that in the cold war the finding of substitutes for total victories and unconditional surrenders were to become the continuing and never-ending national purpose in world affairs.

BIBLIOGRAPHY FOR CHAPTER FOURTEEN

F. R. Dulles, *America's Rise to World Power, 1898–1954* (1955) provides a clear general account and an appraisal of the literature on the subject. Selig Adler, *The Isolationist Impulse* (1957) covers the period from the outbreak of World War I to the date of writing. "The book is not only first-rate diplomatic history but intellectual history as well; it adds a kind of third dimension to the conventional diplomatic treatment." Herbert Feis, *The Road to Pearl Harbor* (1950) is "a remarkably clear and complete job of mapping for us every twist and turn. . . . Mr. Feis starts his recitation in 1937, but he makes it particularly full after April 1940 . . . he has written a book which should remain for some time the standard account. . . ."

Winston Churchill, *The Second World War*, 6 vols., (1948–1953) is the grand account of the conflict, filled with fascinating documentation and carried along by the famous Churchillian prose. R. E. Sherwood, *Roosevelt and Hopkins* (1950) reveals the inner workings of America's wartime diplomacy. For an airing of the main controversy to arise out of this diplomacy, see R. P. Fenne, Jr., ed., *The Yalta Conference.* J. W. Spanier, *American Foreign Policy since World War II* (1960) is "a useful analysis . . . written largely within the context of the Truman-Acheson rationale of world affairs." E. O. Reischauer, *The United States and Japan* (rev. ed., 1962) is "historical writing at its best . . . an understandable analysis of Japanese character. . . . He thinks that our efforts at reform in Japan make communist theories seem old-fashioned and unimaginative by comparison. . . ."

Herbert Agar, *The Price of Power, America since 1945* (1957) is a vigorous, opinionated, and highly rewarding essay. "The apt phrase and caustic comment enliven [the] chronicle of growing maturity, painfully won. Eschewing any attempt to be all-inclusive [Agar] nevertheless creates a sharply lighted picture of a decade filled with tensions and ending in bitter disillusionment." While the emphasis in Agar's survey is on foreign policy, E. F. Goldman, *The Crucial Decade—and After, America, 1945–1960* (1961) concentrates more on the domestic scene. It is throughout "a dramatic, entertaining, and highly useful book. . . . Running through the volume are two major themes: whether the half-century of social and economic reform would be continued and whether we would abandon the traditional concept that there are quick, total solutions to foreign problems and instead accept containment and coexistence as continuing situations . . . told with vividness and insight."

I

The Age of McCarthy
During the first day of the Potsdam Conference, Secretary of War Stimson passed a note to Churchill: "Babies satisfactorily born." At Alamogordo, New Mexico the atomic bomb had been successfully exploded. Three weeks later a second bomb destroyed Hiroshima, killing and wounding more than 160,000. The Russians leaped into the war at once before the third bomb destroyed Nagasaki, and the war ended. The bomb had ended the war; the larger question which the explosions at once raised was whether the bomb would end the world. Although Britain and Canada had cooperated in its creation, the bomb was an American monopoly. What Anglo-

American International Alliances.

Legend:

A – Anzus Treaty
C – Republic of China Treaty
J – Japanese Treaty
K – Republic of Korea Treaty

N – North Atlantic Treaty
P – Philippine Treaty
R – Rio Treaty
S – Southeast Asia Treaty

CANADA N

UNITED STATES
A C J K N P R S

MEXICO R
GUATEMALA R
EL SALVADOR R
HONDURAS R
NICARAGUA R
COSTA RICA R
PANAMA R
ECUADOR R

DOMINICAN REPUBLIC R
HAITI R
COLUMBIA R
VENEZUELA R
PERU R
CHILE R
BOLIVIA R
ARGENTINA R
PARAGUAY R
URUGUAY R
BRAZIL R

GREENLAND N
ICELAND N
NORWAY N
DENMARK N
UNITED KINGDOM N
NETHERLANDS N
BELGIUM N
LUXEMBOURG N
WEST GERMANY N
FRANCE N
PORTUGAL N
ITALY N
GREECE N
TURKEY N
IRAN N

PAKISTAN S
EAST PAKISTAN S
THAILAND S

KOREA K
JAPAN J
TAIWAN C
PHILIPPINES P S

AUSTRALIA AS
NEW ZEALAND AS

American know-how made possible, however, would in time be possible for other nations.

The success of the atomic bomb opened the way for the far more devastating hydrogen bomb and ultimately—theoretically— for the cobalt bomb, a single one of which might be sufficient to destroy all life on earth. Impelled by the fear of absolute extinction, the American government in July, 1946, presented to the United Nations a plan for the universal control of atomic energy. The United States would relinquish its monopoly to the United Nations. It would destroy all existing bombs, and, in common with all other nations, it would submit to perpetual inspection by United Nations teams, to prevent the manufacture of any such weapon in the future. This act of prudent generosity was opposed by the Russians, who were hard at work on an atomic bomb of their own and who refused to submit to inspection.

That Russia would succeed eventually in creating an atomic bomb was assumed, but nobody in authority expected such a development in the near future. The United States rested in the confidence that with its monopoly of the bomb, it was militarily supreme. It reduced the army to below 600,000 men, which allowed it to cut taxes as well. Then in September, 1949, the Truman administration was obliged to inform the American people than an atomic explosion had taken place in Russia. In January, 1950, Truman ordered the Atomic Energy Commission to proceed with the development of a hydrogen bomb. In the meantime both nations busied themselves developing other revolutionary new war machinery, both of them aided by compliant former Nazi scientists, who were no longer permitted such employment in their own native country.

To those who found the news of the Russian bomb incredible an explanation was soon forthcoming. In February, 1949, the British government announced that Klaus Fuchs, an atomic scientist, had confessed to being a Russian spy. For four years, while engaging in atomic research for the British and American governments, Fuchs had forwarded to Russia all of the enormous information at his disposal. The announcement of his confession followed by two weeks the news of the conviction of Alger Hiss, on the grounds, technically of perjury, but actually of spying for Russia during the days of the New Deal.

Hiss, although never a prominent figure in government, had

held various positions of responsibility in the New Deal. At the time he was accused of spying he was serving as head of the august Carnegie Endowment for International Peace. These roles did much to associate him in the minds of Americans both with the idealism of the New Deal and with the more conservative idealism of corporate philanthropy. In appearance and in background he was the very model of the patrician Ivy Leaguer; yet he had been charged by Whittaker Chambers, a confessed former Soviet spy, with systematically forwarding secret information from the State Department to the Kremlin during the 1930s.

Chambers identified Hiss as a former Communist in the fall of 1948 before the House Un-American Activities Committee and returned several months later with the charges of spying. Charges were brought by the New York grand jury, and Hiss went on trial in May, 1949. Following a split decision by the jury a second jury convicted Hiss in January, 1950. By that time it had not been simply Hiss, but a whole generation, which had been on trial. Millions could not believe that events had forced America into those burdensome, dangerous, and crisis-ridden times. A simpler— and for many a more satisfactory—explanation was that there had been a betrayal. Hiss became the personification of this betrayal, and through what he symbolized, many Americans convicted genteel America on the one hand and welfare liberalism on the other of treason to the nation.

To these suspicious Americans this pattern of betrayal was to be seen in ever darker developments. In August, 1949, the State Department issued a white paper announcing the conquest of China by the Communists. Unprepared for this aggrandizement of one quarter of the earth's people, many Americans could find satisfactory explanation only by postulating some deep-laid plot through which America had "lost" China. Then in 1950 the nation enthusiastically launched a "police action" against North Korea, which developed into the fourth bloodiest war in American history.

Into this jittery atmosphere in February, 1950, stepped Senator Joseph McCarthy of Wisconsin, with a talk to the Women's Republican Club of Wheeling, West Virginia. Waving in his hand a letter (which in truth mentioned the names of no Communists), he declared, according to reporters' accounts of the speech, "I have here in my hand a list of 205—a list of names that were known to the Secretary of State as being members of the Com-

munist Party and who nevertheless are still working and shaping
the policy in the State Department." And with that—as much to
his own surprise, apparently, as to anybody's—McCarthy was off
on a four-year career of bully-boy power such as had never before
been witnessed in the history of American demagoguery.

Communism, after frightening the nation briefly following the
first world war, had remained largely dormant as a political issue
until the cold war. Amid the depression conditions of 1932, the
Communist party's candidate, William Z. Foster, had attracted
only a quarter of 1 per cent of the popular vote, and the party
never did so well again. It had enjoyed a measure of success in
attracting intellectuals and radicals during the Lost Generation of
the twenties, but in that respect also it reached the high point
of success in 1932. There followed a growing disillusionment with
its authoritarian tactics. The party had successively greater difficulties explaining away the methodical starvation of the Russian
kulak peasant class, the judicial murders of Red Army generals,
the Nazi-Soviet pact, and the Soviet attack upon Finland.

Still, the thirties was the Popular Front period of international
communism, when party members in the democracies were ordered
to cooperate with reform governments. In America some of them
cooperated by infiltrating an administration which could not bring
itself to take them seriously. Then, with Pearl Harbor, the Reds
became the heroic allies whose later victory at Stalingrad turned
the tide against the Axis. That the Communists were returning to
their bad old ways was a conclusion which the American people
at the close of the war were most reluctant to accept.

In 1946, the year of Churchill's Iron Curtain speech, the Canadian government uncovered a spy ring which had extended into
the United States and had turned over to Russia information concerning nuclear fission. The American government reacted by
creating a Loyalty Commission to screen Federal employees and
to dismiss what came to be known as "bad security risks." Under
the Smith Act, which had been passed in 1940, the government in
1948 indicted leaders of the American Communist party for con-
spiring to advocate the violent overthrow of the government.

Denounced by liberals for trampling on civil rights, the Truman
administration was denounced by right-wing Republicans for suc-
cumbing to Communist influence. "Traitors in high councils of our
own government," declared Representative Richard Nixon of Cali-

fornia, "have made sure that the deck is stacked on the Soviet side of the diplomatic tables." There followed the cases of Fuchs and Hiss, then the Russian atomic explosion, then the fall of Nationalist China, then the invasion of South Korea, and then the rise of McCarthy.

Lacking almost altogether the wit and intelligence of Huey Long, McCarthy probably surpassed Long in the art of heavy-breathing intimidation. Inarticulate but doggedly persistent in his accusations, McCarthy discovered in himself a deadly talent for demolishing reputations through innuendo and slander. Politically all else was beyond him. With all his power he developed no effective organization and associated himself with no political program. When he fell from power he collapsed altogether, leaving nothing behind but a handful of ruined careers and a great deal of bad feeling. For the time being, however, in that atmosphere of bewilderment, resentment, and suspicion, his tactics of relentless accusation were more than sufficient to maintain his reign of terror.

A key to McCarthy's power was his conquest of the United States Senate. When a Senate committee under Millard Tydings of Maryland investigated McCarthy's early charges and declared them false, McCarthy entered Maryland politics during the sena-torial campaign of 1950 and dealt the conservative Southerner Tydings a stunning defeat by questioning his loyalty on the basis of outrageously doctored evidence. That display of McCarthy's personal power persuaded most senators not to stake their careers on a contest with McCarthyism. Thereafter both fear and party advantage persuaded Republican leaders to attempt the impossible task of giving measured and discreet support to the spectacular upstart in their ranks. They were encouraged in this course by appreciable Republican gains in those congressional elections which had featured the defeat of Tydings.

The circumstances plainly were not propitious for Truman's Fair Deal, and Truman, while denouncing McCarthyism out of hand, made the mistake of dismissing the Hiss case as a "red herring," a misjudgment which was used against him to good effect. Then evidences of corruption—gifts of a mink coat and a deep freeze unit in exchange for political influence—served to discredit Truman's administration. The small bribes involved no key figures in the administration, but they added fuel to the grow-ing discontent and to the desire to "clean up that mess in Washington." In "Communism, Korea and Corruption" the Republicans found a winning slogan in the Presidential election of 1952, and in General Eisenhower they possessed an incomparably popular candidate.

Since the close of the war it had been evident to political leaders in both parties that Dwight D. Eisenhower as a candidate for the Presidency could no more be beaten than Grant could have been beaten in 1868. As with Grant, and with Herbert Hoover after World War I, Eisenhower's popularity was the more disturbing to the professionals for the fact that, if he chose to run, nobody knew which party he would choose. In 1948 Democratic party leaders certain in their own minds that Truman could not win, had unsuccessfully urged Eisenhower to accept the Democratic nomination.

In 1952 Republican liberals succeeded where Democratic liberals had failed, and in the Republican convention of that year Eisenhower submitted himself to a bitter struggle against the favorite of the professionals and the conservatives in the party, Senator Taft of Ohio. Supported mainly by the internationalist and the big-business wing of the party, Eisenhower won and launched on a campaign which promised an end to the conflict in Korea and an end to "creeping socialism" at home. His running mate, Richard M. Nixon, had gained his reputation through his role in the conviction of Hiss, and his candidacy served to appease the conservative followers of Taft. The Democrats nominated Governor Adlai E. Stevenson of Illinois, whose witty and eloquent speeches drew fervent support from liberals and intellectuals without convincing the majority of the voters. Eisenhower won handsomely in a campaign which also, narrowly, secured Republican majorities in both houses of Congress.

It may be doubted that Eisenhower's victory contributed appreciably to the Korean peace settlement, which was by then slowly but almost certainly approaching completion. Nor was the Eisenhower administration able to do much to check the "creeping socialism" of the old New Deal reforms. The main positive results of the victory—and certainly they were momentous results—proved to be bipartisan acceptance of the new American role of global responsibility and an end to that McCarthyism at home which had expressed unwillingness to accept the responsibility.

As a member of the party in power, McCarthy continued against the Eisenhower administration the tactics he had employed to such effect against the administration of Truman. Centering his attack upon the State Department he continued his accusations of Communist infiltration, forcing appointments upon Secretary of State John Foster Dulles and forcing the firing, without evidence, of State Department employees. Successful in this, he moved against the Army, accusing a general of coddling Communists. There followed in 1954 a month-long, nationally televised Senate hearing, a vivid exhibition of McCarthy's loathsome technique which rapidly lost him popular support.

The United States Senate thereupon plucked up its courage and condemned McCarthy by a vote of 67 to 22, the fourth such instance in American history. Thereafter ignored by his fellow senators and dropped from the headlines, McCarthy abruptly ceased to exist as a political force. He did not even attend the Republican nominating convention in 1956. He died the year following. By that time Korea had been replaced in the public mind by Egypt, and the Truman Doctrine of aid to Greece and Turkey had been followed by the Eisenhower Doctrine of aid to the nations of the Middle East. Sputnik and intercontinental ballistic missiles tended to persuade doubters that the betrayal of their world was irrevocable and also that it was not to be satisfactorily explained by any simple theory of conspiracy.

II

The Eisenhower Administration   Dwight D. Eisenhower epitomized the ideals of most Americans. He had come out of middle-class, middle America to lead his country in triumph over its foreign enemies. Then, like many another American Cincinnatus before him, he had doffed his uniform to aid his country in peaceful enterprises, serving as president of Columbia University. He was an instinctively religious man and a visibly patriotic one. Under him America would be guided by traditional values rather than current and changing theories. Suspicious of the intellectuals—the "eggheads"—which the New Deal and Fair Deal had harbored, he put his trust in the plain, practical good sense of the business community.

He controlled his righteous anger with difficulty, but he was unaffectedly free with his infectious grin, bringing a degree of good humor into politics during those most troubled times. He had always a great difficulty in expressing what he wanted to say, which was probably an asset in a time when clarity of purpose brought unusually vehement opposition. He inherited a nation more rent by faction than at any time since the Civil War. He bequeathed a nation which had accepted the domestic reforms of F.D.R. and the foreign policy of Truman to such an extent that even the politically ingenious Richard Nixon was at a loss for a political issue in the presidential campaign of 1960.

Himself associated with the Truman foreign policy, Eisenhower chose as his Secretary of State John Foster Dulles, who also had been associated with the postwar diplomatic settlements. As his Secretary of Labor he chose a union official, who was later replaced by a man from management, but on the whole his choice of Cabinet clearly reflected his belief in the Harding dictum that there ought to be less government in business and more business in government.

In the view of Eisenhower, there should be a self-limitation of executive authority, following the aggrandizements of power by Roosevelt and Truman, to the end that the constitutional separation of powers be once again maintained. The nation should return to principles of free enterprise. It was the responsibility of the government to ensure the stable dollar and balance the budget. There should, however, be no reckless return to these true principles. For instance, the farmer should be returned to the world of free competition, but at the same time Eisenhower admonished his Secretary of Agriculture against any dangerously precipitous reductions of price supports.

He appointed a businessman's Cabinet, and it came volubly to the point. His Secretary of Defense, the former president of General Motors, Charles Wilson, wasted no time in unconditionally equating the good of the country with the good of General Motors. His Secretary of the Treasury, the former president of M. A. Hanna and Co., George Humphrey, made it clear at once that the business point of view would inform his Department. His Secretary of Commerce, the industrialist Sinclair Weeks, declared that he had come to Washington to create a "business climate." Secretary of State Dulles, denouncing the policy of containment as cowardice, spoke of liberating peoples in Communist-held countries. He argued for a defense based upon the "massive retaliation" of atomic warfare and a deemphasizing of conventional weapons. He boasted later of having led the nation repeatedly to the brink of war in its diplomatic dealings. And the principles upon which his foreign policy were based, he declared, were those of "openness, simplicity, and righteousness." Like his fellow Presbyterian Woodrow Wilson, he had lost sight of the doctrine of original sin so far as the United States was concerned.

The Eisenhower administration moved at once to effect its counterreforms. A spectacular trip to Korea by the President was followed by the conclusion of hostilities. Price and wage controls, imposed once again during the Korean conflict, were lifted. Control over tidelands oil shifted from the Federal government to that of the states. Federal construction projects diminished, and new checks were placed upon government hiring. TVA, as the leading example of creeping socialism, was to be curbed. Natural resources were to be developed by private rather than by governmental means, and taxes were to be reordered in such a way as to reduce burdens on business. And all was to be accomplished through a cordial cooperation between the executive and the Congress, unmarred by the Rooseveltian and Trumanesque forms of executive dictation.

Eisenhower never altogether departed in his statements from his original views, but in practice he moved afield from them during his eight years in office, and many like-minded men moved reluctantly but inexorably with him. McCarthy presented him with the earliest severe challenge to his principles. For more than a year Eisenhower meticulously refrained from executive coercion of the legislature, while McCarthy, with the acquiescence of Dulles, ordered hirings and firings in the State Department and dictated the censoring of books in the Overseas Information Service. But when McCarthy denounced an Army officer for what amounted to routinely following orders, with respect to a suspected Communist under his command, General Eisenhower retreated from his constitutional position. Slowly and cautiously he brought the government in support of the Army and against the Senator.

In agriculture, price supports were sharply reduced, but then gradually raised again. In the area of public power TVA appropriations were severely cut and TVA was bypassed in a contract with a private Dixon-Yates group to build a power plant on the Mississippi. Public reaction to the revelation of the huge private profits involved, however, resulted in the cancellation of the contract. Eisenhower's

views in the area of public power were more successfully carried
out in the allocating of the power project at Hell's Canyon, Idaho,
to private interests. On the other hand, it was during the Eisenhower administration that the American government finally acquiesced to the construction of the St. Lawrence Seaway jointly with
Canada.

Eisenhower found his administration to be committing the sin of
deficit-spending in spite of itself. The budget was balanced in only
three out of his eight years, and vast new spending programs were
inaugurated. Congress launched also a large public housing program as well as a federal program for school construction. Beyond
that it authorized a highway construction program at a cost of
about 32.5 billion dollars, more than all of the New Deal relief
measures combined. As his second term opened, Eisenhower found
himself battling with a Democratic Congress to defend the largest
budget in peacetime history. That year the nation slumped into an
economic recession, and Eisenhower returned in 1958 to defend an
even larger one.

The administration remained simon-pure on Federal health insurance and—aided by labor scandals—on increased legal controls
over labor unions. Still, as administration officials worked successfully to increase the minimum wage and to bring ten million additional citizens under social security, they were forced to admit that
when you were the party in control of affairs, things looked different. Thus it was the administrating of the New Deal by the reluctant Republicans which won the system final national loyalty.

The nation reacted against the Republican conduct of affairs by
increasing the Democratic majorities in both houses of Congress in
1954, 1956, 1958, and again in 1960, but nothing that his administration did appreciably lessened the popularity of Eisenhower.
For a time, prior to the election of 1956, it appeared that he would
be tragically disqualified for reelection by a severe heart attack. He
recovered remarkably, however, and running this time against a
somewhat less vivacious Stevenson, he was a shoo-in. He doubled
his previous margin of victory to win by almost ten million votes.

There were warnings that Eisenhower's second term would be
fatally incapacitated by continuing struggles between a Republican
administration and a Democratic Congress, but nothing of the sort
occurred. It is true that presidential vetoes were frequent, but it is
also true that the Congress, led by Texans, the Speaker of the

House, Sam Rayburn, and the Senate Majority Leader, Lyndon Johnson, worked in general harmony with Eisenhower's "dynamic conservatism." And the nation, despite rising unemployment and recurrent foreign crises, rested content.

In foreign policy President Eisenhower placed much reliance upon his experienced Secretary of State. Dulles, for his part, despite his active participation in and defense of Truman's foreign policy, now denounced the passive strategy of containment as immoral. Although the conflict in Korea was brought to an end through a compromise with the Chinese Communists, the administration continued to threaten the "unleashing" of the Nationalist Chinese forces on Formosa against the mainland. And while nothing was actually undertaken to remove the Russians from Central Europe, much was said about the freeing of the occupied territories. The stated policy of Dulles was one of constant nudging. "The ability to get to the verge without getting into the war is the necessary art," he declared. "If you cannot master it, you inevitably get into war. If you try to run away from it, if you are scared to go to the brink, you are lost."

In 1954, however, when communism threatened to envelop Vietnam, Dulles did not find the necessary support for intervention among America's allies or within the American Congress or with Eisenhower, and the Communists were allowed to keep what they had won. Dulles made this the occasion for the creation of the Southeast Asia Treaty Organization, a military alliance to contain communism in Asia, but he failed to persuade important Asian nations, including India and Indonesia, to join. In 1956, when Hungary revolted against the Communists, it was bloodily subdued by the Red Army. The American government had excellent reason to suppose that armed intervention by the United States would result in thermonuclear war, and it did nothing. The liberation policy was thus tacitly abandoned and the containment policy returned to.

Probably more important to international relations than the change in the American administration was the change in the Russian leadership. Stalin died in 1953, and, after a mysterious struggle for power, Nikita Khrushchev emerged as the ruler of Russia. There followed signs of a softening of the cold war strategy. The good offices of Russia were used to end the Korean conflict. Russia recognized West Germany and joined the Western allies, not only in signing a peace treaty with Japan, which it was in no position to oppose, but also one with Austria, which it could have wrecked.

Both the United States and the Soviet Union, meanwhile, had perfected hydrogen bombs and were working on intercontinental ballistic missiles. Under these circumstances Eisenhower, declaring he would "wage a war for peace," agreed to a conference in Geneva with Khrushchev. Nothing resulted but a momentarily friendly "Geneva spirit," which quickly was dissipated by events in the Middle East.

The United States was weakened diplomatically in the Middle East by the support it had given to the new nation of Israel. It nevertheless won most Middle Eastern nations to a Western defense system, but it failed with Gamal Abdel Nasser of Egypt. When Nasser turned to Russia for aid, Dulles withdrew American aid. Nasser responded by seizing the Western-owned Suez Canal, and Britain, France and Israel thereupon attacked Egypt. Russia threatened to send "volunteers," and the United States denounced the action of its allies, who then gave up the attempt. The result was general bad feeling among the Western allies and a power vacuum in the Middle East which the American administration attempted to fill through what came to be known as the Eisenhower Doctrine. The United States would lend economic and military aid to Middle Eastern nations threatened by communism.

Even more threateningly the United States faced the rise of Communist influence in the Western Hemisphere as well. Throughout Latin America Communist parties were active and increasing. When a pro-Communist regime came to power in Guatemala the United States forcibly overthrew it, amid bitter Latin-American criticism. Latin America remained impoverished and unstable, and hostile to the United States. Sudden American realization of this hostility occurred in 1958, when Vice President Nixon, on a goodwill tour, was mobbed in several Latin-American countries.

Then, in 1959, Fidel Castro overthrew a pro-American reactionary government in Cuba. Viewed at first as a democratic, patriotic hero, Castro soon revealed himself to be pro-Communist. The Eisenhower administration was still in a condition of indecisive agitation amid the Latin American perplexities when it went out of office. The central difficulty continued to be, as it had been before, that, as Latin-American nations became more democratic, they tended to become more anti-Yankee. Also, as Latin-American conditions were improved, with the aid of American money, the populations increased correspondingly, nullifying the benefits to the people.

Negotiations with Russia to eliminate atomic weapons continued to founder on the Russian refusal to accept inspection, and they became the more futile as Russia, launching the first intercontinental ballistic missile and the first satellite, grew more confident of its ability to beat the United States in the atomic and stratospheric arms race. Russia had demonstrated its superiority in the development of power for rocketry. Otherwise, the evidence indicated, the United States was militarily superior on the basis of its science, technology and, above all, its ability to produce.

The "Geneva spirit" of Russo-American amity, following the summit meeting of 1955, had from the first been an evanescent and wishful thing, and in November, 1958, Khrushchev abruptly concluded the cold war truce with the renewed demand for Western evacuation of Berlin. After a considerable agitation of the issue the Russian government dropped the subject, and in 1959 Khrushchev paid a goodwill visit to the United States. His reception was generally friendly, and he, himself, proved a jovial guest, except for his disapproval on moral grounds of the movie *Can-Can*, his annoyance at receiving insults from the mayor of Los Angeles, and his fretfulness at not being permitted to see Disneyland.

Everything was in readiness for a second summit conference in Paris in the springtime of 1960, when an American U-2 aircraft was shot down while flying over Russia. A remarkable example of Yankee ingenuity, the U-2 was a glider, equipped with a motor, which for some time had been flip-flopping back and forth across Russia, too high for Russian antiaircraft and too slow to be maneuvered against by the swift Russian jets, snapping pictures of everything in sight just like any typical American tourist. Khrushchev made this U-2 incident the angry occasion for breaking up the conference, although he had been aware of these activities long before one of the U-2s had been successfully brought down. The Eisenhower administration made matters worse by reacting with a series of mutually conflicting untruths, which made the administration, with its principle of righteousness in foreign affairs, the butt of international ridicule for the time being.

President Eisenhower had come to office with malice toward none, determined to bind up the nation's wounds and achieve a just and lasting peace. By the time he went out of office his own spirit of goodwill had penetrated the nation to a remarkable extent. That was his greatest achievement. He brought the same spirit, strengthened by a firmness in the right, to foreign affairs, with less success. The course that the United States was pursuing in international relations in January, 1961, was a good deal less clear than it had been in January, 1953. On the other hand, the American people as a whole were now committed to supporting their government in its new world role.

III

<u>Civil Rights</u>   The cold war militarized America to an extent which would have been inconceivable at any time in the nation's previous peacetime history. In the name of security the cold war introduced systems of police control and censorship such as had been generally alien to American peacetime practice. At the same time it placed American democracy critically before the bar of world opinion for the first time. From the beginning the United States had self-consciously stood forth before the world as a good example, but the response of the world had never before been of material importance to it. With the coming of the cold war, the United States, for the first time in its history, was forced to defend its system before the world, against the Communist system.

In this effort it labored under serious disadvantages. To begin with, the United States enjoyed the highest standard of living of any nation in the world, which inevitably made it a stench in the nostrils of the impoverished masses to which it appealed. Equally disadvantageous was the fact that the American people had always been race-conscious, treating as racial inferiors the peoples to whom they were now appealing. The cold war forced Americans to examine their system in the light of world opinion, and in this new light many of them saw in the system grievous faults of which they had formerly been almost unaware. The great sin of American democracy, to which the world situation awakened them, was the old one of its treatment of the American Negro.

With the end of Reconstruction the Southern Negro had been abandoned by the North to shift for himself in the South of the white restoration. Northerners could ill afford to continue their high moral tone on the matter; for wherever Negroes were concentrated in the North, they were badly treated. In the South, meanwhile, the Negroes were left generally in possession of the vote and were not singled out for special legislation.

The late nineteenth century, however, was a time for racial enthusiasms throughout the United States as throughout Europe, and the era of the Spanish-American War was one of mob violence and legislative restrictions against the American Negro. The Southern Jim Crow laws were passed mainly during this period, segregating the Negroes from the whites. In 1896 the United States Supreme Court, in the case of Plessy v. Ferguson, declared that Negroes could be segregated on trains so long as their accommodations were equal. Three years later the Court, in the case of Cumming v. County Board of Education, extended this "separate but equal" interpretation of the Fourteenth Amendment to schools.

The putting of the Negro in his place was implemented at the turn of the century by hundreds of gruesome lynchings and many more acts of terrorism. It was supported also by a racial literature which included works such as The Negro, a Beast and The Negro, a Menace to American Civilization. Nor did the reforming zeal of the Progressive era extend itself to the cause of Negro rights. Theodore Roosevelt made the gesture of inviting the Negro leader Booker T. Washington to the White House, but the furious reaction of his more race-minded Progressive supporters dissuaded him from any further such gestures. Under Wilson racial segregation was introduced into Federal services.

During World War I, 360,000 Negroes served in the armed forces, while many more moved from the South to take war jobs in Northern cities. In the violent aftermath of the war, Negroes in Chicago were slaughtered and tortured in the worst race riots in the nation's history. Negroes in America at that time were in much the same position as Negroes in South Africa, and it was supposed that in both areas they would remain as they were.

Certain Negro leaders in the early twentieth century, however, came to believe that this might not be the case. In 1909 the National Association for the Advancement of Colored People was founded. It departed from the argument of Booker T. Washington that the Negroes should improve themselves to the point where they were acceptable to the white community. Drawing its leadership from Northern Negroes such as the Harvard-trained historian, W. E. B. DuBois, the NAACP launched upon its campaign for equality under the law with whites.

The racist spirit reached its climax in America in the 1920s, and it swept the Negroes along with the Anglo-Saxons. The demagogic

Marcus Garvey organized the Back to Africa movement, which proclaimed Negro racial superiority and called for the formation of a great African Negro nation. Garvey won millions of adherents before he was tried for various swindles and jailed. The NAACP, meanwhile, was gradually gaining support from Northern whites as well as from Northern Negroes.

With the New Deal the Federal government exerted itself on behalf of Negro rights for the first time since Reconstruction. Its efforts, here and there, to provide equal job opportunity on Federal projects, however, amounted to a good deal less than a major program of civil rights reform. More significant was the impact of what the Negroes were doing for themselves to raise their own status in American society. Amid the congenial social atmosphere of the New Deal the "Black Renaissance" took place, which for the first time gave the Negro a position of dignity in American cultural life. There appeared in remarkable profusion during the thirties Negro novelists, poets, playwrights, actors, and concert artists. Negro jazz and Negro spirituals were coming to be viewed with pride as a part of the American heritage, and perhaps the most original of all American contributions to Western culture.

The Black Renaissance took place against the background of German racist atrocities such as Americans had hardly conceived to be possible. These atrocities drove many Americans to reexamine their own racial assumptions. Then, once the nation was at war with Germany, racism was transformed into the ideology of the enemy. In 1941 F.D.R. issued an executive order that "there shall be no discrimination in the employment of workers in defense industries or Government because of race, creed, color, or national origin," and he appointed a Fair Employment Practices Committee to investigate violations of the order.

The war, as its scale was so much larger than that of World War I, brought comparably larger numbers of Negroes into the Armed Forces and into the Northern cities. Between 1940 and 1960 the number of Negroes in the North increased from less than three million to more than seven million. In the South the Negro population remained almost unchanged, but in the South also there was a general exodus to cities such as Atlanta and Birmingham, which left the countryside dotted with deserted farm shanties. Improved job opportunities presented themselves to the Negroes in the Southern as well as Northern cities, and a degree of political participation resulted in addition, but it was the Northern Negro who suddenly became a really significant political force in the nation. By 1960 there were more Negroes in New York than in any other state in the Union, and Negroes were concentrated heavily in all Northern cities as major voting blocs.

Amid the pressures of the cold war, President Truman appointed a committee on civil rights, which reported to him the truth which was becoming obvious to many, that "The United States is not so strong, the final triumph of the democratic ideal is not so inevitable that we can ignore what the world thinks of us or our record." Following the recommendations of the committee, Truman pressed Congress for a permanent Fair Employment Practices Commission, the protection of Negro voting rights, prohibition of segregation in transportation facilities and a Federal antilynching law.

When Southern filibusterers defeated any action, Truman defied the Southern wing of the Democratic party in 1948 to make civil rights for Negroes a major national issue. Shortly before the election of 1948 Truman issued an executive order calling for the integration of the Armed Forces. The pressure of circumstances in Korea brought this into effect there with remarkable results. The Negro soldiers turned into notably better fighters than they had been while in segregated units, and the Southern soldiers accepted integration as a part of army life, and just one more thing to complain about. The surprising success of integration in Korea was followed by a general military integration which constituted a systematic training in racial equality for both Negro and white draftees under favorable conditions.

As early as 1915 the Supreme Court had begun to stir itself to uphold the political rights of Negroes. In that year the Court declared unconstitutional the "grandfather" clauses whereby Southern voters were excused from literacy tests whose forebears had been eligible to vote in 1867. The decision was of little consequence, however, since in the one party South, the primary election was all-important, and the decision did not apply to primaries, which were not provided for in the Constitution. It was not until 1944 that the Court declared the white primary invalid.

In 1938 the Court began to reexamine the question of segregation in the schools in the case of Missouri v. Canada. In the absence of a state law school for Negroes, the Court declared, an otherwise qualified Negro applicant must be admitted to the white law school. In 1950 the Court went beyond this ruling to prohibit the exclusion of Negroes from the University of Texas law school, on the grounds that the state law school for Negroes was not equal in quality to the white one. Then in 1954 the Supreme Court under Chief Justice Earl Warren issued a unanimous decision in Brown v. Board of Education of Topeka, declaring all racial segregation in the schools to be unconstitutional.

"Segregation of white and colored children in public schools," the Court declared, "has a detrimental effect upon the colored children. . . . Separate educational facilities are inherently unequal" and they therefore deprived Negroes of the equal protection of the laws guaranteed by the Fourteenth Amendment. Accordingly, in a sub-sequent decision, the Court ordered the Southern states to desegregate their schools "with all deliberate speed."

Throughout the Deep South, the Court's decisions were met with fierce resistance. White Citizens' Councils were organized to mobilize private opposition, while state governments passed almost innumerable laws to block any moves toward integration. While the Deep South held firm, significant moves toward integration took place in the upper South. Then in 1957 Governor Orval Faubus of Arkansas called out the state National Guard to prevent integration in Little Rock. President Eisenhower countered with Federal troops, and after a delay of more than two years, integration was enforced. Virginia retreated from its program of "massive resistance" and permitted token integration in a few schools chiefly in the northern part of the state, where the population was made up heavily of Federal government workers from Northern states.

More than a half dozen years after the original Court order no integrated school existed in South Carolina, Georgia, Alabama, or Mississippi. Throughout the South, except for completely integrated Washington, D.C., hardly more than one hundred thousand out of three million Negroes attended biracial schools. At the University of Mississippi, in 1962, it required thousands of Federal troops to enforce the admission of a single Negro student, James Meredith, who remained guarded night and day by Federal officers as he pursued his studies. Meanwhile, integration has proceeded peacefully in most Southern colleges.

It was the observation of the Swedish sociologist Gunnar Myrdal, in his massive study of the American Negro, that "the Negro prob-

lem is not only America's greatest failure but also America's incomparably great opportunity for the future. . . . The century-old
dream of American patriots, that America should give to the entire
world its own freedoms and its own faith, would come true.
America can demonstrate that justice, equality, and cooperation are
possible between white and colored people." This is an ideal which
is obviously far from having been achieved either in the North or
the South. Nevertheless, the advancing status of the Negro in
American society is one of the major social changes of the nation's
recent history and one which could never have been predicted on
the basis of the woeful history of the American Negro from the
end of Reconstruction to the coming of the Great Depression.

IV

American Science   Intellectually the twentieth century has been the age
of science in America. This rise in the status of science
could hardly have been predicted from what had gone before any
more than could the much more modest rise in the status of the
Negro. In both cases the main causes were the same: the advance
of industry and the coming of the hot and cold wars.

Business support did much to give pure science the respectability
in the twentieth century which it had lacked in the days of Joseph
Henry. By the turn of the twentieth century the relevance of pure
science to industrial advance was becoming obvious. The great
American mathematical physicist, Willard Gibbs, living just before
the dawn of the new day, had gone unhonored in his own country,
and even within his own university, Yale. In Germany, however,
where the practical application of science to industry was better
understood, Gibbs' scientific papers, notably his paper "On the
Equilibrium of Heterogeneous Substances," received a more appre-
ciative audience. One result was the strengthening of Germany
during the First World War through its application of Gibbs'
theories to the synthetics industry. By that time American industry
had wakened to possibilities which had not previously occurred
to it.

General Electric established a research laboratory in 1900, and
Du Pont followed two years later. The third of the largest of the
research laboratories, that of Bell Telephone, was instituted in
1925. Toward the close of the nineteenth century, Leo H. Baekeland

came to America from Belgium and, through his scientific investigations, created the Bakelite industry. Du Pont hired a manic depressive wizard, Wallace H. Carothers, whose genius created the synthetic rubber industry in the twenties and nylon in the thirties, revolutionizing the entire textiles industry through the introduction of chemical fibers.

Industrial competition for scientists gave them a stronger position in the nation's universities, while it forced industry to allow them, in industrial laboratories, much the same freedom which they would enjoy in a university. Then, during the New Deal, the Federal government entered the competition for their services, notably in the Department of Agriculture, under the agricultural scientist, Henry A. Wallace. Finally, with World War II, the scientist became the savior of the nation and, possibly, the destroyer of the world. In any event his prestige had reached its zenith.

It was the more recently established universities which mainly had taken the lead in physics and, by the time of World War II, in nuclear physics. The University of Chicago had dominated the field during the first quarter of the twentieth century, to be overtaken by the University of California and the California Institute of Technology, in fierce competition for Nobel Prize winners, followed by Massachusetts Institute of Technology and Columbia University.

In nuclear physics, as in other areas of science, the United States had the advantage of the rest of the world in its greater wealth and technical development. The age had arrived when the main advances in science required an enormous economic outlay. The leading pioneer in this new age was Ernest O. Lawrence of the University of California, who, though no theoretical scientist, won the Nobel Prize for his construction in 1929 of the Cyclotron, the atom smasher which broke loose particles in an electrical field by moving them at higher and higher speeds. Similarly, in astronomy advances in knowledge depended on the wealth and technical capacity which could produce the telescope with its 200-inch reflector on Mount Palomar in California. Even in botany, new knowledge was to be derived from construction of a million-dollar Phytotron, a greenhouse with controlled environmental conditions.

By the eve of World War II, research in nuclear physics, mainly in Germany and Italy, had demonstrated the possibility of creating a nuclear explosion. The United States, which had not led in this field, had gained enormously from Nazi and Fascist persecution.

Refugee scientists in America at the time of Pearl Harbor included Albert Einstein, Niels Bohr, Enrico Fermi, and Leo Szilard, in addition to many others. In 1939 Einstein and others revealed to Roosevelt the possibility of constructing an atomic bomb, and Roosevelt authorized the Manhattan Project, with a budget of two billion dollars. To those who worried about the chancy venture he explained that, if it worked, Congress would never investigate it, and if it did not, Congress would never investigate anything else.

At the eve of World War II Germany led in rocket technology as well as nuclear physics, and it was providential for the Allies that Hitler encouraged research on the V-2 "buzz bomb" at the expense of research on an atomic weapon. The basic principles of space flight had been laid down by Sir Isaac Newton, but until World War II they had been applied only to science fiction. During the 1920s an American, Robert Hutchins Goddard, had done important work in the field of rocketry, but he had been generally dismissed as a fool.

By mid-century the war-inspired technological developments had turned space travel into a practical possibility. For the United States, as for Russia, the spoils of war had included German scientists, experienced in the development of buzz bombs, who were put to work on space projects. In October, 1957, the American program was much accelerated following news that the Russians had launched Sputnik into orbit. The United States followed with Explorer I in January, 1958. In the space race since then Russia has had the huge advantage of a superior fuel which permits the launching of satellites far heavier than can be managed by the Americans.

Progress in the more peaceful sciences naturally has been slower, but science generally has gained greatly from the scientific cold war. The Russians, with Sputnik, have given Americans a greater respect for education and, more than that, for knowledge, than ever characterized the nation before. The National Science Foundation and other government agencies for intellectual activity enjoy an acceptance today which was looked for in vain by Thomas Jefferson and John Quincy Adams.

The founding of graduate schools in America antedated the interest of industry in pure science, and the early academic contributions to science were not affected by practical considerations. They were influenced more, as had been the case in colonial times, by the unique opportunities which America provided. Because of the presence of interesting Indians, anthropology had been a strong American field from earliest times, and in the late nineteenth and early twentieth centuries Americans made important contributions in this area, aided by the variety of peoples which the New Immigration brought to the nation.

Beginning in 1908 Franz Boas conducted a study of immigrants and their children for the Federal government. The results of his study, which indicated significant bodily changes in second generation Americans, demolished old ideas concerning inherent racial characteristics. Boaz and his students went on to found the area of social anthropology and to destroy the idea of an invariable evolutionary development of races or societies.

At Harvard, during the same period, William James made contributions in the field of psychology which were probably of greater importance than his contributions in the field of philosophy. His *Principles of Psychology*, published in 1890, presented a theory of emotions, that bodily changes follow immediately upon perception rather than as a response to perceptions. In the field of literature James's work was pervasively influential in contributing the idea of the stream of consciousness.

A pole apart from James in his ideas was the psychologist J. B. Watson, who in 1913 published an enormously influential article, "Psychology as the Behaviorist Views It." Leader of the school which has been unkindly but usefully designated as "rat psychology," Watson, discarding the mind as an active agency, studied man in terms of his conditioned responses. As with the psychology of William James, the behavioral psychology of Watson made a strong impact upon literature, notably in the writings of Ernest Hemingway, which deal with behavior rather than feelings. Watson, himself, became an advertising executive, and by no means the least of his influence upon American society has been the massive attempt at hidden persuasion in advertising to which the American public has subsequently been subjected.

Freudian psychiatry made an even more momentous impact upon twentieth-century American thought. By the close of the nineteenth century the medical profession had long forgotten the early, and for a time influential, writings of Benjamin Rush on the relation of mental disturbance to physical illness. American doctors at the turn of the twentieth century were taught to assign physical causes to all mental as well as physical diseases. In 1909 Sigmund Freud delivered a series of lectures at Clark University which received important American attention, on the one hand from academic supporters and on the other from some who rejected "pornographic tales about pure virgins."

Acceptance of the validity of psychiatry, however, was so rapid in the United States as to surprise Freud himself. In 1910 the Psychopathological Society was founded under the encouragement of the leading American Freudian, A. A. Brill. By the time of the Lost Generation, Freud had all but superseded Marx and Darwin as the prophet of the age, and the knowing ones were explaining themselves to each other in terms of the id, the ego, and the superego. At the same time the field of social work was being revolutionized by psychiatry.

In the course of World War II, the behaviorists, with their belief in the automatic responses of humans, were gone one better by the cyberneticists, with their achievement of human responses by machines. Norbert Wiener of the Massachusetts Institute of Technology directed the development of machines which could predict the future positions of enemy planes in order to direct antiaircraft fire upon them. From there, machines were created with the automatic responses of living creatures. An electro-mechanical rat was constructed, for instance, which was capable of solving a rat's maze more quickly than a living rat. Unlike atomic energy, which was initially thought of only in terms of destruction, the war-born developments in electronic automation were from the first seen as revolutionary industrial developments. Rapidly applied to a wide variety of industries, automation went far toward transforming American production in the years following the war. A rough index of its importance was the increase in the use of electricity in America by 160 per cent during the decade after the war.

Throughout American history, until the twentieth century, science had proved itself to be the enemy of religion. Although Puritan ministers had eagerly accepted Newtonian science as further revelation of God's works, the main influence of the New Science had been away from the original Puritan orthodoxy. In the nineteenth century, Darwinian science, with its explicit denial of the Book of Genesis, had been seen at once as the enemy, and those who came to terms with it necessarily compromised their original beliefs in order to do so.

The scientific findings of the twentieth century, however, tended in the other direction. The theory of relativity was incomprehensible to all but the specialists as the theories of gravity and of evolution had not been. Under the scrutiny of scientific investigation the universe became more mysterious rather than less so. But more than that, the possibility of an atomic Armageddon created disturbing second thoughts among many who had looked upon science and technology as the dutiful servants of man.

The forties and fifties saw a resurgence of religion in America, after three-quarters of a century of retreat. Church membership rose from about 45 per cent in the mid-twenties to about 60 per cent in the mid-fifties. Among the nonevangelical Protestant sects, the neo-orthodoxy of Reinhold Niebuhr became increasingly influential, with its return to the doctrine of original sin and of the helplessness of the individual to save himself or his society by the force of his own will. But it was the evangelical old orthodoxy, notably the Baptist churches, which made the greatest gains in membership.

The age saw also the rise of new fundamentalist sects, such as the Church of the Nazarene, the Pentecostal Assemblies, and the Jehovah's Witnesses. The leading figure in this resurgent evangelism was Billy Graham, preaching in the tradition of George Whitefield of colonial times to bring sinners to Christ through whatever church they might wish to join. However much the movement was accompanied by jukebox claptrap about "the man upstairs," the power of religion was undeniably on the rise in the nation.

The giving up of their diplomatic isolation seems to have moved the American people to give up their cultural isolation as well. The generation which followed World War II witnessed a proliferation of art galleries and symphony orchestras throughout the nation. Television introduced millions of Americans to the art forms of Europe, including those of the cold war enemy, Russia, to which they had formerly never been so widely exposed. The early ballet productions on television were met with an onslaught of indignant telephone calls protesting what the men were doing to the women. When it was explained that this was a traditional art form, however, the American people accepted it, as they were accepting so much else that was new to them. It was a historical landmark in the history of the fine arts in the United States when the New York Philharmonic Orchestra was, for the first time in its history, led by an American-born director, Leonard Bernstein.

But the willingness of America to accept the old culture of Europe was as nothing compared to the avid acceptance by Europe of the new culture of the conquering United States. The trumpet of Louis Armstrong was heard throughout the Old World, and the walls came tumbling down. High, low, and demisociety in Europe was quick to catch the latest American hit tune and the latest American dance step. Although fastidious Americans blushed for the cultural front which their countrymen were presenting to the world, the world—much of it, at least—was happily drinking in the new culture from the "Land of Coca-Cola."

V

Kennedy Administration The relative political calm of Eisenhower's closing year in office was broken by a presidential campaign, outwardly devoid of clear-cut political issues but covertly dominated, for much of the electorate, by the volatile issue of whether a Catholic should be admitted to the Presidency.

John F. Kennedy of Boston was the second son in one of the most remarkable political families in American history in a region characterized by political family dynasties: Adamses, Saltonstalls, and Cabots. His father, Joseph P. Kennedy, early achieved great wealth and became a patron of politics and a leading supporter of Franklin Roosevelt, being rewarded by appointment as chairman of the Securities and Exchange Commission and later as Ambassador to Great Britain. John Kennedy's mother, Rose Fitzgerald Kennedy, came from a politically prominent Massachusetts family, and it was the ambition of the Kennedys that the eldest son, Joseph, Jr., would distinguish himself nationally as a statesman. This ambition was blasted when Joseph, Jr., was killed in action in World War II. Thereafter, the hopes of the family centered upon John F. Kennedy, who had, himself, narrowly missed death during the war, as commander of a PT boat.

John Kennedy was an energetic intellectual, whose first published work, *Why England Slept*, appeared during his senior year at Harvard, and, at the same time, he was a handsome young man with a penchant for café society. These were qualities which were not seemingly very well suited to the requirements of ward politics in Boston. It turned out, however, that Kennedy was a born political campaigner as well, and he won his election to the House of Representatives in 1946 at the age of 29. Serving for two terms in the House, he won election to the Senate in 1952 by a narrow margin. Six years later, he won reelection by a prodigious landslide.

In the Democratic convention of 1956, Kennedy was narrowly defeated for the vice-presidential nomination, and almost from that moment on, he launched his campaign for the Presidency, tirelessly assisted by his numerous and politically brilliant family. Entering the Democratic primaries in 1960, the Catholic J.F.K. won an astonishing victory in the overwhelmingly Protestant state of West Virginia, aided by a quality reminiscent of F.D.R., amid extremely depressed mining conditions. Leading from this show of strength, he went on to win the presidential nomination in the convention on the first ballot.

Opposing Kennedy in the general election was Vice President Richard M. Nixon, like Kennedy, a young man who had risen rapidly to his position, through the House and the Senate. Chiefly at issue during the campaign—the religious issue being disavowed by both candidates—was the recession at home and the Castro take-over of Cuba abroad. A noteworthy political innovation in the 1960 campaign was the series of televised debates between the candidates. No significant differences of opinion emerged from the debates, but it was generally conceded in the national press, that Kennedy's performances were the more impressive. It was later generally conceded that these debates had given Kennedy his margin of victory, especially since, prior to the debates, Nixon had been much the better known of the two men nationally.

Kennedy won the election by a hair's breadth. It later appeared from analysis of the voting returns, however, that this narrow decision had been the result of a massive majority of white Protestant votes for Nixon against an even larger majority of the votes of Negroes and of second and third generation Americans for Kennedy. Having thus narrowly refuted the political axiom that a Catholic could never be President, Kennedy was at pains throughout his Presidency to insist upon the strictest observance of the doctrine of separation of church and state, most notably in the area of Federal aid to parochial schools. By this policy, he aroused the opposition of some leading members of the Catholic Church, but he did much to allay the suspicions and win the support of many who had opposed his election on the grounds of his religion. In this, he was greatly aided by the fact that his administration occurred during the reign of Pope John XXIII, whose humane and ecumenical reign brought a mood of harmony to the Christian world, unprecedented in modern times.

The youngest man ever elected to the Presidency in the nation's history, Kennedy gathered around him a group of young, conspicuously Harvard-oriented intellectuals, chief among them, his younger brother, Robert Kennedy, whom he appointed as Attorney General. These men were highly conscious of themselves as spokesmen for the new generation, born in this century and tempered by depression and war, as Kennedy proudly announced in his inaugural address. They were confident that they could open up the "New Frontier" of mid-twentieth-century opportunities to the American people. They faced, however, a Congress which was dominated by that same coalition of conservative Republicans and conservative Democrats which had successfully contained the Second New Deal in the late thirties and which had throttled Truman's Fair Deal in the late forties. Kennedy's New Frontier, which inherited much from Truman's Fair Deal, met much the same fate during Kennedy's Presidency.

Kennedy failed in his efforts to win Congress to his "medicare" program, just as Truman had failed to achieve a similar program of public medical insurance. The fight for Federal aid to education became involved in the controversy over aid to parochial schools and foundered. Kennedy was somewhat more successful in his smaller-scale programs of aid to depressed areas and of job-rehabilitation for men thrown out of work by automation. In 1962, he won a dramatic victory against the steel industry when he successfully mobilized the government against a scheduled price increase in steel. The industry managed to increase prices later, however, piecemeal and rather on the quiet.

The general failure of the administration to achieve its domestic reforms was no doubt in part due to the fact that economic conditions throughout Kennedy's administration had shown steady, if unspectacular, improvement. The ideal of full employment was still far from being reached, however, and widespread economic hardship remained, especially within the Negro communities of the nation. Throughout Kennedy's years in office, Negro groups voiced their demands with increasing urgency, for equality of job opportunities, and, even more, for equality in civil rights. Accordingly, the administration fought in 1963 for a tax reduction to stimulate the economy and a civil rights measure to improve the position of the Negro in American society. Both bills remained deadlocked in Congress at year's end.

As had been the case with Truman, Kennedy won a much greater measure of congressional support in foreign than in domestic affairs. Indeed, his one major victory in domestic affairs, the massive space program, was overwhelmingly endorsed by Congress largely in the context of foreign affairs, to enhance American world power and prestige by beating Russia to the moon. It would be far from true to say that foreign policy had been elevated above party politics; nevertheless, except for a growing congressional disposition to whittle away at foreign aid measures, whenever Kennedy called for congressional support in the cold war, he got it.

The first major diplomatic development under Kennedy was the disastrous U.S.-sponsored Bay of Pigs fiasco. Cuban refugees, trained under the direction of the Central Intelligence Agency, were overwhelmingly defeated in their efforts to invade Cuba at the Bay of Pigs and overturn the pro-Communist Castro regime. To some extent, this catastrophe was removed from party controversy by the fact that the invasion plans had initially been undertaken during the Eisenhower administration. The invasion itself, however, had been a Kennedy administration undertaking, and it was argued by leading Republicans that failure to provide the invaders with air support had brought about the defeat. This was to remain as a source of political dispute.

The problem of Cuba was later brought home to the American people, as no other problem had been since the Korean conflict, when President Kennedy went before a national television audience to tell it that Russian missile-launching bases were under construction on Cuban soil and that stockpiles of Russian missiles were already stored there, capable of carrying nuclear warheads to American cities. Kennedy announced that he had placed the Armed Forces on the alert throughout the world, and that he had blockaded Cuba. All Russian vessels sailing to Cuba would be halted and inspected, and those carrying equipment for nuclear warfare would be turned back. The blockade, furthermore, would continue, until the Russian missiles and missile sites in Cuba were removed. As a tense world waited for possible nuclear war, Russian ships, bound for Cuba, turned from their course, and Premier Khrushchev announced that the President's demands would be met.

Complaints were later voiced in Congress about the lack of on-the-spot inspection, to insure the removal of atomic equipment, and about the Russian military and technical personnel which remained on the island. Never afterwards, during the Kennedy administration, however, did the Russians make remotely so aggressive a move anywhere in the world. A lessening of cold war tension followed the Cuba "confrontation," and this relaxation was expressed, in 1963, by the signing of an agreement between the United States and Russia, as well as other nations, to ban nuclear bomb testing, except in underground areas. France and Red China were the notable abstainers from this agreement.

A further result of the second Cuban crisis, favorable to the United States, was the reaction against Castro on the part of many Latin-Americans, who had formerly looked upon him as a nationalistic reformer and who now looked upon him as a puppet of the Soviet government. The Alliance for Progress, meanwhile, proceeded at a disappointingly slow pace in its programs for raising Latin-American standards of living and encouraging greater cooperation among the several Latin-American states.

America's role in the Far East has become an increasingly ambivalent one, since the Korean conflict, presenting ever more perplexing problems for which solutions, certainly, have not been found. The United States remains committed to defend the government on Formosa, with its increasingly aged and hostile ruler, Chiang Kai-shek. It is committed to the sustaining of impoverished South Korea and to the guaranteeing of its independence from Communist North Korea, where the far richer natural resources produce a dramatically higher standard of living. Most perplexingly of all, it has been drawn ever more deeply into Southeast Asian affairs, which became increasingly unstable in the course of the Kennedy administration.

Initially intending, apparently, to extend cautiously limited technical and military aid to nations of Southeast Asia, the United States became increasingly involved in the military affairs of South Vietnam, as the grueling Vietnamese war with the Communist Viet Cong continued indecisively. Eventually, nearly 17,-000 American military personnel were committed to the struggle which the Ngo Dinh Diem regime was waging against the Communists. The Diem regime, in the opinion of American observers, had originally held forth promise of maintaining a stable, non-Communist government, but reports of violent suppression began to filter out of Saigon in increasing volume.

These stories of atrocities were vividly dramatized to the world in a series of self-immolations by fire, on the part of protesting Buddhist monks. Then, Diem's sister-in-law, the influential Mme. Ngo Dinh Nhu, wrote a letter to the *New York Times,* delighting in what she called the "Buddhist barbecues" in Vietnam. The United States had been embarrassed before by the company it kept internationally, for various reasons, but it had never found itself involved with anything quite like the "Dragon Lady," as the delicately beautiful Mme. Nhu immediately came to be known. While Henry Cabot Lodge worked in Saigon to achieve some kind of solution to an incredible situation, Mme. Nhu toured the United States, appealing to fascinated audiences on behalf of the Diem government. As she was completing her tour and preparing to return to her country, Vietnamese generals overthrew the Diem regime and established a military junta, which at once freed prisoners and revoked oppressive laws. The United States, whether rightly or not, received a large measure of credit for the *coup d'état,* but the war with the Viet Cong went on indecisively, as before. Cambodia, meanwhile, ordered out the American advisers and launched upon the usual anti-American campaign.

Europe continued prosperous and stable through Kennedy's Presidency, but under rapidly changing circumstances, which altered her relationship with America in ways which obliged the United States to find a new, and as yet unformulated, role in the Atlantic Community. The Common Market proceeded apace during those years, to unify the economy of Western Europe. It was inevitable that a degree of political unification would accompany this revolutionary customs union, but President Charles de Gaulle of France made it increasingly clear that, for him, the prime purpose of the Common Market was to create a third power in the world to rival the United States and the Soviet Union. De Gaulle forced the exclusion of Great Britain from the Common Market, and France became the third nation in the world to share the atomic bomb. De Gaulle became increasingly hostile to NATO and to America's leading role in the defense system of Western Europe.

At the close of 1963, Walter Lippmann summarized the character and accomplishments of the Kennedy administration. He noted that "we must begin with the brutal fact that the big hopes and promises of the New Frontier are at a standstill." It was not that "John F. Kennedy lacked eloquence and persuasiveness or that he was not shrewd enough as a political manipulator."

> It is that we have come again into one of those periods, recurrent in our history after the exertions of war, when the presidency is diminished.
> . . . Enormously popular though he was, he could not arouse in the people the energy to propel them across the New Frontier.

In foreign affairs, Lippmann continued, events taught President Kennedy that the influence of the United States in the world had diminished irretrievably, since the immediate postwar years, and that new arrangements would be necessary to meet America's new world situation. In the meantime,

> He achieved one thing brilliantly, which is changing the course of events, and that has been to convince the Soviet Union that it must perforce and that it can comfortably and honorably live within a balance of power which is decidedly in our favor. For that John F. Kennedy will long be remembered.

Midday on November 22, 1963, in the course of a motorcade through Dallas, Texas, President Kennedy was assassinated. He was 47. He was the fourth American President to be assassinated, and, within the twentieth century alone, he was the fourth President upon whose life an attempt had been made.

President Kennedy had served under gunfire and had very nearly been killed during World War II, and he was thoroughly conversant with American history, including the history of the dangers of the Presidency. Accordingly, upon receiving the Democratic nomination in 1960, he chose his vice-presidential running mate with care. He surprised most people by selecting the majority leader of the Senate, Lyndon B. Johnson, who had been his leading rival at the convention. In part, he chose Johnson as being the running mate most likely to save votes, which would otherwise be lost by a Catholic candidate from the urban Northeast. In part, as Kennedy said privately, at the time, he chose Johnson as the man who, in his estimation, was best fitted to lead the country, in the event of his own death.

Born in Texas ranch country in 1908, Johnson had entered politics in 1931, as secretary to a congressman. Like President Kennedy, he had won his seat in the House of Representatives at the age of 29, running on a thoroughgoing New Deal platform. Except for wartime service in the Navy, during which he won the Silver Star for gallantry in action, Johnson remained in the House until 1948. In that year, he won a seat in the Senate by a margin of 87 votes. There, four years later, at the age of 44, he was elected majority leader by his Democratic colleagues, the youngest man of either party ever to hold the position.

During the later Eisenhower years, Johnson achieved the height of his reputation as the politician's politician, bringing the Republican administration and the Democratic Senate majority into harmony with one another on many issues. He was praised as a moderate and a skillful compromiser; yet in 1954, he had organized the Democratic senators in support of the condemnation of Senator Joseph McCarthy, and in 1957 he had steered through the Senate the first civil rights bill to be enacted in 80 years.

As Vice President, Johnson had been given a more active role and kept himself better informed than almost any other Vice President in history. Shortly after President Kennedy's assassination, Johnson went before the television cameras to promise to "do my best. That is all I can do." An hour later, in the plane which had flown the Presidential party to Texas, he was sworn in as the nation's thirty-sixth President and was at once flown back to Washington to take up his duties as Chief of State.

BIBLIOGRAPHY FOR CHAPTER FIFTEEN

For general accounts of the cold war and of postwar domestic politics, see the relevant books listed at the close of the previous chapter. To them may be added John Lukacs, *A History of the Cold War* (1961) and H. A. Kissinger, *Nuclear Weapons and Foreign Policy* (1957). R. H. Rovere, *Senator Joe McCarthy* (1959) is perhaps the best account of the man and the phenomenon, by the Washington correspondent of *The New Yorker* magazine.

Two studies of mid-century American society, F. L. Allen, *The Big Change* (1952) and C. W. Mills, *The Power Elite* (1956) may profitably be contrasted with each other. Allen describes a half century of democratic advance in terms of the spread of the suffrage, the diffusion of wealth among the masses, the replacement of serving girls by household appliances, and the democratizing impact of mass production. Mills describes an irresponsible clique of generals, admirals, senators, and corporation executives operating under cover of the cold war out of reach of the masses, who, under any circumstances, are manipulated by this group for its own purposes. Each—arguing, of course, on a different level—presents a persuasive thesis supported by solid and usually interesting information.

There are some scholarly contemporary observers who are willing to confess to at least a measure of Allen's optimism. J. G. Galbraith, for instance, in his *American Capitalism: The Concept of Countervailing Power* (1962 ed.) presents the thesis that concentrations of power in the economy tend to inspire the creation of opposing concentrations, which check them. D. M. Potter, *People of Plenty: Economic Abundance and the American Character* (1954) presents an optimistic view of America based upon the thesis implicit in the subtitle. A. M. Schlesinger, Jr., *The Vital Center* (1962 ed.) and Daniel Bell, *The End of Ideology: On the Exhaustion of Political Ideas in the Fifties* (1959) retain hope of continuing moderate reform in the direction of wider democracy. In recent years, however, the scholarly doubters have received a wider hearing with such gloomy analyses as Vance Packard, *The Hidden Persuaders* (1950), W. H. Whyte, Jr., *The Organization Man* (1956), Martin Mayer, *Madison Avenue, U.S.A.* (1958).

Probably the most influential study in this genre has been David Riesman et al., *The Lonely Crowd* (1950), which sees individualistic "inner-directed" values increasingly replaced by changing and readily manipulated mass values. The deepening pessimism of the theologian Reinhold Niebuhr expresses itself in *The Irony of American History* (1952), which sees recurrent disaster arising out of a national spiritual inadequacy, repeatedly manifesting itself in a fatally false self-image of national virtue and self-sufficiency. Walter Lippmann, a semiofficial spokesman for American intellectuals for half a century, concluded in *The Public Philosophy* (1955) that new safeguards against democracy were necessary for the good of society.

The new concern for civil rights for Negroes has produced a flood of literature on the subject. From the historical point of view the best introduction is C. V. Woodward, *The Strange Career of Jim Crow* (1955). "The author, an acknowledged specialist in the post-Reconstruction history of the South, has exploded a myth, widely accepted as historic fact, that the Southern system of Negro segregation with all its ramifications was established by the revered 'Redeemers' who . . . restored white supremacy in the former Confederate states." Included among the other recent literature on the subject is the Pulitzer prize-winning novelist R. P. Warren's *Segregation: The Inner Conflict in the South* (1956), M. J. Butcher, *The Negro in American Culture* (1956), and R. W. Logan, *The Negro in the United States* (1957). W. J. Cash, *The Mind of the South* (1941) remains an extraordinarily persuasive and vivid account of Southern white society and its relation to the Southern Negro.

T. H. White, *The Making of the President, 1960* (1961) is a detailed piece of political reporting, while J. M. Burns, *John Kennedy: A Political Profile* (1959) is a generally sympathetic account by the author of the best one-volume biography of Franklin Roosevelt. J. F. Kennedy, *The Strategy of Peace* (1960) presents his preconvention views on foreign policy.

CHRONOLOGY

EXPLORATION

Internal Political Events	International Politics and Diplomacy	Economic and Social
	790(?): Irish monks reach Iceland	
	981(?): Norsemen discover Greenland	
	1002(?): Leif Ericson reaches North America	
	1492: Columbus discovers West Indies	
	1493: Papal line of demarcation; second voyage of Columbus	
	1494: Treaty of Tordesillas between Spain and Portugal	
	1497: John Cabot explores Newfoundland coast	
	1498: Third voyage of Columbus	
	1499: Alonzo de Ojeda and Amerigo Vespucci discover mouth of Amazon	

1502:	Fourth voyage of Columbus
1513:	Balboa discovers Isthmus of Panama
1519–1521:	Cortés conquers Mexico
1519–1522:	Magellan circumnavigates globe
1521:	Ponce de Leon attempts settlement in Florida
1534–1541:	Cartier explores St. Lawrence River
1539–1543:	Hernando de Soto discovers Mississippi River
1577–1580:	Sir Francis Drake circumnavigates globe
1583:	Sir Humphrey Gilbert attempts settlement of Newfoundland
1584:	Sir Walter Raleigh attempts settlement of Roanoke Island
1603:	Champlain explores St. Lawrence River

Internal Political Events	International Politics and Diplomacy	Economic and Social
	1606: Charters granted to Virginia Companies of London and of Plymouth	
1607: Founding of Jamestown		
1608: Founding of Quebec		
	1609: Hudson discovers Hudson River	
		1612: Tobacco planted commercially in Virginia
		1619: First Negroes brought to Virginia
1619: First representative assembly in Virginia		
1620: Plymouth Colony founded; Mayflower Compact		
1621: New Netherlands founded		
1624: Virginia charter revoked; Virginia becomes a royal colony		
1627: Finns and Swedes settle region of the Delaware		
	1629: Massachusetts Bay Company obtains charter	

1630: Massachusetts Bay Colony founded		**1630–1642:** Great Migration of 16,000 to New England
1634: Settlement of Connecticut and Maryland		
1636: Roger Williams founds Providence		**1636:** Harvard College established
1636–1637: Pequot War		
1638: New Haven settled		**1638:** Antinomian Controversy: Anne Hutchinson banished from Massachusetts
1639: Fundamental Orders of Connecticut		
	1641–1660: Great Rebellion and Interregnum in England	
		1647: Massachusetts General Court provides for public education
	1651: First Navigation Act	
	1660: Reenactment of Navigation Act	
	1662: Connecticut charter granted	**1662:** Halfway Covenant in Massachusetts
	1663: Rhode Island and Carolinas receive charters; second Navigation Act	
1664: Dutch colony of New Netherlands becomes English colony of New York		

Internal Political Events	International Politics and Diplomacy	Economic and Social
1675–1676: King Philip's War		
1676: Bacon's Rebellion		
1682: Settlement of Pennsylvania		
1684: Massachusetts loses charter		
1686: Edmund Andros appointed governor of New England; Dominion of New England created		
1689: Overthrow of Andros following Glorious Revolution in England	**1689–1697:** King William's War	**1692:** Salem witchcraft trials
	1696: British Board of Trade established	**1693:** William and Mary College founded
	1699: Woolens Act	**1701:** Yale College founded
	1702–1713: Queen Anne's War	**c. 1726–c. 1756:** Great Awakening
1719–1729: Carolinas reorganized into two royal colonies	**1733:** Molasses Act passed	
1733: Georgia founded	**1739–1748:** King George's War	**1746:** Founding of Princeton
	1745: Capture of Louisbourg	
	1754–1763: French and Indian War	
	1759: Fall of Quebec	
1761: James Otis attacks Writs of Assistance	**1762:** Louisiana transferred from France to Spain	

1762–1766: Pontiac's Conspiracy	**1763:** Proclamation Line	
1763: Patrick Henry argues the the Parsons' Cause	**1763–1765:** Grenville Ministry in England	
1764: Beginning of nonimportation	**1764:** Sugar Act; Colonial Currency Act; first Quebec Act	**1764:** Brown University founded
1765: Patrick Henry's resolutions in Va. House of Burgesses; Stamp Act Congress: *Declaration of Rights and Grievances*	**1765:** Stamp Act; Quartering Act	
	1766: Repeal of Stamp and Sugar Acts; passing of Declaratory Act	
1767: Revival of nonimportation	**1767:** Townshend Acts	
1767–1771: Regulator Movement in North Carolina protests lack of western representation in Assembly		
1770: Collapse of nonimportation; Boston Massacre	**1770:** Repeal of Townshend Acts except for tax on tea	
1772: Gaspee affair; formation of standing committees of correspondence	**1772:** Crown assumes payment of governors and judges in Massachusetts	
1773: Va. House of Burgesses appoints a Provincial Committee of Correspondence; Boston Tea Party		

Internal Political Events	International Politics and Diplomacy	Economic and Social
1774: Suffolk Resolves; First Continental Congress	**1774:** Coercive Acts: Boston Port Bill; Massachusetts Government Act; Administration of Justice Act; Quartering Act; second Quebec Act	
1775: Second Continental Congress; Washington appointed commander-in-chief of Continental Army	**1775:** Battles of Lexington and Concord, Ticonderoga, Crown Point, and Bunker Hill; siege of Boston	
1776: Declaration of Independence	**1776:** British evacuation of Boston; battles of Long Island, White Plains, and Trenton	**1776:** *Common Sense* published
1777: Articles of Confederation drawn up	**1777:** Battles of Princeton, Bennington, Saratoga, and Brandywine	
1777–1778: Conway Cabal attacks Washington's conduct of the war	**1777–1778:** Winter at Valley Forge	
	1778: Treaties of commerce and alliance with France; Lord North's final peace offer rejected; battle of Monmouth	
	1779: George Rogers Clark captures Vincennes; Spain enters the war	

476

1780: French army under Rochambeau arrives at Newport; battles of Camden and King's Mountain; treason of Benedict Arnold

1781: Cornwallis surrenders at Yorktown

1782: Lord North resigns; Holland recognizes U.S. independence; preliminary articles of peace signed

1783: Final peace terms with England

1785: Land Ordinance for Northwest Territory

1786: Virginia Statute for Religious Freedom

1787: Northwest Ordinance

1787–1788: *Federalist Papers* published

1781: Articles of Confederation adopted

1786: Annapolis Convention

1786–1787: Shays' Rebellion

1787: Constitutional Convention

1788: Ratification of the Constitution

Internal Political Events	International Politics and Diplomacy	Economic and Social
WASHINGTON'S ADMINISTRATIONS (1789–1797)		
1789: Judiciary Act		
1791: First ten amendments to Constitution ratified	**1790:** Nootka Sound Treaty gives Britain claim to Oregon Territory	**1790–1791:** Hamilton's Fiscal Program: Report on Public Credit; Funding Bill; Assumption Bill; creation of Bank of the United States; Report on Manufactures
c. 1793–c. 1800: Beginning of organized political parties	**1793:** France declares war on Great Britain; Washington's Proclamation of neutrality; Genêt arrives in America	**1793:** Fugitive slave law; Eli Whitney invents cotton gin
1793: Giles Resolutions		
1794: Whiskey Rebellion	**1794:** Jay's Treaty	
1796: John Adams-Jefferson campaign; Washington's Farewell Address	**1795:** Pinckney's Treaty	
JOHN ADAMS'S ADMINISTRATION (1797–1801)		
1798: Alien and Sedition Acts:	**1797:** XYZ Affair	

1798–1800: Undeclared naval war with France

1800: Treaty with France

Virginia and Kentucky Resolutions; Eleventh Amendment ratified

1800: Jefferson–John Adams election

1801: John Marshall appointed Chief Justice of the Supreme Court and holds post until his death, 1835

JEFFERSON'S ADMINISTRATIONS (1801–1809)

1801–1805: Tripolitan War

1803: Louisiana Purchase

1803: Marbury v. Madison

1803–1806: Lewis and Clark expedition

1803–1804: Northern confederation scheme and Essex Junto

1804: Twelfth Amendment ratified

1804: Hamilton-Burr duel

1804–1807: Burr Conspiracy

1807: Chesapeake-Leopard affair arouses American anger against Britain over naval impressments; Embargo passed

1808: African slave trade prohibited

1809: Embargo repealed; Non-Intercourse Act passed

479

Internal Political Events	International Politics and Diplomacy	Economic and Social
MADISON'S ADMINISTRATIONS (1809–1817)	1810: Macon's Bill No. 2; West Florida annexation proclamation	1811: Defeat of bill to re-charter Bank of the United States; Fletcher v. Peck
1811: Battle of Tippecanoe	1812–1815: War of 1812	
	1812: American attempts to sieze Canada	
	1813: Perry's victory on Lake Erie; second American advance on Canada	
1814: Hartford Convention	1814: British burn Washington; fail to capture Baltimore; Peace of Ghent	
	1815: Battle of New Orleans	1816: Second Bank of the United States chartered; protective Tariff of 1816 passed
MONROE'S ADMINISTRATIONS (1817–1825) ("Era of Good Feelings")	1817: Rush-Bagot Agreement	1817: National Road completed to Ohio
	1818: Canadian boundary settlement and agreement with Britain for ten-year joint occupation of Oregon; Andrew Jackson's Florida campaign	1818: Tariff of 1818 raises protective duties
1820: Missouri Compromise; Maine admitted	1819: Transcontinental Treaty with Spain	
1821: Missouri admitted	1821: Mexican independence	

1819:	Panic of 1819; Dartmouth College v. Woodward; McCulloch v. Maryland
1824:	Tariff of 1824 raises duties, Gibbons v. Ogden
1825:	Completion of Erie Canal
1828:	"Tariff of Abominations"

1822:	Congressional resolution for recognition of new Latin-American republics
1823:	Monroe Doctrine
1826:	Panama Congress issue

| 1824: | "Corrupt bargain" election |

JOHN QUINCY ADAMS'S ADMINISTRATION (1825–1829)

| 1828: | Election of Jackson |
| 1828–1829: | Workingman's parties organized in Philadelphia and New York |

DEMOCRACY, EXPANSION, AND CONFLICT

| 1830: | West Indian trade reopened to American ships |

| 1830: | Maysville Road veto |
| 1831: | Garrison begins publication of *The Liberator*; Nat Turner slave insurrection in Virginia; invention of McCormick reaper |

JACKSON'S ADMINISTRATIONS (1829–1837)

| 1830: | Webster-Hayne debate; emergence of Anti-Masonic party |
| 1831: | Peggy Eaton affair and reorganization of Jackson's Cabinet |

481

Internal Political Events	International Politics and Diplomacy	Economic and Social
1832: Jackson-Clay election		**1832:** Tariff of 1832 retains protection principle; Jackson's Bank Bill veto
1832–1833: Nullification crisis		**1832–1833:** Compromise tariff and Force Bill
1833: Creation of Whig party; Senate resolutions of censure against Jackson		**1833:** American Antislavery Society founded; Removal of Indians from Fla. and Ga.
1834: Emergence of radical Locofoco party in New York		
1836: Election of Van Buren; first congressional "gag rules" against antislavery petitions	**1836:** Texas independence	**1836:** Specie Circular; distribution of surplus revenue among the states
1837: Censure of Jackson expunged from Senate journal		**1837:** Panic of 1837; Charles River Bridge Case
VAN BUREN'S ADMINSTRATION (1837–1841)	**1837–1842:** Border conflicts with Canada concluded by Webster-Ashburton Treaty, 1842	**1838:** Beginnings of underground railroad
1840: Harrison-Van Buren "log cabin and hard cider" campaign		**1840:** Independent Treasury Bill

HARRISON'S ADMINISTRATION (1841)

1841: Harrison dies less than a month after taking office; John Tyler succeeds to the Presidency

TYLER'S ADMINISTRATION (1841–1845)

1842: Dorr Rebellion in Rhode Island

1845: Native American Party formed

POLK'S ADMINISTRATION (1845–1849)

1846: Wilmot Proviso

TAYLOR'S ADMINISTRATION (1849–1850)

1850: Compromise of 1850 proposed; enacted after Taylor's death

---

1845: Annexation of Texas

1845: Polk's elaboration of Monroe Doctrine

1846: Oregon Treaty with England

1846–1848: Mexican War

1847: Nicholas Trist mission to Mexico

1848: Treaty of Guadalupe Hidalgo

1850: Clayton-Bulwer Treaty

1841: Preemption-Distribution Act; repeal of Independent Treasury

1845–1847: Irish potato famine drives emigrants to America

1846: Walker Tariff; revival of Independent Treasury system

1848: Gold discovered in California

1849: Immigration of German '48ers

Internal Political Events	International Politics and Diplomacy	Economic and Social
FILLMORE'S ADMINISTRATION (1850–1853)		
1850: Nashville Convention; Compromise of 1850		1852: *Uncle Tom's Cabin* published
PIERCE'S ADMINISTRATION (1853–1857)	1853: Gadsden Purchase	
1854: Kansas-Nebraska Act; formation of Republican and Know Nothing parties	1854: Ostend Manifesto; treaty of commerce and friendship with Japan; Canadian reciprocity treaty	
1856–1858: "Bleeding Kansas"		
1856: Buchanan-Frémont election		
BUCHANAN'S ADMINISTRATION (1857–1861)		1857: Dred Scott case; Tariff of 1857 lowers rates to 20%
1858: Kansas rejects proslavery Lecompton Constitution; Lincoln-Douglas Debates		1859: John Brown's raid on Harpers Ferry; discovery of Comstock Lode
1860: Lincoln, Douglas, Breckinridge, and Bell election; secession of South Carolina		
LINCOLN'S ADMINISTRATIONS (1861–1865)	1861–1865: Civil War	
1861: Confederate States of America established; Joint Committee on the Conduct of the War created		1861: Morrill Tariff; income tax imposed

	1861: Fort Sumter; First Battle of Bull Run; Trent Affair	
1862: Legal Tender Act; Homestead Act; Morrill Land Grant College Act; Pacific Railroads Act	**1862:** Second Battle of Bull Run; Antietam; Shiloh; Fredericksburg	**1862:** Preliminary Emancipation Proclamation
	1862–1863: Disputes with England over construction of Confederate raiders	
1863: National Banking Act; New York draft riots	**1863:** Battles of Chancellorsville, Vicksburg, Gettysburg, Chickamauga, and Missionary Ridge	**1863:** Final Emancipation Proclamation; first Union conscription Act; Prize cases
	1864: Battle of the Wilderness; Sherman's march	**1864:** Wade-Davis Bill pocket vetoed by Lincoln (National Union Party)-McClellan election
	1865: Surrender of Lee's forces at Appamattox; final capitulation of Confederate forces under Johnston and Kirby Smith in May	**1865:** Assassination of Lincoln

Internal Political Events	International Politics and Diplomacy	Economic and Social
JOHNSON'S ADMINISTRATION (1865–1869)		**1865–1866:** Black Codes
1865: Thirteenth Amendment ratified Joint Committee of Fifteen created		**1866:** Freedmen's Bureau bill; founding of Ku Klux Klan; founding of National Labor Union; *Ex parte* Milligan
1866: Civil Rights Bill, Fourteenth Amendment proposed		
1867: Military Reconstruction Acts; Tenure of Office Act	**1867:** Purchase of Alaska	**1867:** Stanton *v.* Georgia; Mississippi *v.* Johnson
1868: Omnibus Bill; Impeachment of Johnson; Grant-Seymour election; Fourteenth Amendment ratified		
GRANT'S ADMINISTRATIONS (1869–1873)		**1869:** Knights of Labor formed; attempted gold corner; Texas *v.* White
1870: Fifteenth Amendment ratified	**1869–1872:** *Alabama* claims	
1871: Overthrow of Tweed Ring in New York	**1870:** Santo Domingo affair	**1870–1871:** Legal Tender Cases
1872: Amnesty Act; Liberal Republican movement	**1871:** Treaty of Washington	**1872:** Credit Mobilier; Tariff of 1872 lowers duties slightly
	1872: Geneva arbitration award to U.S.	

1875: Civil Rights Act; Whiskey Ring investigation

1876: Disputed Hayes-Tilden election

HAYES'S ADMINISTRATION (1877–1881)

1877: Formal end of Reconstruction and withdrawal of Federal troops from Florida, Louisiana, South Carolina

GARFIELD'S ADMINISTRATION (1881)

1881: Assassination of Garfield and succession to Presidency of "Stalwart" Republican, Arthur

ARTHUR'S ADMINISTRATION (1881–1885)

1883: Pendleton Civil Service Act

1884: Cleveland-Blaine campaign

1873: Panic of 1873; Coinage Act

1874: Climax of Granger movement which began in 1867

1875: Specie Resumption Act

1878: Bland-Allison Act; Greenback-Labor movement

1879: Resumption of specie payments

1882: Chinese Exclusion Act

1883: Civil Rights Cases; Tariff of 1883

	Economic and Social
1886:	Haymarket Affair; American Federation of Labor formed
1890:	Sherman Anti-Trust Act; Sherman Silver Act; McKinley Tariff
1891:	Forest Reserve Act
1893:	Panic of 1893; repeal of Sherman Silver Purchase Act; formation of Anti-Saloon League
1894:	Pullman and American Railway Union strikes; Coxey's Army; Wilson-Gorman Tariff
1895:	Income tax cases
1896:	Plessy v. Ferguson
1897:	Dingley Tariff

	International Politics and Diplomacy
1889–1890:	First International American Conference
1893:	Hawaiian revolution
1895:	Cuban rebellion; Venezuela boundary dispute
1898:	DeLôme Letter; sinking of the *Maine*; Spanish-American War; annexation of Hawaii

Internal Political Events

CLEVELAND'S ADMINISTRATION (1885–1889)

1887: Interstate Commerce Act

HARRISON'S ADMINISTRATION (1889–1893)

1890: Force Bill

1892: Rise of People's (Populist) party

CLEVELAND'S ADMINISTRATION (1893–1897)

1896: McKinley-Bryan "battle of the standards" election.

McKINLEY'S ADMINISTRATIONS (1897–1901)

1899–1902: Philippine insurrection
1899: Open Door Note
1900: Chinese Boxer Rebellion
1901: Platt Amendment

1900: Currency Act (Gold Standard Act)
1901: Formation of United States Steel Corporation

1901: Insular Cases; Assassination of McKinley and succession of Theodore Roosevelt

THEODORE ROOSEVELT'S ADMINISTRATIONS (1901–1909)

PROGRESSIVE ERA

1901: Hay-Pauncefote Treaty

1902: United Mine Workers strike; Newlands Act

1903: Panamanian revolution; Hay-Bunau-Varilla Treaty

1903: Elkins Act; Wright brothers make first flight

1904: Roosevelt Corollary to Monroe Doctrine

1904: *Shame of the Cities* published

1905: Roosevelt's peace-making efforts in Russo-Japanese War

1905: Lochner v. New York; International Workers of the World formed

1906: Pure Food and Drug Act; Meat Inspection Act; Hepburn Act

Internal Political Events	International Politics and Diplomacy	Economic and Social
		1907: Panic of 1907
		1908: Aldrich-Vreeland Act authorizes temporary national banking system; Muller v. Oregon
		1909: Payne-Aldrich Tariff
TAFT'S ADMINISTRATION (1909–1913)		
1910: Roosevelt's Osawatomie ("new nationalism") Speech; Ballinger-Pinchot controversy	1910: Dollar Diplomacy	
1911: La Follette organizes National Republican Progressive League	1911: Marines land in Nicaragua	1911: Dissolution of Standard Oil and American Tobacco trusts
1912: Roosevelt's Progressive ("Bull Moose") party; Wilson-Roosevelt-Taft election		
WILSON'S ADMINISTRATIONS (1913–1921)		
1913: Sixteeenth and Seventeenth Amendments ratified	1913: Bryan's "Cooling Off" treaties	1913: Underwood Tariff; Federal Reserve Act

1916: National Defense (Adamson) Act	**1914:** Vera Cruz invasion; ABC intervention; Panama Canal opened	**1914:** Federal Trade Commission established; Clayton Anti-Trust Act
	1915: Sinking of *Lusitania*	**1916:** Federal Farm Loan Bank Act
1917: Draft Act; Espionage Act	**1916:** Expedition into Mexico	**1917:** Government administration of railroads; War Industries Board
	1917: Unrestricted German submarine warfare; Zimmerman note; U.S. entrance into World War I; purchase of Virgin Islands	
1918: Eighteenth Amendment ratified; Volstead Act	**1918:** Wilson's Fourteen Points; armistice	**1919:** Steel strike
	1919: Versailles Treaty	**1920:** Esch-Cummins Railroad Act; Merchant Marine Act; Palmer raids and "red scare"
	1920: Defeat of Versailles Treaty by Senate	

THE TWENTIES AND THIRTIES

	1921: Separate peace with Germany	**c. 1920–c. 1926:** Revival of Ku Klux Klan

HARDING'S ADMINISTRATION (1921–1923)

1921: Immigration Act

491

Internal Political Events	International Politics and Diplomacy	Economic and Social
1923: Death of Harding	1921–1922: Washington Conference	1922: Fordney-McCumber Tariff
COOLIDGE'S ADMINISTRATIONS (1923–1929)		
1924: Teapot Dome scandal; Soldiers' Bonus Act; Immigration act	1924: Dawes Plan	1925: Scopes trial
	1927: Attempts to outlaw war; Geneva naval conference	1927: Sacco and Vanzetti executed
1928: Hoover-Smith election	1928: Kellogg-Briand Pact	1929: Wall Street crash; Agricultural Marketing Act
HOOVER'S ADMINISTRATION (1929–1933)	1930: London Naval Conference	1931: Smoot-Hawley tariff
	1931: Debt and reparations moratorium	1932: Reconstruction Finance Corporation; Bonus March on Washington; Norris Anti-Injunction Act
	1932: Stimson Doctrine	
FRANKLIN D. ROOSEVELT'S ADMINISTRATION (1933–1945)	1933: Good Neighbor policy proclaimed; Soviet Russia recognized	1933: The "Hundred Days": Securities Act; Emergency Banking Relief
1933: The "Hundred Days"; Twentieth and Twenty-first Amendments ratified		

Act and Banking Act; Home Owners Loan Corporation; Gold repeal joint resolution; Agricultural Adjustment Act; Farm Credit Act; Federal Emergency Relief Administration; TVA; National Industrial Recovery Administration

1934: Frazier-Lemke Bankruptcy Act; Crop Loan Act; Cotton and Tobacco Control Acts; Silver Purchase Act; Civil Works Emergency Relief Act; Railroad Pension Act; Reciprocal Tariff Act; Johnson Debt Default Act; Communications Act

1935: Wagner Labor Relations Act; Social Security Act; Public Utility Holding Company Act; Wealth Tax Act; Works

1935: Neutrality act

1935: "Second New Deal"

493

Internal Political Events	International Politics and Diplomacy	Economic and Social
		Progress Administration; Rural Electrification Administration; Schechter case
1936: Roosevelt-Landon election		**1936:** Soil Conservation and Domestic Allotment Act; U.S. v. Butler
1937: Roosevelt's "court-packing" plan	**1937:** Neutrality Act; Roosevelt's "quarantine the aggressors" speech	**1937:** Emergence of CIO; Wagner-Steagall public housing act; business recession; NLRB v. Jones & Laughlin
	1938: Lima declaration of hemispheric defense	**1938:** Fair Labor Standards Act; Second AAA

HOT AND COLD WARS

1939: Invasion of Poland; Declaration of Panama; Amendment of U.S. Neutrality Act of 1937

1940: Selective Service Act; Smith Act; Roosevelt-Willkie election

1943: Connally-Fulbright resolutions favoring U.S. participation in post-war international organization

1944: Roosevelt's election to fourth term

1940 Nazi conquest of Western Europe; embargo on iron and steel shipments to Japan; Rome-Berlin-Tokyo pact

1941: Lend-Lease Act and subsequent extension of act to Russia; Atlantic Charter; attack on Pearl Harbor and declaration of war against Japan, Germany, Italy

1942: Anglo-American invasion of North Africa; Battles of the Coral Sea and Guadalcanal

1943: Casablanca Conference; victory in North Africa; invasion of Sicily and Italy; invasion of Gilbert Islands

1944: Invasion of Normandy and Southern France; Battle of the Bulge; recapture of Guam; invasion of Mariana Islands and of Leyte; Second Battle of the Philippine

1942: War Industries Board; War Production Board; War Labor Board; Office of Price Administration

Internal Political Events	International Politics and Diplomacy	Economic and Social
	Sea; Dumbarton Oaks Conference	
1945: Death of Roosevelt	**1945:** Yalta Conference	
TRUMAN'S ADMINISTRATIONS (1945–1953)	**1945:** Victory in Europe; Invasion of Okinawa; atomic bombs dropped on Hiroshima and Nagasaki; Russia declares war on Japan; Victory in Asia; San Francisco Conference; Potsdam Conference	
	1946: Paris Peace Conference	**1946:** Removal of most price controls
1946: Republican victory in congressional elections	**1947:** Truman Doctrine; Marshall Plan	**1947:** Taft-Hartley Act
1947: Unification of Armed Services	**1948:** Vandenburg Resolution favors U.S. participation in regional security associations	
1948: Truman-Dewey election	**1948–1949:** Berlin Blockade	

1949: NATO; Mutual Defense Assistance Act

1950: Brussels Conference Invasion of Korea

1951: Japanese peace treaty signed; Korean peace talks begin

1953: Death of Stalin; Korean armistice

1954: Southeast Asia Treaty Organization

1955: Geneva summit meeting

1957: Russia launches Sputnik I

1950: Conviction of Alger Hiss; rise of McCarthy to national prominence

1951: Dismissal of MacArthur; McCarran (Internal Security) Act; ratification of Twenty-second Amendment

EISENHOWER'S ADMINISTRATIONS (1953–1961)

1953: Defeat of isolationist Bricker Amendment

1954: Army-McCarthy hearings; Senate condemnation of McCarthy

1956: Eisenhower-Stevenson election

1953: Removal of wage and price supports established during Korean Conflict

1954: Corporate tax reductions; Brown v. Board of Education of Topeka

1955: Unification of AFL and CIO

1957: Little Rock school integration crisis

Internal Political Events	International Politics and Diplomacy	Economic and Social
KENNEDY'S ADMINISTRATION (1961–1963)	**1958:** U.S. launches Explorer I	
	1961: Bay of Pigs invasion; Alliance for Progress program in Latin America; Peace Corps established	
	1962: John Glenn orbits the earth; Cuban crisis	**1962–1963:** Growing Negro demands for equal rights culminate in march on Washington "for jobs and freedom"
1963: Assassination of Kennedy	**1963:** Limited nuclear test ban treaty concluded; Vietnam crisis worsens	**1963:** Token school integration in all Southern states; James Meredith graduates from the University of Mississippi
JOHNSON'S ADMINISTRATION (1963–)		

INDEX

AAA, 388, 389
ABC powers (Argentina, Brazil, and Chile), 335, 403
Abernethy, Thomas P., 121
Abolitionism (see Antislavery)
Adams, Charles Francis, 16, 246, 247
Adams, James Truslow, 17
Adams, John, 42, 47, 66, 71, 76, 103, 110, 112, 143
Adams, John Quincy, 139, 140, 146, 200, 456
Adams, Samuel, 41, 68, 83
Adamson Act, 326, 333
Adkins v. Children's Hospital, 356
Administration of Justice Act, 70
Agassiz, Louis, 306
Agrarian reform (see Agriculture; Granger movement; Populism)
Agricultural Adjustment Act, 388, 389
Agricultural Marketing Act, 388
Agriculture, 36, 209-210, 258, 410, 440
Alabama, 142
Alabama (ship), 282-283
Alamo, 200
Alaska, 202, 290
Albany Congress, 44
Albany Plan, 71
Albany Regency, 145
Aldrich-Vreeland Act, 332
Algonquin Indians, 51, 62
Alien and Sedition Acts, 111, 114
Allen, Ethan, 74
Alliance, 287
Alliance for Progress, 463
Altgeld, John P., 274, 275
Alvarado, Pedro de, 7
Amendments to Constitution, first Ten (Bill of Rights), 76, 90
Twelfth, 110, 112
Thirteenth, 231
Fourteenth, 138, 231
Fifteenth, 231, 245
Sixteenth, 330
Seventeenth, 385
Eighteenth, 351
Nineteenth, 352
America First Committee, 406
American Anti-Slavery Society, 190
American Colonization Society, 190

American Federation of Labor (AFL), 275, 280, 361, 390
American Philosophical Society, 42
American Revolution (see Revolutionary War)
American Tobacco Company, 328
Ames, Oakes, 247
Anderson, Sherwood, 367
Andrews, Charles M., 72
Andros, Sir Edmund, 24
Anglican Church (see Church of England)
Animal magnetism, 186
Annapolis Convention, 88
Anthropology, 457
Antietam, Battle of, 221, 225
Anti-Imperialist League, 290
Anti-Masonic party, 157, 184
Antinomianism, 16
Antislavery, 94, 149, 190-193, 226
Architecture, 45, 371
Argentina, 403
in ABC powers, 335, 403
Aristotle, 41
Arkansas, 208, 453
Armada, 5
Armstrong, Louis, 460
Army, U.S. in 1895, 284
in World War I, 340
in World War II, 409, 414
since World War II, 437
Arnold, Benedict, 74, 118
Aroostook War, 201
Arthur, Chester A., 251, 267
Articles of Confederation, 72, 81-82
Ashburton, Lord, 202
Asia, 4, 6
Assemblies, colonial, 50
Assumption of state debts, 102
Astor, John Jacob, 171, 202
Astoria, 202
Atlantic Charter, 416
Atlantic and Pacific Railroad, 242
Atomic bomb, 418, 435, 437, 447-448, 456
Atomic Energy Commission, 437
Austerlitz, Battle of, 123
Austin, Moses, 199
Austin, Stephen, 199
Australia, 411
Austria, 406
Automobiles, 362

499

Calvert, Cecilius, Lord Baltimore, 11, 12, 23
Calvert, George, Lord Baltimore, 11
Calvin, John, 15
Cambodia, 465
Cameron, Simon, 244
Canada, 211, 282, 435, 439
Canadian boundary controversy, 200-201
Capone, Al, 351
Caribbean (see Latin America; individual nations)
Carnegie, Andrew, 244, 260, 300
Carolinas, 18
Caroline (ship), 201
Carothers, Wallace H., 454
Carroll, Charles, of Carrollton, 169
Carson, Kit, 215
Cartier, Jacques, 8
Casablanca, 416
Cash, W.J., 220
Cass, Lewis, 206
Castro, Fidel, 447, 463-464
Catholic Church, 3, 4, 7, 11-12, 302-304
Catholicism, 354, 384, 461-462
Central Pacific Railroad, 242, 247, 256, 259
Cervera, Pascual, 288
Chambers, Whittaker, 438
Champlain, Samuel de, 8
Chancellorsville, Battle of, 225
Chandler, Zachary, 228
Charles II, 11, 17-19
Charleston, 34, 154
Charlotte Temple (novel), 175
Charter of privileges, 21, 76
Chase, Salmon P., 222
Chase, Samuel, 115
Chattanooga, Battle of, 225
Chautauqua, 312
Chesapeake (ship), 123
Chiang Kai-shek, 416, 418, 429
Chicago, 172
Chile, 335, 403
China, 292, 303, 342, 359, 405
    Communist 429-431, 438, 446
    Nationalist, 429, 446
Christian Church, 186
Christian Science, 94
Church and state, 94
Church of England, 11, 13, 39, 40, 47, 50, 94
Church of the Nazarene, 459

Churchhill, Winston, 417, 425-427
Churubusco, Battle of, 205
Cincinnati, Order of the, 84, 108
CIO, 391
Cities (see Urbanization)
Civil rights, 449-454, 462-463
Civil Rights Act, 228
Civil Rights Bill, 467
Civil War, 217-226
    See also Confederacy; Secession; individual battles)
Civil Works Administration (CWA), 387
Civilian Conservation Corps (CCC), 384, 387
Claflin, H.B., 171
Claiborne, William, 23
Clark, William, 197
Clay, Henry, 135, 141, 146, 149, 154, 157-159, 193, 203, 207
Clayton Antitrust Act, 333
Cleveland, Grover, 269, 273, 284, 286, 325, 332-334
Clinton, De Witt, 125, 143, 145-147
Coal, 240-241
Cobalt bomb, 437
Cochran, Thomas C., 259, 262
Coercive Acts, 69
Coin's Financial School, 277
Cold War, 449, 463-464
Colonial Currency Act, 69
·Colored Alliance, 276
Columbia College, 47, 455
Columbus, Christopher, 6, 7
Commerce, medieval, 5
Commerce and industry, 28, 34-37, 136, 168-170, 259-260, 360-363
Commerce Department, 355-356
Committee to Defend America by Aiding the Allies, 406
Committee of Fifty-one, 70
Committee on Public Information, 339, 347
Committees of Correspondence, 69
Common Market, 465
Communism, 427, 442, 446
Communist party, American, 349, 392, 395, 439
Compromise of 1850, 207-208, 211, 213
Compromise of 1877, 249-250
Comstock Lode, 256-257
Confederacy, 211-222
Confederation Congress, 84

Jeffersonian republicanism, 104, 112-114, 119, 150-151
Jehovah's Witnesses, 459
Jensen, Merrill, 73, 93
Jewett, Sarah Orne, 313
Jews, 22, 37, 303, 384
Jim Crow laws, 450
John XXIII, Pope, 462
Johns Hopkins University, 310
Johnson, Andrew, 227-229, 245
Johnson, Hiram, 325
Johnson, Hugh S., 393
Johnson, Lyndon B., 466-467
Johnson, Tom, 325
Johnston, Joseph, 226
Josephson, Matthew, 262
Judiciary Act of 1789, 104, 115

Kansas, 208, 213
Kansas-Nebraska Act, 193, 213, 215
Keating-Owen Child-labor Act, 333
Kellogg-Briand Pact, 359
Kelly, George, 368
Kennedy, John F., 460-466
Kennedy, Joseph P., 460
Kennedy, Joseph P., Jr., 460
Kennedy, Robert, 462
Kennedy, Rose Fitzgerald, 460
Kentucky, 119, 145, 223
Key, David M., 250
Keynes, John Maynard, 384, 397
Khrushchev, Nikita, 446-447
King, Ernest J., 411
King, Rufus, 87
King George's War, 51
King William's War, 51
King's Mountain, Battle of, 80
Knights of Labor, 274
Know-Nothing party, 172, 215
Knox, Frank, 407
Korea, 429, 444
    South, 429, 440, 463
Korean War, 425, 429-431
Ku Klux Klan, 229, 303, 350
Kuhn, Loeb, and Company, 279

Labor, 170-171, 274-276, 349-350, 361, 390-391, 423, 424, 445
La Follette, Robert M., 325, 354
Land acts of 1796, 1800, 1804, and 1820, 145
Land companies, 62
Land grants, 172, 242-243

Lansing, Robert, 337
Larkin, Thomas O., 203
Latin America, 141, 283, 334-335, 403-404, 446, 463
Laud, William, 22
Laurens, Henry, 65
Lawrence, Ernest O., 455
Lawyers, 66-67
League of Nations, 341, 342, 357, 405, 418
Learned societies, 312
Lee, Arthur, 79
Lee, Richard Henry, 75
Lee, Robert E., 225
Leisler, Jacob, 25
"Lend-Lease" bill, 407
Lenin, Nikolai, 99
Leopard-Chesapeake incident, 123
Lewis, John L., 350, 391, 423
Lewis, Meriwether, 197
Lewis, Sinclair, 366, 369
Lexington and Concord, Battle of, 71, 73
Leyte Gulf, Battle of, 414
Liberal Republicans, 247, 249, 250, 252, 267
Liberty bonds, 339
Liberty League, 394
Liberty party, 203
Lilienthal, David, 390
Lincoln, Abraham, 216, 217, 222-224, 226, 227
Lindsay, Vachel, 368
Linnaeus, Carl, 42
Lippmann, Walter, 466
Literature, 176-180, 312-316, 366-371
Little Bighorn, Battle of the, 257
Lloyd, Henry Demarest, 260, 309
Lloyd George, David, 341
Locke, John, 75, 112
Locofocos, 157
Lodge, Henry Cabot, 288
Lodge, Henry Cabot, Jr., 465
Lome, Dupuy de, 287
London, Jack, 316
Long, Huey, 392, 395, 440
Longfellow, Henry Wadsworth, 177-179, 312, 313
Lords of Trade, 24
Lost Generation, 364, 367
Louisbourg, 51
Louisiana, 142
Louisiana Purchase, 116
Louisiana Territory, 140, 142, 197

Lowell, James Russell, 177, 179, 312, 313
Loyalists, 94
Lumber industry, 35
Lundy's Lane, Battle of, 126
Lusitania, 336-337
Lutheran Church, 34
Lyceum, 312

McAdoo, William Gibbs, 338, 354
MacArthur, Douglas, 411, 431
McCarthy, Joseph, 425, 438, 441, 444, 467
McClellan, George B., 225
McCormick, Cyrus, 239
McCormick reaper, 210, 240
McCulloch *v.* Maryland, 137-138, 154
McDonald, Forest, 93
MacDonough, Thomas, 126
McGillivray, Alexander, 62
McKinley, William, 278, 279, 287, 289, 321-323
McLean, John, 147
McLeod, Alexander, 201
McLoughlin, John, 202
McMaster, John Bach, 87
Macon's Bill No. 2, 124
Madero, Francisco, 334
Madison, James, 89, 90, 92, 104, 111, 114, 123, 124, 127, 139
Magellan, Ferdinand, 6-7
Maine, 142
Maine (battleship), 287
Maine laws, 189
Malone, Dudley Field, 306
Management, scientific, 360-361
Mangum, Willie P., 159
Manhattan project, 456
Mann, Horace, 172, 187, 189
Manorial system, 3
Marbury *v.* Madison, 114, 137
Marcy, William L., 212
Mariana Islands, 414
Marion, Francis, 80
Marshall, George C., 411, 422, 427, 428
Marshall, John, 112, 114, 115, 119, 136-139
Marshall Islands, 414
Marshall Plan, 425, 428
Martin, Joseph, 431
Maryland, 11, 23, 25, 32, 35, 88, 137-138, 222

Mason, George, 76, 77, 90
Mason, John Y., 212
Massachusetts, 13-15, 22, 24, 25, 49, 50, 65, 76, 94, 127, 143
Massachusetts Government Act, 69-70
Massachusetts Institute of Technology, 455
Masters, Edgar Lee, 368
Mather, Cotton, 45-46
Mather, Increase, 42
Maury, Matthew, 175
Maximilian, Emperor, 282
Maximum Employment Act, 423
Mayflower, 13
Mayflower Compact, 13, 75
Maysville Road Bill veto, 152
Meade, George, 225
Mellon, Andrew, 352, 356
Melville, Hermann, 172, 180, 226, 312, 313
Mencken, H. L., 367, 370
Mercantilism, 32, 59
Meredith, James, 453
Mesmerism, 186
Methodist Church, 39, 183-184
Mexican War, 204-205
Mexico, 199-200, 203, 211, 281, 334-335, 403
Meyers, Marvin, 162
Michigan, 208
Middle East, 427, 446
Midnight judges, 114
Midway, Battle of, 412
Midway Island, 411
Militia, 126
Millennialism, 185-186, 189
Miller, Arthur, 368
Miller, Perry, 17
Miller, William, 185, 186
Missiles, 447, 456, 463
Mississippi, 142
University of, 453
Missouri, 142, 223
Missouri *v.* Canada, 452
Missouri Compromise, 141-142, 213
Mitchell, John, 327
Molasses Act, 31, 63
Monetary policy (*see* Banking)
Monopolies (*see* Trusts)
Monroe, James, 130, 135, 145, 427
Monroe Doctrine, 139-141, 403
Montcalm, Marquis de, 53
Montejo, Francisco de, 7
Montgomery Ward, 255

Moody, John, 280
Moore, Marianne, 369
"Moral diplomacy," 335
Moravian Church, 39
Morgan, J.P., 274, 280, 299, 300, 327
Morgan, William, 157
Morgan and Company, 157
Mormon Church, 185
Morrill Land Grant Act, 242-243
Morris, Gouverneur, 83
Morris, Robert, 77
Morrow, Dwight, 403
Motley, John Lothrop, 177
Mount, William Sidney, 176
Mount Vernon meeting, 88
Muckraking, 260, 324
Mugwumps, 269
Munich, 401
Munn v. Illinois, 255
Murdock, Kenneth, 17
Murray, "Alfalfa Bill," 325
Music, 175, 459
Mussolini, Benito, 405
Myers, Gustavus, 262
Myrdal, Gunnar, 453-454

NAACP, 450, 451
Nagasaki, 435
Namier, Lewis, 72
Napoleon, 116, 124
Napoleon III, 282
Narragansett Indians, 23
Nashville Convention, 207
Nathan, George Jean, 367
National Alliance, 276
National Association for the Advancement of Colored People, 450-451
National Banking Act, 243
National Labor Reform party, 247
National Labor Relations Act, 390-391, 424
National Labor Union, 247, 274
National Origins Act, 304
National Recovery Act, 384, 387, 389, 390, 393
National Republicans, 157
National Science Foundation, 456
Nationalism (see Imperialism; Isolationism; Nativism)
Nativism, 172
NATO, 428, 465
Natural resources, 240-241

Natural rights, 307
Naval Office, British, 67
Naval stores, 32
Navigation Acts, 23, 24, 33, 60
Navy, U. S., 340, 412, 409
Negroes, 48, 384, 425
    civil rights, 449-454, 462-463
    suffrage, 143, 231, 245
    (See also Antislavery; Slavery)
Netherlands, 5, 22, 23
Neutrality Act, 403-405
Nevada, 256, 257
Nevins, Allan, 220, 262
New Deal, 381-397, 451, 462
    philosophy of, 382-385
    (See also Roosevelt, Franklin Delano)
New England, 12-17, 124
    (See also individual states)
New England Confederation, 23
New England Emigrant Aid Society, 213
New France, 51, 53, 57, 59
New Frontier, 462, 466
New Harmony, 187
New Haven, colony of, 16
New Jersey, 19, 39
New Jersey Plan, 90
New Netherlands, 19, 23
New Orleans, 118, 139
    Battle of, 127
New York, 19-20, 25, 35, 36, 65, 67-69, 82, 91, 142-144, 172
New York Association for Improving the Condition of the Poor, 188
New York Central Railroad, 171, 259
New York City, 35, 143, 299
New York Stock Exchange (see Wall Street)
New York World, 286
Newburgh Addresses, 83
Newfoundland, 8
Newport, 37
Newspapers, 65, 66, 286-287, 312, 365, 406
Newton, Sir Isaac, 42
Nicaragua, 403
Nicholson, Francis, 25
Nicolls, Richard, 19
Niebuhr, Reinhold, 459
Nixon, Richard, 439-441, 443, 461
Non-Importation, 68, 69
Non-Intercourse Act, 123, 124
Norris, Frank, 315-316
North, Lord, 61, 69, 79, 80

Russia, 282, 421
(*See also* Soviet Union)
Russo-Japanese War, 292
Rutgers College, 47

Sacco-Vanzetti case, 350
St. Lawrence River, 8
St. Lawrence Seaway, 445
St. Leger, Barry, 77
"Salary grab," 247
Salem, 14
Sandburg, Carl, 368
Santa Anna, Antonio López de, 200
Santo Domingo, 246, 284
Saratoga, Battle of, 77, 80
Saroyan, William, 368
Schecter Poultry Corporation
Case, 393
Schlesinger, Arthur Mier, Jr., 162
Schlesinger, Arthur Mier, Sr., 73,
218
Schools (*see* Education)
Schurz, Carl, 228, 246, 249, 269
Schwartz, Delmore, 369
Science, 42, 174-175, 305, 310,
415, 454-458
Scientific management, 360-361
Scioto Company, 118, 172
Scopes trial, 306
Scotch-Irish, 37-38, 40
Scott, Winfield, 211
Secession, 217, 241
Securities and Exchange Act, 386
Security Council, United Nations,
418, 419, 430
Sedition Act, 339, 347
Segregation, 452-453
Senate, U.S., 89, 269, 342, 440, 442
Separatists, 13
Seven Years War, 51
Seventh Day Adventism, 184-185
Sevier, John, 117, 118, 135
Seward, William, 157, 208, 222, 282
Seymour, Horatio, 245-269
Shapiro, Karl, 369
Shays' Rebellion, 50, 86-88
Sherman, John, 253
Sherman, William T., 225
Sherman Antitrust Act, 272, 275,
328, 333
Sherman Silver Purchase Act,
272-274
Shipbuilding, 35
Silliman, Benjamin, 175

Simpson, Jerry, 277
Sinclair, Upton, 392
Singer, Isaac M., 239
"Sit-down strikes," 391
Slave trade, 191
Slavery, 11, 18, 21, 34, 36, 48, 120,
141, 206-208, 209, 215-216, 218
(*See also* Antislavery; Negroes)
Slidell, John, 203
Smith, Alfred E., 354
Smith, Gerald L. K., 392
Smith, John, 9, 45
Smith, Joseph, 184-186
Smith Act, 439
Smith College, 312
Smuggling, colonial, 60
Social classes, 47-49, 172-174, 209,
299-300, 363
Social Gospel, 305
Social Security Act, 394, 445
Socialist party, 339, 392
Society of Friends (*see* Quakers)
Solomon Islands, 414
Sons of Liberty, 65, 68, 69, 70, 108
Soulé, Pierre, 212
South Carolina, 18, 25, 32, 34, 51,
136, 153, 206, 230
South Carolina Exposition, 153
South Korea, 429, 440, 463
(*See also* Korean War)
South Vietnam, 463-465
Southeast Asia Treaty Organization
(SEATO), 446
Southern Alliance, 276
Southern society, 209-210
Soviet Union, 401, 416, 421, 426,
431, 435, 437, 446, 456, 463-464,
466
(*See also* Russia)
Spain, 5, 8, 80, 139-140, 281, 282
Spanish-American War, 285-289
Specie Circular, 158
Sputnik, 456
Stalin, Josef, 416, 426, 428
Stalwarts, 248-250
Stamp Act, 64-66, 68
Stamp Act Congress, 65
Standard Oil Company, 260-262,
309, 328, 333
Stanford, Leland, 259, 299, 311
Stanford University, 311
Staple Act, 24
Stassen, Harold E., 419
State capitals, 77
State constitutions, 76, 142-144

513

Turner, Frederick Jackson, 120, 160, 219
TVA, 384, 389-390, 407
Twain, Mark, 314, 316
Tweed, William Marcy, 248
Tweed Ring, 248
Tydings, Millard, 440
Tyler, John, 159, 160, 200

U-2 aircraft, 448
Unemployment, 462
  (*See also* Depression)
Union League clubs, 245
Union Pacific Railroad, 241-242, 247, 256, 259
Union party, 227
Unions (*see* American Federation of Labor; Congress of Industrial Organizations; Labor)
United Automobile Workers, 423
United Mine Workers, 280, 327, 350, 391
United Nations, 418-419, 421, 437
  in Korean War, 430
  UNESCO, 419
United States Bank, 115, 127, 137-138, 160
United States Steel Corporation, 279, 280, 349, 362
United States *v.* E.C. Knight and Company, 272
University of California, 455
University of Chicago, 311, 455
University of Michigan, 311
Urbanization, 36, 172, 297-301, 363
Utah Territory, 185
Utopianism, 186-187

V-2 rockets, 456
V-J Day, 421
Valley Forge, 77
Van Buren, Martin, 145, 147-148, 152, 153, 159, 160, 200, 203, 206
Vandenberg, Arthur M., 419, 427, 428
Vanderbilt, Cornelius, 248, 259
Vanderbilt, William, 326
Venezuela, 284-285
Vera Cruz, 335
Versailles Peace Conference, 341-343, 401
Vicksburg, 225

Viereck, Peter, 369
Vietnam, 446
  South, 463-465
Vikings, 1, 3
Vinland, 1
Virginia, 9-11, 22, 23, 32, 41, 71, 88, 91, 94, 286, 453
  (*See also* House of Burgesses)
Virginia Company, of London, 9
  of Plymouth, 9
Virginia and Kentucky Resolutions, 111, 124, 153
Virginia Military District, 117
Virginia Plan, 90
Virginia Resolves, 68
Volstead Act, 351, 382

Wabash, St. Louis and Pacific Railroad *v.* Illinois, 270
Wade, Benjamin F., 228
Wade-Davis Bill, 227
Wagner, Robert, 390-391
Wagner Labor Relations Act, 393, 424
Walker, William, 212
Wall Street, 269, 274, 280, 327, 333, 349, 378, 386
Wallace, Henry A., 420, 424, 426, 455
Wallace, Henry C., 353
Walpole, Robert, 34
War of 1812, 122-127, 177
War Hawks, 126
War Industries Board, 338-362
War Labor Board, 410
War Manpower Commission, 410
War Production Board, 410
Ward, John, 162
Ward, Lester, 308
Warner, Charles Dudley, 314
Warren, Earl, 453
Washington, Booker T., 384, 450
Washington, George, 36, 62, 74, 88, 101, 108, 141
Washington, D.C., 115
Washington Conference, 358
Washington Treaty, 283
Watauga Association, 117
Watson, J.B., 457
WCTU, 352
Wealth Tax Act, 393, 394
Weaver, James B., 255, 277
Webster, Daniel, 135, 143, 147, 149, 154, 158, 160, 202, 207

514

Webster, Noah, 174
Webster-Ashburton Treaty, 201
Webster-Hayne debate, 152-153
Weed, Thurlow, 147, 157, 158
Wellesley College, 312
Wertenbaker, Thomas Jefferson, 19
Wesley, John, 39
West, Benjamin, 44
West Indies, 31
West Virginia, 461
Western Design, 23
Western lands, 82, 84
Western Reserve, 117
Westward expansion, 122, 142, 208
  (See also Frontier)
Weyler, Valeriano, 286
Whig party, 150, 158
  (See also Republican party)
Whiskey Rebellion, 108
Whiskey Ring, 246
White, Hugh L., 159
White, William Allen, 324
White Citizens Council, 453
Whitefield, George, 39, 40
Whitman, Walt, 177-178, 180,
  312, 313
Whittier, John Greenleaf, 177, 179
Wiener, Norbert, 458
Wilbur, Richard, 369
Wilder, Thornton, 368
Wilderness, Battle of the, 226
Wilkinson, James, 118, 119
William III, 24, 47, 51
William and Mary College, 311
Williams, Roger, 15-16

Williams, Tennessee, 368
Willkie, Wendell, 407, 419
Wilmot, David, 206
Wilmot Proviso, 206
Wilson, Woodrow, 291, 303, 325,
  331-343, 347-348, 352, 357, 450
Wilson v. Mason, 137
Winthrop, John, 14
Wirt, William, 157
Wisconsin, 208
Wisconsin Progressivism, 325
Wise, Isaac M., 303
Wolfe, Thomas, 370
Woman's rights, 352-353, 363-366
Women's Christian Temperance
  Union (WCTU), 352
Workingmen's parties, 171
World War I, 335-340, 383-384
World War II, 408-416

XYZ Affair, 111

Yale College, 47, 182
Yalta Conference, 417-418, 426
Yazoo land fraud, 138
York, Duke of (see James II)
Yorktown, Battle of, 80
Young, Brigham, 185
Young America, 211

Zenger, John Peter, 66
Zimmerman note, 337

515

DATE DUE